Alta California

Western Histories
William Deverell, series editor
Published for the Huntington-USC Institute on California and the West
by University of California Press and the Huntington Library

1 *The Father of All: The de la Guerra Family, Power, and Patriarchy in Mexican California*, by Louise Pubols

2 *Alta California: Peoples in Motion, Identities in Formation, 1769–1850*, edited by Steven W. Hackel

Alta California

Peoples in Motion, Identities in Formation, 1769–1850

Edited by Steven W. Hackel

Published for the Huntington-USC Institute on California and the West
by University of California Press, Berkeley, California, and
the Huntington Library, San Marino, California

Copyright 2010 The Henry E. Huntington Library and Art Gallery and
   University of California Press
All rights reserved.
Series jacket design by Lia Tjandra
Interior design by Doug Davis
Copyediting by Susan Green, Jean Patterson, and Sara K. Austin
Image research by José Sánchez
Indexing by Jean Patterson

Printed in the United States by McNaughton & Gunn
15 14 13 12 11 10   1 2 3 4 5

Library of Congress Cataloging-in-Publication Data
Alta California : peoples in motion, identities in formation, 1769–1850 / edited by Steven W. Hackel.
   p. cm. — (Western histories ; 2)
Includes bibliographical references and index.
ISBN 978-0-87328-242-0 (alk. paper)
 1. California—History—To 1846. 2. California—History—1846–1850.
3. California—Social conditions. 4. California—Ethnic relations. 5. Group identity—California—History. 6. Ethnicity—California—History. 7. Identity (Psychology)—California—History. 8. Borderlands—California—History.
9. Frontier and pioneer life—California. 10. Spain—Colonies—America—History.
I. Hackel, Steven W. II. Huntington-USC Institute on California and the West.
 F864.A47 2010
 305.8009794—dc22
                    2009053827

Contents

List of Illustrations — vii

Introduction
Steven W. Hackel — 1

Part 1 Franciscan Identity in the Eighteenth-Century Borderlands

What They Brought: The Alta California Franciscans before 1769
Rose Marie Beebe and Robert M. Senkewicz — 17

Franciscan Missionaries in Late Colonial Sonora: Five Decades of Change and Conflict
José Refugio de la Torre Curiel — 47

Part 2 After the Village: Indian Identity in Alta California

"Raise your sword and I will eat you": Luiseño Scholar Pablo Tac, ca. 1841
Lisbeth Haas — 79

Identity through Music: Choristers at Missions San Jose and San Juan Bautista
James A. Sandos — 111

Part 3 Borderland Identities of Soldiers and Settlers

Becoming Californio: Jokes, Broadsides, and a Slap in the Face
Louise Pubols   131

Genetics and the *Castas* of Colonial California
John R. Johnson and Joseph G. Lorenz   157

Part 4 The Spanish Borderlands:
Comparing National Perspectives

Fantasy Heritage: California's Historical Identities and the Professional Empire of Herbert E. Bolton
Albert L. Hurtado   197

A New Borderlands Historiography: Constructing and Negotiating the Boundaries of Identity
David J. Weber   215

Identities and the Usable Pasts of Colonial Borderlands: Spanish Historians and the North Pacific Frontiers of the Spanish Empire
Sylvia L. Hilton   235

Selected Bibliography   325

Contributors   331

Index   335

ILLUSTRATIONS

Jules Tavernier, *Carmel Mission on San Carlos Day—1875*	cover
Page from the Mission Santa Clara Book of Baptisms	4
Colegio de San Fernando	31
Mission Santiago de Jalpan	33
Ruins of Mission San Fernando Rey de España de Velicatá	39
Pablo Tac's "Conversion of the San Luiseños"	85
Two of Pablo Tac's Luiseño-Spanish dictionary booklets	90–91
Pablo Tac's note to Cardinal Mezzofanti	93
Pablo Tac's dictionary booklet, fols. 134v–135r	96–97
Pablo Tac's drawing of two dancers	101
Fragment of one of Pablo Tac's final pages	105
Herbert E. Bolton, St. Francis Hotel, San Francisco, 1945	199
Herbert E. Bolton at age sixteen or seventeen	207

STEVEN W. HACKEL

Introduction

This volume has its origins in historical documents and identity-changing interactions initiated two hundred and forty years ago with the establishment of Mission San Diego on July 16, 1769. On that day the Franciscans inaugurated the first mission in what would eventually be a chain of missions that stretched from San Diego to just north of San Francisco. More than a year and a half later, in the first months of 1771, the Kumeyaay allowed the missionaries to baptize a few of their children at Mission San Diego.[1] Most likely the first Indian baptized at San Diego was a three-year-old boy whom the padres named "Francisco Antonio"; he was the son of a village leader who himself would be baptized in 1771 or 1772 and named "Carlos."[2] In the eyes of the missionaries, baptism and the bestowal of a Spanish name signified an identity shift that began to transform an Indian into a Spaniard, a pagan into a Catholic. In keeping with Catholic practice, the names of these Kumeyaay and the sacraments they received would have been duly recorded by the Franciscans in the mission's baptism register. The details of these first baptisms at San Diego and those of some five hundred other Kumeyaay are not known to us today in full because the register in which the padres recorded them was destroyed in 1775 when Carlos and Francisco Antonio's uncle, Francisco, led an attack that killed Father Luis Jayme and burned the mission to the ground.[3] Soon after the attack, however, the Franciscans painstakingly reconstructed the baptism register from memory in a volume that survives to this day.

By the time missionaries began to recreate the baptism register of Mission San Diego, Franciscans had established four more missions in California: San Carlos Borromeo (1770), San Antonio de Padua (1771), San Gabriel Arcángel (1771), and San Luis Obispo (1772). In these early years, missionaries baptized more than one thousand Indians, believing that they were cultivating in them the rudiments of a Spanish

Catholic identity. In the coming decades, the padres would establish sixteen more missions as well as a chapel at the presidio of Santa Barbara and a church in the pueblo of Los Angeles. At all of these sites, just as at Mission San Diego, missionaries dutifully administered and meticulously recorded thousands of sacraments. In so doing, they contributed to a set of records that would encompass nearly the entirety of the region's colonial population. While there is no countervailing set of records from Indians describing colonial California,[4] these baptism, marriage, and burial registers constitute an amazingly thorough record of the lives of the Indians, soldiers, settlers, and missionaries of colonial California. And although there has been heated debate during the last two hundred and forty years over the goals, the morality, and the legacy of the mission enterprise and its effects on California Indians, scholars have never doubted the importance of the sacramental registers to an understanding of the people of Alta California.[5]

California Mission Sacramental Registers

California Franciscans, of course, created the sacramental registers for their own purposes, not those of future historians. During the early modern period, the Catholic Church required all Catholic priests, including missionaries along the Spanish frontier of North America, to record in detail all of the sacraments they administered. This not only reduced the likelihood that missionaries would re-baptize an individual but also ensured that they did not violate canonical guidelines that disallowed Catholic marriages between closely related individuals. The sacramental records also allowed the Franciscans to demonstrate to a cash-strapped and over-extended Spanish state a quantitative if not qualitative record of the advance of Catholicism in Alta California. Thus, when California missionaries baptized an individual—whether an Indian adult or a newborn Spanish child—they recorded that person's given Spanish name, godparents, place of origin, age, parents, siblings, and, when applicable, the individual's children and marital status, as well as any other family relations or facts that they considered relevant to that person's identity. Furthermore, in California, as an aid to recordkeeping, missionaries assigned each baptism a unique number, beginning with the number one for the first baptism at each mission. Similarly, when they married or buried someone and performed the associated sacraments, missionaries recorded that individual's Spanish name, age, marital status, place of baptism, family relations, and, when known, their baptism number and mission of baptism. Franciscans also assigned marriage and burial records unique numbers at each mission. Thus, at any given time, the missionaries could determine how many baptisms, marriages, and burials they had performed at each mission. The padres also believed that these records gave them a clear way of identifying individual Indians within the growing ranks of neophytes at each mission.[6]

Remarkably—given the political instability of California as it shifted from Spanish to Mexican rule, and then to U.S. statehood—the baptism, marriage, and burial records for California's twenty-one missions, the Santa Barbara presidio, and the Los Angeles Plaza church survive with but a few exceptions. Altogether, the sacramental registers from these sites contain records on more than 100,000 baptisms, 70,000 burials, and 28,000 marriages that the Franciscans administered between 1769 and 1850. Collectively, these mission registers contain not only much of the information necessary to reconstruct the lives of tens of thousands of Indians and settlers but also the raw materials for the discovery and writing of larger and more intimate histories of colonial California.

A prerequisite for these new histories was a workable system that would allow scholars to access the information in the sacramental registers. Throughout much of the twentieth century, scholars skilled in reading eighteenth-century Spanish handwriting consulted mission records here and there as they sought to piece together the lives of notable Californians and the mission Indian communities of the region.[7] Some, like genealogists Thomas Workman Temple and Marie E. Northrop, devoted decades to the careful study of mission records and the creation of genealogies of the families of the "Californios," the non-Indian settlers of the region.[8] In the 1960s and 1970s, scholars of California Indians turned to the sacramental records to examine Indian population decline.[9] And in the 1980s and 1990s, a new generation of historians and anthropologists—emboldened by the power of the microprocessor and emerging database software—brought together a desire to document the tremendous diversity and depth of Indian life in early California with an interest in creating data sets of linked records for individual missions and then clusters of related missions. These could shed light on events previously unseen by historians and perhaps even by historical actors themselves. In this regard, Randall T. Milliken, who works on the missions and Indians of Northern California, and John R. Johnson, who studies the missions and Indians of the Santa Barbara region, were pioneers.[10]

In the mid-1990s, after working on my own databases of the records of Missions San Carlos and San Gabriel, I became aware of the need for a comprehensive database that would bring together the sacramental records of all the missions into a uniform and integrated system. Such a database would include the records, not just of Indians or Californios,

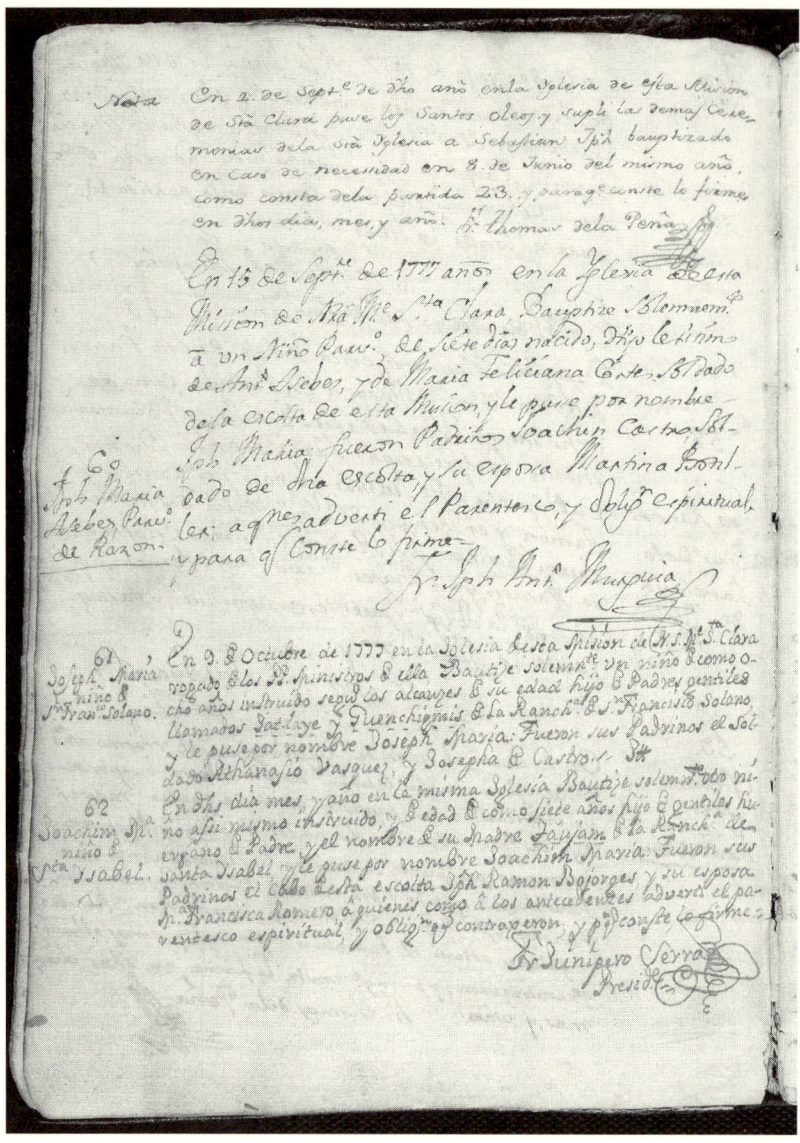

A page from the Mission Santa Clara Book of Baptisms in which Fathers Tomás de la Peña, José Antonio Murguía, and Junípero Serra recorded baptisms. Tomás de la Peña records that Sebastian José, an Indian whom the Franciscans had baptized without the full ceremonies because they believed he was gravely ill, has now been given a complete baptism. José Murguía states that he has baptized the seven-day-old child of a soldier serving as a guard at the mission. And Junípero Serra writes that he has baptized two young boys from villages in the vicinity of Mission San Clara. Courtesy of Santa Clara University Archives.

but of all the people of early California who came within the scope of the missions. Without this comprehensive and integrated database, it was impossible, many of us reasoned, to see the movements of Indians and settlers from one part of the province to another or to grasp various social processes and patterns of historical change that unfolded across all of the missions, presidios, and pueblos of colonial California. The creation of this comprehensive database required institutional support, as it was too vast an undertaking for one person or even a group of researchers. In 1998, just when this project was being conceptualized, Robert C. Ritchie, W. M. Keck Foundation Director of Research at the Henry E. Huntington Library, saw the importance of this endeavor. With his backing and the institutional support of the Huntington, the Early California Population Project (ECPP) was born.[11] It would prove to be a Huntington-led collaborative project, one that would involve numerous scholars, a team of data-entry personnel, grants from a wide range of institutions, and nearly a decade of work. Following the completion of an online version of this database in the summer of 2006 and its installation on the Huntington's website, the project has been used by an increasingly wide range of scholars, genealogists, historians, teachers, Indian groups, and government agencies.[12] All have profited from easy access to mission records like those initiated at San Diego so long ago that had remained beyond the reach and use of nearly everyone for centuries.

The ECPP database presents a trove of data on individuals and families and on the social structure of the missions and pueblos. But above all, the mission sacramental records speak to a colonial world that was in motion. Indians, soldiers, and settlers were moving from place to place, and the very institutions that had sustained Indian culture and society for centuries, if not millennia, as well as those that had promoted Spanish society and Spain's colonization in the New World, were in flux. To study these mission records, therefore, is to gain insight into a world in which Indians moved from village to mission, from mission to mission, and often from mission to pueblo and presidio. The records reveal that soldiers and settlers were even more mobile than Indians, on account of the demands of military or settler life. One also sees not only the demographic collapse of Indians and the expansion of Californio families but also the workings of Catholicism in the daily lives of early California residents and the boundaries and contours of the emerging social, political, economic, and racial systems that structured the lives of Indians, soldiers, and settlers.

In this crucible of change that was Alta California, individual and community identities could not help but be transformed. It comes as no surprise, therefore, that when the Huntington convened a conference in the fall of 2006 to celebrate the completion of the Early California Population Project, two overarching themes—motion and identity—emerged most forcefully in the scholarly papers that were presented. This volume, *Alta California: Peoples in Motion, Identities in Formation*, presents substantially revised essays from that conference. Collectively, the contributors seek a deeper comprehension of how missionaries, Indians, soldiers, and settlers understood themselves, how they pursued various roles and identities, and, finally, how scholars of differing identities and backgrounds have studied and understood identity within the Spanish Borderlands.

Identity in Early California

Until recently, the study of identity was not a preoccupation of historians of early California.[13] The earliest scholarship on the region focused on Spanish missionaries and government officials who helped to create California.[14] In the first half of the twentieth century, scholars began to examine the institutional foundations of California in work that focused most closely on Spanish missions and presidios. In the mid-twentieth century, anthropologists began to deepen their understanding of California's Indian groups, and Catholic Church historians continued their work on the leading missionaries of colonial California.[15] By the 1970s, historians and anthropologists began to work together in new ways to uncover how Indians responded to the growth and expansion of Spanish institutions in California. Most recently, scholars have begun to trace how the institutions of Spanish California emerged out of broader currents of thought and ideologies central to colonial Mexico and early modern Spain.[16]

In this volume as well as in other recent scholarship, historians are moving beyond questions of how Europeans transplanted familiar institutions to the New World and are exploring how Indians, Europeans, and Creoles lived and understood themselves within the colonial world. Scholars of early America beyond California have long been interested in identity, and it seems fair to say that the publication in 1987 of a volume of essays, *Colonial Identity in the Atlantic World, 1500–1800*, edited by Nicholas Canny and Anthony Pagden, was a watershed event.[17] As the first editors to gather essays on the creation of identity in the various regions of the Atlantic World, Canny and Pagden outlined a series of questions that have dominated the field for a generation. The volume cohered around what the editors described as a need to shift from a focus on the relationship between the movements toward independence and the formation of a national identity to a study of the factors that encouraged "transplanted European communities to begin to think of themselves as in some ways distinct and separate from the mother country."[18] A related approach, which focused on the emergence of Creole identity and colonial subjectivity, has been particularly important to scholars of colonial Spanish America.[19] It continues to dominate the field and has recently caught the attention of literary scholars.[20] This rich scholarship on colonial and Creole identity has recently been joined by an increasing number of books and articles that examine how Indians maintained and transformed their own identities during the colonial period.[21]

In recent years, historians have also come to embrace the notion that individuals can have multiple identities and loyalties, depending on time, place, and context.[22] More specific to the Spanish Borderlands, work is now emerging on the instability of political loyalty and the emergence of national identity across the Gulf Borderlands in the years of intense imperial rivalry before, during, and after the American Revolution.[23] Scholars have also paid close attention to the conflicting identities among settlers during the first half of the nineteenth century in Texas that were spawned by the U.S. economy and Spanish and Mexican systems of governance and patronage.[24] Yet, as important as questions of Creole identity, national loyalty, and U.S. economic expansion are to students of many regions of colonial America, the study of identity in colonial California carries its own particular insights and regional variations.

For many reasons, social and political developments in colonial California had their own trajectory, and thus so did the formation of individual and community identity in the region. European settlement of Alta California did not begin until 1769, long after much of North America had been colonized and settled by Europeans. Spain and then Mexico held sway in California, unchallenged in the absence of an imperial rival, until the Mexican-American War. And although scholars working on Spanish America have begun to devote attention to the intersection of race and identity,[25] the varied and numerous categories of race and caste prevalent in much of New Spain never fully materialized in Alta California during the colonial period.[26] There were in fact very few people living in the province who had actually been born in Spain, and most soldiers, settlers, and Franciscans in California ignored the typical Spanish racial *casta* categories so prevalent in central Mexico. Instead, they saw all the local Indians as *indios* and identified themselves and their brethren as Californio, *español*, or *gente de razón*.[27]

A quick look at the database of the Early California Population Project shows how narrowly social, racial, and ethnic categories—and thus important aspects of individual and communal identity—were defined in colonial California, at least by the Franciscans. In Alta California, missionaries performed more than 100,000 baptisms, and about 15,000 of these were of non-Indians of various races and nationalities. In only about 5,271 of these records did the padres explicitly identify the race or ethnicity. Of these, they classified nearly all as gente de razón. Remarkably, the padres classified only fifteen children they baptized between 1769 and 1850 as español. Moreover, in the mission records, there are only sixteen instances when missionaries recorded newborns as *mestizo*, even though a *minimum* of 152 children were born in the missions to marriages that joined a gente de razón father and a California Indian mother. Thus the padres' categories were not only few, they were also malleable.

A similar simplification of racial categories in colonial California can be found in the relatively small number of matrimonial investigations that survive from the period. The padres performed and recorded these examinations for all marriages of non-Indians to determine whether the bride and groom were entering marriage of their own volition and whether any canonical impediments to the marriage existed. What seemed to matter most to the missionaries who wrote these reports was the groom's occupation, the bride's and groom's places of residence, and whether or not the bride and groom were of legitimate birth. Racial and ethnic status seemed largely irrelevant to the padres, even in cases where the bride and groom were clearly mestizo. For example, in the matrimonial investigation at Mission Santa Barbara of José Miguel Pico and María Casilda de la Cruz in 1794, the padres made no mention of Pico's racial or ethnic status, even though in the census of 1790 his father is identified as mestizo, his mother Maria Jacinta as *mulatta*, and his brothers as mulattos.[28]

The fault line that divided Indians from others in Alta California was just one factor that influenced identity formation in the region. As the essays in this volume suggest, while Spanish missionaries saw in Alta California an opportunity to create a Catholic Church that was based on what they had known in Spain, most colonists crafted an evolving institutional, corporate, regional, or group identity, and they looked to family lineage and drew upon local circumstances for self-definition rather than the standards and cultural norms and institutions of the Iberian peninsula. In Alta California, as throughout most of the Spanish Borderlands, soldiers' and settlers' identity-forming and -affirming decisions and affiliations were most likely also motivated by networks of kinship and a desire for economic well-being. For Indians, clearly, membership in a mission community was identity-changing, but Indians' needs to find and pursue a strategy of survival and cultural continuity in the midst of change determined where and how they found a place in the colonial world, and how they understood their place in it.

In this volume, four separate sections take up various aspects of identity as it relates to early California and the study of the Spanish Borderlands. Part 1 explores the origins of the identities of California's first missionaries and examines the development of Franciscan missionary techniques as well as the lives of the leading Franciscans. Rose Marie Beebe and Robert M. Senkewicz argue that for Father Junípero Serra, California was a stage upon which he could act out an identity that "owed far more to the history of Spain and central Mexico than to anything or anyone that actually existed in Alta California." Thus, to Beebe and Senkewicz, Serra, a man of uncommon education and accomplishment by the time he went to Alta California, lived a life that was in many ways shaped more by his youth in the Old World than by his adulthood in New Spain. Because of his role establishing the first missions in colonial California, his constant sparring with the region's governors, and the movement within the Church to proclaim him a saint, Serra stands apart in the historiography of early California, even as he has come to represent all California missionaries. But as José Refugio de la Torre reminds us in his essay, Franciscan missionaries—even though they were all members of a distinctive order with demanding rules—often disagreed and were not all alike, and their individual, group, and corporate identities were shaped as much by personal experience as by the goals and projects that so animated their lives. Most important, de la Torre shows us not only how missionaries' goals reflected differences among individuals but also how these goals varied over time as successive generations of missionaries sought to spread their own brand of mission-based Catholicism to the far reaches of New Spain's colonial north.

Missionaries of course came to California to indoctrinate Indians into Catholicism, and the essays in part 2 suggest how the colonial encounter offered new avenues for the expression of Indian identity. In her portrait of Pablo Tac, Lisbeth Haas illustrates that Indian identity in California could be at once Catholic, oppositional, and indigenous. Tac was clearly exceptional in that he, unlike any other California Indian who lived during the colonial period, left his own written account of life in the California missions. Tac's own narrative in the hands of Haas speaks to the ability of many California Indians to maintain a sense of individual, tribal, and communal identity within "a world of defeat." Individuals like Tac balanced a sense of self that combined a comprehension of the colonial hierarchies at work in California with possibilities for "equality, liberty, and citizenship" within the emerging Republic of Mexico. Pablo Tac was not alone among California Indians in crafting part of his identity at the missions through close ties with the Franciscans. For, as James A. Sandos reveals in his careful and novel study of the choristers and musicians at Missions San Jose and San Juan Bautista, the missions afforded Indians with musical abilities special opportunities to combine old and new beliefs and practices and to join, in Sandos's words, "a privileged social and spiritual world." Sandos's essay not only explores the relationship between music and individual identity in the missions but also, for the first time, identifies many of the Indians in colonial California whose lives and selves cohered around music and song.

As part 3 discusses, for soldiers and settlers who moved to Alta California, identity was more a matter of culture and power than race and ethnicity. As Louise Pubols argues, political identity in Mexican California was immensely complicated for soldiers and settlers. They were united in their belief that they were a people apart from the Indians of the region, but they had a harder time determining their true political loyalties. The region had passed from Spain to Mexico a mere two generations after its birth, before any strong ties had been constructed between the frontier and the governing metropolis. Thus, despite a collective caste consciousness, the region's *pobladores* did not forge or share a common national identity. Rather, by the 1840s, most native-born non-Indian men in California asserted a fictional Spanish descent, a nominal identification with the Republic of Mexico, and a fierce pride in their identity as "Californio," a cluster of ideas and behaviors explored by Pubols. Whereas Pubols examines the cultural foundations of an emerging regional Californio identity in Mexican California, anthropologists John R. Johnson and Joseph G. Lorenz deploy new scientific techniques rooted in the study of mitochondrial DNA to reveal the degree to which the Californios' cultural identity masked their mestizo genetic origins. Johnson and Lorenz's explorations of the deep ancestry of California's soldiers and settlers suggests not only the Sonoran and Sinaloan origins of the Californios but that identity in colonial California was a cultural construction, not a biological inheritance.

Part 4 of this volume moves from history and the study of colonial California to historiography and an examination of how historians during the twentieth century, proceeding from a variety of perspectives and motives, shaped the identity of the field of the Spanish Borderlands. In a blend of historical research and personal narrative, Al Hurtado examines how Herbert Eugene Bolton, the pioneering historian who created the field of Spanish Borderlands history, built a professional empire that sought for the first time to give Spain's colonial North American possessions their proper place in the narrative of American history. Though he lauds Bolton's goal, Hurtado discovers in him a shrewd political tactician who was willing to perpetuate California's "fantasy heritage" in order to create his own professional empire. This fantasy heritage was the modern-day incarnation of the racial fictions and spurious notions of cultural purity that defined Californio identity and that are so carefully explicated in this volume by Pubols, Johnson, and Lorenz.

The history of the concept of "identity" and the degree to which scholars have applied it to the study of the Spanish Borderlands before 1848 are the focus of David J. Weber's wide-ranging historiographical essay. In his survey of twentieth-century Borderlands scholarship from Bolton through the linguistic turn, Weber observes that scholars of the Borderlands have long concentrated on Spanish and Mexican "character" and its response to the environment and Indians of the northern frontier. Weber concludes that the more modern concept of identity is both useful and necessary to capture "realities for which contemporaries had no useful vocabulary." In the essay that draws this volume to a close, Sylvia L. Hilton reveals how the national and nationalist perspectives of Spanish scholars have shaped Spanish scholarship on the Borderlands. In a work that is both monumental and microscopic, Hilton surveys and synthesizes more than 250 years of scholarship. In so doing, she helps illuminate the degree to which historians and their scholarship can be said to have identities of their own. Like the people historians study, Hilton argues, historical scholarship is the product of time and place and the outcome of competing loyalties and evolving subjectivities. This volume then, in all of its parts, illuminates the vital and dynamic nature of identity in Spanish and Mexican California and the central importance of identity as a topic of inquiry in studies of the shaping of the larger field of Spanish Borderlands history.

From conceptualization through completion, this volume has been a pleasure, one now enhanced by the opportunity to acknowledge those people and institutions who have made this work possible. This volume's indebtedness to Roy Ritchie and the Huntington Library is enormous, and it is suggested over the preceding pages. In planning the conference that became this volume I had the very useful advice of William B. Taylor, David J. Weber, and Walter Brem, three scholars whose generosity and knowledge match their enthusiasm for the study of the Borderlands. Janet Fireman, David Igler, Fredrika J. Teute, Peter C. Mancall, William B. Taylor, and series editor William Deverell provided wise counsel and encouragement as this volume took shape. For a quiet office for my work on this project and others, as well as a never-ending supply of engaging conversationalists, I thank the Huntington Library Research Division. The staff of the Huntington Library Press—Sara K. Austin, Jean Patterson, and the incomparable Susan Green—eased my job as editor through their careful work, unstinting standards, good cheer, and tireless enthusiasm. Finally, while this volume was a collective and collaborative effort among the authors whose work is presented here, compiling and editing these essays took time and energy, and more time and more energy. Without the love, support, and encouragement of Heidi Brayman Hackel it would not have been possible.

Notes

1. Zephyrin Engelhardt, *San Diego Mission: The Missions and Missionaries of California* (San Francisco: James H. Barry, 1920), 39.

2. For the records of these baptisms, see the Early California Population Project, http://missions.huntington.org, Francisco Antonio, San Diego bapt. no. 1, and Carlos, San Diego bapt. no. 35.

3. Francisco, San Diego bapt. no. 32. On this rebellion, see Steven W. Hackel, *Children of Coyote, Missionaries of Saint Francis: Indian-Spanish Relations in Colonial California, 1769–1850* (Chapel Hill: University of North Carolina Press, 2005), 258–61; and James A. Sandos, *Converting California: Indians and Franciscans in the Missions* (New Haven, Conn.: Yale University Press, 2004), 55–68.

4. This is not to say that Indian views of colonial California are non-existent. See, for example, Steven W. Hackel, "Sources of Rebellion: Indian Testimony and the Mission San Gabriel Uprising of 1785," *Ethnohistory* 50, no. 4 (2003): 643–69, and the essay by Haas in this volume, "'Raise your sword and I will eat you': Luiseño Scholar Pablo Tac, ca. 1841."

5. During the Spanish period, missionaries and soldiers clashed over the role of the missions and the degree to which the padres could control and punish Indians. Those conflicts deepened during the colonial period until the 1830s, when mission secularization stripped the Franciscans of most of their authority over Indians. On late twentieth-century debates over the missions and mission historiography, see James A. Sandos, "Junípero Serra's Canonization and the Historical Record," *American Historical Review* 93, no. 5 (1988): 1253–69.

6. This method of recording and identifying individual Indians in registers was simply a recordkeeping system; Indians did not know their own baptism numbers and continued to identify themselves by their native names or, later, by their given Spanish names.

7   James Culleton, *Indians and Pioneers of Old Monterey: Being a Chronicle of the Religious History of Carmel Mission Considered in Connection with Monterey's Other Local Events and California's General History* (Fresno, Calif.: Academy of California Church History, 1950).

8   Marie E. Northrop and Southern California Genealogical Society, *Spanish-Mexican Families of Early California, 1769–1850*, 1st ed. (New Orleans: Polyanthos, 1976); Marie E. Northrop and Southern California Genealogical Society, *Spanish-Mexican Families of Early California, 1769–1850*, 2nd ed. (Burbank, Calif: Southern California Genealogical Society, 1987).

9   Sherburne F. Cook and Woodrow W. Borah, *Essays in Population History: Mexico and the Caribbean*, 3 vols. (Berkeley: University of California Press, 1971–79).

10 Randall Milliken, *A Time of Little Choice: The Disintegration of Tribal Culture in the San Francisco Bay Area, 1769–1810* (Menlo Park and Novato, Calif.: Ballena Press, 1995); John Richard Johnson, "Chumash Social Organization: An Ethnohistoric Perspective" (PhD diss., University of California, Santa Barbara, 1988).

11 For full discussions of the creation of the database, see Steven W. Hackel, "Early California Population Project Report," *Journal of California and Great Basin Anthropology* 26, no. 1 (2006): 71–74; Steven W. Hackel and Anne Marie Reid, "Transforming an 18th-Century Archive into a 21st-Century Database: The Early California Population Project," *History Compass* 5, no. 3 (2007): 1013–25.

12 See, for example, the recent essay by Sara Peelo, "Baptism among the Salinan Neophytes of Mission San Antonio de Padua: Investigating the Ecological Hypothesis," in *Ethnohistory* 56, no. 4 (2009): 589–624; the essay by Sandos in this volume, "Identity through Music: Choristers at Missions San Jose and San Juan Bautista"; and Quincy Newell, *Constructing Lives at Mission San Francisco: Native Californians and Hispanic Colonists, 1776–1821* (Albuquerque: University of New Mexico Press, 2009).

13 For works that do take up the issue of identity in early California, see Lisbeth Haas, *Conquests and Historical Identities in California, 1769–1936* (Berkeley: University of California Press, 1996); Barbara Voss, *The Archaeology of Ethnogenesis: Race and Sexuality in Colonial San Francisco* (Berkeley: University of California Press, 2008).

14 Hubert Howe Bancroft, *California*, 7 vols. (San Francisco: A. L. Bancroft & Co., 1884–90); Zephyrin Engelhardt, *Missions and Missionaries of California*, 4 vols. (San Francisco: James H. Barry Company, 1908–15).

15 See the voluminous work of Robert F. Heizer. See also the work of the Franciscan historian Maynard J. Geiger, including *The Life and Times of Fray Junípero Serra, O.F.M.; or, The Man Who Never Turned Back, 1713–1784, a Biography* (Washington, D.C.: Academy of American Franciscan History, 1959).

16 Hackel, *Children of Coyote*; Sandos, *Converting California*; and Beebe and Senkewicz, "What They Brought: The Alta California Franciscans before 1769," in this volume.

17 Nicholas Canny and Anthony Pagden, eds., *Colonial Identity in the Atlantic World, 1500–1800* (Princeton, N.J.: Princeton University Press, 1987). For a discussion of the changing meaning of the term *identity* in scholarship, see Philip Gleason, "Identifying Identity: A Semantic History," *The Journal of American History* 69, no. 4 (1983): 910–31. For other important studies of identity in colonial America, see Michael Zuckerman, "The Formation of Identity in Early America," *William and Mary Quarterly* 34, no. 2 (1977): 183–214; Jack P. Greene, *Imperatives, Behaviors, and Identities: Essays in Early American Cultural History* (Charlottesville: University Press of Virginia, 1992); Ronald Hoffman, Mechal Sobel, and Fredrika J. Teute, eds., *Through a Glass Darkly: Reflections on Personal Identity in Early America* (Chapel Hill: Published for the Omohundro Institute of Early American History and Culture by the University of North Carolina Press, 1997).

18 Canny and Pagden, eds., *Colonial Identity in the Atlantic World*, 5.

19 David A. Brading, *The First America: The Spanish Monarchy, Creole Patriots, and the Liberal State, 1492–1867* (Cambridge: Cambridge University Press), 1991.

20 Ralph Bauer and José Antonio Mazzotti, eds., *Creole Subjects in the Colonial Americas: Empires, Texts, Identities* (Chapel Hill: Published for the Omohundro Institute of Early American History and Culture by the University of North Carolina Press, 2009).

21 This scholarship is exceptionally broad and deep. For a recent work on these issues in the Californias, see Lee M. Panich, "Missionization and the Persistence of Native Identity on the Colonial Frontier of Baja California," *Ethnohistory* 57, no. 2 (2010): 225–62.

22 Greg Dening, "Introduction: In Search of a Metaphor" and "Histories of Self," in *Through a Glass Darkly*, 1–5, 9–12.

23 Gene Allen Smith and Sylvia L. Hilton, eds., *Nexus of Empire: Negotiating Loyalty and Identity in the Revolutionary Borderlands, 1760s–1820s* (Gainesville: University Press of Florida, 2010).

24 Andrés Reséndez, *Changing National Identities at the Frontier: Texas and New Mexico, 1800–1850* (Cambridge and New York: Cambridge University Press, 2005).

25 Andrew B. Fisher and Matthew D. O'Hara, eds., *Imperial Subjects: Race and Identity in Colonial Latin America* (Durham, N.C.: Duke University Press, 2009).

26 Rosamaría Toruño Tanghetti, "Licit and Illicit Unions: Engendering Mexican Society," in *A Companion to California History*, ed. William Deverell and David Igler (Chichester, U.K., and Malden, Mass.: Wiley-Blackwell, 2008), 127–44.

27 William M. Mason, *The Census of 1790: A Demographic History of Colonial California* (Menlo Park, Calif.: Ballena Press, 1998), 45–76.

28 Matrimonial Investigation of José Miguel Pico and María Casilda de la Cruz, Father Esteban Tapis, Mission Santa Barbara, October 31, 1794, and Father Miguel Sanchez, November 6, 1794, San Gabriel Mission Matrimonial Investigation Records, McPherson Collection, Honnold/Mudd Library, Claremont Colleges, Claremont, Calif.; Mason, *Census of 1790*, 85.

PART 1
FRANCISCAN IDENTITY IN THE EIGHTEENTH-CENTURY BORDERLANDS

ROSE MARIE BEEBE AND
ROBERT M. SENKEWICZ

WHAT THEY BROUGHT: THE ALTA CALIFORNIA
FRANCISCANS BEFORE 1769

For a long period beginning in the nineteenth century, historians of California generally characterized missionaries during the Spanish and Mexican eras in one of two ways: as heroic agents of civilization or nefarious purveyors of destruction. The heroic interpretation became dominant in works influenced by the Spanish Revival movement, and it was also evident in the writings of the great Franciscan historians Zephryn Engelhardt, Maynard J. Geiger, and Francis F. Guest, all of whom based their work on the trove of documents at the Santa Barbara Mission Archive-Library. In the 1980s and 1990s, the nefarious interpretation became especially pronounced, due to a number of books that appeared in connection with the controversies surrounding the proposed canonization of Junípero Serra and the commemoration of the Columbus quincentenary.[1]

In the past fifteen years, however, mission historians have consciously shifted their perspective to focus on Indians. In this new framework, the missionaries have been, very properly, de-centered. They tend to be regarded as an important set of people who—along with soldiers and settlers—made up part of the context and shaped part of the environment in which native Californians were active agents. As one set of actors among many, they were shaped in complex ways by all those with whom they interacted. Thus it is possible to see them in a more nuanced light.[2]

This essay is in that vein, for we endeavor to move beyond celebration or condemnation. Using Junípero Serra as an exemplar, we seek to determine how a person's identity as a Spanish Franciscan might affect both his choice to become a missionary in New Spain and how he lived out that choice. For Serra and his religious brothers, one of the most exciting things about Alta California was that they were in the first group of Spanish colonists to arrive there. They believed that elsewhere in New Spain, settlers, soldiers, and officials had oppressed the native peoples and inhibited the spread of the gospel. They thought that Alta California offered them a chance to set things right. They idealized Alta California as a fertile and inviting field. These missionaries did not realize that their assessment was deeply colored by the militant religious suppositions they had brought from early modern Spain and by their struggles with other Spanish colonists over how to treat indigenous peoples, a question that had divided religious and civil authorities in New Spain since the early sixteenth century. They viewed Alta California and its inhabitants through a lens that owed far more to the history of Spain and central Mexico than to anything or anyone that actually existed in Alta California. What Junípero Serra wanted to accomplish with the native peoples of Alta California was shaped by what he and his order had learned from their experiences in Mallorca, Mexico City, the Sierra Gorda, and Baja California.

We chose to focus on Serra because he was father president of the Alta California missions, because his activities produced a rich documentary record, and because he has come to symbolize the entire California missionary enterprise. However, a cautionary note is in order. Serra's voice was not the only missionary voice. Indeed, even during his lifetime, his views were far from unchallenged. In 1771 his former student and closest missionary companion, Francisco Palóu, wrote to Mexico City to criticize Serra for wanting to establish too many missions too quickly. In 1775 his religious superior in Mexico City, exasperated by Serra's tendency to act without sufficient consultation, publicly chastised him and severely limited his powers in a strongly worded letter that he sent to all the California missionaries. We can learn much about the missionary experience by examining Serra—but not everything. His fellow missionaries could and did disagree with him. Tensions within the missionary community were more common than is often realized.[3]

Petra

Since this volume is occasioned by the completion of the Early California Population Project, let us introduce Junípero Serra with two baptismal entries contained in that marvelous database. One, dated December 26, 1770, records Serra's first baptism in Alta California. It reads:

> In the name of the Father, the Son, and the Holy Spirit. Amen
> On December 26, 1770, in the church of this mission,
> San Carlos de Monterrey, I solemnly baptized a boy,

about five years old, the son of gentile parents who willingly presented him to the Catholic Church. And I named him Bernardino de Jesús. His godfather was Lieutenant Don Pedro Fages, an officer of the Company of Catalonian Volunteers and commander of the Royal Presidio of this port. I reminded him of the spiritual bond and obligation he entered into. And in order for it to be on record, I signed it.
      Fr. Junípero Serra

Why did Serra name the first Indian he baptized in Alta California Bernardino? The answer most likely lies in the village of his birth, Petra, on the eastern side of the Mediterranean island of Mallorca. Petra had two churches. One was named San Pedro. This is where Miguel José Serra was baptized on November 24, 1713. The other church, where young Serra attended a Franciscan grammar school, was named San Bernardino.[4]

Another entry records a baptism he performed on September 3, 1782. It reads:

> On September 3, 1782, in the church of this mission, San Carlos de Monterrey, I solemnly baptized a girl, about thirteen years old, the daughter of gentile parents from Sargenta-Ruc, the same parents of the boy Leonardo, number 300 in this book. I gave her the name María de Buen-año, (in honor of Most Holy Mary of my beloved homeland). Her godmother was María del Carmen Chamorro, wife of Corporal José Marcelino Bravo. I advised her of her responsibilities. And in order for it to be on record, I signed it.
>   Fr. Junípero Serra

Here the reference to Mallorca ("my beloved homeland") is explicit. The name Serra gave the child was an allusion to a devotion to Mary under the title of "Bonany" (Catalán for "Buen Año" [good year]). This was a Mallorcan devotion dating from 1609, a year of bountiful harvests after many years of drought. The "good year" was attributed to the villagers' prayers to Mary. A chapel to Mary was built outside of Petra to commemorate the happy result. As it happened, the harvest at Mission San Carlos was projected to be a poor one in September 1782. This baptismal record suggests that Serra hoped to encourage the Virgin to act in Monterey Bay as he believed she had acted in Petra. Half a century after he left his ancestral village, its traditions were still very much a part of Junípero Serra.[5]

Petra was a very old rural settlement; its roots may have reached back to Roman times. Serra was proud of its history. In 1748 he boasted that his village was one of the four oldest *villas* on the island. Serra grew up close to the land in a region where the forces of nature determined much about the quality of life. Cycles of drought had long been a fact of life on Mallorca. During the Middle Ages, Mallorca had won the right to alleviate famines by trading for wheat among the Muslims of southern Spain and northern Africa. Engaging in such commerce thus became one of the traditional privileges (*fueros*) of the island. Drought likely featured among Serra's last memories of Mallorca. In 1747, two years before he left for the Americas, the harvests began to fail. By the end of the 1740s, the island's farmers were bringing in only one-sixth of the amount of wheat they had harvested only a few years earlier. A number of the wealthier Mallorcan families left for the mainland and their absence appears to have contributed to a further decline in the local economy.[6]

These Mallorcan agricultural catastrophes left a permanent mark on Serra. His correspondence demonstrates his insatiable desire to leave no detail of the agricultural and economic development of the missions unattended. Large sections of his 1773 *representación* to the viceroy, which is mostly remembered for Serra's successful appeal to get Pedro Fages replaced as military commander of Alta California, were devoted to the issues of maintaining and supplying the struggling missions. Serra's remarks covered a range of topics, such as the necessity of immediately readying a new frigate, the best way for invoices to be drawn up at San Blas, and the reasons why the missions needed another forge and a blacksmith.[7]

Another aspect of life in Petra continued to influence Serra. After around 1720, it appears that the production of textiles increased notably in the rural areas of the island. In Mallorca, as elsewhere in Europe, most of this work was done by women. Figures are hard to come by, but it appears that between 1720 and 1755, when Serra was growing up in Petra, studying and teaching in Palma, and traveling widely throughout the Mallorcan countryside as a preacher, textile exports from the island almost tripled. Women therefore played an especially important economic role in the communities in which Serra lived and worked during this period. For Serra and the Mallorcans who accompanied him to the New World, the well-ordered rural community included women who were engaged in weaving and other forms of domestic production. In his laudatory biography of Serra, Palóu described his and Serra's missionary activities in the Sierra Gorda from 1750 to 1758 in terms that harked back to their experiences in the Balearic Islands. Under Serra's leadership, he said, "the harvests increased and became so abundant that some was left over," and the native women were employed "in tasks befitting their sex, such as spinning, weaving, making stockings, knitting, sewing, and so forth." In some ways, Serra's journey to the New World represented a journey back to Petra.[8]

Becoming Junípero

Serra left Petra when he was fifteen years old. He then spent a year studying with one of the canons of the cathedral in Palma. He applied for admission to the Franciscans soon after he celebrated his sixteenth birthday but his petition was denied. The reason may have been that people named "Serra" had been identified and punished by the Mallorcan Inquisition from the end of the fifteenth century until at least the beginning of the seventeenth century. Serra reapplied about six months later and was accepted. He spent a year as a novice, a period during which he lived in a Franciscan community and studied Franciscan spirituality. In September 1731, he formally became a Franciscan by taking solemn vows of poverty, chastity, and obedience. On this occasion, he changed his name to Junípero.[9]

It was not unusual for young religious to take the name of a favorite saint or a holy person when they took their vows. They might add that name to their given name, as a type of middle name. In this way they were expressing their devotion to a significant figure in their religious development. However, it was unusual for them to use that new name in place of their given name. Of all the Mallorcan Franciscans who came to the New World, Serra seems to have been the only one to have done that. What was the significance of this choice?[10]

Brother Junípero was one of the companions of Francis of Assisi, the founder of the order. Brother Junípero was known for patience, humility, and simplicity. None of these are qualities that one spontaneously associates with Junípero Serra. Perhaps Serra knew himself well enough to realize that these were qualities that he would always have to struggle to attain. If so, then his choice of name suggests that he anticipated that life as a member of a religious order would be a challenging struggle to attain a series of ideals.[11]

The name Junípero also had general connotations of strength. Francis is supposed to have once said, "Would that I had a forest of Junipers."

Perhaps this aspiration was personal as well, for Serra himself was small and slight and always seemed to be pushing himself to compensate for a lack of physical prowess. As a novice, he had been embarrassed that he was too short to reach a lectern to perform a regular duty of the novices—turning the pages of the book for the friar who was leading the chant.[12]

Finally, a local variety of the juniper plant, *ginebró*, flourished in the Mallorcan countryside. The choice of the name thus may also be another reference to his childhood and his place of birth—Serra's way of saying that his new identity as a Franciscan would incorporate his older one as a resident of rural Mallorca.[13]

For centuries Spaniards and other Europeans had been changing indigenous names of people and places in the Americas to European names as an expression of the new colonial relationship. As we have seen, Serra did the same thing in California, but he had first done it to himself. In Serra, we encounter a man for whom adopting a new name to express a new identity and a new relationship was a normal part of life.

Ramón Llull

After Serra finished his novitiate on the outskirts of Palma, he moved into the city. He studied and taught at the university named for one of the most famous Mallorcans, Ramón Llull. Theologian, philosopher, mystic, poet, scholar, and the author of over one hundred works, Llull was born in Mallorca in 1232 and died in 1315. He was a member of the third order of Saint Francis, a group designed for those who wished to cultivate Franciscan spirituality in their lives without becoming priests, brothers, or sisters. Llull's tomb was in the great Franciscan church in Palma, Sant Francesc, in whose convent Serra lived for almost twenty years.[14]

Llull was very interested in missionary work to the Muslims of North Africa. He traveled there a number of times to engage Muslim scholars and leaders in conversation and to preach there. In this he was reminiscent of Francis of Assisi, who had once traveled to Egypt to preach to Sultan Melek el-Kamel. In 1276, Llull even started a school on Mallorca to train missionaries in Arabic.[15]

Llull's reputation in official church circles waxed and waned over the centuries after his death, but in Mallorca he was always regarded very favorably. The university in Palma, founded in 1483, was named the "Estudio General Lulliano." Even after its name was officially changed in 1526, it continued to be called the "Lullian university." In 1721 a definitive edition of Llull's works was completed in Germany, and this gave rise to what one Llull scholar has termed a "flurry" of publications in Mallorca:

between 1720 and 1750, at least forty-three editions of various Llull works were published on the island.[16]

This growing of interest in Llull was part of a larger cultural development in Mallorca in the first decades of the eighteenth century. Since being conquered by King Jaime I of Aragón in 1229, Mallorca's primary association with the Spanish mainland had been with that northeastern region of the Iberian Peninsula. Like most Aragón-related jurisdictions, Mallorca favored the claim of Hapsburg Archduke Charles over that of the Bourbon Duke of Anjou, Philip, in the succession controversy at the beginning of the eighteenth century. Mallorca felt that the Hapsburgs would be more likely than the Bourbons to retain the traditional local privileges (fueros) that the island had enjoyed. When the War of the Spanish Succession (1701–14) ended with Philip on the throne, he was quick to extend his control over Mallorca. In 1714 the royal fleet appeared off of Palma and an army landed on the eastern coast. In 1715 the army entered Felanitx, about ten miles south of Petra. The conquest was achieved in short order and the traditional local privileges were superceded by a decree known as the Nueva Planta, issued in 1715. This was one of a series of decrees propagated in a number of localities by which the Bourbons imposed their central authority. The Mallorcan version of the Nueva Planta reduced local power, including the power of the Church.[17]

The new authorities took additional steps to exert control over the island. In 1721 the commander general ordered his troops to fan out through the countryside to put down remnants of local resistance. In the countryside, people often took refuge in churches, but the Bourbon troops disregarded the right of sanctuary and routinely entered churches to make arrests. And, in 1747, two years before Serra left for the New World, the army swept through Palma and forcibly conscripted a large number of young men, who were sent to join the royal forces in the siege of Naples.[18]

In the context of these events, the revival of interest in Llull can be seen as part of the reassertion of what one historian has termed an "insular nationalism" in the face of Bourbon initiatives. In another cultural assault, the Bourbon centralizers and the early patrons of the Spanish Enlightenment who were associated with them tended to disparage local cults. Benito Jerónimo Feijóo, one of the leading exponents of this trend, ridiculed Llull's most significant work, the *Ars Magna*, scornfully noting that in Mallorca, Llull was venerated as a saint and his words were regarded as "the trumpet of the Holy Spirit." Antoní Ramón Pascual, a colleague of Serra's at the Lullian University, published a two-volume response to Feijóo and defense of Llull in 1749–50.[19]

As a result of the association of Llull with Mallorcan pride, one of the major annual events in Mallorca became the sermon preached on Llull's feast day, January 25, in the church of Sant Francesc. On January 25, 1749, that sermon was preached by none other than Junípero Serra. A copy of it has not survived, but Palóu tells us that a retired faculty member said that the sermon should be "printed in letters of gold." The sermon connects Serra very closely with the local tradition of Mallorca and suggests that he was among those who opposed the centralization and the military efforts that were used to enforce it.[20]

By the time Serra arrived in New Spain, the tensions between missionaries and soldiers had a long history. Indeed, events in New Spain are sufficient to explain the quarrels between Serra and a series of military officers in Alta California. Serra's antipathy to the military, however, was particularly intense compared with other missionaries. It figured in a number of conflicts, but perhaps most forcefully in the disputes he had with military commander Fernando de Rivera y Moncada in the mid-1770s. Their quarrel was ferocious. When Serra wrote Rivera and rather sanctimoniously expressed the hope that God might forgive Rivera for all the trouble he was causing Serra, Rivera shot back that Serra was the one who needed divine forgiveness. He told Serra to stop whining: undiplomatically, he asked for "less noise." Serra was particularly irked when, in an echo of Bourbon behavior in Mallorca, Rivera personally entered a room that was being used as a chapel at the San Diego presidio and arrested a baptized Indian who had been one of the leaders of the 1775 Kumeyaay revolt and was claiming sanctuary there.[21]

"The Other"

As in many places in Spain, Mallorca's own identity was closely associated with struggles against the "other." The Inquisition had been set up on the island at the same time that it was established in the rest of the Iberian Peninsula in the fifteenth and sixteenth centuries. But at least in its formal activities, the Inquisition was less active after about the middle of the sixteenth century. The next hundred years were a time of economic troubles for both Spain and Mallorca. This period climaxed around 1650, when a plague ravaged the island, killing as much as 20 percent of the population. Prosperity began to return to Spain in the second half of the seventeenth century. The coastal areas were the first to experience this, and Mallorca participated in it. However, the gradual rise in prosperity appears to have increased tensions on the island, sparking some resentment against the *conversos* (baptized Catholics of Jewish descent), who were the backbone of Palma's commercial class. These people found themselves targeted.[22]

In 1675, the Inquisition condemned a Jewish man fleeing from North Africa to be burned alive in Palma. It conducted mass arrests and trials in 1679 and, in an auto-da-fé in 1691, burned three conversos alive. The Inquisition also seized large amounts of property as part of this persecution. According to Henry Kamen, the confiscations were the largest in all three centuries of the Spanish Inquisition. The moves against the conversos, who were called *chuetas*, a derogatory term probably derived from the diminutive of an old Mallorcan word for "Jew," basically involved the seizure and redistribution of much of the commercial wealth of Palma.[23]

During the entire eighteenth century, conversos could live only in a specific part of the city. Autos-da-fé were held in Palma in 1722 and 1724, although no one was executed in connection with them. However, open hostility to the conversos continued throughout the eighteenth century. For example, in 1755 the Inquisition in Mallorca published a list of all the people on the island whom it had punished since 1645. Also in 1755, a 1691 book by the Jesuit Francisco Garau, describing in gruesome detail the executions at the end of the seventeenth century, was republished in Palma. In 1772 the chuetas of Mallorca addressed a formal petition and protest to King Carlos III, who issued three decrees in the 1780s forbidding various forms of discrimination against them.[24]

During the 1740s, Serra was a *comisario* (investigator) of the Inquisition.[25] His formal participation mainly involved examining works for their orthodoxy to determine whether they should be published, a task not explicitly related to the treatment of conversos. Living in a city with a large and identifiable converso population, however, affected how Serra and Spaniards with similar experiences looked upon the fundamental task of a missionary: conversion. To put it simply, association with the Inquisition and residence in a city known for its anti-converso actions caused Serra and those like him to suspect the authenticity of conversions. The more the Inquisition took action against so-called Judaizantes, the more it raised doubts about the sincerity of the "conversion" of the conversos.

In this context, any deviation from the officially sanctioned norms of Christian behavior would be regarded as a deliberate turning away from the true religion. Much of Serra's later disagreements in Alta California with Governor Felipe de Neve revolved around Neve's attempts to hasten what he regarded as the assimilation of the indigenous peoples by creating meaningful positions of local authority for them within the colonial order. Serra objected to this because he was convinced that these Indians were, in their own fashion, secret Judaizantes, that is, people who were holding on to their traditional ways after baptism. In 1780 Serra bitterly complained to Neve that Baltazar, a baptized Indian who had been elected *alcalde* at Carmel, had proven to be a "deserter . . . inciting the people here, meeting personally with those who leave here with permission, and thereby trying to swell the members of his band." In Serra's judgment, Baltazar's behavior had proven that his conversion was insincere, and he was not the only false convert. At both San Gabriel and San Luis Obispo, Serra complained, the office of alcalde had been bestowed on native leaders who had not totally renounced their native traditions. These natives' sexual activity was central to his complaints. He called Baltazar an "adulterer." He also stated that the San Luis Obispo alcalde "kidnaped another man's wife and took off with her," and grumbled that the San Gabriel alcalde, Nicolás, "was supplying women to as many soldiers as asked for them."[26]

When contemporary historians, archaeologists, or anthropologists look at the two-millennia-long history of Christian evangelization, some conclude that most populations targeted by missionaries neither wholly accept nor wholly reject Christianity. In missionary preaching, Christian concepts were necessarily interpreted through the prism of indigenous religion. Christian words gained new meaning as they were filtered through indigenous vocabulary and grammar and as Christian elements were incorporated into an indigenous worldview. The result of all this was often a spirituality that was neither simply Christian nor simply indigenous, but was a fundamentally new blend of the two. Historians of European religion have taught us that the "spread" of Christianity there was often really the creation of a new type of religion. The religion that was created and often re-created in constantly evolving forms was derived from both Christian and pre-Christian elements.[27]

Some Christian missionaries acknowledged this constant dynamic. Jesuit missionaries to China in the sixteenth and seventeenth centuries largely based their evangelization strategies on emphasizing commonalities between Christian and local religious traditions. Sixteenth-century Franciscans in central Mexico did the same. But in Alta California, the early missionary approach tended to be less accommodating, in part because of Serra's suspicions about converts, derived from his association with the Inquisition in Mallorca.[28]

Some of Serra's contemporaries attempted to adopt a somewhat open view to indigenous forms of expression and to lay the groundwork for a less confrontational understanding of native California culture and religion. Thanks to the work of the late Alan Brown, we know that Juan Crespí's diaries recorded many detailed scenes of native life. But Brown also demonstrates how systematically both Palóu and Serra excised precisely those sections before allowing the diaries to be circulated. Father Vicente de Santa María's descriptions of native life in the San Francisco Bay region were rendered in an open and, for his day, generous fashion. Perhaps that was one of the reasons Serra branded him as "rather difficult to manage." Serra's background, by contrast, could make him somewhat uninterested in native spirituality and religion. For him, the persistence of these traditions created the temptation to backslide. In his mind, the Christian California Indians were like the chuetas of Mallorca, and he was always suspicious of them when they were out of sight. For instance, in a mission's early years, when the nascent complex was not a self-sustaining agricultural entity, priests had to allow mission residents periodic trips to their own home villages and landscapes. Serra tolerated this, but only barely. When he thought an individual was taking too long in returning, he would grow angry if the soldiers did not immediately organize a search party and go out after the "fugitive."[29]

Serra's distrust of native beliefs and traditions did not persist among all the Franciscans who came after him. The Ohlone people who were painted by Georg Heinrich von Langsdorff as they danced at Mission San Jose in 1806 or the Petaluma people whom Louis Choris depicted as dancing in the plaza of Mission Dolores a decade later did so with at least the tacit approval of the resident missionary. Among these more tolerant Franciscans was the priest in charge at Mission San Luis Rey, Antonio Peyri, a Catalán who arrived in Alta California twelve years after Serra's death. Peyri had been living among the same group of native people for twenty-nine consecutive years, and he appears to have accepted the persistence of indigenous traditions. His approach was somewhat different from Serra's. When Auguste Duhaut-Cilly visited Mission San Luis Rey in 1827, he witnessed a native dance there and remarked of the Indians, "Although they may all be Christians, they retain many of their former beliefs, which the padres, as a matter of policy, pretend not to notice."[30]

Jews were not the only "other" represented in eighteenth-century Mallorca. The island had originally been conquered from the Moors by King Jaime I in 1229. The memory of the event was rekindled in 1732, when Spanish forces conquered the city of Oran on the North African coast. To celebrate this victory a grand celebration was held in Palma. The parades included many student and university groups, including students from the Lullian university. As part of the festivities, a group of Moorish slaves who were held on the island were paraded through the streets of the city in which Serra was living as a young Franciscan student. The Reconquista, when Islam was driven from the Iberian Peninsula, was still alive. Thirty-seven years later, in 1769, after Portolá left San Diego for Monterey, Serra decided to dedicate the fledgling mission on July 16. This was the date of the famous victory of King Alfonso VIII over the Almohades at Navas de Tolosa in 1212. Serra aimed to repeat the Reconquista, this time driving non-Christian native religion out of Spanish California.[31]

John Duns Scotus

At the Lullian University, Serra held the chair of Scotistic philosophy, named for the thirteenth-century Franciscan theologian John Duns Scotus. In the broad sweep of medieval theology and philosophy, Scotus was not typical. Indeed, he was rather eccentric, which was why the sarcastic name given to the followers of Duns Scotus has survived in the word "dunce." For instance, he rejected the widely held synthesis of one of the most influential Christian medieval theologians, Anselm of Canterbury, about the doctrine of the redemption wrought through Christ, since he thought it placed insufficient emphasis on the boundless love of God for humanity. In his theology, Scotus, in common with many Franciscans, emphasized the will over the intellect. His philosophy and theology also tended to emphasize the qualities of relationships and aesthetics over the most static scholastic categories of substance and judgment. He explicitly understood moral goodness in terms of musical harmony and used the image of chords on a harp to underscore his insistence that morality involves, above all, a proper relationship among human actions. In another passage he spoke of the morally good act as a work of art, in which proportion and balance combine to produce something that is aesthetically pleasing.[32]

Serra's insistence on the catechetical benefits of art and music and his almost obsessive concern with obtaining good works of art from Mexico for the California missions stemmed in part from his absorption of Scotus. In addition, Scotus's emphasis on relationships and his insistence on the Trinity as the model of relationships gave Serra's Petra experience a philosophical and theological grounding. Well-ordered communities did no less than reflect the very nature of God.[33]

Among Franciscans, Scotus was best known for his vigorous theological defense of the Immaculate Conception. Scotus's justification of this idea provided the basis for the Vatican's eventual acceptance of it as a Catholic doctrine. In the seventeenth century, the Immaculate Conception was championed both by Franciscans and, for their own reasons, by the Hapsburg monarchs of Spain. Devotion to the Immaculate Conception was an important part of Serra's identity, which helps explain his embrace of the works and writings of Sor María de Jesús de Agreda, best known for her alleged bilocations to New Mexico in the 1620s. Sor María was a member of the Conceptionists, a Franciscan group that was particularly devoted to the notion of the Immaculate Conception. She had said that God had revealed to her that Native Americans would be converted to Catholicism at the mere sight of Franciscans. She also said that other Franciscans had miraculously preached to some Indian nations during the seventeenth century. Serra regarded himself as literally following in their miraculous footsteps. At Mission San Antonio in the early 1770s, the missionaries reported that a very old Indian woman had said that her parents had told her when she was young that a man dressed like the missionaries and preaching the Christian gospel had come to the region many years ago. Serra and Palóu believed that this man had been one of the Franciscans to whom Sor María had referred.[34]

Leaving Mallorca

Serra spent over eighteen years in academic life in Palma as a student and a teacher. He did extremely well in that career. Yet, at some point in the 1740s, when he was entering his mid-30s, he seems to have begun to become discontented with academics. It was not measuring up to his expectations and he felt that his own spiritual life was becoming stale. We have only Palóu's account of Serra's interior struggle, but it was obviously based on intimate conversations with Serra. According to Palóu, Serra "re-kindled in his heart those desires which had stirred him as a novice, but which had been deadened because of his preoccupation with study." In this crisis, Serra chose as his model the recently canonized San Francisco Solano, who had left Spain for a missionary career at the then-advanced age of forty. As a Mallorcan Franciscan who walked by the missionary Llull's tomb almost every day, for Serra the path to rekindling his religious zeal lay across the sea. When he arrived at his residence in Mexico City, his first request was to be allowed to live with the novices, whose life in the community was the most rigorous and whose youthful fervor Serra desired to reclaim. One of Serra's most famous phrases, taken from a letter he wrote soon after he departed Mallorca, was "go forward, never turn back." In fact, Maynard J. Geiger subtitled his biography of Serra *The Man Who Never Turned Back*. Yet, in a very fundamental fashion, Serra's journey to the Americas was a type of journey backward, a quest to recover for himself the religious fervor he felt his academic career had stifled.[35]

Mexico

On January 1, 1750, Serra arrived at the Apostolic College of San Fernando in Mexico City. The apostolic colleges were a comparatively recent development among the Franciscans in New Spain. They were an attempt to help the order recover for itself the intensity and perceived successes of the golden age of missionary activity in the sixteenth century after what was regarded as a stagnant time in the following century. These schools were modeled on colleges founded on the Iberian Peninsula starting in 1680. The Iberian missionary colleges were created to train and support the increasing number of men then engaged in itinerant ministry within Spain itself, preaching in the countryside to renew religion among the faithful.[36]

The colleges were brought to the New World by a Mallorcan, Antonio Llinás. Like Serra, Llinás was something of a restless academic. He was twice turned down for positions at the university in Palma and he went to New Spain to accept a lectureship there. After teaching at Franciscan schools in Querétaro, Celaya, and Valladolid, Llinás experienced a religious transformation himself in 1675. He related that he had a vision in which God had shown him "the manifest deceptions of this miserable world." So he went to Spain and consulted with the minister general of the order, José Ximénez Samaniego, a former spiritual director to Sor María de Jesús de Agreda and her biographer. From that experience, Samaniego already had developed a certain interest in New World missions. Llinás and Samaniego decided that the opening of apostolic colleges in the Americas could be an important way of renewing the Franciscan missionary enterprise there. Among Llinás's first recruits for this new enterprise were twelve Mallorcan Franciscans who enlisted in the cause in 1682.[37]

The first college was founded in Querétaro. Llinás had developed an interest in organizing missionary activity in the Sierra Gorda, and Querétaro was the gateway to that region. The college was named Santa Cruz, after a cross that supposedly had been erected on the location by an early missionary after the conquest of the region by the Spaniards in 1531. Thus

Colegio de San Fernando, Mexico City. Photo by Maynard J. Geiger, O.F.M.
Courtesy of the Santa Barbara Mission Archive-Library.

the founders of the first apostolic college consciously harked back to an earlier period of missionary activity. Two other apostolic colleges were eventually founded in Mexico: Nuestra Señora de Guadalupe in Zacatecas in 1707 and San Fernando in Mexico City in 1733. When Serra arrived at San Fernando, he found his perfect match. A man seeking personal renewal had found an institution, the apostolic college, dedicated to institutional renewal.[38]

Sierra Gorda

After spending six months at the Apostolic College of San Fernando, in July 1750 Serra and Palóu were both sent to the mission of Jalpan in the Sierra Gorda. They spent the next eight years there and, for part of that period, Serra served as father president of the Sierra Gorda missions.

Both Serra and the apostolic colleges aimed to restore something they felt had been lost—they were looking for the past. In the Sierra Gorda, they found the past, but not the one they were seeking; instead they encountered what they regarded as a repetition of an unsavory part of the colonial past in New Spain. The story behind this perception started around the time of the founding of the College of San Fernando, as important voices in New Spain were beginning to wonder if the mission-presidio system had outlived its usefulness. In the 1720s, Pedro de Rivera, the military commander of Veracruz, had made an inspection tour of the northern presidios. He wrote a report concluding that the presidios were becoming too expensive to maintain. He also argued that, in some of them, soldiers were simply acting as *mayordomos* for the missions and were being forced to perform inappropriate tasks. He wrote that at one presidio, "The soldiers do nothing except assist the nearby three missions. Since they are not doing the job of military men, the presidio should be eliminated." As Rivera's report was being circulated and discussed over the next decade, similar accusations were being leveled against the missions. Staff members of the Ministerio de Guerra y Hacienda were complaining that the missions were also costing too much, especially because missionary salaries had to be paid from the treasury. In the 1740s, such views were shared by both the viceroy (the first Revilla Gigedo) and the auditor of the ministry (the Marqués de Altamira). In José de Escandón they found the man to carry out a different method of colonization.[39]

Escandón arrived in Querétaro in 1721 as a low-ranking army officer and he gradually established himself as an important figure in the region. His name appears in the public records as both a purchaser and seller of

Mission Santiago de Jalpan. Courtesy of Robert H. Jackson, Mexico City.

slaves in the city. He also became the owner of an important textile factory in Querétaro. Escandón undertook military campaigns against the Jonace and other Indians of the Sierra Gorda as early as 1735. His success in these campaigns helped him move up the military ranks, and he became a colonel in 1740. In 1741 he was placed in charge of the Sierra Gorda. As one of his first tasks, Escandón sought to congregate the Indians into missions, and he looked to the College of San Fernando for assistance.[40]

The College of San Fernando's first experience in the region was the year before, in 1740, when it founded a mission at Vizarrón, about halfway between the city of Querétaro and the highlands occupied by the Pame people. The existence of this mission is what encouraged Escandón to consider the College of San Fernando when he was thinking of missionaries for the highlands. Escandón assigned the college five missions—Santiago de Jalpan, Nuestra Señora de Purísima Concepción del Agua de Landa, San Francisco del Valle de Tilaco, Nuestra Señora de la Luz de Tancoyol, and San Miguel Arcángel de Concá. In his biography of Serra, Palóu implied that these missions were all new, but the mission at Jalpan was already in existence. The Franciscans took it over from an Augustinian priest, Lucas Cabeza de Vaca.[41]

The first few years of the College of San Fernando's experience with the Sierra Gorda were quite trying. Originally, the college did not have enough men to staff the five missions. Priests from the College of Santa Cruz in Querétaro had to fill in. In addition, two severe epidemics ravaged the region in the late 1740s, and four of the Fernandino priests perished in them in 1746–47. The future of the Fernandino mission enterprise in the region did not appear to be very solid.[42]

Yet, that fragility was not a concern for Escandón and the government ministry in Mexico City. He repeatedly stated that he did not foresee an extensive formal mission period for the churches that he was setting up. In 1747 he reported that in a short time the missions could easily be converted into *curatos*, or regular parishes. According to historian Lino Gómez Canedo, Escandón's plan was for the colonists and the Indians to live close to each other, and for the colonists to be the primary agents of the assimilation of the Indians to the Spanish empire. Colonists would be attracted by offers of land, which meant that the missions could never become large landowners. If such a colonization effort succeeded, it could be carried out at little cost to the treasury.[43]

In the 1740s, the College of San Fernando did not have the resources to oppose Escandón's plan. The Fernandinos were not entirely happy with Escandón's government in the region. In 1742, for example, they denounced the use of Jonace people as involuntary laborers on the haciendas of two regional officials. But practical considerations forced them to temper their criticisms of his plans for temporary missions since the college did not have abundant manpower to send to the area in any case. The four missionary deaths the college suffered in the late 1740s put further severe strains on its ability to staff all of the missions. Therefore, the college found that it had to acquiesce with regard to Escandón's plans. In 1748, for example, Guardian José Ortés de Velasco, who founded the first Fernandino mission in 1740, San José de Vizarrón, agreed that the Sierra Gorda missions would soon be able to be turned into parishes and delivered to the bishop.[44]

In 1751, a year after Serra's arrival in Jalpan, Escandón proposed the establishment of a civil settlement, the Villa de Herrera, near the mission lands. Soon settlers were complaining to him that they were unable to take possession of the lands they had been promised because the Indians (supported by the missionaries) were there and would not leave. Escandón exchanged a series of angry letters with the missionaries over the next few years until a compromise was engineered by military officer Vicente de Posadas in 1754. The settlers were given land around Saucillo, slightly farther away from Jalpan, while the mission itself was allotted its own land in the Tancama Valley. A 1762 Franciscan document still reported with irritation that the Villa de Herrera was "practically right in the middle of the five missions."[45]

Unfortunately, we do not know Serra's reaction to this situation because very few Franciscan letters from the Sierra Gorda have survived. Of those that have come to light, none were written by Serra or Palóu. There are only a few hints. In a 1776 letter, Serra made a cryptic reference to "the time of the disputes" with Escandón. Most interestingly, we also know that in 1752 Serra traveled to Mexico City and got himself appointed as an officer to the Inquisition in New Spain. Because of his previous experience with the Inquisition in Mallorca, this was a natural move for him to make after he heard rumors that two women of the area were engaged in some sort of demon worship. It is also possible, however, that he was trying to equip himself with additional jurisdictional powers for potential use against the settlers.[46]

When the College of San Fernando was finally able to devote greater manpower to the Sierra Gorda missions, it attempted to resist Escandón's goal of turning the missions into parishes, a goal it had only reluctantly supported in the 1740s. In 1761, for example, some settlers in Escanela, just south of Jalpan, tried to stimulate secularization proceedings, and the then-president of the missions, Juan Ramos de Lora, resisted vigorously. The very next year, Serra and Palóu joined two other friars in stating that "considerable time, patience, and effort" would be necessary before the missions could be handed over to a bishop.[47]

By this time, Escandón had long since left the Sierra Gorda. In gratitude for undertaking the colonizing task there and for his success in keeping costs down, Escandón was rewarded with the title Conde de Sierra Gorda in 1749. He was also given the opportunity to colonize Nuevo Santander, the area south of Texas on the Gulf Coast of New Spain.[48] There he was able to more fully develop the strategy he had initiated in the Sierra Gorda. He jettisoned the mission-presidio system in favor of a large number of pueblos of settlers. The missions were mostly reduced to simple churches and the missionaries became little more than chaplains to the settlers, much to the horror of the friars from the Apostolic College of Guadalupe in Zacatecas who staffed the missions. In this strategy, Escandón was reflecting Bourbon policy in New Spain, since by this time, most missions in central Mexico had already been secularized.[49]

One result of this method was that settlements were frequently raided by the Indians whose lands were being taken, and the Indians were attacked in turn by the settlers (who doubled as militia) and soldiers. The authorities declared a sixteenth-century style "war of fire and blood" against the Indians. Captured Indians were often sent to the haciendas of the military leaders or to the textile works in Querétaro, where they labored as virtual slaves. The Indians who resisted had the choice of exile or extermination. By the end of the eighteenth century, no more than 1,700 of the approximately 25,000 Indians who had lived in the area at the beginning of the colonization activity were still there. According to Patricia Osante, the legal privileges granted to Escandón in this endeavor were very reminiscent of those granted to sixteenth-century Spanish colonizers.[50]

The Fernandinos followed all these developments closely. They believed that diminishing the power of the missions would return New Spain to a very undesirable past. Escandón's policies seemed to them to repeat the exploitation of the native peoples that had marked the first decades of Spanish colonization in the New World. In the narrative of Spanish expansion that was shared by most religious orders and that dated from the sixteenth-century writings of Bartolomé de las Casas, indigenous peoples needed to be grouped into missions to protect them from such oppression. Now, they feared, the brutal past had sprung to life again.

The college eventually accepted secularization of the Sierra Gorda missions in 1770, but that was only to free up men for the Alta California enterprise, which had begun the year before. California was the place where they were going to make their statement. Serra had come to the New World looking to recover the religious zeal of his own past. In New Spain he had found representations of two separate pasts. Escandón's methods recalled the oppressive colonial past, when conquistadores had virtually enslaved the native peoples. The apostolic colleges' activities recalled the missionary response to that oppressive past, when heroic friars gathered the native peoples into self-sustaining Christian communities in which they would be protected from secular domination. In California, first in Baja California and then in Alta California, Serra meant to make what he regarded as his order's heroic past come once again to life.[51]

Baja California

When the Jesuits were expelled from New Spain in 1767, the Fernandinos jumped at the chance to assume control of the seventeen missions the Jesuits had founded between 1697 and 1767 in the southern two-thirds of Baja California. Like most people in New Spain, they did not know very much about the peninsula, but they did know that the Jesuits had managed to attain a considerable degree of control over the military and that Baja California had not attracted a large number of civilian settlers. The balance of power, in other words, was reversed from that in the Sierra Gorda. This state of affairs explains an odd occurrence that happened while Serra and his fellow Franciscans were at Tepic waiting for a boat to take them on the next leg of the trip from Mexico City to Baja California. There were other Franciscans in the port as well, one group from the Apostolic College of Santa Cruz in Querétaro and the other group from the Province of Jalisco. Both of these groups were bound for the former Jesuit missions in Sonora, where Jesuits had waged hard struggles against settlers and soldiers for decades.[52]

Suddenly, the viceroy ordered that the assignments were to be changed. The Jaliscans were to go to Baja California and the Fernandinos were to go to Sonora. The reason given was that since the Fernandinos and the Queretans were from apostolic colleges, they would probably be able to work better together in Sonora. The Jaliscans, coming from another type of Franciscan institution, should be the ones to work separately in Baja California.

Serra was furious. He quickly dispatched Palóu and another friar to Guanajuato so that they could personally lobby Visitor General José de Gálvez against the change. The effort was successful and the viceroy rescinded his earlier order. We suspect that the impetus for the proposed change in destinations was Manuel de Ocio, a Baja California entrepreneur who had long quarreled with the Jesuits about their significant control over the few settlers in Baja California. Ocio owned property in Guadalajara and his son had just married into a prosperous Guadalajara family. Ocio may well have hoped that Franciscans from the Guadalajara region might be more amenable to allowing settlers greater influence than yet another missionary group headquartered in Mexico City, as the Jesuits had been. But Serra's strong reaction to the proposal indicated that for him, Baja California had a particular attraction. With missionaries dominant over settlers, it was the mirror opposite of the Sierra Gorda.[53]

When Serra and his fellow Franciscans arrived in Baja California, they soon discovered that its missions were in very bad shape. Four years of drought and other natural disasters, including plagues of locusts, had afflicted the Baja California peninsula in the mid-1760s. Nonetheless Gálvez, who personally came to Baja California in 1768, wanted the missions there to supply the expedition to the north that he was organizing. Therefore, he chose to present the poverty of the Baja California missions as being only a temporary state of affairs. He had to argue that these missions could afford to contribute to the northern expedition while still functioning. So he concocted a fiction that the poverty of the missions was the result of the greed of the *comisionados* who had been temporarily placed over them by Gaspar de Portolá after the Jesuits had left but before the new missionaries had arrived. These comisionados, the story went, had despoiled the missions. The Franciscans went along with the account that Gálvez put forth. A version of it appears in Palóu's *Historical Memoirs of New California*. In that volume, this story is used as an object lesson: only missionaries can be trusted with the mission temporalities.[54]

Thanks to the research of Harry Crosby, we know the identities of these comisionados. They were generally soldiers from the presidio at Loreto. Not one of them ever enriched himself with mission plunder. The commander of the Loreto presidio was Fernando de Rivera y Moncada. He had been in that post since 1751, and he knew each of these soldiers extremely well. The missionaries' acceptance of the story of their alleged greed was probably one of the things that poisoned the relationship between Rivera and Serra. In fact, the poverty of the Baja California

Ruins of Mission San Fernando Rey de España de Velicatá. Photo by Maynard J. Geiger, O.F.M. Courtesy of the Santa Barbara Mission Archive-Library.

missions was not temporary, and their continuing decline was one reason the Fernandinos were quite happy to unload them on the Dominicans in 1772.[55]

But for Serra, the story contained an important moral. If the Franciscan missions in Alta California were to be as successful as he judged the Baja California missions to have been, the soldiers should have no independent authority at the missions, which should be exclusively under missionary control. The military had as little place in his vision of a re-established heroic age of missions as settlers did.

In May 1769, Serra and Portolá departed from Baja California's most northerly mission outpost and headed overland for San Diego. Shortly after the journey began, an event occurred that made a great impact on Serra. This is how he described it in his diary:

> On May 15...I had a great consolation...While I was within the little shelter of my dwelling place, I received notice that gentiles were coming and were already near. I praised the Lord and kissed the ground, giving thanks to His Divine Majesty that after so many years of longing He granted me the grace of being among them in their own land. I went forth and immediately found myself in the company of a dozen Indians, all men, all of whom were adults with the exception of two boys, the one about ten years old, the other about sixteen. Then I saw what I could hardly begin to believe when I read about it or was told about it, namely that they go about entirely naked like Adam in Paradise before the fall.[56]

After nineteen years in the New World, for the first time Serra was finally entering upon the full-fledged missionary experience of being the first to work among non-Christian peoples in their own land. For as we have seen, the Pame among whom he had worked in the Sierra Gorda had been evangelized well before he and the Fernandinos arrived. Also, the indigenous peoples in Baja California among whom he had spent the past year had been evangelized decades before by the Jesuits. Serra was quite literally overwhelmed by this new experience. Finally, he was experiencing what he had hoped to encounter when he departed for America.

Junípero Serra would meet the inhabitants of Alta California as a man in search of his own past and his order's past. He would meet them as a man who, in his own mind, was fighting on their behalf against what he deemed to be the oppressive practices from the colonial past, which had erupted into the present. Many of the ways in which he would wage that fight had been forged as a result of the perspectives he had acquired during his long journey from Petra to Palma, then to Mexico City, the Sierra Gorda, and Baja California. He carried each of these places with him as he entered Alta California.

Notes

The authors would like to thank the Academy of American Franciscan History, especially its director, Dr. Jeffrey M. Burns, for support of their work on Junípero Serra.

1. This trend was evident in the first systematic history of California written by a North American, Franklin Tuthill's *History of California* (San Francisco: H. H. Bancroft & Co., 1866). It persisted in various forms in the great multi-volume histories of Hubert Howe Bancroft and Theodore H. Hittell of the nineteenth century, and into the twentieth century in the work of historians like Zoeth Skinner Eldredge. A good example of the "mission revival" approach can be found in Helen Hunt Jackson, *Father Junípero and the Mission Indians of California* (Boston: Little, Brown, 1902). For an example of the anti-mission approach, see Rupert and Jeanette Costo, *The California Missions: A Legacy of Genocide* (San Francisco: The Indian Historian Press, 1987).

2. See, for example, Douglas Monroy, *Thrown Among Strangers: The Making of Mexican Culture in Frontier California* (Berkeley: University of California Press, 1990); Lisbeth Haas, *Conquests and Historical Identities in California, 1769–1936* (Berkeley: University of California Press, 1995); Albert Hurtado, *Intimate Frontiers: Sex, Gender, and Culture in Old California* (Albuquerque: University of New Mexico Press, 1999); James A. Sandos, *Converting California: Indians and Franciscans in the Missions* (New Haven, Conn.: Yale University Press, 2004); Kent G. Lightfoot, *Indians, Missionaries, and Merchants: The Legacy of Colonial Encounters on the California Frontier* (Berkeley: University of California Press, 2005); Steven W. Hackel, *Children of Coyote, Missionaries of St. Francis: Indian Spanish Relations in Colonial California, 1769–1850* (Chapel Hill: University of North Carolina Press, 2005).

3. Francisco Palóu to Rafael Verger, October 19, 1771, in Francisco Palóu, *Cartas desde la península de California, 1768–1773*, ed. José Luis Soto Pérez (Mexico: Editorial Porrúa, 1994), 179; "Circular Letter of Fray Francisco Pangua, Guardian of San Fernando, to the Missionaries of California, Mexico, February 7, 1775," in Junípero Serra, *Writings of Junípero Serra*, ed. and trans. Antonine Tibesar, O.F.M., 4 vols. (Washington, D.C.: Academy of American Franciscan History, 1955–56), 2:459–63; Rose Marie Beebe and Robert M. Senkewicz, *Tensions Among the Missionaries in the 1790s* (Bakersfield, Calif.: California Mission Studies Association, 1996).

4. This record is San Carlos baptism no. 1 in the Early California Population Project database. The sacramental register in which the full record is contained is located in the Archives of the Diocese of Monterey, in Monterey, California. We thank Br. Lawrence Scrivani, SM, for locating this record and the record mentioned in the next paragraph for us when he served as archivist. Maynard J. Geiger, O.F.M., *The Life and Times of Fray Junípero Serra, OFM, or, The Man Who Never Turned Back, 1713–1784, A Biography*, 2 vols. (Washington, D.C.: Academy of American Franciscan History, 1959), 1:5, 10; Maynard J. Geiger, O.F.M., *The Serra Trail in Picture and Story* (San Francisco: Franciscan Fathers of California, 1960), 4–5.

5   San Carlos bapt. no. 750, Early California Population Project; Serra, *Writings*, 4:157, 269.

6   Serra, *Writings*, 4:298–99; Jaime Lladó Ferragut, "El Siglo XVII en Mallorca," in *Historia de Mallorca*, ed. J. Mascaró Pasarius, 5 vols. (Palma: Mascaro Pasarius, 1975), 2:209–17; Román Piña Homs, "Del Decreto de Nueva Planta a las Cortes de Cádiz," in Pasarius, *Historia de Mallorca*, 2:321; Gabriel Alomar Esteve, *Ensayos sobre historia de las Islas Baleares, hasta el año 1800* (Palma: Luis Ripoli, 1979), 365–66.

7   Hubert Howe Bancroft, *History of California*, 7 vols. (San Francisco: The History Co., 1884–90), 1:416; Serra, *Writings*, 1:294–329.

8   Carlos Manera, "Manufactura téxtil y comercio en Mallorca, 1700–1830," *Revista de historia económica* 6, no. 3 (1988): 523–55; Francisco Palóu, *Life of Fray Junípero Serra*, ed. and trans. Maynard J. Geiger, O.F.M. (Washington, D.C.: Academy of American Franciscan History, 1955), 32–33.

9   Geiger, *Serra*, 1:18–22; Sandos, *Converting California*, 33; Baruch Braunstein, *The Chuetas of Majorca: Conversos and the Inquisition of Majorca* (New York: KTAV Publ. House, 1972), 139–81.

10 Maynard J. Geiger, O.F.M., "The Mallorcan Contribution to Franciscan California," *The Americas* 4, no. 4 (1947): 141–50.

11 Regis J. Armstrong, O.F.M. Cap., J. A. Wayne Hellmann, O.F.M. Conv., William J. Short, O.F.M., eds., *Francis of Assisi: Early Documents*, 4 vols. (Hyde Park, N.Y.: New City Press, 1999–2002), 3:125, 333.

12 Palóu, *Life of Fray Junípero Serra*, 5, 321.

13 Alomar Esteve, *Ensayos*, 393.

14 E. Allison Peers, *Ramon Lull, A Biography* (London: Society for Promoting Christian Knowledge, 1929); Anthony Bonner, ed. and trans., *Doctor Illuminatus: A Ramón Llull Reader* (Princeton, N.J.: Princeton University Press, 1993).

15 Bartolomé Escandell Bonet, *Baleares y América* (Madrid: Editorial Mapfre, 1992), 292–93; Kieran McCarty, "Before They Crossed the Great River: Cultural Backgrounds of the Spanish Franciscans of Texas," *Journal of Texas Catholic History and Culture* 3 (1992): 37–43; Bonner, *Doctor Illuminatus*, 13.

16 Palóu, *Life of Fray Junípero Serra*, 309; Bonner, *Doctor Illuminatus*, 59, 69–70; the number forty-three was derived from the online card catalogue of the Biblioteca Nacional de España, at http://catalogo.bne.es.

17 Piña Homs, "Del Decreto de Nueva Planta," 292–308.

18 Ibid., 263–64, 319–21; Alomar Esteve, *Ensayos*, 364.

19 Peers, *Ramon Lull*, 391; Bonner, *Doctor Illuminatus*, 70–71.

20 Palóu, *Life of Fray Junípero Serra*, 6.

21 Serra, *Writings*, 2:365–71, 448; 3:443; Rivera called for "less noise" (*menos ruido*) in Fernando de Rivera to Junípero Serra, October 26, 1775, in Fernando de Rivera y Moncada, *Diario del capitán comandante Fernando de Rivera y Moncada, con un apéndice documental*, ed. Ernest J. Burrus, SJ, 2 vols. (Madrid: Ediciones J. Porrúa Turanzas, 1967), 2:406.

22 Henry Kamen, "Vicissitudes of a World Power," in *Spain: A History*, ed. Raymond Carr (Oxford: Oxford University Press, 2000), 166; Alomar Esteve, *Ensayos*, 359; John Lynch, *Bourbon Spain, 1700–1808* (Oxford: Basil Blackwell, 1989), 8; Henry Charles Lea, *A History of the Inquisition of Spain*, 4 vols. (New York: The Macmillan Company, 1922), 1:335, 3:306.

23 Henry Kamen, *Inquisition and Society in Spain in the Sixteenth and Seventeenth Centuries* (Bloomington: Indiana University Press, 1985), 232; Henry Kamen, *The Spanish Inquisition: A Historical Revision* (New Haven, Conn.: Yale University Press, 1998), 150; Braunstein, *Chuetas of Majorca*, 69–70; on the term *chueta*, see Kenneth Moore, *Those of the Street: The Catholic-Jews of Mallorca* (Notre Dame, Ind.: University of Notre Dame Press, 1976), 22. Families of those who were persecuted by the Inquisition in Mallorca suffered discrimination up to the twentieth century. See Moore, *Those of the Street*, 159–204.

24 Angela S. Selke, *The Conversos of Majorca: Life and Death in a Crypto-Jewish Community in XVII Century Spain*, trans. Henry J. Maxwell (Jerusalem: Magnes Press, Hebrew University, 1986), 3–5; Kamen, *Inquisition and Society*, 234; Lea, *A History of the Inquisition of Spain*, 2:213, 3:307; Braunstein, *Chuetas of Majorca*, 122, 125.

25 Sara T. Nalle, "Inquisitors, Priests, and the People during the Catholic Reformation in Spain," *Sixteenth Century Journal* 18, no. 4 (1987): 559–60.

26 Serra, *Writings*, 3:406–17; see also Steven W. Hackel, "The Staff of Leadership: Indian Authority in the Missions of Alta California," *William & Mary Quarterly* 54, no. 2 (1997): 347–76.

27 Lamin Sanneh, *Translating the Message: The Missionary Impact on Culture* (Maryknoll, N.Y.: Orbis Books, 1989); Richard Fletcher, *The Barbarian Conversion: From Paganism to Christianity* (Berkeley: University of California Press, 1999); Ramsay MacMullen, *Christianity and Paganism in the 4th to 8th Centuries* (New Haven, Conn.: Yale University Press, 1997).

28 On China, see Liam Matthew Brockey, *Journey to the East: The Jesuit Mission to China, 1579–1724* (Cambridge and London: The Belknap Press of Harvard University Press, 2007); on central Mexico, see Francisco Morales, "Franciscanos ante las religiones indígenas," in *Franciscanos en América*, ed. Francisco Morales (Mexico City: Conferencia Franciscana de Santa María de Guadalupe, 1993), 87–102, and Jaime Lara, *Christian Texts for Aztecs: Art and Liturgy in Colonial Mexico* (Notre Dame, Ind.: University of Notre Dame Press, 2008); for these types of developments in Sonora, see José Refugio de la Torre Curiel, "Conquering the Frontier: Contests for Religion, Survival, and Profits in Northwestern Mexico, 1768–1855" (PhD diss., University of California, Berkeley, 2005), 244–320, and his essay in this volume.

29 Juan Crespí, *A Description of Distant Roads: Original Journals of the First Expedition into California, 1769–1770*, ed. and trans. Alan K. Brown (San Diego: San Diego State University Press, 2001); John Galvan, ed., *The First Spanish Entry into San Francisco Bay, 1775* (San Francisco: John Howell, 1971), 11–76; Serra, *Writings*, 3:317 (for Santa María); 2:284–87, 3:411 (for "fugitives").

30 Auguste Duhaut-Cilly, *A Voyage to California, the Sandwich Islands and Around the World in the Years, 1826–1829*, ed. and trans. August Frugé and Neal Harlow (Berkeley: University of California Press, 1999), 119.

31 Lladó Ferragut, "El Siglo XVII en Mallorca," 311–12; Palóu, *Serra*, 75.

32 Mary Beth Ingham, *The Harmony of Goodness: Mutuality and Moral Living According to John Duns Scotus* (Quincy, Ill.: Franciscan Press, 1996), 55–72; Mary Beth Ingham, *Scotus for Dunces: An Introduction to the Subtle Doctor* (St. Bonaventure, N.Y.: Franciscan Institute Publications, 2003), 83.

33 See, for instance, Serra, *Writings*, 1:187, 221, 225; 2:311, 431; 3:55, 91.

34 Iván Martínez, "The Banner of the Spanish Monarchy: The Political Use of the Immaculate Conception," in *Un privilegio sagrado: La concepción de María Inmaculada: Celebración del dogma en México/A Sacred Privilege: The Conception of Mary Immaculate: The Celebration of Dogma in Mexico* (Mexico City: Museo de la Basílica de Guadalupe, 2005), 123–54. We wish to thank Margo Gutiérrez, Assistant Head Librarian, Benson Latin American Collection, University of Texas Libraries, for finding us a copy of this article. Clark Colahan, *The Visions of Sor María de Agreda: Writing Knowledge and Power* (Tucson: University of Arizona Press, 1994); Serra, *Writings*, 1:267; Palóu, *Serra*, 112.

35 Palóu, *Life of Fray Junípero Serra*, 8; Serra, *Writings*, 1:3, 9.

36 Michael McCloskey, O.F.M., *The Formative Years of the Missionary College of Santa Cruz of Querétaro, 1683–1733* (Washington, D.C.: Academy of American Franciscan History, 1955); Félix Saiz Díez, *Los colegios de propaganda fide en Hispanoamérica* (Madrid: n.p., 1969); Carlos León Mujal, "Out of the Apocalypse to Alta California: Franciscans in the New World, 1524–1833" (PhD diss., University of California, Berkeley, 2002), 155–69.

37 McCloskey, *Missionary College of Santa Cruz*, 16; Escandell Bonet, *Baleares y América*, 241–43.

38 Isidro Félix de Espinosa, *Crónica de los Colegios de Propaganda Fide de la Nueva España*, ed. Lino Gómez Canedo (Washington, D.C.: Academy of American Franciscan History, 1964), 103–39; Ellen Gunnardóttir, *Mexican Karismata: The Baroque Vocation of Francisca de los Ángeles, 1674–1744* (Lincoln, Neb.: University of Nebraska Press, 2004), 98.

39 Thomas H. Naylor and Charles W. Polzer, eds., *Pedro de Rivera and the Military Regulations for Northern New Spain, 1724–1729: A Documentary History of His Frontier Inspection and the Reglamento de 1729* (Tucson: University of Arizona Press, 1988), 158; Patricia Osante and Rosalba Alcaraz Cienfuegos, *Nuevo Santander: Un acercamiento al origen de Tamaulipas* (Victoria, Mexico: Gobierno del Estado de Tamaulipas, 1999), 68; María del Carmen Velázquez, *El marqués de Altamira y las provincias internas de Nueva España* (Mexico City: Colegio de México, Centro de Estudios Históricos, 1976), 33–65; Patricia Osante, ed., *Testimonio acerca de la causa formada en la colonia del Nuevo Santander al coronel Don José de Escandón* (Mexico City: Universidad Nacional Autónoma de México, 2000), vi; Patricia Osante, *Orígenes del Nuevo Santander, 1748–1772* (Victoria, Mexico: Universidad Autónoma de Tamaulipas, 1997), 146.

40 Osante, *Testimonio*, ix; Luz Amelia Armas Briz and Olivia Solís Hernández, eds., *Esclavos negros y mulatos en Querétaro, siglo XVIII: Antología documental* (Querétaro, Mexico: Gobierno del Estado de Querétaro, Oficialía Mayor, Archivo Histórico de Querétaro, 2001), 63–64.

41 Lino Gómez Canedo, *Sierra Gorda, un típico enclave misional en el centro de México, siglos XVII–XVIII* (Querétaro, Mexico: Ediciones del Gobierno del Estado de Querétaro, 1988), 61, 79, 81–85; Palóu, *Life of Fray Junípero Serra*, 25.

42 Gómez Canedo, *Sierra Gorda*, 115.

43 Ibid., 81; Velázquez, *El marqués de Altamira*, 59.

44 Gómez Canedo, *Sierra Gorda*, 58, 121, 216; on the college's efforts to recruit men in Europe, see Rose Marie Beebe and Robert M. Senkewicz, "Uncertainty on the Mission Frontier: Missionary Recruitment and Institutional Stability in Alta California in the 1790s," in *Francis in America: Essays on the Franciscan Family in North and South America*, ed. John Schwaller (Berkeley, Calif.: Academy of American Franciscan History, 2005), 307.

45 Gómez Canedo, *Sierra Gorda*, 96–98; Fray Joseph García, Fray Francisco Palóu, Fray Pedro Pérez de Mezquía, and Fray Junípero Serra, "Estado de las misiones de la Sierra Gorda en 1761," San Fernando de México, January 11, 1762, in Gómez Canedo, *Sierra Gorda*, 240; Lino Gómez Canedo, "Fray Junípero Serra y su noviciado misional en América (1750–1758)," in Lino Gómez Canedo, *Evangelización, cultura y promoción social: Ensayos y estudios críticos sobre la contribución franciscana a los orígenes cristianos de México (siglos XVI–XVIII)*, ed. José Luis Soto Pérez (Mexico City: Editorial Porrúa, 1993), 913.

46 Serra, *Writings*, 3:59, 1:19.

47 García et al., "Estado de las misiones," 243.

48 María Elena Galaviz de Capdevielle, "Descripción y pacificación de la Sierra Gorda," *Estudios de historia Novohispana* 4 (1971): 137; Velázquez, *El marqués de Altamira*, 57; David J. Weber, *The Spanish Frontier in North America* (New Haven, Conn.: Yale University Press, 1992), 194; Francis F. Guest, "Mission Colonization and Political Control in Spanish California," in *Hispanic California Revisited*, ed. Doyce B. Nunis Jr. (Santa Barbara, Calif.: Santa Barbara Mission Archive-Library, 1996), 87–114.

49 William B. Taylor, *Magistrates of the Sacred: Priests and Parishioners in Eighteenth Century Mexico* (Stanford, Calif.: Stanford University Press, 1996), 83–86; David J. Weber, *Bárbaros: Spaniards and Their Savages in the Age of Enlightenment* (New Haven, Conn.: Yale University Press, 2005), 107–9.

50 Osante, *Testimonio*, x, xxix; Osante, *Orígenes del Nuevo Santander*, 147, 234; Osante and Alcaraz Cienfuegos, *Nuevo Santander*, 82.

51 Gómez Canedo, *Sierra Gorda*, 121–22, 243; Palóu, *Life of Fray Junípero Serra*, 36–37.

52 Francisco Palóu, *Historical Memoirs of New California*, ed. and trans. Herbert Eugene Bolton, 4 vols. (Berkeley: University of California Press, 1926), 1:13–16; Francisco Palóu, *Recopilación de noticias de la Antigua y de la Nueva California (1767–1783)*, ed. José Luis Soto Pérez (Mexico City: Editorial Porrúa, 1998), 17; Gómez Canedo, *Evangelización*, 621–22.

53 Harry Crosby, *Antigua California: Mission and Colony on the Peninsular Frontier, 1697–1768* (Albuquerque: University of New Mexico Press, 1994), 362–63.

54 Harry W. Crosby, *Gateway to Alta California: The Expedition to San Diego, 1769* (San Diego, Calif.: Sunbelt Publications, 2003), 13–14, 38–41; Palóu, *Historical Memoirs of New California*, 1:32–37.

55 Harry W. Crosby, *Doomed to Fail: Gaspar de Portolá's First California Appointees* (San Diego, Calif.: San Diego State University, Institute of Regional Studies of the Californias, 1989); Palóu, *Historical Memoirs of New California*, 1:236–40.

56 Palóu, *Life of Fray Junípero Serra*, 65. Here we are following Geiger's translation, with the exception of the word *gentiles*, which we render by the word "gentiles," which we think retains more of the biblical connotations Serra and most other missionaries intended. Geiger, on the other hand, followed the Bolton convention of translating this word as "pagans" or "heathens."

JOSÉ REFUGIO DE LA TORRE CURIEL

Franciscan Missionaries in Late Colonial Sonora: Five Decades of Change and Conflict

In 1768, almost a year after the expulsion of the Jesuits from New Spain, the Franciscan friars from the Apostolic College of Querétaro took over most of the Sonoran missions located between the Yaqui Valley and the Gila River. Most of that year, about ten months, was consumed by an arduous journey across the lowlands of Nueva Galicia, Guadalajara, Lower California, and the Sierra Madre. The first missionaries from Querétaro arrived in Sonora in June of that year.[1]

Legally and morally, one historian has explained, "Spain regarded the conversion of Indians to Christianity as its central enterprise in the New World."[2] To that end, José de Gálvez and Viceroy Teodoro de Croix had decided to entrust the bishop of Durango with the administration of the southernmost Sonoran mission districts and to restaff the rest of the Jesuit missions with Franciscan friars. The Franciscan presence in New Spain's northern frontier was considered instrumental to imperial objectives, while at the same time it was expected to work to the advantage of local populations.[3] In theory, the goal was to promote the expansion of the Spanish settlements in far-off lands, and at the same time to transform the day-to-day lives of the Indians.[4]

In practice, however, most of the non-indigenous settlers and local authorities gradually became convinced that a good missionary minded spiritual concerns only, leaving issues of an economic or political nature in the hands of laypersons. But from the perspective of the Indians, as recent discussions have shown, the presence of the missionaries was advantageous when they were claiming rights to their lands, calling for protection, or reorganizing their communities.[5] A great many explanations have been proposed to define the characteristics and functions of eighteenth-century missionaries in northern New Spain. These constructions attest to the various ways in which Spanish authorities, would-be settlers, and Indians needed or wanted the friars to act—more than the ways they actually did act. Even in recent times, it has been a common practice to refer to the missionaries in northern New Spain collectively as Jesuits, Franciscans, or Dominicans—as if these designations conveyed a single repertoire of beliefs, attitudes, and practices in all regions and at all points in time.[6] Such representations or usages reflect the kind of identity that was assigned (then and now) to the friars as missionaries.[7]

This essay aims to engage in a larger discussion about the construction and transformation of group identities in northern New Spain by focusing on the Franciscan case in Sonora. Between 1768 and the late 1790s, two generations of Franciscans arrived in the region. Despite some differences in their attitudes and actions, in most respects they shared the conviction that the rules and precepts of their religious order were not incompatible with the administration of the temporalities—namely, the economic production of the mission, the organization of the daily life and labor of the Indians, and the secular possessions and property of the Church. These two generations linked the "apostolic zeal" of their order to direct control of the mission Indians' labor and productive capacity and to the expansion of the Spanish and Christian empires. They passionately believed that their role as apostolic missionaries required them to organize not just the religious lives of the Indians but virtually all aspects of their existence. A third group of Franciscans, who are the focus of the last portion of this essay, arrived in Sonora in the early years of the nineteenth century. They saw their role quite differently. They saw themselves as undertaking the responsibility for the Indians' religious lives only, and did not want to be involved in the daily management of labor and production. They saw themselves as working for the religious transformation of the Indians, and they therefore believed that the Crown should fund their efforts. They also acknowledged that their functions had become less central to society, as cultural ties between Indians and colonizers grew stronger and tensions deepened between missionaries and Indians over matters of labor, belief, and practice.

Identity formation of course touches upon every aspect of daily life, and involves issues as varied as gender, ethnicity, spirituality, and class, all of which are the focus of separate areas of study. However, my primary concern here is both self-definition and differentiation among the members of an apparently homogenous group of clergymen. As I will show, the Queretan friars serving the Pimería Alta missions[8] developed different strategies of socio-religious work, depending on the ways in which they perceived self-definition operating among other groups, on how they understood their own work, and on the way they viewed themselves, compared to other friars participating in the same venture. In other words, different groups of missionaries had distinct identities, based on various and sometimes contrasting agendas.[9]

As recent studies of California missions show, internal divisions within the ranks of the missionaries reveal deep differences in personality, ideas, and ways of understanding corporate functions. For instance, Beebe and Senkewicz, in their study on the Franciscans of the College of San Fernando sent to California, analyze the characteristics of different generations of Franciscans.[10] Borrowing insights from this case, I contend that Queretan missionaries distinguished themselves from the rest of the Spanish settlers and from the Xaliscan friars who were also assigned to the missions in Sonora. Furthermore, in doing so, the Queretans faced internal divisions because of the coexistence, in the late eighteenth century, of contradictory ways of understanding missionary work within their own institution. Examined through the lenses of social identity, these fissures reveal the ways in which the Queretan missionaries sought to define and defend the repertoire of attitudes, beliefs, and norms of conduct that were to characterize their order. At the same time, these fissures suggest the ways in which these missionaries tried to adapt to the demands of a changing society.

It is well known that the principles and precepts that governed the lives and deeds of the Franciscan friars were first laid down in the thirteenth century, when the order of St. Francis and the vows of poverty, chastity, and obedience were approved and sanctioned by the papacy.[11] Subsequent reforms to the order, and the creation of new branches within the Franciscan family, added further restrictions and modes of behavior that determined the general character of this religious group in the eyes of the societies in which the friars were immersed.[12] In the sixteenth century the Spanish Crown issued a series of decrees and royal orders governing the structure and operation of the religious orders in the Americas, including the privileges and limits of the members, both as individual persons and as part of a community.[13]

These written codes compose the legal framework that delineated the institutional body of the Franciscans. Beyond those constructions, local practices and environments—as well as the nature of the interaction between local communities and friars—were also important in the formation of Franciscan group identity. The Sonoran case explored here shows how the first Franciscan missionaries from the Apostolic College of Querétaro developed a particular group identity, partially influenced by the institutional constraints of the order, but mostly constrained by the ways in which they adapted to mission life in the context of the growing consolidation of other forms of Spanish settlement on New Spain's northern fringes. The divergent attitudes of three generations of Queretan friars examined here toward the administration of mission temporalities, control of Indian labor, and daily life within the mission provide examples that illustrate how Queretan Franciscan group identity changed over time.

Temporalities and Franciscan Poverty

One of the main problems that the Franciscan administrations faced in northern New Spain was the management of mission properties (*temporalidades*). Upon their arrival in Sonora, the Queretan missionaries found that their authority to use mission resources for their sustenance was subordinate to the will of local officials. However, their timely requests to the College of Querétaro, which responded rapidly, and José de Gálvez's 1769 decree entrusting the friars with the administration of temporalities improved prospects for those missionaries. Because of the acknowledgment of the precarious conditions in that frontier region, the Queretans managed after 1769 to gain not only control of the temporalities but also the right to intervene in the social organization of the towns under their care, to monitor dealings between Indians and Spaniards, and to ensure that the Indians farmed individually and fulfilled their obligation to work three days per week on community lands.[14] Thanks to these privileges, by 1771 the Queretans at San Xavier del Bac and Ati had managed to accumulate large quantities of cattle and grain.[15] At other missions the Queretans reorganized communal labor, supervised construction projects in their missions, and generated considerable material resources.[16]

For mission residents, however, the Queretans' handling of the mission economy proved a difficult burden. Unpaid labor was the bone of contention: it triggered discord between Indians and missionaries, and it provoked residents' complaints about the excesses of the fathers. As a result of the gradual demographic decline of these population centers in the late eighteenth century, the situation worsened, because the pressures of agricultural production and ranching fell upon a constantly shrinking base of Indian laborers.

For the first generation of Queretans in Sonora, managing the temporalities was also a way to secure the congregation and conversion of Indian groups. Father Francisco Garcés, who most clearly exemplifies the views of his generation, declared that this form and method of administration would require that the missionary "speak with the hands." To accomplish this, the missionary would have to combine his work on the communal lands with close supervision of the Indians' work, and would furthermore need to distribute food and commodities to the Indians efficiently, to ensure their participation in daily prayers.[17] According to Father José Soler, another member of this founding generation, the Queretan "form and method" of administration was "the most conducive" route, both to subsistence for mission residents and indoctrination of the Indians.[18]

As these examples suggest, soon after their arrival in Sonora the Queretans had incorporated the administration of temporalities as a distinctive feature of their socio-religious project. In time, however, in response to the many critics of the mission regime, the members of the second generation of Queretans in Sonora developed a more elaborate system for controlling local resources. A document dating from 1780 reveals the ways in which the Queretans were to define the relation between mission work and the handling of temporalities. In this document, Father Antonio Barbastro, the president of the Queretans in Sonora, drafted what he termed "the method that should be observed in the communication of sacraments, prayers, and instruction of the Indians." "We are to be poor and to appear as such," the letter stipulated. In this missive, Barbastro explained that it was entirely legitimate for the missionaries to accept alms, "as long as it is not the missionary [himself] who receives the money," and as long as they were applied to the needs of the Indians. In administering a mission's common property, the fathers were to make sure that the Indians worked regularly and did not sell their products cheaply. Nonetheless, popular opinion characterized the fathers who carried out this oversight as virtual "administrators of estates," who were in violation of both canon and common law.

Barbastro did not share this view, however, reasoning that what the Queretans were doing in Sonora was "nothing more than counseling the [Indian] governor as to what is best, and replacing, not his master ... as does the administrator, but his lack of wits, as he does so out of charity, unlike the administrator." In his approach to the issues of managing money and purchasing and selling goods, Barbastro distinguished two types of commerce. If it became necessary for a friar to actually handle money in the execution of such transactions, a third party representing the missionary would have to receive the payment itself. On the other hand, if agreements were based on the exchange of goods (as occurred in most cases), then the missionaries themselves could handle the transactions, as often as was deemed necessary. Barbastro explained that barter (*trueque*) allowed them "to purchase in the same way as we may sell; and thus we can establish a price for an article, sell it, and even look for a buyer." Finally, he made it clear that the prime beneficiary of Indian labor was to be the mission church:

> because the personal services that the Indians provide for the growth and conservation [of the churches] is admitted in place of the tithes, first fruits, [and] ecclesiastic fees... [T]hey are obliged to pay like all other Christians, for the sustenance of the mission church and its minister, and in conformity with this, if the church has needs then such goods may not be invested in any other thing.

If a surplus remained, once the needs of the church and the minister had been taken care of, it could be used to succor the Indians, beginning with widows, orphans, and the sick, and then including the entire community.[19] In this lengthy exposition, Barbastro established the moral foundations of the exploitation of Indian labor and authorized the commercial relations in which the missionaries were implicated.[20] By the same token, Barbastro authorized the friars to barter with the goods they listed in their annual requisitions (*memorias de géneros*), and this became perhaps the most common commercial practice among them, though one that the Jesuits had prohibited on various occasions.

On a symbolic level, what was the significance of retaining control over mission temporalities? An example from the Ópata mission of Bacadehuachi provides a glimpse of the instrumental role that this privilege played in the construction of group identity among the missionaries. In contrast to the Queretan missionaries in the Pimería Alta, where the Franciscans' access to and control of mission produce gave them the power to distribute charity, the Xaliscan missionaries stationed in the Opatería no longer performed this function. Being a blue-robed missionary in Sonora in the late eighteenth century implied a situation of dependency in which the role of relief-provider was played by laypersons—including mission Indians. Father Francisco Caballero, missionary of Bacadehuachi, for example, was unable to get access to the above-mentioned sources of funds, but in his position of authority over the local population, he could also make a request to the captain of the Ópata Indians of that town for sustenance. He promised to pay for these provisions in due time, once his annual stipend was paid from the royal treasury in Arizpe.[21]

Thus, the Queretans contemporary with Father Barbastro, the *misioneros apostólicos,* or gray-robes, enjoyed an atypical position within their communities. Unlike the Xaliscans, their southern neighbors, they did not have financial hardships. Nor were they faced with local authorities closely supervising daily activities, as was the case in the Opatería. Queretans did not have among their ranks friars as detached from missionary activities as the blue-robed *gachupines,* who sided with the bishop of Sonora in the 1780s when criticism of mission regimes in northern New Spain was at its height.[22] Or at least that is what the Queretans thought in the late 1780s, before Commandant General Pedro de Nava reformed the methods of administering temporalities and government of mission Indians in the Provincias Internas.[23]

Reaction against Pedro de Nava's Reform

In 1794, Pedro de Nava ordered that instead of providing personal labor, all male Indians under fifty years of age would cooperatively support the missionaries by donating half a *fanega* of corn, or twelve *reales*. De Nava's decree sought to abolish "the ancient method of community" in Indian towns that had been congregated into mission settlements ten years earlier, or more. This meant that only recently converted populations would conserve the existing form of government, and those only for a period not longer than ten years. Moreover, the goal was to treat Indians as owners of their cattle, their lands, and the products of their labor, thus putting them on the same footing as the Spaniards and other groups. Like the rest of the population, the Indians would be free to accept work in any form that they wished (including attending to the missionaries), but their employers would be obliged to pay them for their labor.[24] Finally, the commandant general decreed the division of communal lands, leaving one part to be worked for the common benefit of the town, while the other fields were to be distributed in individual plots among the Indians of each locality.[25]

The widely varying impact of these reforms was matched only by the considerable differences in the settings in which they were applied and in the opinions of missionaries with respect to their implementation.[26] But in all cases, the reforms decreed by de Nava attempted to address the increase in the non-Indian population along New Spain's northern frontier in the late eighteenth century, and its growing demand for agricultural lands and laborers.[27] Against this backdrop, it is hardly surprising that the regions in Sonora where the reforms were implemented most rapidly (the central valleys and the piedmont, seat of the missionary district of the province of Xalisco) were also those that registered the highest number of claims to land by private individuals in the early nineteenth century.[28]

In the Pimería Alta, de Nava's reforms meant not only taking administrative functions out of the clergy's hands but also, and above all, standardizing policies in the missions along the frontier with those in other population centers in Sonora (all of which had been founded at least ten years earlier). This new policy jeopardized plans by the Queretans to establish missions between Alta California and New Mexico, and the reactions of the fathers, of course, were not long in coming. De Nava's 1794 decree was soon answered by a series of reports and presentations designed to demonstrate the deleterious effects that this policy would have for the advance of Spanish settlement into the Gila and Colorado river valleys. However, the Franciscans' response to the new reform soon revealed that the missionary enterprise in the Pimería Alta was seriously compromised by differences in criteria between the two groups of clergymen, the Queretans and the Xaliscans. The challenge that those missionaries faced in the late eighteenth century was whether to tolerate the policies sanctioned by custom and to administer mission properties directly, as had been the norm during the Jesuit period, or to attempt to adjust Sonoran reality to the spirit of Franciscan principles.

How are we to understand these divisions among the Queretans, the members of one of the most disciplined ecclesiastical institutions in New Spain? In this period, it would be inappropriate to refer to the dichotomy between peninsular and Creole Franciscans that several years later would mark the epoch of Mexican independence, as members of both of these camps could be on either side of the question of Nava's reforms. The rupture that divided the Queretans was in fact expressed in terms of familiarity with the frontier societies, through allusions to their experience in mission activities, and, in a wider sense, through distinctions between "older" and "younger" missionaries.[29]

By the mid-1790s, Father Francisco Antonio Barbastro was the spokesperson for the second generation of Queretans in the Pimería Alta,[30] those who had arrived on the eve of the creation of the Custody of Sonora[31] in 1783 and had survived the period during which the bishop, Father Antonio de los Reyes, had attempted to reform the mission regime in northern New Spain.[32] In addition to Barbastro, Fathers Baltasar Carrillo, Francisco Iturralde, Francisco Moyano, Juan Bautista Llorens, Lorenzo Simó, and Juan Santiesteban were the missionaries of the "old school" who, upon receiving news of the recent reform of mission government, simply acknowledged receipt of the commandant's dispositions and assured de Nava that they would suspend their administration of mission properties as soon as they had completed the last construction projects they had undertaken.[33] Perhaps owing to their long experience in those provinces, or perhaps because they were aware that in Sonora, decrees approving and then derogating such matters were being issued one after another, the "older" missionaries concluded that they could survive the policy changes of the civil authorities simply by pretending to fulfill them.[34] Years of experience had led those priests to reconsider their posture regarding the government of the missions; though they supported, in principle, managing communal properties through agents and depositaries (*procuradores* and *depositarios*) as their constitution mandated, experience had taught them that accounts and holdings had to be handled personally to guarantee the material and spiritual progress of the missions. Nonetheless, after persistent rumors and criticism from residents over this system of management, fatigue set in: perhaps it would be better in the long run to abandon direct administration if matters were not going to improve.

This posture contrasted sharply with the ideas of the second generation of missionaries who arrived in the Pimería Alta in the early 1790s. While they shared the older friars' ideal of expanding the missions toward the Gila and Colorado rivers, they insisted that the missions retain only indirect control of temporalities, through agents and depositaries. The new missionaries also insisted upon exercising the principles of authority consecrated in the old method of government in the mission towns. Among this new generation, Father Diego Miguel Bringas would play a fundamental role in articulating what they considered to be the most appropriate method of moving their socio-religious project forward. Moreover, it was Father Bringas who went to the missions in the Pimería Alta as a *visitador*: to evaluate the work of the older missionaries, to become familiar with the problems those missions were confronting, and to discover the roots of the accusations that some of the new missionaries had made to the Discretory of the College of Querétaro against their older colleagues.

Let us now examine the terms in which this generational rupture developed. After dissolving the short-lived Custody of San Carlos de Sonora in 1791, Barbastro had initiated negotiations with the bishop of Sonora, the commandant general, and the intendant of Sonora to allow his college to take possession of the old missions and attempt, once again, to establish missions in the area around the Gila and Colorado rivers.

Barbastro opined that their arrival should reflect great poverty: they should take only a few agricultural implements, and they should leave the cattle at the missions in the Pimería Alta to avoid possible raids by Indians. Efforts should be made to attract a few Spanish families to settle around the missions, though they would be prohibited from living inside the Indian towns. Above all, however, Barbastro argued that the Franciscans should exercise universal jurisdiction (*omnímoda jurisdicción*) over the missions of those new establishments.[35] A military escort would not be necessary, he said, because in those lands it was actually more dangerous to be accompanied by soldiers than to travel alone. Furthermore, he argued, if the local authorities did not support the venture because they did not favor the coexistence of Indians and Spaniards, then that was even better for the friars, as they would be able to enter those new territories on their own, as their forebears had done.[36]

Barbastro proposed that the new mission district be placed entirely under the "universal jurisdiction" of the missionaries, extending into that region the same mode of governance that he himself had sanctioned for the Pimería Alta. But the College of Querétaro opposed the plan for two reasons: they had begun to question the rectitude of the traditional mode of government over which Barbastro presided, and they considered it "inconvenient" to commit to the Gila and Colorado river venture without the approval of the Crown. Influenced by these two arguments, the members of the Discretory opted to draw out the process, promising only to study Barbastro's proposals "in due time." Wizened by age, Barbastro knew that this meant that the Discretory had subtly rejected his project. He realized that times had changed, and that it was difficult for the younger priests, who had no direct experience of missionary work in far-off provinces, to understand the needs of frontier missions.[37]

While discussion of Barbastro's proposal continued, the College of Querétaro received reports from individual missionaries in Sonora containing accusations of improper handling of properties and monies by Barbastro and his fellow Franciscans, and citing other abuses that put "the souls of those older missionaries in peril." Concerned about these reports, and made uneasy by Barbastro's form of government, in March 1795 the fathers of the Discretory of the Querétaro College appointed Father Diego Miguel Bringas—until then the college's chronicler—to visit the missions in the Pimería Alta. The objectives of his visit, Bringas was instructed, were twofold. First, he was to pull the missions out of their temporal and spiritual ruin by convincing the local authorities to allow the missionaries to continue managing the temporalities, and by correcting the "excesses" he encountered through whatever means he deemed necessary. Second, he was specifically entrusted with the task of finding a way to expand the missions into the Papaguería region.[38] Historians have traditionally regarded this second task as the most important aspect of Bringas's visit to the Pimería Alta, partly because he was accompanied on his journey by nine missionaries who expected to take charge of the new missions.[39] But the earnest entreaty that the visitador sent to the king in 1796 to win his support for the establishment of new missions there, and the attendant publicity, has held greater weight for most historians.[40] We should not, however, lose sight of two facts: such dreams did not materialize; and the primary motive behind Bringas's visit was to resolve serious problems in the internal organization of the Pimería Alta missions.

The "excesses" that Father Bringas was sent to correct were linked to the generational rupture mentioned above. The Discretory had invested Bringas with full powers to remove missionaries from their office and to order their return to Querétaro, along with whatever measures he felt were appropriate to remedy the condition into which those missions had fallen. In other words, the Discretory had sent Bringas not only to verify the status of the situation in Sonora but also to remove the older friars from their missions, as they recognized later when they supported Bringas's laconic diagnosis: "There is no other remedy than to recall those priests who have grown old here amidst these faults of observance."[41]

As a matter of fact, Bringas had been sent to the Pimería Alta just a few weeks after the college had demanded that Barbastro explain the accusations leveled against him by Father Francisco Villaseca, a recently arrived missionary. Villaseca had declared it probable that the friars assigned to those missions did not obey the rules: they possessed herds of animals; they openly bought and sold merchandise; and the president of the missions—Father Barbastro—was aware of everything that was going on, had consented to it, and even encouraged these practices by his own example. Finally, Villaseca accused Barbastro of constructing a house in Aconchi at a monumental cost. As far as Barbastro was concerned, the accusations against him clearly reflected the enormous gulf that existed between those missionaries who were accustomed to life on the frontier and those who had but recently arrived:

> When a European priest comes to [the New World], he sees and hears many things that cause him grave dissonance, ... naked Indians, women showing their breasts,

indolent, filthy people, a language they do not understand; he sees the minister at the altar but also in the corral, feeding the chickens; selling lard, candles, soap, rags, etc. He sees him receiving everything he is given, ... [and] judges everything as illicit, at times verging on sin ... As he sees the minister doing all these things with no remorse, he judges him obstinate and incapable of repair; and finds no other solution than to return to the convent. It does not occur to him to inquire conscientiously but only to report to the prelate. Thus, he dishonors the missionaries, worries the prelates, and causes a tempest so powerful that even the forests are devastated.[42]

The defense that Father Barbastro presented to his superiors was quite simple: the oldest argument elaborated to criticize the labors of the missionaries assigned to Sonora, he asserted, was that it was impossible for them to observe the rules of the Franciscan order. It had been used, he said, by Father Antonio de los Reyes in his attempts to promote reform, and several priests continued to use it as an excuse, "some in order to get away, others to avoid coming." The problem was that in order to survive on those missions it was necessary for the missionaries to administer mission properties and conduct transactions in the name of those establishments, even though many of them found such activities repugnant. With respect to the house in Aconchi, Barbastro explained that efforts had been going on for several years to promote the establishment of the Third Order of Penitence[43] in that town, and it was for this reason that he had built the house and chapel. In conclusion, Barbastro emphasized, he was sure that he had disproved all the accusations against him, and that the entire episode had been nothing more than a ploy devised by Villaseca to facilitate his return to the college. In closing his defense, Barbastro put the following words into Villaseca's mouth: "This life is not fit for me, there is no stipend ... So, how shall I get out [of Sonora]? Though I return to the college without license, I shall say that I have come to avoid condemnation." Barbastro concluded by reaffirming the disposition required of those priests who went to work in Sonora, implicitly praising the quality of the older missionaries and criticizing the prejudices of the younger ones: "One must arrive prepared to suffer labor and hardships, for if one recalls [life at] the college then all is lost ... ; it is here, here where even the most valiant lion must bow his head."[44]

Though Barbastro was successful in his defense, his presence in the Pimería Alta was no longer deemed necessary by the Discretory.[45] In fact, the time would come when the Discretory would instruct the visitador, Diego Bringas, to sound out the commandant general "with great dissimulation and prudence" to see if he was disposed to remove Barbastro from those provinces. Though Barbastro's return to the college never came to pass, his resignation from the post of president of the missions in the Pimería Alta was accepted. In 1795 Father Bringas named Father Francisco Iturralde to replace Barbastro, in recognition of Iturralde's long tenure there.[46]

The trouble between Villaseca and Barbastro was not an isolated incident in the Pimería Alta, as the conflict that emerged between older missionaries and newer ones led to similar accusations in several different places in that mission district. For example, Father Lorenzo Simó was accused by one recently arrived missionary, Father Ángel Collazo, of living with a woman in Cucurpe, Bacoachi, and Caborca.[47] In another case, upon his arrival in Sonora, the visitador, Bringas, immediately proposed that two of Barbastro's allies, Fathers Narciso Gutiérrez and Antonio Díez, return to Querétaro, though his plan was frustrated when Iturralde and Barbastro interceded on their behalf and took them in as "auxiliaries" on their respective missions.[48]

Despite these disagreements, which were quickly resolved through diplomatic means, Father Bringas's *visita* took place in relative tranquility from July to December of 1795.[49] Afterward, he drafted a report in which he attempted both to curry the favor of the king and to conserve the administration of temporalities in the Pimería Alta. He argued that those towns represented ongoing conversions (*conversiones vivas*), even though they had been founded more than one hundred years earlier, and he made an effort to show that they constituted a veritable "frontier of heathenism." Bringas's report also requested the Crown's financial support for the establishment of new missions in the area around the Gila and Colorado rivers, and he petitioned that the responsibility for that venture not be left to local authorities. He cited the case of 1781 that, he believed, had resulted in the deaths of several missionaries and settlers at the hands of the Yuma Indians.[50] Bringas argued that they should follow the method consecrated by experience and entrust the organization of those communities to the missionaries, providing them with adequate military escorts and authorizing two friars for each mission.[51] Upon Bringas's return to the College of Querétaro, the establishment of the new missions became a priority for the Discretory, and in the following years the responsibility for promoting this matter among the civil and ecclesiastical authorities of the Viceroyalty fell squarely upon his shoulders, as did the task of securing various sources of financing for that enterprise.[52]

With the visitador back in Querétaro, the conflicts among the Franciscans in the Pimería Alta increased in intensity once again, and a storm of opposing arguments raged across the province. Iturralde, the recently named president of the missions, found himself facing more and more problems in ordering their spiritual and temporal administration, as the initiatives of the missionaries often ran counter to his dispositions. In 1797, this led to a confrontation between Father Florencio Ibáñez and President Iturralde, and the former was consequently granted leave to return to the college one year later.[53] In 1798, Father Pascual Rodríguez became disenchanted with the prospects in Sonora and "bowed his head," just three years after accompanying Father Bringas to Sonora. He asked for, and received, permission to abandon the Pimería Alta and return to Querétaro.[54]

Father Barbastro died in the town of Aconchi in June 1800,[55] taking the very backbone of the Queretan missions in Sonora with him, as it was he who had brought cohesion to the second generation of its missionaries. Although Barbastro was survived by a few of his contemporaries, by the early nineteenth century some of them had returned to Querétaro and others had broken their affiliation with the college. A few of them remained in the Pimería Alta, but only to be cared for during their illnesses and old age by younger missionaries.[56] Thus, a third generation of Franciscans came to work in the region, the final contingent of missionaries who came from Spain to take charge of the missions.[57]

A New Contingent Arrives as Missionary Administration Concludes

In the early years of the nineteenth century, the clergy at the College of Querétaro concluded once again that it was necessary to revitalize missionary activities in Sonora. Mission reform and the expansion into Papaguería would hardly have seemed novel objectives by then, but they still fired the imagination of the Discretory, which considered them to be longstanding goals. This new reform movement was led by Father Juan Bautista Ceballos who, curiously, had remained aloof from the missionary experience in Sonora but was convinced of the need to "reform the customs" of his fellows stationed in those far-off lands. Father Ceballos, who was for several years part of the Discretory of Querétaro, was sent to visit the college's missions in 1809.[58] After drawn-out negotiations in Querétaro and Mexico City to obtain the necessary funds and to convince other Franciscans to accompany him to the Pimería Alta, Father Ceballos and his entourage finally began their journey in December 1812, arriving in Sonora in mid-1814.[59] The visitador's traveling companions were Fathers Pedro Ruiz, Francisco Fontbona, Miguel Montes, and Matías Creo, the "young blood" that would soon encounter great difficulty in melding with the older priests in those mission districts.

The importance of Ceballos's visit lies in the changes he introduced in the mission towns in the Pimería Alta. Given the historical moment in which his visita took place, it fell to Ceballos to organize the missions in the Pimería in accordance with the constitutional regime promulgated in 1812 in Spain. Upon his arrival in Sonora, Ceballos found that according to the Constitution of Cadiz (1812), national *alcaldes* had been elected to replace the old local authorities (the Indian governor and other justices). A fervent supporter of this system of government and of putting the Indians on an equal footing with other settlers, Father Ceballos promoted the idea that the missions should pay the Indians for their labor, "as they do with non-Indian workers," and, moreover, that the missions should carry out their obligation to distribute individual plots of land to the Indians.[60] Those dispositions received a warm welcome in such towns as San Ignacio, Cocóspera, Tumacácori, and Tubutama, which were administered by the newly arrived missionaries. However, it was quite a different story with the older missionaries.

Friction between the visitador and the new president of the Pimería Alta missions, Father Francisco Moyano, did not take long to surface. In Ceballos's view it was clear that Moyano would never accept these new measures in Oquitoa and San Xavier del Bac because he was "stuck on the idea that the Indians should work for him, receiving nothing in return," and because his accustomed way of fulfilling his obligation to aid the Indians was to give them thin blankets, for which he charged a *fanega* of wheat.[61] After his visita in the Pimería Alta, Father Ceballos went to the town of Ures, where he intended to establish a seminary-like convent (*hospicio*) for the missionary districts of Sonora.[62] By early 1815 these reforms of the governing system for mission towns had been derogated by the Spanish government and, as on previous occasions, the mission towns simply returned to the old system of governance and the practice of electing indigenous governors and alcaldes.[63] But the 1814 reforms had left a noticeable mark on the Pimería Alta. On the one hand, Indians from several missions had taken advantage of the freedoms consecrated in the Cadiz Constitution and fled from their towns, while those who had opted to remain refused to be treated as neophytes under missionary tutelage. On the other hand, Ceballos's visita had polarized relations between the missionaries in the Pimería Alta to such a degree that neighborliness and the norms of conduct among the Queretan brethren became marked by increasing intolerance.

As in earlier years, this disjuncture between the older and younger missionaries stationed in the Pimería Alta would soon become evident in bitter disputes, mutual recrimination, and even desertions by some missionaries in circumstances that scarcely befitted their religious investiture. One of the first signals of disquiet among older missionaries came from Father Juan Bautista Llorens just a few months after the conclusion of Ceballos's visita. As far as Llorens was concerned, it was clear that the visita had completely upset the Pimería Alta region, because its arguments in favor of freedom for the Indians had prevented the missionaries from carrying out their ministry in those towns.[64] After the visita it became virtually impossible to convince the Indians to attend Mass or the Doctrine, and even more difficult to convince them to remain in their towns; even the Pápagos who frequented those towns no longer stayed with the missionaries for those same reasons. "There is no one among the older fathers who does not regret these events," lamented Father Llorens in early 1815, as everything on the missions had been reduced "to liberty [and] land distribution."[65] Under these circumstances, Father Llorens lost interest in remaining at the college's missions, and informed his father guardian that he had been accepted by the province of Xalisco and wished to leave the college, to "change the habit of a [Franciscan of the Apostolic] College" for the blue robe of the Xaliscans and serve on one of their Sonoran missions.[66]

Together with Llorens, Fathers Francisco Moyano, Narciso Gutiérrez, and Diego Gil also made their disillusionment with these prospects known: they knew that the visita was a stratagem that Ceballos had wielded "against the old missionaries," and for this reason they attempted through all available means to ensure that the dispositions dictated by Father Ceballos during his visita did not take effect.[67] Nor had the prefect been wasting his time: upon his arrival in Sonora he had explained to the guardian of the College of Querétaro that the missionary who was mainly responsible for the abuses he was trying to correct in Sonora was Father Gil. "Most of the blame lies with Father Gil," Ceballos had observed, and with this sentence sealed Father Diego's fate: he was soon recalled to the college.[68]

Amid this disorder at the hands of the Franciscans in the Pimería Alta, the residents of the missions continued to strengthen ties of dependence with the nearby ranches and mines, while the Spanish settlers near the missions continued to acquire lands in the vicinity. It is difficult to say whether the problems among the missionaries were symptoms of these developments or if the gradual separation of the indigenous population from the mission regime was facilitated by the internal conflicts of the Sonoran missionaries. What was clear was that as the nineteenth century wore on, these two processes gathered momentum. It would be difficult to recall a clearer case of disobedience and rebelliousness in the Pimería Alta than the one involving Father Francisco Fontbona, who in 1815 traveled to several of the missions dressed as a layman, mounted on horseback, attending fiestas here and there, ignoring his father president, and engaging in fisticuffs with anyone who got in his way.[69]

Equal alarm arose, at least among the older missionaries, when also in 1815 one of their young fellows threatened Queretan brethren and local authorities at gunpoint. The young friar wished to move to a town other than the one to which he had been assigned, and drew the weapon to try to force their consent. To the utter consternation of the older missionaries—and the delight of those who were transmitting timely reports of misadventures that were really none of their concern—Father Matías Creo, the protagonist of the incident, accompanied his show of bravura with a prolonged series of public insults hurled at the president of those missions (then Father Francisco Moyano) over a period of several days.[70] Far greater surprise was caused by the reaction of Ceballos, the prefecto comisario, who had been sent to Sonora to "reform the customs" of the missionaries. Ceballos devoted his efforts to returning the older friars to the College of Querétaro because they did not support his visita—all the while tolerating outrageous conduct by the missionaries he himself had introduced into Sonora. Several months after these incidents, Ceballos alleged in his own defense that "the missionaries who have been accused are not as bad as they seem to have been portrayed to the Discretory."[71] In his opinion, a week of spiritual exercises would suffice to correct the path of the new friars, while it was better that the older missionaries—including the president of the missions—be sent back to Querétaro because of their errors in handling the missions' assets, "though this was not to be taken as punishment."[72]

Ceballos's visita caused a deep rupture in relations among the missionaries but there was another telling consequence of this episode: the acceptance by the Indians of the offer to equalize their rights with those of the Spanish settlers. Though the meaning of equality and liberty for the citizenry had long been debated in Spanish courts, for the residents of mission towns it was clear that these concepts were to be understood as freedom of possession and freedom of transit in that frontier area. Through his advocacy of these constitutional principles, Father Ceballos had unintentionally set in motion one of the processes that would precipitate the end of the mission regime in the nineteenth century. Once these freedoms had been granted to mission residents, it proved impossible to retract them and to subject the Indians once again to the authority of the missionaries.[73]

Changing Settings, Contrasting Personalities

The first two generations of Franciscans who arrived in Sonora before 1800 were in general agreement about their complex roles within the missions. They perceived little contradiction between the precepts of their religious order and the administration of temporalities, and believed in a broad continuity between the control of their communities and the expansion of the Spanish and Christian empires. In their own view, they were to act both as community builders and relief providers. Like the missionaries examined by Beebe and Senkewicz in their essay in this volume, these Franciscans confronted their new challenges while deeply rooted in their past experiences.[74] In contrast to these earlier generations, a third group of friars understood their duties differently, considering that their proper sphere should be religious matters only, and not mission temporalities. The consolidation of Spanish settlements (ranches, mining sites, villages) in the areas surrounding the missions, the development of stronger economic and cultural ties between Indians and colonizers, the growing tensions between missionaries and Indians over matters of labor, belief, and practice—all of these changes made the new missionaries aware that their role in the daily management of Indian lives was becoming peripheral. They criticized their predecessors for a dual failure—neither anticipating these changes nor taking steps to accommodate them.

The Sonoran case here examined is in some ways analogous with examples from other regions, where the institution was deeply shaken by the collision between old and new forms of mission administration.[75] The struggles between *padres viejos y nuevos* in Sonora confirms what Beebe and Senkewicz have observed about late eighteenth-century California missions: at the dawn of the colonial period missions were not only affected by external criticisms, but they were also internally weak, fragile, and divided.[76] Overlooking these internal disruptions, they contend, provides a biased picture of the development of mission history: in

California, their argument goes, the result has been that some scholars consider the relative economic success of the missions inevitable. In the same vein, the decline of Sonora missions has long been considered a natural one, because after the expulsion of the Jesuits in 1767 those towns' wealth, produce, and livestock virtually disappeared within a couple of years.[77] Again, focusing on the personalities of the missionaries and the changing contexts in which they worked, and on the gradual transformation of frontier societies, gives a more nuanced picture of the final decades of mission life in northwestern New Spain.

In Sonora there was a time when the missionaries identified themselves with the old method of administration, an eclectic manifestation of the practices, customs, norms, and exemptions that regulated the ways in which missionaries interacted with all social groups related to mission life (resident Indians, Indians not affiliated with the mission, *vecinos*, soldiers, miners, merchants, and missionaries). In other words, the old method of government was at the core of the identity of missionaries as a social group.

But in the view of Bourbon reformers, by the late eighteenth century most of the mission districts in Spanish America no longer needed, or wanted, the intervention of clergymen in temporal matters. In fact, local ordinances like Pedro de Nava's 1794 decree established a watershed indicating what the new posture of missionaries should be. In daily life, mission residents played a crucial role in this redefinition of social identities, whenever they demanded autonomy in annual elections, refused to work for the missionaries, contested the friars' authority, or pledged allegiance to local vecinos.

In the later eighteenth century into the early nineteenth, Queretan missionaries gradually accepted that their role had to change because their situation had evolved, becoming increasingly precarious. They acknowledged that there were "old" and "new" ways of doing things that were not necessarily better or worse, just as wine is not better or worse than vinegar: they simply have different properties, and can be used in contexts that may enhance or undermine their natural attributes. Gray-robed missionaries did not degrade over time; but the communities of Spanish America developed in a way that they did not plan, and they had to adapt.

Notes

1 The first Queretan missionaries sent to Sonora are listed in *Nómina de los religiosos asignados para recibir algunas de las misiones de Sonora*, Archivo Franciscano de la Provincia de Michoacán [henceforward AFPM, AQ], Letter K, leg. 14, no. 4. This group of Franciscans left Querétaro on August 5, 1767.

2   David J. Weber, *Bárbaros: Spaniards and Their Savages in the Age of Enlightenment* (New Haven and London: Yale University Press, 2005), 93.

3   José de Gálvez, "Copia de las ordenes comunicadas a los Padres misioneros apostólicos de la Santa Cruz de Querétaro," Ures, September 29, 1769. Biblioteca Nacional de México, Fondo Franciscano, 40/912.

4   In his superb study on the policies regulating the relations between Spaniards and Indians, David J. Weber examines how this ideal of religious and cultural conversion often collided with local realities. Some Indians found that life in missions was unbearable, while others willingly remained there; some missionaries kept Indians confined, while others allowed them to come and go freely. These inconsistencies were partly consequent on the attempt to implement a program of acculturation in complex and diverse contexts. Weber notes that "for Spaniards, making Indians rational meant putting them in order ... by congregating them in Spanish-style communities, or *reducciones*. Indians who did not live in settled communities appeared to Spaniards as 'vagabonds' who lived 'licentious and brutal life, without a trace of order'"; *Bárbaros*, 91–95.

5   The process that Cynthia Radding terms the "colonial pact" is an example: Indians negotiated their allegiance to king and Church in exchange for protection and support; as part of this pact, Indians were able to use colonial institutions (such as tribunals and judges) to respond to Spaniards' encroachments on their lands, thus defending what they saw as their ethnic spaces. See Radding, *Wandering Peoples: Colonialism, Ethnic Spaces, and Ecological Frontiers in Northwestern Mexico, 1700–1850* (Durham, N.C.: Duke University Press, 1997), 8, 12–13; and "Cultural Boundaries between Adaptation and Defiance: The Mission Communities of Northwestern New Spain," in *Spiritual Encounters: Interactions between Christianity and Native Religions in Colonial America*, ed. Nicholas Griffiths (Lincoln: University of Nebraska Press, 1999), 116–35. Borrowing from Radding, Susan Deeds explains such patterns of interaction through the concept of mediated opportunism, "a framework tailored to understanding how material and mental barriers limit the capacity for change" among Indian groups; see Deeds, *Defiance and Deference in Mexico's Colonial North: Indians under Spanish Rule in Nueva Vizcaya* (Austin: University of Texas Press, 2003), 6. See also Lisbeth Haas's essay in this volume, in which she analyzes the case of Pablo Tac, a Luiseño Indian who used the resources and institutional channels of the Catholic Church to compose a narrative of Luiseño history. He conveyed Luiseño perspectives on their own defeat while affirming the equality between Indians and Spaniards—and Tac's own power as a scholar to represent Luiseño language and experience.

6   See, for instance, Sylvia L. Hilton's comments, in her essay in this volume, on Spanish historiography on missions and missionaries in northern New Spain. This ambiguity, or lack of precision, as David J. Weber explains in this volume, stems in part from historians' interest in defining the character of geographical regions that encompassed sets of populations; the focus on identities among Borderlands historians, Weber contends, is a more recent development and began with the interest in ethnic groups and subgroups, from the perspective of the "insider."

7   My use of the concept of identity is informed by the way that Henri Tajfel, John Turner, and Richard Jenkins have defined social identity. From Tajfel and Turner I borrow the idea that a set of psychological and sociological factors determines when and why individuals identify with and behave as part of social groups by means of internal and external processes of categorization, identification, and comparison. Jenkins's insights into social identity are usefully applied to the Franciscans, in particular here *vis-à-vis* relations and people's understandings of themselves and of others. See *Social Identity and Intergroup Relations*, ed. Henri Tajfel (Cambridge: Cambridge University Press, 1982); John C. Turner, *Rediscovering the Social Group: A Self-categorization Theory* (Oxford: Oxford University Press, 1987); and Richard Jenkins, *Social Identity* (London and New York: Routledge, 1996).

8   The Pimería Alta was the vast region of Sonora north of Cucurpe and south of the Gila River. It was named after the Pima Indians occupying this area, although the adjective "alta" was added to separate this area and its inhabitants from the portion of central Sonora where "Pima bajo" Indians resided.

9   Adopting the categorization of identities proposed by Manuel Castells, I view the efforts of an entire generation of Sonoran missionaries in terms of "project identity." As I will show, they tried to reorganize their local communities according to a redefinition of what it meant, from their own perspective, to be a missionary. In Castells's formulation, identity building may be classified as project identity "when social actors ... build a new identity that redefines their position in society and, by so doing, seek the transformation of overall social structure." Castells distinguishes two other forms of identity building, "legitimizing" and "resistance" identities; see Castells, *The Power of Identity* (Malden, Mass., and Oxford: Blackwell, 1997), 8.

10 Rose Marie Beebe and Robert M. Senkewicz, "Uncertainty on the Mission Frontier: Missionary Recruitment and Institutional Stability in Alta California in the 1790s," in *Francis in the Americas: Essays on the Franciscan Family in North and South America*, ed. John F. Schwaller (Berkeley, Calif.: Academy of American Franciscan History, 2005), 295–322.

11 *La Regla de los Frailes Menores*, ed. Hermenegildo Binanchi (Tolosa, Spain: Editorial Guipuzcoana, 1924).

12 A spiritual movement that originated among the Franciscans in the thirteenth century advocated strict adherence to the rules and precepts of the order, an attempt to return to its earliest ideals; see Lázaro Iriarte, *Historia Franciscana* (Valencia: Editorial Asis, 1979), 99–105. Another wave of revivalism among the Franciscans came in the seventeenth century, with the promotion of new institutions committed to religious conversion. In 1622 Pope Gregorio XV founded the Congregation for the Propagation of the Faith (Propaganda Fide), aiming to promote better instruction and preparation for missionaries. On March 12, 1682, the minister general of the Franciscans authorized Father Antonio Linaz to establish the first seminar modeled according to the spirit of the Congregation. Father Linaz had tried for a number of years to persuade the Franciscan authorities in Spain of the need to revitalize and regenerate evangelization in New Spain; his goal was to establish a seminar to prepare missionaries for the conversion of the Indians of Querétaro and San Luis Potosi, a

project realized in 1683 with the founding of the College of Querétaro, the first institution of this type in the Americas; see Cuauhtémoc Esparza Sánchez, *Compendio histórico del Colegio de Propaganda Fide de Nuestra Señora de Guadalupe Zacatecas* (Zacatecas, Mexico: Universidad Autónoma de Zacatecas, 1974), 13–14; Isidro Félix de Espinosa, *Crónica de los Colegios de Propaganda Fide de la Nueva España* (Madrid: Academy of American Franciscan History, 1964), bk. 1, chap. 12; Antolín Abad Pérez, *Los Franciscanos en América* (Madrid: MAPFRE, 1992), 88–89; Félix Sáiz, "La expansión misionera en las fronteras del imperio español," *Franciscanos en América*, ed. Francisco Morales (Mexico: Conferencia Franciscana de Santa Maria de Guadalupe, 1993), 188–90.

13   A series of concessions granted in 1493 by the papacy to the Spanish monarchs recognized the *patronato* of the Spanish Crown over the Church in its trans-Atlantic possessions, which in theory gave the king complete jurisdiction over the structure and functioning of this institution. The rights and duties thus acquired by the Crown included, among others, the evangelization of its dominions, the collection of tithes, and the right to present candidates to all cathedrals and ecclesiastical benefices. With regard to the mendicant orders, the Crown tried to subject the friars to the bishops, although in missionary districts this policy tended to be more flexible; see J. H. Elliott, *Empires of the Atlantic World: Britain and Spain in America, 1492–1830* (New Haven and London: Yale University Press, 2006), 68; Alberto de la Hera, *Iglesia y Corona en la América Española* (Madrid: MAPFRE, 1992), 188–89; Paulino Castañeda Delgado, "Los franciscanos y el Regio Vicariato," in *Actas del II Congreso Internacional sobre los Franciscanos en el Nuevo Mundo* (Madrid: DEIMOS, 1988), 317–59. Although the missionaries depended on the support of the Crown to finance their activities in the Americas, they regularly disputed the ways in which the patronato could affect them. For examples of these conflicts during the sixteenth century, see *Códice Mendieta: Documentos Franciscanos siglos XVI y XVII*, ed. Edmundo Aviña Levy (Guadalajara: Edmundo Aviña, 1971); Georges Baudot, *La pugna franciscana por México* (Mexico: CONACULTA, 1990), 37–57.

14   Bancroft Library, Father Marcelino da Civezza Collection [henceforward BL, FMCC], 201–11.

15   In early 1771 Father Garcés reported that he had purchased some four hundred head of cattle for the mission at San Xavier del Bac; Father Francisco Garcés to Father Mariano Buena y Alcalde, San Xavier del Bac, February 20, 1771, AFPM, AQ, Letter K, leg. 14, no. 6. At Ati, Father José Soler wrote in 1772 that the mission had almost three thousand pesos in gold, silver, and reales, generated through dealings with the mining town of La Ciénega; Father Joseph Soler to Father Juan Crisóstomo Gil de Bernabé, Ati, May 26, 1772, BL, FMCC 202–10.

16   "Copia de la visita hecha este año de 1775 por el P fr. Juan Díaz," BL, FMCC 201–5. Although we lack records documenting the production, consumption, and circulation of mission goods in the Pimería Alta, testimonies on the various construction projects and equipping of churches characteristic of the missions there in the late eighteenth century suggest a gradual recovery of local economies in that period. See, for example, BL, FMCC, 202–4, and AFPM, AQ, Letter K, leg. 18, no. 17.

17   AFPM, AQ, Letter K, leg. 14, no. 6.

18   Father José Soler to Father Romualdo Cartagena, Pitiqui, August 12, 1773, BL, FMCC, 201–28.

19   Father Francisco Antonio Barbastro to the missionaries of the Pimería Alta, Tubutama, April 30, 1780, AFPM, AQ, Letter K, leg. 16, 2nd portion, no. 3.

20   This brought tremendous relief to economically important missions, such as that of Caborca; according to one Franciscan, as soon as the Spanish settlers found out that the Indians were planting, "they would implore [the missionary] to receive money in advance," in order to ensure that they would receive the product. Father Florencio Ibáñez to Father Esteban Salazar, Saric, May 29, 1783, AFPM, AQ, Letter K, leg. 16, no. 12.

21   In this case from 1794, José Marcial, captain of the Ópata Indians of Bacadehuachi, collected 154 pesos and 7 reales at the *caja real* in Arizpe, which represented half of the stipend of Father Caballero. The money was paid to Marcial in July of that year in return for the goods he had given Caballero between January and June 1794. Archivo General de Indias [henceforward AGI], Guadalajara, 451.

22   On the comparison of forms of internal government between Xaliscan and Queretan missionaries, see Francisco Antonio Barbastro to guardian father Esteban Salazar, Saric, November 4, 1781, AFPM, AQ, Letter K, leg. 16, 2nd portion, no. 7. Differences between Xaliscans and Queretans on the relations between missionaries and local authorities are mentioned in Francisco Antonio Barbastro to Father Diego Ximénez, Tubutama, June 17, 1783, AFPM, AQ, Letter K, leg. 16, 2nd portion, no. 19.

23   As a result of his visit to New Spain, José de Gálvez envisioned the creation of an autonomous military command that brought together all the provinces of New Spain's northern frontier in order to strengthen its defenses and to promote the Spanish settlement in those far-off areas. Thus, the Comandancia General de Provincias Internas was created by decree on May 16, 1776, and Teodoro de Croix (a nephew of Viceroy Marquis de Croix) was appointed as its first titleholder. He held the responsibilities of governor and commandant general of the provinces of Nueva Vizcaya, Sonora, Sinaloa, and the Californias (including the subaltern governments of Coahuila, Texas, and New Mexico). See Luis Navarro García, *Don José de Gálvez y la Comandancia General de las Provincias Internas del Norte de Nueva España* (Seville: Escuela de Estudios Hispano-Americanos, 1964), 275.

24   As in other regions of the viceroyalty, the aim of local authorities was to eliminate the personal services that the Indians had long been providing to the fathers, and to force the missionaries to pay Indians for their work. An example of this policy is found in the Nuevo plan de administración for the Nayarit missions, approved by Viceroy Marqués de Branciforte in 1794, after three years of conflicts over these issues between the Franciscans from the province of Xalisco and the Audiencia of Guadalajara; see José Refugio de la Torre Curiel, *Vicarios en Entredicho: Crisis y Desestructuración de la Provincia Franciscana de Santiago de Xalisco* (Zamora, Mexico: El Colegio de Michoacán, 2001), 283–85. It is highly probable that these reform projects along the frontier of New Spain echoed ideas on redistributing land to the Indians and generally modifying the colonial administrative apparatus that José del Campillo y Cossío had

expressed in Spain in the mid-eighteenth century, compiled and published in 1789 in his *Nuevo sistema de gobierno económico para la América*; those ideas were widely accepted both on the peninsula and in New Spain. See Enrique Florescano and Isabel Gil Sánchez, "La época de las reformas borbónicas y el crecimiento económico, 1750–1808," in Daniel Cosío Villegas, *Historia General de México*, vol. 1 (Mexico: El Colegio de México, 1976), 488.

25 Pedro de Nava, Chihuahua, April 10, 1794, AFPM, AQ, Letter K, leg. 16, 2nd portion, no. 103. The response of Father Barbastro, president of the Queretan missionaries, is in AFPM, AQ, Letter K, leg. 16, 2nd portion, nos. 97, 99.

26 In Texas, pressures exercised by the civilian population hastened the enactment of these reforms. In 1793, the Franciscans were excluded from handling temporalities in San Antonio de Valero, and by the following year this measure had been extended to the rest of the Texas missions. Some analyses have intimated that this measure constituted a "partial secularization" of the Texas missions, and that this left them at the mercy of "secular avarice," "unscrupulous townspeople," and "land speculators." It is clear that the secularization of the missions was not related to the management of their material goods but rather to the maturation of the process of indoctrination and the turnover of spiritual care to the faithful from the regular clergy to the secular clergy. Moreover, control of the temporalities did not imply donating land to groups of settlers avid for material resources, but the incorporation of the Indian population into a network of social exchange that implied much more complex measures than simply taking their land away. The comments discussed here are from Felix D. Almaraz, *The San Antonio Missions and Their System of Land Tenure* (Austin: University of Texas Press, 1989), 6, 8–19; and Almaraz, "San Antonio's Old Franciscan Missions: Material Decline and Secular Avarice in the Transition from Hispanic to Mexican Control," *The Americas* 44, no. 1 (July 1987): 1–4.

27 In New Mexico between 1779 and 1784, the vecino population increased by more than 16.2 percent per year. After 1790, they began to apply for grants to unsettled lands in order to found new villages; see Ross Frank, *From Settler to Citizen: New Mexican Economic Development and the Creation of Vecino Society, 1750–1820* (Berkeley and London: University of California Press, 2000), 47, 119.

28 According to some estimates, from 1770 to 1829 these regions were responsible for 46 percent of all land claims registered in the entire territory of Sonora; see Saúl Jerónimo Romero, *De las misiones a los ranchos y las haciendas: La privatización de la tenencia de la tierra en Sonora, 1740–1860* (Hermosillo, Mexico: Gobierno del Estado de Sonora, Secretaría de Educación y Cultura, 1995), 123–35.

29 As on other mission frontiers, the rupture was provoked by the maturation of the first group of missionaries, who had been pioneers in the region, and their confrontation with a second group of clergy who arrived with a new perception of the way to perform their ministry. In their study of the California missions, Beebe and Senkewicz identify these conflicts as marking the conformation of four groups, or generations, of missionaries. Conspicuous among these friars were the "padres descontentos," a group of missionaries who "became the symbols of all that was problematic" in the College of San Fernando and its missions; Beebe and Senkewicz, "Uncertainty on the Mission Frontier," 305.

30   A Spaniard probably born around 1734 in the villa of Cariñena (Aragon), he arrived in Mexico in 1770, stayed at the College of Querétaro for a couple of years, and then went to the missions in Sonora around 1773; Lino Gómez Canedo, "Estudio Introductorio," in Francisco Antonio Barbastro, *Sonora hacia fines del siglo XVIII* (Guadalajara, Mexico: Librería Font, 1971), 9–10.

31   The Custodia de Sonora (1783–91) was part of Bishop Antonio de los Reyes's reform of Sonoran missions. In theory it was meant to be a single missionary jurisdiction that would bring together the Queretan and the Xaliscan missions, placing all the missionaries under the direct supervision of a new superior (*custodio*) and the bishop of Sonora. On the ups and downs of this project, see José Refugio de la Torre Curiel, "Conquering the Frontier: Contests for Religion, Survival, and Profits in Northwestern Mexico, 1768–1855" (PhD diss., University of California, Berkeley, 2005), 159–64.

32   Between 1767 and the end of the 1770s, a first generation of Franciscans can be identified: those sent by the College of Querétaro to take charge of the former Jesuit missions. From the late 1770s to the creation of the Custody of San Carlos in 1783, a second generation of Franciscans appeared in Sonora, including Father Barbastro. By the 1790s, the second generation of Franciscans in Sonora had nearly been supplanted, following the deaths of several priests and the return of several friars that Bishop de los Reyes had brought from Spain to found his Custody. The transition from this generation to that of the newly arrived missionaries of the third generation would be characterized by a number of conflicts, a long series of personal attacks, and differing criteria for evangelization and mission administration. Yet among the members of the third generation of missionaries some individuals immediately identified themselves with the "older missionaries" and even became their close collaborators, including Fathers Narciso Gutiérrez and Antonio Diez, who in the early nineteenth century were involved in serious confrontations with recently arrived friars.

33   This was the case of the missions at San Xavier, Cocospera, Santa Magdalena, Saric, and Santa Teresa. In his petition to the commandant general, the Queretan president indicated that the required permission would be effective for only one year—sufficient time, in his estimation, to conclude the construction of those churches. See Barbastro to Commandant General Pedro de Nava, Aconchi, April 29, 1794, AFPM, AQ, Letter K, leg. 16, 2nd portion, no. 103. Despite these proposals, by 1798 the missionaries in the Pimería Alta were still managing the missions' assets, though they had received notice that they would soon have to turn them over. See Father Francisco Iturralde to Father Francisco Miralles, Tubutama, March 3, 1798, BL, FMCC, 203–24.

34   Father Barbastro had commented specifically on this matter on one occasion: "Since the *comandancia* was established there has been a flood of providences that still fall by the bucketful, with order being scarcely observable . . . Last year, I clearly told the commandant general face-to-face: 'Sir, it is well that [you] grant this and that providence, but I am not asking for providences . . . [but] the fulfillment of those already given. Your Lordship can be sure that [your providences] will not be fulfilled, because those of your antecessors have not been fulfilled either'"; Barbastro to Father Juan Francisco Rivera, Aconchi, December 3, 1793, AFPM, AQ, Letter K, leg. 16, 2nd portion, no. 102.

35   Barbastro to Father Juan José Sáenz y Gumiel, Aconchi, January 31, 1791, AFPM, AQ, Letter K, leg. 16, 2nd portion, no. 71.

36   Father Antonio Barbastro to Father Juan José Sáenz y Gumiel, Aconchi, August 29, 1792, AFPM, AQ, Letter K, leg. 16, 2nd portion, no. 86; Father Antonio Barbastro to Father Juan José Sáenz y Gumiel, Aconchi, January 25, 1793, AFPM, AQ, Letter K, leg. 16, 2nd portion, no. 90.

37   On one occasion he reflected: "To the misfortune of the poor missions and missionaries, very few of the friars who make up the Discretory have been at the missions"; Father Antonio Barbastro to the Discretory of the College of Querétaro, Aconchi, July 30, 1793, AFPM, AQ, Letter K, leg. 16, 2nd portion, no. 93.

38   "Poder, instrucciones, comisión para visitar las misiones de la Pimería Alta y facultad para desfiliar en caso necesario que dio el V Discretorio al visitador que envió a Sonora, 1795." March 30 and 31, 1795, AFPM, AQ, Letter K, leg. 18, no. 10.

39   The missionaries who accompanied Bringas were Fathers Pascual Rodríguez, Mariano Bordoi, Pedro Amorós, Francisco Cobas, Angel Alonso de Prado, Andrés Sánchez, Pablo Mata, Andrés Garaigorta, and Ramón López, AFPM, AQ, Letter K, leg. 18, no. 11.

40   The translation and publication of Bringas's report, dated 1796, has played an important role here; see *Friar Bringas Reports to the King: Methods of Indoctrination on the Frontier of New Spain, 1796–1797*, ed. Daniel S. Matson and Bernard L. Fontana (Tucson: University of Arizona Press, 1977).

41   The Discretory of the College of Querétaro to Father Diego Bringas, Querétaro, March 7, 1796, AFPM, AQ, Letter K, leg. 18, no. 21.

42   Father Antonio Barbastro to Father Juan Alias, Aconchi, February 22, 1795, AFPM, AQ, Letter K, leg. 16, 2nd portion, no. 109. The metaphor alludes to the severe impact provoked by the accusations against old missionaries: even the best-regarded missionaries were likely to lose their credit and reputation under these repeated attacks, succumbing like some strong structures do when nature's forces hit badly.

43   This was the association of laymen (*terciarios*) gathered under the spiritual direction of Franciscan friars, devoted to pious ends and to the salvation of one's soul through penitence.

44   Father Antonio Barbastro to Father Juan Alias, Aconchi, February 22, 1795, AFPM, AQ, Letter K, leg. 16, 2nd portion, no. 109.

45   It was clear to Barbastro that he had lost favor with the Discretory of the college, and the incident with Brother Villaseca confirmed his impression. In his correspondence with a friar at the college, he wrote: "I know clearly, father guardian, that I lost [favor with] the Discretory, and therefore everything I propose and say will always be seen as suspicious"; Barbastro to the Guardian of Querétaro College, Aconchi, July 24, 1795, AFPM, AQ, Letter K, leg. 16, 2nd portion, no. 118.

46   For the same reason, the Discretory of the college opposed this appointment, as it would have placed another of the old missionaries in the presidency, and this time, one who had always been very close to Father Barbastro; see The Dis-

cretory of the College of Querétaro to Father Diego Bringas, Querétaro, March 7, 1796, AFPM, AQ, Letter K, leg. 18, no. 21. Iturralde was informed of his appointment in September 1795; Father Diego Bringas to Father Francisco Iturralde, Aconchi, September 13, 1795, BL, FMCC, 202–52.

47 Father Antonio Barbastro to the Discretory of the College of Querétaro, Aconchi, May 19, 1795, AFPM, AQ, Letter K, leg. 16, 2nd portion, no. 112.

48 The Discretory of the College of Querétaro to Father Diego Bringas, Querétaro, March 7, 1796, AFPM, AQ, Letter K, leg. 18, no. 21. Father Francisco Iturralde to Father Sebastián Ramos, Tubutama, May 31, 1797, AFPM, AQ, Letter K, leg. 18, no. 23.

49 Father Diego Bringas, "Testimonio de la visita efectuada a las ocho misiones de la Pimería alta," AFPM, AQ, Letter K, leg. 18, no. 17.

50 AFPM, AQ, Letter K, leg. 18, no. 25.

51 Bringas, "Testimonio de la visita," AFPM, AQ, Letter K, leg. 18, no. 17.

52 Father Diego Bringas to Commandant Pedro de Nava, Chihuahua, March 15, 1796, AFPM, AQ, Letter K, leg. 18, no. 28; see also "Diligencias que hizo el Venerable Discretorio para conseguir que se consignasen a beneficio de las misiones del colegio las limosnas que dejó el difunto capitán don Francisco de Zúñiga, 1800–1804," AFPM, AQ, Letter K, leg. 18, no. 37.

53 Santa Teresa, December 4, 1797, BL, FMCC, 203–21. After fifteen years working at those missions, Father Ibáñez was expelled from Sonora by President Iturralde because, as he told the college, "in truth [Ibáñez] is not fit for the missions"; Father Francisco Iturralde to Father Francisco Miralles, Tubutama, May 4, 1798, BL, FMCC, 203–26.

54 BL, FMCC, 203–26.

55 Gómez Canedo, "Estudio Introductorio," 9.

56 For example, Father Iturralde returned to Querétaro at some point after Barbastro's death, and around 1813 was interim president of his Colegio; BL, M-A 25:3, document 1. Fathers Juan Bautista Llorens and Lorenzo Simó were accepted in the province of Santiago de Xalisco in 1797, and both continued to work in the Sonoran missions until their deaths, though assigned to Basarac and Bacadehuachi, respectively; Biblioteca Pública del Estado de Jalisco, Colección de Manuscritos, book 50-V, fols. 59, 80.

57 De la Torre Curiel, *Vicarios en entredicho*, 339.

58 BL, M-A 25:3, document 16.

59 BL, M-A 25:3, document 9.

60 BL, M-A 25:3, document 13.

61 Ibid.

62 BL, M-A 25:3, document 15.

63 Father Francisco Moyano to Father Diego Miguel Bringas, Oquitoa, June 4, 1815, BL, M-A 25:3, document 8.

64 Father Juan Bautista Llorens to Father Diego Miguel Bringas, San Xavier del Bac, April 4, 1814, BL, M-A 25:4, document 6.

65 Father Juan Bautista Llorens to Father Diego Miguel Bringas, San Agustín del Tucson, January 4, 1815, BL, M-A 25:3, document 5.

66 At that time, the Franciscan province of Xalisco administered missions among the Ópata and Pima bajo Indians in Sonora. In these areas the Indian population was more hispanicized than that of the Queretan district, and missions were practically bereft of temporalities; thus, the activities of Xaliscan missionaries there closely resembled the daily life of parish priests. Unlike the Queretans, Xaliscan missionaries did not claim to be driven by the apostolic zeal of Propaganda Fide corporations, and for that reason they did not find the religious administration of these towns so troublesome.

67 Father Narciso Gutiérrez to Father Diego Gil, May 28, 1815, BL, M-A 25:4, document 7.

68 Father Juan Bautista Ceballos to Father Diego Miguel Bringas, San Francisco Xavier del Bac, July 7, 1814, BL, M-A 25:3, document 13.

69 BL, M-A 25:4, document 6. Due to various scandals, and his refusal to allow Father Francisco Madueño to carry out a juridical inquiry into his conduct in the Pimería Alta, Father Fontbona was recalled from the missions by the College of Querétaro in 1817 and taken prisoner, to be returned to Spain; Archivo de la Real Audiencia de Guadalajara Ramo Criminal, 131-2-1979, 1817.

70 Father Narciso Gutiérrez to Father Diego Gil, unknown place, April 26, 1815, BL, M-A 25:4, document 8. Father Matías Creo to Father Diego Miguel Bringas, Saric, January 23, 1815, BL, M-A 25:3, document 7.

71 Father Juan Bautista Ceballos to Father Diego Miguel Bringas, Ures, June 14, 1815, BL, M-A 25:3, document 15.

72 Ibid.

73 Years later, the indigenous captain of Caborca, Enrique Tejeda, together with the alcalde of that town and an Indian named Juan Antonio Valenzuela, the alcalde of Pitiquito, wrote to the president of the missions that, beginning in 1814, when "freedom was granted so that as vecinos we would be equal in lands and fruits of the fields with the vecinos [of Spanish origin], the Christian subjection that we had enjoyed from our Father ministers for our spiritual and temporal good began to be lost." One of the problems with these freedoms, the three men avowed, was that every time a minister attempted to defend the Indians from abuses at the hands of the Spanish settlers, the latter invoked the argument of equality among vecinos and Indians, which made the intervention of third parties in favor of the latter quite useless; Enrique Tejeda to Father José María Pérez Llera, Caborca, February 28, 1835; Archivo General del Estado de Sonora, Fondo Ejecutivo, vol. 62, exp. 10.

74 Thus, the Mediterranean background of Serra accounts for the creation of his own identities as Mallorcan, as follower of important Catholic theologians, and as Franciscan—all of which would surface in his Californian experience. In their essay in this volume, Beebe and Senkewicz observe: "Junípero Serra would meet the inhabitants of Alta California as a man in search of his own past and his order's past. He would meet them as a man who, in his own mind, was fight-

ing on their behalf against what he deemed the oppressive practices from the colonial past, which had erupted into the present."

75 For a comprehensive analysis of the reactions to the new method of government of the missions in the Spanish possessions, see Weber, *Bárbaros*, 116–37.

76 Beebe and Senkewicz, "Uncertainty," 298.

77 As Patricia Escandón observes, "one year after the expulsion of the Jesuits, the mission system in Sonora clearly revealed symptoms of what was to be its ultimate disintegration"; "Los problemas de la administración franciscana en las misiones sonorenses, 1768–1800," *Actas del IV Congreso Internacional sobre los Franciscanos en el Nuevo Mundo* (Madrid: DEIMOS, 1993), 283.

Part 2
After the Village: Indian Identity in Alta California

LISBETH HAAS

"Raise your sword and I will eat you":
Luiseño Scholar Pablo Tac, ca. 1841

Between 1834 and 1841, a young Luiseño scholar named Pablo Tac, while studying in Rome to be a missionary, wrote the first grammar and dictionary of the Luiseño language as well as a history of his people after their conversion to Catholicism.[1] Tac had grown up at Mission San Luis Rey de Francia (in present-day north San Diego County) during the 1820s, a prosperous period for the mission, following Mexico's independence from Spain in 1821. More than 2,000 people lived around the mission in the coastal valley or at San Antonio de Pala, an *asistencia* farther inland.[2] Other Luiseño Christians continued to live in their historic territories in villages with non-Christian relatives and neighbors. This pattern differed from that of most California missions, at which those baptized were, in the language of colonial policy, "reduced" to live at the mission proper. By law, indigenous communities continued to hold title to their ancestral land and maintained a degree of self-governance. The Spanish imposed a system of tribute and labor for the king on most indigenous communities, but in California, colonization had not proceeded to that point. Converts labored at the missions and presidios for little or no direct compensation. Confined within the missions and subject to a coercive labor system, they received rations. The missions also claimed the lands of those baptized as mission property. After 1834 the Mexican government, in turn, secularized most of the mission land and turned it over to the state. But many Luiseños remained in their villages and on ancestral land during the Spanish and Mexican eras; this helped some Luiseño bands retain both their land and their language.

Pablo Tac's expressions of legal, historical, and social identities, which have been discussed in previous studies,[3] are consistent with material David J. Weber has found on the notion of identity in contemporary scholarship. In his essay in this volume, Weber argues that identities are now understood to have been "more variable and mutable than

Bolton's generation had suggested"; scholars have found that "identities were not simply shaped by one's origins... Instead they were situational, fluid, and multiple."[4] Tac identified as a "Quechnajuis," meaning from his ancestral territory of Quechla, where the Franciscans established Mission San Luis Rey (1798). Tac identified other Luiseños by their specific territories of origin, such as Temecula and Pala. He also identified himself and others as San Luiseño, people from the larger swath of Luiseño territory. He described indigenous people from other missions by the name of their mission or tribe. In his dictionary he identified "Appache" as "a caste of People" (fol. 111v). Tac referred to the Spanish system of *castas*, which ascribed various legal and social positions to people in the Americas. He writes about the Apache tribe, which he describes as being from Sonora. But in Mexico, Apaches came to symbolize "savage" and non-Catholic peoples who remained independent and hostile to the Mexican nation.[5] Tac also referred to Apaches in this way (fol. 153). He used the term *indio* to refer to all indigenous people, including Luiseños. Indio was a social and legal position that set them apart from non-Indians, though some groups—for example the Tlaxcaltecans of central Mexico—negotiated a non-tributary status and other privileges that placed them legally and socially outside the category of indio.

In his essay in this volume, James A. Sandos demonstrates that the mission itself created new social positions and bodies of knowledge that influenced indigenous people's identities. Sandos beautifully conveys the importance of choristers and musicians within indigenous mission communities, whose populations favored them as godparents and witnesses in baptism. At Mission San Jose the choristers often served as godparents, second in popularity only to sacristans, who helped officiate at the mass.[6] New identities emerged among settlers as well. Louise Pubols's essay traces the prominence of Spanish identity among an otherwise multiracial and multiethnic group of soldiers and settlers. By 1810, she argues, "the non-Indian inhabitants of California had forged a common identity as Spaniards despite their disparate origins."[7] Studying the difficulty of forging a strong allegiance to Mexican nationalism among the residents of California, she recounts the emergence of a regional Californio identity that embraced all things Spanish.

Tac's writings about history and the colonial era, and about Luiseños and Spaniards, are of particular interest in this volume because they were the basis of his views of identity. Furthermore, Tac's manuscript—the history, grammar, and dictionary—offers concepts, categories of analysis, and subjects that provide a sense of the past difficult to find in the writing of his missionary and military contemporaries.⁸ The themes, places, people, and events he identifies reveal a world of defeat for Luiseños, in which they had lost formal political control over their land and governance yet still exerted certain forms of power and authority. Tac's history emphasized indigenous forms of power under colonialism and at the mission during the Mexican era that began in 1821. His work reflects its moment, when political ideas about equality, liberty, and citizenship were fought over and debated in California, Mexico City, Rome, and other places he lived. He writes with conviction about Luiseño equality despite the colonial hierarchies that he grew up with at the mission. He understands equality as existing within difference, which is a particularly complex and important idea, as equality was increasingly perceived as a right gained through one's purported sameness.⁹

Colonial Settlement and Defeat in Luiseño Territory

Spain and Mexico never controlled more than a narrow part of the California coast, but the occupation of a tribal territory by a mission, presidio, or town brought livestock that destroyed seed fields and stream beds that had provided sustenance for centuries, if not longer. Sometimes the occupation of a place for the mission, pasture, and fields occurred by negotiated agreement; sometimes it was without consent. In either case, the loss of land rights eroded the political autonomy of a tribe, even if the occupiers' presence initially seemed to foster greater wealth through trade and gifting. Foreign seeds and weeds easily invaded seed fields and coastal mountain ranges. While new foods were sometimes welcomed, the effect on native plant life varied.

The Spanish eventually prohibited the burning of agricultural fields and areas they viewed as pastureland, further eroding the ability of tribes to manage traditional crops. The missionaries would give passes for people to return to their territories to cultivate and harvest, fish and hunt, but if pass-holders were late in returning, the missionaries might send other natives or soldiers from the mission to bring them back and punish them with a whipping.

New diseases became endemic and resulted in a dramatic loss of life within the missions, creating significant change in indigenous society over time, as Steven W. Hackel has demonstrated for the Monterey Bay area.¹⁰ Spanish illness defied traditional means of healing. In many territories, disease caused huge numbers of deaths long before the Spanish settled. Indeed, between the time that the Spanish passed through the coastal part of Luiseño territory in 1769 and their settlement there in

1798, many natives died and others became gravely ill. In Chumash territory, thousands of people died between 1769 and 1782, when missions began to be established in the major coastal villages. Warfare *between* villages, owing to the role of some of them in spreading diseases brought by Spanish settlers, increased.

The Spanish presence had an enormous impact on basic aspects of identity, initiating demographic, political, economic, and environmental changes, creating a "time of little choice," as Randall Milliken called it.[11] First affecting the territories in the immediate vicinity of missions, presidios, and towns, the repercussions were experienced at ever-greater distances. Indigenous societies divided over what to do: some people joined the mission, while others refused to do so for one or more generations. Ancient societies along the coast lost control of most of their land within a half-century or less after colonization began in 1769.[12] Defeat meant losing those lands and political autonomy to become indios and minors under the law.

For twenty-six years after 1769, the Spanish moved through Luiseño territory between San Diego and all points northward. They traveled along the Camino Real, a large dirt trail that linked the north to the south, with expeditions of livestock, goods, translators, workers, settlers, and soldiers. The Spanish records were silent about the region and inhabitants of what became Mission San Luis Rey until they began to explore it again for that mission's site in 1795.

By 1795, some Luiseño leaders and others in the population had been baptized, and affiliated to nearby missions. In 1783, for example, the leader from the village of Guechi, in the valley where the mission would be founded, was baptized during a life-threatening illness. He sent his sons to Mission San Diego to ask the missionary to perform the Catholic ceremony.[13] Some Luiseños had already moved to Missions San Juan Capistrano or San Gabriel to the north, or to Mission San Diego to the south. They seem to have chosen the missions closest to their homelands, and they may have done so in response to family crisis provoked by illness and death.

When the Spanish returned in 1795, they found that the populations in villages in the valley near the Camino Real, as well as others in the interior at Pala (about seven miles over coastal mountains), wanted the mission to locate among them.[14] The political discussions that took place within each territory and between people in different Luiseño territories remain absent in records I've found, but the people who lived near the Camino Real again welcomed the Spanish in 1797. Father Fermín Francisco de Lasuén said a "numerous and amiable" population greeted them. He wrote of their "bravery and spirit of sacrifice to work and accommodate [the expedition] in the most courteous way."[15] They actively recruited the missionaries and succeeded in impressing them. Lasuén wrote, "these pagans are such that, taking into account all the Indians who are subject to us, they are the ones who are outstanding for peaceful dispositions and for a friendly attitude toward our people. They are longing for a mission." "Without fear of being mistaken," he emphasized that "none of the others have equaled these in grasping the purpose of our efforts."[16]

Illness had severely impacted Luiseño society. Its spread was facilitated by the movement of the Spanish through Luiseño territory on the Camino Real for the previous twenty-six years, and by inter-village ritual, trade, and marriage networks.[17] The increase in sickness may have made it seem imperative, at least to some leaders, to build a mission to gain access to economic power and possible medical assistance. Unfortunately, the missions became centers for contagion. Father Lasuén wrote of going to Luiseño territory in 1797 and of having baptized "some of their sick," but he didn't convey a sense of the magnitude or nature of the disease.

In February and March 1798, a few months prior to the mission's founding, the entire valley seems to have been stricken by an epidemic of fever or flu that was spreading through the southern California missions. Lasuén recorded the illness only as incidental to the larger story concerning preparation for the mission's founding. He had asked Father Fuster at San Diego to go to the region and ask its inhabitants to build "four or five little huts ... [and] do a little planting" at the spot around the cross. He suggested inducing them to do so "by distributing food to the pagans." The missionary contacted the "chief of the district," on whom they counted for a smooth settlement and through whom labor arrangements could be made. Too ill to meet with Fuster, the leader sent a representative who reported the population in the area sick and "more or less incapacitated, and that for the moment nothing could be done."[18] Lasuén himself reported the incident after twenty days of his own illness, from which he recovered due to "rather potent medicine," without which he might have died.[19]

The Spanish records are silent on any effects of the illness at San Luis Rey, but Pablo Tac later recorded, "there had been five thousand souls with all their countries near, but for an illness that came to California, two thousand souls died and three thousand remained."[20] The Spanish left hints of the severe effects of illness each of the many times they noted illness or reflected on the many deaths among native people. But Tac alone spoke of it as a fundamental part of Luiseño colonial history.

The mission was founded on June 13, 1798, in the territory of Quechinga at the place "known as Tacayame,"[21] which meant "volunteered" and "clearly heard."[22] The population grew quickly as people sought affiliation. Within a week of the founding of San Luis Rey, seventy-seven persons had been baptized and twenty-three others received instruction from a blind prayer leader from Mission San Juan Capistrano, who was a native of Luiseño territory. These twenty-three adults attended "punctually morning and evening from the very day of the founding." By August 1, 1798, three principal chiefs and their wives from neighboring villages were under instruction, with twenty-nine others.[23]

The blind prayer-leader worked with other translators to render Christian prayers and doctrine into Luiseño and instructed the first adults who entered the mission "in their own language."[24] Their translation of *God* seems to have drawn on a concept that existed in the region. In Tac's dictionary the word for God is translated into *Chañichñis*, the name of a central deity who gave many of the dances, other ritual practices, and structures of leadership and authority to coastal populations (fol. 121r).[25] The attributes and history of the Catholic deity are not shared by Chañichñis, who expressed a concept of God highly influential in native thought and culture during the colonial era.[26] The translation placed Luiseño Christianity into a framework that would sustain indigenous practices and ideas. The fuller significance of Chañichñis remained unclear to the non-Luiseño speaker, while Luiseños learned about Catholic doctrine through this and other translations of Spanish Catholicism.

But "Conversion"—the title of Tac's history, which he repeats a number of times—is about the Spanish settlement and the building of the mission, and emphasizes work and new forms of authority. Religious conversion per se is not the theme. In each rendition of his story of "Conversion" (which he treated as convergent with Spanish settlement), Tac emphasized that the Spanish brought Chañichñis to the Luiseños, and that they accepted him. The overarching story told under "Conversion de los San Luiseños" is about the new order of things, or the political defeat of the Luiseños, and how they nonetheless retained some power, for example through alliance and baptism.

By the end of 1806—in the first eight years of the mission—more than 1,158 Luiseños had been baptized from the towns in the immediate vicinity of the mission along the Lower San Luis Rey River, such as Quechinga and Pumusi, the towns of Pablo Tac's father and mother. The valley could not sustain a population much larger than it already had at

> Conversion de los San Luiseños
> de la
> Alta California.
>
> Despues que quitaron las Missiones a los Padres Jesuitas de la California, vinieron los Padres de la Religion de S. Francisco, y de S. Domingo, los primeros para la Alta California, los segundos para la baja California, California es una, dividida en dos partes es decir Baja California, y alta California asi llamada por el Señor Don Cortez, que fue el primero que la halló.
>
> La Baja California empieza desde la Mission de S. Lucas, hasta la Mission de S. Diego, desde la Mission de S. Diego la Alta California, hasta mas arriba de Monte Rey.
>
> Se sabe de la historia que los primeros que se fueron para la California de los Missioneros, fueron los P. Jesuitas, y el primer entre ellos el Padre Salva tierra, Juan renombrado en la historia de la California por sus obras de Dios.
>
> Llegaron los Padres de la Religion de S. Domingo en la baja California, y los Padres de la Religion de S. Francisco en la Alta. Los Padres Franciscanos de los que yo aqui hablo

One of the three beginnings of Pablo Tac's "Conversion of the San Luiseños."
Biblioteca dell'Archiginnasio, Bologna.

contact, and Father Lasuén decided to "reduce" only the people in that valley to live at the mission proper. The new asistencia at Pala provided land for a large farm and orchards, a chapel, livestock grazing, and artisan workshops, but most people baptized there would continue to live in their territory. Similar mission outposts, gardens, orchards, and grazing lands existed near other village sites, to the northwest at San Mateo, and to the northeast at Temecula. Thus, although relatively few Luiseños lived at the Mission San Luis Rey, and long before most Luiseños had been baptized or otherwise affiliated to it, the mission's economy and influences reached into distant parts of the region.

In part it was the structure of Luiseño society that enabled the mission to extend its economy so far beyond the coastal valley where it sat, and to do so quickly. As the pre-colonial Luiseño population had expanded over the centuries in the region, groups of people forged new territories. Each territory remained politically autonomous, but the Luiseños also developed a broader sense of ethnic territory, and a web of family and clan relations connected different politically autonomous tribes to each other. The relationships fostered by marriages that took place among people from Topome and Quechinga, two large villages, probably made it easier for the mission at Quechinga to establish an agreement with village leaders at Topome to cultivate crops there. The mission renamed the densely populated Topome region Santa Margarita, and by the 1810s the population cultivated fields, orchards, and grazing lands for the mission.

By the time of Tac's birth in 1821, Mission San Luis Rey had become the most prosperous of the California missions. Its population continued to grow during Tac's youth. By 1827, 2,663 Christian Luiseños lived among the still-significant non-Christian Luiseño population. The mission considered its boundaries to encompass the territory of its converts. By such reckoning, the mission's lands extended 11 leagues north to south and 15 leagues east to west, and harbored 22,610 cattle, 27,412 sheep, 1,120 goats, 1,501 horses, and more than 500 pigs and mules.[27] For decades, the mission's extensive production enabled it to trade with Spanish ships. After independence, it traded with ships from North and South America and Europe. Luiseño Christians supported the presidio of San Diego with corn, beans, wheat, lard, soap, blankets, mantles, and shoes.

Equality, Knowledge, and Silence

Antonio Peyri had worked at Mission San Luis Rey de Francia since his arrival in California in 1798, but with Mexican independence, he sought to return to Spain. News of independence and celebrations of the new republic began in California in March 1822, when the Plan de Iguala arrived in a special mail, designating September 16, 1821, as Independence Day, and creating an empire under Agustín de Iturbide. A Mexican commissioner of the empire, Doctor Don Agustín Fernández de San Vicente, also arrived in California in March 1822, to announce independence and the laws of the nation. He presided over festivities and instituted new representative legislatures and bodies in cities, towns, and for the territory. On April 11, 1822, Father Payeras, head of the Alta California missions, and ex-Prefect Father Sarría went to Monterey and swore allegiance to the new government.

Missionary Peyri was one of twenty who wanted to leave California when Mexican independence was announced, signing a petition that included a category for those who "fervently" desired to go.[28] Peyri placed himself in that group, as did Boscana and the other missionaries from San Luis Rey, San Juan Capistrano, San Juan Bautista, Santa Cruz, San Jose, and Santa Ines. One of two missionaries from San Buenaventura, La Purísima, San Antonio, Santa Clara, and Soledad also fervently wished to leave. Some of the old and infirm wished to stay rather than travel great distances. Other older missionaries wished to stay in order to have a role in the change, but only fifteen of thirty-five expressed their willingness to stay in California.

It took Peyri nearly a decade to receive permission to leave Mission San Luis Rey. When he finally did, he decided to take Pablo Tac and Agapito Amamix, another Luiseño youth, to assist him on the journey and to study and return as parish priests or missionaries to California. The young men left their ancestral village site and the mission community where they were born to train to be missionaries. It looked like the mission would certainly change and possibly become an Indian parish, with most of the land distributed among the indigenous and settler populations. Many Christians who were integrated into the mission's economy lived within their native villages. Luiseños held on to many tribal lands, but their land rights became particularly tenuous at various moments, including during the Mexican era.

Political turmoil engulfed California at the time Tac, Amamix, and Father Peyri left on January 17, 1832. The population at San Luis Rey expressed a militant politics for Indian equality and Indian rights to the mission and their territories. They had done so increasingly with the support of the liberal Governor José María de Echeandía, who arrived in California in 1826. Tac must have witnessed the political conflict at the mission, heard people speak against the power and wealth of the Church, and for the redistribution of its riches to build the nation.

They found similar conflicts in Mexico City, where they lived for about two years before departing for Spain in the winter of 1834. They also encountered in Barcelona the turmoil and anti-Church sentiment that they had witnessed in Mexico. Peyri found a place for them at the Collegium Urbanum de Propaganda Fide in Rome.[29] The college welcomed them for being "from distant lands, Indigenous and of legitimate birth, and well mannered."[30] These were Peyri's words. Peyri's concern over pure blood, legitimate birth, and good comportment suggested that colonial roles would follow the two youths to Rome in 1834, even though the casta system had been abolished in Mexico in 1824.

The Collegium Urbanum occupied a city block of Vatican land in Rome in a neighborhood that had long been an international quarter. The building was constructed around a central patio and a large internal courtyard for the horses and carriages. With narrow streets that wound up hilly inclines, the quarter contained foreign embassies to the Vatican interspersed with a dense cluster of churches, monasteries, shops, and residences. It faced the Plaza Español, where steps led up to an old church overlooking Rome.

Tac's experiences would have been familiar to others at the college. Many of the other youths shared histories marked by social and political turmoil, colonialism, and the emergence of modern states and liberal thought. Many had witnessed anti-imperial and national struggles based on new political ideas in their homelands in the Ottoman, Russian, British and French empires. Some students came from Albania, Persia, Cypress, Mesopotamia, Constantinople, Bulgaria, and other areas of the Ottoman Empire where Roman Catholics formed a minority population. Persia, Mesopotamia, and Constantinople had historic Christian populations, some from the era of the Crusades. Many of these places had recently undergone wars and rebellions from internal and external challenges to Ottoman rule. Other students came from Dalmatia, Scotland, Byelorussia, and Dublin. A few indigenous students came from the Mississippi Valley and Great Lakes region of the United States, where Jesuit missions had long existed. Tac would have heard about political change in former empires and new nations in Europe, the Middle East, and Asia from his fellow students.

Tac and Amamix studied grammar in 1834 and 1835. Amamix took ill and was nursed at the college's villa at Tusculano, just outside Rome, but unfortunately died of a high fever on September 26, 1837.[31] He was buried in the subterranean crypt of the monastery church.[32] Tac studied

Latin grammar for four years—from 1834 to 1838—and then took year-long courses in rhetoric (1838–39), humanities (1839–40), and, after recovering from a serious fever, philosophy (1840–41). On February 2, 1839, Tac made his first vows to join the priesthood while studying humanities.

While Tac studied, he wrote. He produced a partial Luiseño-Spanish dictionary and grammar for the vast collection of languages held by Vatican librarian Cardinal Carlos Giuseppe Mezzofanti, a linguist who had been a professor of ancient languages at many universities before he began to work for the Vatican in 1814. In 1833, near the time when Tac arrived, the pope appointed him custodian of the Vatican Library. Mezzofanti's collection of grammars included Chinese, Danish, Ethiopian, Greek, French, English, Algonquin, Aymara (Andean), Arabic, Italian, and what he called "Californese" (Luiseño). For each language, Mezzofanti had manuscripts copied by assistants and grammars written by students, and he collected printed language material. The files varied in size and content, but Tac's file stood out, distinct from the rest.[33]

No other manuscript in Mezzofanti's archive compares to Tac's in terms of its length, its comprehensive nature, the history it tells, and the quality of its written voice. Tac developed a humorous but poetic tone and addressed his readers as if personally. He referred to Luiseños as "we." The grammatical notes and dictionary fragments written by other students amounted to a few dozen pages at most, whereas Tac wrote about 250. Only Tac completed a substantial grammar and a history. He also created three dictionary booklets (see figures on next page). A number of his pieces, such as a dialogue between "blood and rabbit," express Luiseño oral traditions and poetic sensibility.

Tac had perhaps heard Luiseño elders discuss Indian equality in California, and had seen power shift with the arrival of the Mexican-appointed Governor Echeandía, who passed the provisional plan for the emancipation of mission Indians in California in 1826. Echeandía, the first liberal governor to arrive in Mexican California, was a popular figure in the indigenous political communities at San Luis Rey and San Diego during Tac's era. To the Indian citizen he stood for Indian citizenship and political autonomy, the return of lands, the distribution of mission goods, and Indian equality. In his dictionary Tac records three definitions for the word "liberal." He translated *alauis* as "liberal," and "to be liberal," *alauimoquius* as "he who was liberal" (fol. 110v).

Tac seemed to have a politics that embraced equality without conflating it with sameness. In translating between Luiseño and Spanish in the grammar and dictionary, he often established equivalences between the two systems of thought and expression, but sometimes he could not

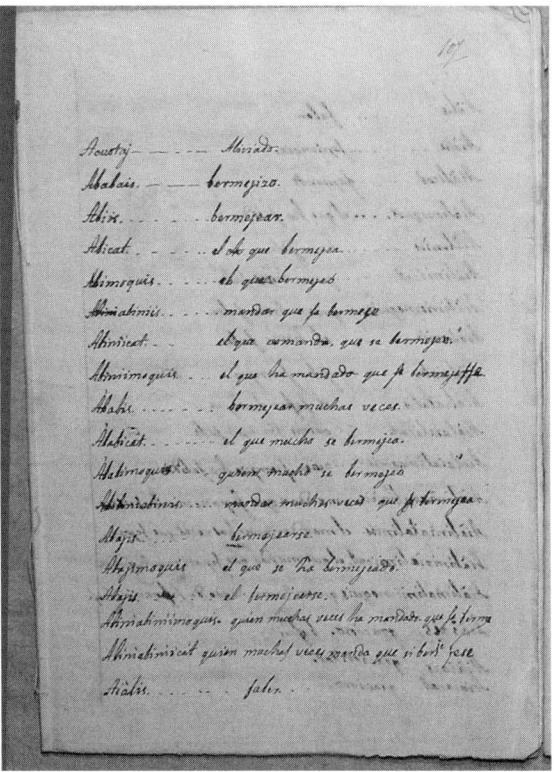

The first of Pablo Tac's three Luiseño-Spanish dictionary booklets, fol. 107. A delicate linen ribbon binds each of the three booklets. These booklets document some of the Luiseño words with beginnings from A to Cu. Biblioteca dell'Archiginnasio, Bologna.

do so, and in fact difference pervades the manuscript: Tac uses grammatical examples that distinguish between how something is said "by the Spaniards" and "by us." For example, while the Spanish use *usted* (the formal for "you"), "we refer to our fathers and leaders as 'tu,'" the familiar or informal reference for "you" (fol. 37r).[34] Difference did not create Indian subordination for Tac, however; rather, it identified and pointed to distinct cultural, ritualistic, and intellectual systems.

Tac also acknowledged that particular meanings might be lost in translation to Spanish, while some words might not be translatable at all.

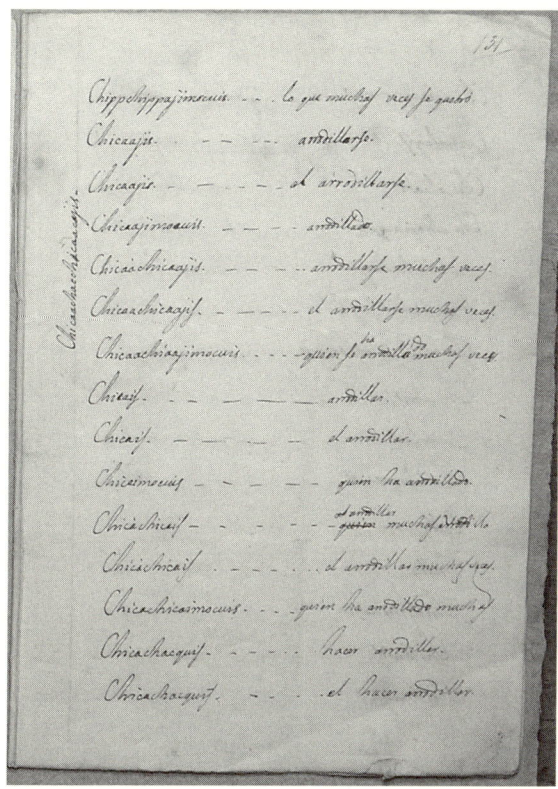

Pablo Tac, Luiseño-Spanish dictionary booklet, fol. 131. Biblioteca dell'Archiginnasio, Bologna.

Perhaps he decided some words should only be rendered with a translation that kept their meaning obscure. Though Tac acknowledged the difficulty of rendering Luiseño accurately, scholars have found that his grammatical rules and orthography reflect current knowledge of the language and its logic.[35]

Tac claims authorship of these pieces when he writes from the perspective of "we," a reference that embraced more than one group for Tac. He also wrote directly to Mezzofanti, in a note written on a cut folio, placed at about the center of the manuscript. Tac addressed Mezzofanti as "your Excellency," saying:

> Everything that I know about this language I have taught your Excellency; if something is missing, which

> I think it is, which often happens when you are writing in another time that could end. I'll teach you more, but who can teach what they don't know? What I knew, I taught, what I didn't know, I've left behind. Better to be quiet than to speak in lies. Now we'll collect the papers and begin writing the rules again as we are able.
>
> (Fol. 96)

Tac's statement expressed poetically something that he faced as a scholar: the sense that colonialism may have caused irrecoverable losses in traditional forms of speech and the life they gave voice to, which he refers to as a "time that could end." Perhaps he also alluded to an unbridgeable distance between himself and the lived experience of his language, as if certain parts of it might be lost to his memory.

If Tac expressed doubt about the completeness of his Luiseño grammar, which embodied a mode of analysis that he learned in Rome, he did not extend those hesitations to his history about the "Conversion de los San Luiseños." He wrote this history by drawing on Luiseño forms of narration, as will be discussed shortly. The note to Mezzofanti also had a playful element characteristic of Tac's style; stating that he had written everything he knew, he suggested that he would "collect the papers and begin writing the rules again."

Above all, the passage speaks to the way truth and lies remained a core problem in colonial relations. Writing as a scholar in a post-colonial era, Tac claimed to write outside the realm of deception. Deception ran deep in Spaniards' representation of Luiseños, a current that is evident from even a brief look at documents written by the missionary Peyri. He deplored Indians for their traditions, beliefs, and practices, and lamented that even those converts who seemed most sympathetic to Spanish Catholicism remained "always Indian."[36] Peyri referred many times to his inability to penetrate the silence he encountered when he tried to get information about the logic and meaning of Luiseño ceremonies and dances, finding the Indians "reticent, deceitful, and reserved."

In fact, silence formed an important part of Luiseño culture. Only experts could properly and safely exercise spiritual and practical knowledge.[37] Secrecy protected access to many forms of supernatural power so that it could not be misused. Certain ceremonies took power back from those who, the elders judged, had misused it.[38] Secrecy also guarded knowledge that individual specialists possessed.[39] Religious belief and ritual guarded the gathering and storing of specialized knowledge of plant and land man-

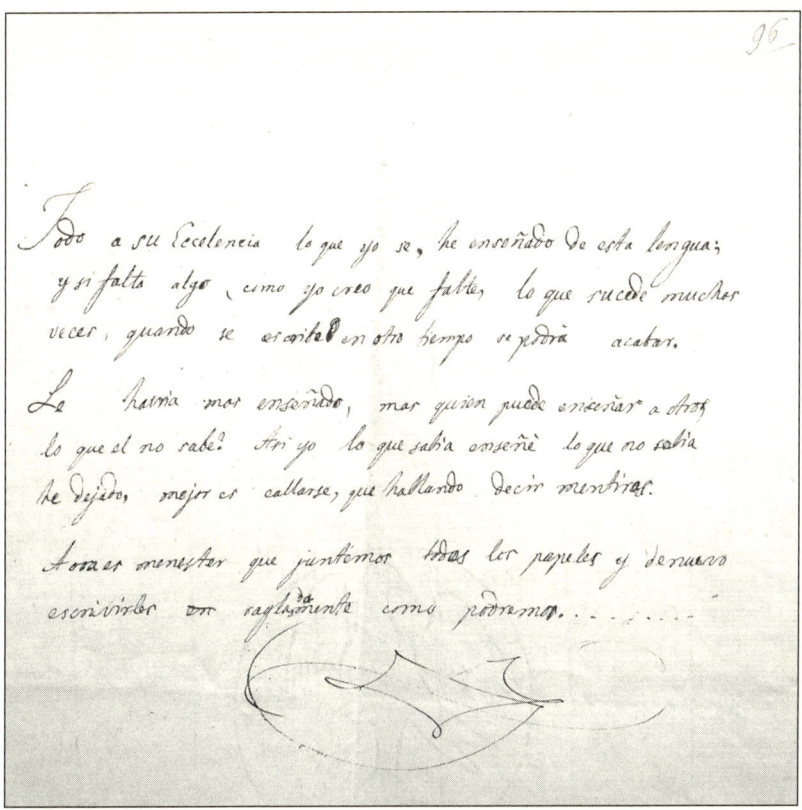

In the midst of writing his manuscript, Pablo Tac left a note to Cardinal Mezzofanti, the Vatican librarian and linguist for whom he created the grammar, dictionary, history, poems, and other fragments of Luiseño. He addresses Cardinal Mezzofanti as "your Excellency." Biblioteca dell'Archiginnasio, Bologna.

agement, for example, crucial knowledge in a semi-arid environment.[40] The population compensated those who exercised specialized knowledge. Even during the mission era, individuals would be paid for healing, or for their help in procuring an abundant harvest, or for making rain.[41]

The secrecy that left the intricacy of Luiseño religion and belief beyond the grasp of outsiders like Peyri also derived from aspects of the language itself. As in many areas of California, a council of learned elders spoke a ceremonial language that the majority of people did not understand. But even someone like Tac, who does not seem to have been initiated or apprenticed by a Luiseño elder, knew many words related to the sacred. Still, these words needed a lengthy interpretation in Spanish to render them intelligible.

Castilian did not have adequate words or concepts to express in a single term many of the Luiseño ideas about the sacred world, but these were conveyed among the words Tac placed in his dictionary.[42] He translated many words that had elaborate ceremonial meaning with the simplest Spanish word.[43] *Assuot*, for example, referred to the golden eagle. Perhaps to avoid writing the sacred word, Tac translated it as "eagle" (fol. 112v). He translated *chacajis* as "to cry." *Chacajis* refers to the deep sorrow expressed in ritualistic weeping (fol. 120v).[44] Tac translated *chappiis* as "to stop raining," though, as Eric Elliott indicates, it is a ceremonial word designating the being who makes it rain and stop raining (fol. 121v). Tac translated *chuiis* as "to burn," but it refers specifically to Luiseño cremation, a practice the Spanish attempted to replace with Christian burials into mass and unmarked graves in the mission cemetery (fols. 136v–137r).

Though the word *as* refers to both domesticated animals and the shaman's familiar spirit, Tac translated it only as "animal," a seemingly innocuous definition, but not a simple reference (fol. 112r). During the colonial period the horse and cow became synonymous with *as*, the shaman's familiar. The metamorphosis of the livestock—who were so closely associated with Luiseño political defeat—into shaman spirits minimized the role that they played for the Spaniards, while it augmented the power of shamans. It drew the horse and cow into the world of the Luiseño sacred. Translation alone could not render the meaning of Luiseño words linked to the realm of the sacred. For example, the word *chocorris*, to be like a mountain, had five verb forms, including *chocorrimocuis*, he who makes them act like a mountain (fol. 134v). Mountains entered the enactment of the sacred in dance. Some people also returned after death as stones and rocks. But "to be like a mountain" had no equivalent in the Spanish culture of the sacred, nor did Spanish have an equivalent verb that expressed the significance of the action.

The grammar and dictionary affirm Luiseños' persistent access to a sacred world, a set of concepts, bodies of knowledge, and systems of authority that gave them power during this era. As did all Luiseños, Tac had a specific and partial access to Luiseño cultural and historical knowledge. But as he wrote in the passage quoted earlier, "What I knew, I taught, what I didn't know, I've left behind."

Power despite Defeat

Most documents left by the missionaries and military in California are virtually silent about the areas of thought and life where Luiseños exercised leadership. In contrast, Tac's manuscript focuses on places defined by their social, political, and spiritual value: in the territory of Quechla, in the spaces of dance, at the ball game, and in the home. His history focuses on the Luiseño figures who wielded authority. Tac lamented the political defeat of his ancestors and the loss of political power by the leaders who allowed the Spanish to settle. He emphasized the importance of the elders and their traditional forms of knowledge and power. He also documented the presence and significance of those who spoke and dressed as Spaniards and rode on horseback—men who moved more easily between cultures, languages, and political systems, even as they maintained their allegiance to other Luiseños. These people played a similar role to Tac's in moving between cultures and in shaping memory and recording knowledge during a time of extreme change.

Tac embraced a shamanic concept of power—one in which power could be accessed by ritual practice and specialized knowledge, and wielded according to both social and natural laws. Despite Luiseños' political defeat, the shaman could access power to provoke change, including transformations in the social and political sphere as well as in individual lives.[45] Accessing forms of such knowledge and power often involved the use of datura or other hallucinogenic substances that produced trance-like states that enabled ritual leaders and commoners, in particular circumstances, to enter a supernatural plane. Tac described the use of datura in boys' coming-of-age dances, which he discusses twice in his manuscript. The "dream helpers," or shamans' familiars who guided people through their journeys, are represented on rock paintings found throughout the region. The images could be returned to for an invigoration of the memory and power derived from the journey.[46] Power could also be accessed through dance and other rituals.

The authority Luiseño men hold in the "Conversion de los San Luiseños" differs from that reflected in the other three stories in Tac's history—on the "Ball game," "What is Done Everyday," and "Dance." Some of the stories appear almost anecdotal, and yet they show how Luiseños dealt with their losses—the change in their power after defeat, and the areas that offered them rejuvenation. In writing on the ball game, Tac emphasized twice that the games "serve us well," but he doesn't explain why. Tac announced, "there is a game called *uauquiii*, meaning ball game with a game stick. We'll begin there." After describing it, he related the story of one game that took place between the San Luiseños and the San Juaneños (to the south of Mission San Luis Rey) that turned into a fight. The incident ended comically, and the Spanish soldiers arrived afterward.

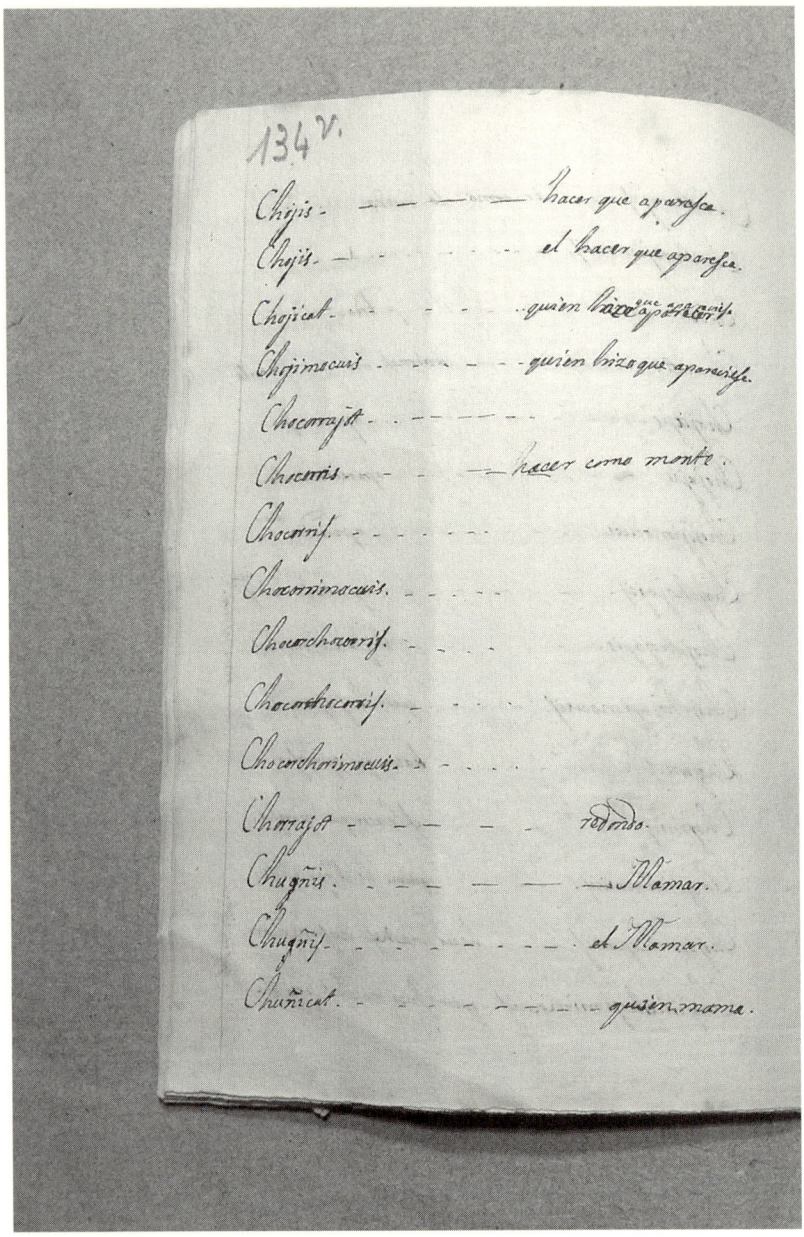

Open folios 134v–135r on the inside of one dictionary booklet. Biblioteca dell'Archiginnasio, Bologna.

135

Chuñimocuis	quien ha mamado.
Chunchuis	mamar muchas veces.
Chunchumis	el mamar muchas veces.
Chunchunimocuis	quien ha mamado.
Chunniniis	hacer que mame.
Chunniniis	el hacer que mame.
Chunninimocuis	quien hizo para que mamese.
Chujis	Esupir.
Chujis	gargajo.
Chujimocuis	quien ha esupido.
Chujchujis	Esupir muchas veces.
Chujchujis	el Esupir muchas veces.
Chujchujmocuis	quien ha esupido.
Chujinis	hacer que esupa.
Chujinis	el hacer que esupa.

This is the first time the soldiers appeared in Tac's history, and he represented them trembling in fear. They "trembled and attempted to end it with words," but the fight had already subsided. The guard of the thirty Luiseños, an Indian who, Tac reported, "spoke like the Spaniards," directed himself to the crowd while saying to the soldiers "raise your sword and I will eat you, but in his language" (fol. 60r). Only the Luiseños, Juaneños, and the reader could have understood the Luiseño guard's subversion of the soldiers' authority through verbal wit. I used this quote in the title of this essay to emphasize Tac's humor and authority.

In the story "What is Done Everyday" Tac placed the Luiseño home in the mission village at the center of action. The daily life of the family was structured around work determined by the needs of the mission, including schooling for the young men and labor in textiles for the young women. But the paternal authority of the Luiseño father, and the cooking and care provided by the mother, remained pivotal to the families' well-being and life within the household (fol. 66r–v). While work at the mission dominated daily activity, emotion resided in the home, where people laughed, cried, told stories, ate, and slept together. Tac conveyed the story with longing and nostalgia. Emotion rarely entered his other stories.

Responding to the world of political defeat and the losses of autonomy and life, sorrow and lamentation seem to shadow the pages of Tac's grammar. He used the verb "to cry" relatively frequently in examples interspersed throughout the grammar. *Namis* means "to cry," and one can say *n'an'is'* meaning "tears," "heavy crying," and "to cry." *Namiis*, to cry, distinguishes further between the cry of the child and that of the adult. For a man the verb *Naiis* (or *nanis*) expresses the greater degree of sorrow— *Laai op Nac*, the man cries (fol. 69r–v). And among his examples, he wrote "for you, I always cried" (fol. 35r), "my mother cries for my oldest brother," and "my father cried."[47] When crying first appears toward the beginning of the grammar in the example, "there was a man who always cried," Tac set it against the example of someone who always laughs, but "cry" reappears in many more examples, while laughter does not.[48]

One grammatical example reads, "Why do you cry, I cry for my father who was eaten by coyotes" (fol. 69r). Shortly thereafter, Tac supplied another example: "they say that over there are coyotes and that they paint, write, and sing very well, who would believe it (fol. 72v). To understand the implications of these examples, we should note that the Spanish used painting, writing, and singing as a cultural basis for Christianization. Translators gave one Luiseño word, *Nauis*, three equivalents in Spanish: to signal, to paint, and to write (fol. 82r). In fact, Luiseños did not have a tradition of writing, canvas painting, or melodic song, which did feature in the choral and liturgical singing that they came to participate in. They had an extensive oral tradition, sand and rock painting related to ritual (that could both represent and embody sacred meaning), and chants and other songs that accompanied dance or told stories. But to signal, paint on canvas, and write remained connected to the colonial world. Through those two grammatical examples, Tac suggested a connection between death and the Spanish presence through a Coyote, or trickster, tale. In another example, Tac wrote, "He says, but we don't know the truth of his wisdom, that he wanted to kill the foreigners near his country."[49] The grammar, when read for its content rather than to examine the structure of the language, offers anecdotal, poetic, and humorous reflections that often suggest, through subtle means of storytelling, the more devastating sides of the Spanish presence.

Dance

Twice in his history, Tac wrote about dance, one of the most important ways native people at the missions continued to access knowledge and power. Tac's emphasis on dance as part of the daily life and history of the missions was echoed in the writings of Father Gerónimo Boscana, who wrote an ethnographic study of San Juan Capistrano during Tac's lifetime, and missionary Peyri from San Luis Rey. All three documented the integral role dance played at the missions. Boscana wrote of dances that lasted for days on end. "Hardly a day passed without some portion of it being devoted to this insipid and monotonous ceremony," he wrote, "as on all the feast days of the Indians, dancing was the principal ceremony."[50] Like missionary Peyri, Boscana recorded that dance took place for every conceivable reason: to celebrate, rectify, acknowledge, and change conditions.

Dance offered a way for indigenous populations at the missions to continue to access power despite their defeat by the Spaniards. In the traditions of southern California, the figure Chinigchinich had given Luiseños and Juaneños some of the most important dances performed during the colonial and Mexican eras. Chinigchinich conveyed the laws and established rites and ceremonies for the preservation of life through dance.[51] Within this tradition, dance produced knowledge and regenerated power.

Despite its significance, colonial indigenous dance rarely appeared in the Spanish archives concerning the missions. In keeping with the European insistence on divorcing bodies "from their capacities to theorize," the missionaries and colonial officials lacked the language and concepts to value or analyze dance as a way to gain knowledge and change the balance of power.[52] In California as elsewhere, Europeans confronted societies that still allowed the body to produce knowledge through dance and to render the spiritual world into corporal existence. Colonial officials recorded little more than the mere existence of movement, sound, ritual, and bodily practices like dance and tattooing. Relying on those meager records and their own assumptions, historians virtually wrote dance out of life at the missions, even where indigenous sources such as Tac's history, or the rare ethnography written by Boscana, focused on its prominence.[53]

When Europeans mention dance at the missions, they never offer the details that could point to its significance.[54] When Tac, like Chumash Fernando Librado Kitsepawit, wrote about dance, he described the connection of the dances to the cosmological order and supernatural world. Both Tac and Librado give such details as the exact location, season, and time of day when the dances took place, the direction from which the dancers entered, the exact direction in which the dancers moved, where the dancers directed their gestures, and whether the dancers looked up or down. Tac and Librado also emphasized that the song determined the movement.[55]

This native way of relating the directionality employed in the dance reflected the concerns of Luiseño and Chumash astrologers that structures, ritual areas, and ceremonies "[conform] to their perception of the cosmos."[56] Librado also emphasized that the older dancers insisted strictly upon proper movement and upon using only the paint, feathers, and regalia specific to each dance's iconography. This exactness conforms to the requirements of "divine animation," in which supernatural beings and animal spirits choreographed their own presence through the steps and could be recognized through the visual cues associated specifically with them.[57]

Dance constituted group identity in ongoing ways and helped natives to conceptualize changes in that identity. Reflecting on its relationship to identity, Tac noted that dance took place "in many ways according to the type of Indian." He considered the dances that he had seen the Yuman and Apache Indians perform when they passed through the missions on trade expeditions or with Spanish troops, and on the dances of Indians at Missions San Diego, San Juan Capistrano, San Gabriel, San Fernando, and San Carlos Borromeo. All "also have their dances different one from the others." That Tac identifies broad ethnic identities through dance is consistent with the role dance has played in many cultures, constituting a "site of confrontation and negotiation of identities."[58]

Pablo Tac's drawing of two dancers. Tac wrote about dancing twice in his history. Biblioteca dell'Archiginnasio, Bologna.

The elaborate preparation for dance involved the cultivation of particular abilities and crafts: trade in goods, gathering feathers in the thousands, and the skills of feather, stone, bone, wood, basket, and shell work. All these were needed to make the elaborate regalia worn and carried during the dance. Elders held the knowledge about the production and application of body paint, and they weaved the baskets used in dance ceremonies. They also cultivated techniques for gathering, preparing, and administrating the potentially deadly hallucinogenic substance that dancers still used during the mission era. The knowledge, authority, and skill of many people sustained dance practice. Those people, skills, and practices remain outside most documents and histories of the missions, yet are central to Tac's history.

Tac's dictionary records many words related to dance. The verb *aluuiis*, for example, meant "to look above" (fol. 110v); dancers looked up in the Chinigchinich dance that Tac described. The dictionary offers fifteen common actions related to *aluuiis*. The word *caquis* meant the voice of the raven, a sacred bird in Luiseño religion connected to Chinigchinich ritual: dance, song, and other ceremonies required the voice of the raven. Tac provided nine verb forms of the word, including "he who makes the voice of the raven"; *caquinis*, "to order that the voice of the raven be made"; *caquiniimoquis*, "he who orders that someone make-like the voice of the raven"; and "he who makes the voice of the raven many times" (fol. 119r–v).

The dictionary illustrates how Luiseño translators brought dance practice into the daily life of Luiseño Christians. The verb *cheiis* meant historically "to dress with a *cheiat* for dance." Made of precious feathers, the *cheiat* was worn in a number of important dances. During Tac's era *cheiis* developed a more general meaning, "to dress" (fol. 126v), and was used in reference to European garb. Wearing the clothing made at the mission and purchased through trade constituted a symbol of being Christian. Textiles were among the most common imports to the missions, and textile factories and workrooms existed at each, creating cloth and clothing from the wool of each mission's many sheep, and producing cotton cloth where that plant grew, as in San Diego. Using the verb *cheiis* to make reference to the Christian practice of dressing brought the language of dance ritual into the daily language of Christians. In the twentieth century Luiseño speakers once again used the word *cheiis* only in reference to dance regalia; it no longer made reference to the act of dressing.[59]

Similarly, Chinigchinich became established in the Luiseño language as a historic figure, but Chinigchinich dance and ritual practices common during Tac's era seem to have ceased by the late nineteenth century. By then, the noun appeared as *Changichngish*, meaning a sacred being.[60] An early twentieth-century Luiseño dictionary still referred to Chinigchinich as "the name of the most important god in the Luiseño religion," referring to historical practices.[61] Though Luiseños appear to have always been monotheistic, they used another name (and concept) for God—*Chamyuuugawish*—during the twentieth century.[62]

Within the Tradition of Native Scholars

Many indigenous scholars who, like Tac, documented their communities' pasts, wrote relatively little about the Spanish invasion itself. Indigenous documents in central Mexico, for example, often recorded the conversion to Catholicism by incorporating a patron saint into the retelling of an otherwise unbroken past. Stephanie Wood found that records embodying indigenous memory and identity "perhaps selectively emphasize pride in their own leadership and ancestry, their own creation stories, and the moments in history that strengthened their communities and autonomy, their own heroism and even their own conquests."[63]

Though Tac emphasized defeat and the new supremacy of the missionary and God, he assigned Luiseños a specific part in the Christian story: "For us the son of God came down from the skies and also died for us."[64] Tac placed Luiseños within the larger Christian teleology, even as he identified a Christian God who held qualities different from those of the Spanish God, by giving the translation of God as Chiñichñis, a being in native religion who gave some of the very dance practices performed at the mission. Though writing about political loss, furthermore, Tac still defined the territory of the mission as belonging to "us," referring to "our land" and to "Quechla."

In setting the history in his ancestral territory of Quechla, and in focusing on the alliance between the missionary and chief that enabled the Spanish to stay, Tac showed native-Spanish alliances to be crucial to Spanish settlement. As is common among Indian scholars, he placed his own ancestral territory, and the mission village, at the center of his story. Tac used "we" to refer to descendants from that territory and to those who lived at the mission. He also wrote of San Luiseños, an identity grounded in affiliation with the mission and in historic connections among Luiseño speakers across a large territory. He distinguished San Luiseños from the other native people he wrote about. As noted earlier, he defined *Appache*, for example, as "a caste of people," referring to the Spanish system of castas that prescribed legal and social standing for people in the Americas (fol. 111v). He also distinguished Indians, as a group, from Europeans.

The narrative of a violent conquest that produced destruction and total loss generally appeared in European rather than native writing. In indigenous writing, defeat did not preclude access to power, authority, or property, as is evident from the many petitions and legal documents concerning native people's rights in the Spanish and Mexican archives.[65] In this and other respects, Tac's writing resembled that of other native scholars whose work suggested "a transformation and Europeanization of a way of seeing that remained faithful to ancient canons."[66] Indigenous writers commonly mastered the content and form of colonial grammars and narrative form, and collaborated in writing grammars and doctrine.[67] As did other Indian writers, Tac mastered Spanish orthography and knew how to construct a grammar. He used those skills to leave a record of his language and society as a nineteenth-century scholar but also acted within a tradition of indigenous writers from earlier eras.

Tac produced the Luiseño grammar and dictionary during an era when Indian writers began to publish more frequently in their own languages and in national or imperial languages. The Cherokee scholar Sequoyah developed a Cherokee writing system in 1808, for example, and in 1821 the Cherokee nation adopted Sequoyah's alphabet as its own.[68] Many Cherokee wrote to defend their land and political autonomy, and to stop their forced removal from the south during the 1830s.[69] In Massachusetts, Pequot orator and intellectual William Apess made a living through his writing during an era when writers had just begun to earn enough to support themselves.[70] During the nineteenth century, the unified Hawaiian court's close ties to Protestant missionaries created intellectuals who worked in both traditions. Some of the strongest scholars of native Hawaiian language, culture, and history associated with the court, wrote in their native language, and yet professed Christianity and translated the Bible and prayers.[71]

Tac's writing stands among these and other nineteenth-century native intellectuals who, as translators and interpreters before them, used their knowledge and skills to move between worlds, and to produce records of their histories and language.[72] Like these other scholars, Tac not only rendered his language in written form but also presented a way of understanding the colonial world in which he grew up. The spaces that formed the setting for his history—Quechla, the ball field, the place of the dance, and the home of the Christian Indian in the mission village—rarely appeared in other documents of the era. Throughout his manuscript, Tac asserted native authority and power as they existed among the elders and among newer authority figures who, like Tac, had found ways to represent cultures and to move between them.

Tac never returned to Mission San Luis Rey. He died in Rome in December 1841. Mezzofanti took possession of the manuscript, and it became part of his collection. With Mezzofanti's death in 1849, the manuscript was sent to Mezzofanti's birthplace in Bologna, Italy, with the rest of the archive.

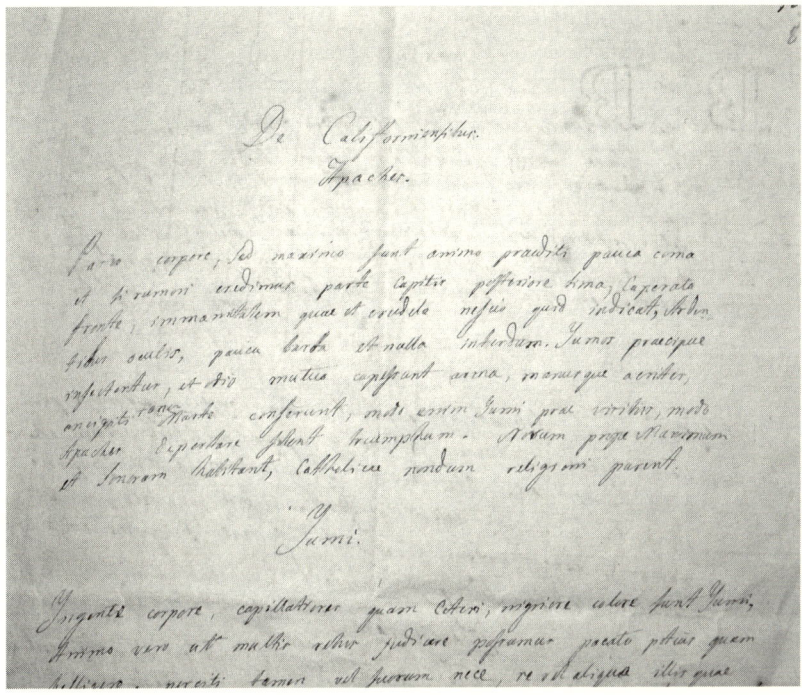

A fragment of one of Pablo Tac's final pages, fol. 153. These include four short ethnographic sketches of California Indian people, written in Latin for Mezzofanti's vast collection. Biblioteca dell'Archiginnasio, Bologna.

Notes

1   "Prose Lingua Californese—Studi grammaticali sulla lingua della California," Fondo Speciale Giuseppe Mezzofanti, box 3, folder 1, Biblioteca Comunale dell'Archiginnasio, Bologna (hereafter BCAB), fol. 71. Further references to this work will appear in the text. Also see the microfilm of the manuscript: Pablo Tac, "Studi grammaticali sulla lingua della California," ca. 1835, MS. Film no. 255, microfilm reels 1–6, Huntington Library (hereafter HL). Pablo Tac's birth date remains unknown; his baptism as an infant on 15 January 1822 is recorded in Padrón II of Mission San Luis Rey.

2   An asistencia was a kind of "proto-mission," without a resident padre.

3   See Steven W. Hackel, *Children of Coyote, Missionaries of Saint Francis* (Chapel Hill: University of North Carolina Press, 2005), 241–42; James A. Sandos, *Converting California* (New Haven: Yale University Press, 2004), 154–55; and Lisbeth Haas, *Conquests and Historical Identities in California* (Berkeley: University of California Press, 1995), 15–19.

4   See the essay by Weber in this volume.
5   See Nicole Guidotti-Hernández, "Transnational Histories of Violence during the Yaqui Indian Wars in the Sonora/Arizona Borderlands: The Historiography," presented at the Instituto Tepoztlán for the Transnational History of the Americas, Tepoztlán, Mexico, 2009.
6   See the essay by Sandos in this volume.
7   See the essay by Pubols in this volume. Barbara Voss considers related themes at the presidio of San Francisco in *The Archaeology of Ethnogenesis: Race and Sexuality in Colonial San Francisco* (Berkeley: University of California, 2008).
8   The entire manuscript will be published in the original and in translation in Lisbeth Haas, ed., *The Writing of Luiseño Scholar Pablo Tac* (Berkeley: University of California Press, forthcoming).
9   For an excellent critique of the politics of universalism for the way it obscures difference and prejudice, and the right to be equal and different, see Joan W. Scott, *The Politics of the Veil* (Princeton: Princeton University Press, 2007). For a complementary study of indigenous politics in Mexico during these years, see Florencia Mallon, *Peasant and Nation: The Making of Postcolonial Mexico and Peru* (Berkeley: University of California Press, 1995).
10 See Hackel, *Children of Coyote*, esp. 65–123.
11 See Randall Milliken, *A Time of Little Choice: The Disintegration of Tribal Culture in the San Francisco Bay Area, 1769–1810* (Menlo Park, Calif.: Ballena Press, 1995).
12 Building on the literature concerning microbes and the military in colonial ventures, Steven W. Hackel calls the movement into the missions and the tremendous loss of life a "dual revolution." See Hackel, *Children of Coyote*, 65–123.
13 Florence Connolly Shipek, "A Strategy for Change: The Luiseño of Southern California" (PhD diss., University of Hawaii, 1977), 43; Early California Population Project, http://missions.huntington.org, San Diego bapt. no. 996, December 24, 1783.
14 Father Juan Mariner of Mission San Diego, "Diario," 26 August 1795, Santa Barbara Mission Archive-Library (hereafter SBMAL); and Father Zephyrin Engelhardt, *San Luis Rey Mission* (San Francisco: James H. Barry Co., 1921), 3–5.
15 Father Francisco Lasuén to Governor Diego de Borica, 28 March 1797, no. 117, Taylor Collection, HL.
16 Fermín Francisco de Lasuén to Father Pedro Callejas, 21 October 1797, San Diego, in *Writings of Fermín Francisco de Lasuén*, ed. and trans. Finbar Kenneally, 2 vols. (Washington, D.C.: Academy of American Franciscan History, 1965), 2:51.
17 Shipek, "A Strategy for Change," 67–68. See also Constance Goddard DuBois, "The Religion of the Luiseño Indians of Southern California," *University of California Publications in American Archaeology and Ethnology* 8 (1908): 69–108.
18 Lasuén to Don Diego de Borica, 14 April 1798, Mission San Buenaventura, in Kenneally, ed., *Writings*, 2:78; and Lasuén, 14 April 1798, no. 133, Taylor Collection, HL.

19 Lasuén to Father Miguel Lull, 17 April 1798, Mission San Buenaventura, in Kenneally, ed., *Writings*, 2:79.

20 Pablo Tac, "Prose Lingua Californese," MS. Microfilm 255, reel 4, frame 90 (fol. 92 in MS.), HL. He writes this in the last and final version of the story about the mission, not in any of the other versions. Approximately three thousand Luiseños would convert to Christianity, and over a thousand others would be born to Christian parents by the time Tac and Agapito Amamix left for Rome.

21 Lasuén to Don Diego de Borica, 13 June 1798, in Kenneally, ed., *Writings*, 2:84–85.

22 See John R. Johnson and Stephen O'Neil, *Final Report: Descendants of Native Communities in the Vicinity of Marine Corps Base Camp Pendleton* (Santa Barbara, Calif.: Santa Barbara Museum of Natural History, 2001), 28. They quoted Trinidad Soto, who had spoken to John P. Harrington in the earlier part of the twentieth century.

23 Engelhardt, *San Luis Rey Mission*, 16.

24 Lasuén to Don Diego de Borica, 20 June 1798, in Kenneally, ed., *Writings*, 2:87.

25 The words that follow go back to deeper roots than the colonial era. They relate "to scold," "to talk back to," "kicking," at the same time they refer to a celebration or party.

26 Father Gerónimo Boscana wrote the one ethnography produced by a missionary in California during the early 1820s. Boscana, *Chinigchinich: A Revised and Annotated Version of Alfred Robinson's Translation of Father Gerónimo Boscana's Historical Account of the Belief, Usages, Customs and Extravagancies of the Indians of this Mission of San Juan Capistrano Called the Acagchemem Tribe* (Banning, Calif.: Malki Museum Press, 2005).

27 Engelhardt, *San Luis Rey Mission*, 53. Engelhardt published Father Antonio Peyri's "Report for the California Territorial Legislature," December 22, 1827.

28 November 19, 1822 petition to Father Payeras, in Donald Cutter, ed. and trans., *Writings of Mariano Payeras* (Santa Barbara, Calif.: Bellerephon Books, 1995), 337–38.

29 They were listed among 111 students at the Collegii in the *Catalogus Alumnorum* —1819 to 1837—Collegii Urbani qui AB Anno MDCCC XXXVII (Roma: Collegii Urbani, 1837): en typographeo, Archive of the Collegium of Propaganda Fide (hereafter CPF).

30 Letter from Antonio Peyri to Don Estevan Anderson, April 16, 1836, Vallejo Collection, C-B 3:1, Bancroft Library.

31 Letter no. 1587, "America—Estau Unitita," vol. 4, p. 343, 1853, CPF. They are sending death notices in response to the prince's letter of inquiry of February 15. Also see notice of his illness in *Catalogus Alumnorum*, 22, CPF.

32 Engelhardt, *San Luis Rey Mission*, 86.

33 "Poesia Californese con traduzione spagnolo—sigunda la lingua de Californese," Fondo Speciale Giuseppe Mezzofanti, "scritti varii," box VII, folder 186, BCAB. For contemporaneous reflections on Mezzofanti, see C. W. Russell, *The*

Life of Cardinal Mezzofanti (London: Longman, Brown, 1858); and Nicholas Wiseman, *Recollections of the Last Four Popes and of Rome in Their Times* (New York: Joseph F. Wagner, ca. 1850s).

34 These comparisons are especially prominent in the grammar on fols. 33r–51v.

35 See Sandra Chung, "Remarks on Pablo Tac's *La Lingua degli Indi Luiseño*," *International Journal of American Linguistics* 40 (1974): 292–307 at 297.

36 Father Antonio Peyri and Father Francisco Suñer, "Preguntas y Respuestas," December 12, 1814, SBMAL.

37 Raymond C. White, "Religion and Its Role among the Luiseño," in *Native Californians: A Theoretical Perspective*, ed. Lowell J. Bean and Thomas C. Blackburn (Ramona, Calif.: Ballena Press, 1976), 355–77.

38 See Shipek, "A Strategy for Change"; Don Laylander, ed., *Listening to the Raven: The Southern California Ethnography of Constance Goddard DuBois* (Salinas, Calif.: Coyote Press, 2004), 130–31; and DuBois, *The Religion of the Luiseño Indians*, 69–186.

39 Shipek, "A Strategy for Change," 34, 41. On pay, see Boscana, *Chinigchinich*.

40 Shipek, "A Strategy for Change," 97.

41 See White, "Religion and Its Role among the Luiseno"; Boscana, *Chinigchinich*.

42 White, "Religion and Its Role among the Luiseño," 356.

43 Eric Elliott, interview by Lisbeth Haas, January 13, 2007. Elliott studied Luiseño as a historical and contemporary language and reconstructed it in writing with Luiseño elders. See Villiana Calac Hyde and Eric Elliott, *Yumáyk yumáyk = long ago* (Berkeley: University of California Press, 1994) and "Dictionary of Rincón Luiseño" (PhD diss., University of California, San Diego, 1999). Elliott teaches Luiseño. He also helped to write the bilingual Luiseño-English curriculum at the school on the Pechanga reservation, run by and for members of the Pechanga band of Luiseño Indians.

44 Elliott, interview.

45 See Lowell J. Bean, "Power and its Applications in Native California," in *California Indian Shamanism*, ed. Sylvia Vane and Lowell J. Bean (Menlo Park, Calif.: Ballena Press, 1992), 21–32.

46 David Whitley, *A Guide to Rock Art Sites: Southern California and Southern Nevada* (Missoula, Mont.: Mountain Press Publishing, 1996), 22; and "Shamanism and Rock Art," *Cambridge Archaeological Journal* 2 (1992): 89–113 at 91. See Ken Hedges, "Shamanistic Aspects of California Rock Art," in *California Indian Shamanism*, 67–88. Also see R. C. White, "Luiseño Social Organization," *University of California Publications in American Archaeology and Ethnology* 48 (1963): 91–194; and Campbell Grant, *The Rock Paintings of the Chumash* (Santa Barbara, Calif.: Santa Barbara Natural History Museum and EZ Nature Books, 1993).

47 Tac, "Prose Lingua Californese," MS Microfilm 255, reel 3, frames 16 and 12, HL.

48 See, for example, ibid., MS Microfilm 255, reel 2, frames 17, 26, and 27; and reel 3, frames 16 and 20, HL.

49 Ibid., MS Microfilm 255, reel 3, frame 20, HL.

50 Boscana, *Chinigchinich*, 57.

51 Ibid., 34.

52 Ellen Goellner and Jacqueline Shea Murphy, eds., *Bodies of the Text: Dance as Theory, Literature as Dance* (New Brunswick, N.J.: Rutgers University Press, 1995), xii. See especially Susan Foster, "Textual Evidances," 231–47.

53 Officials occasionally attempted to prohibit dance, sometimes controlled when it could take place, and occasionally punished dancers who they were told were involved with healing or other forms of "witchcraft." Their attempts to prohibit dance caused at least one uprising at Mission San Gabriel, and most wrote about it as a mere "diversion" of the Indians. Neither Peyri nor Boscana seems to have attempted to limit the performance of dance.

54 See G. H. von Langsdorff, *Voyages and Travels in Various Parts of the World During the Years 1803, 1804, 1805, 1806, and 1807* (London: Henry Colburn, 1812); and Louis Choris, *Voyage pittoresque autour du monde, avec des portraits de sauvages d'Amérique, d'Asie, d'Afrique, et des îles du Grand Océan; des paysages, des vues maritimes, et plusieurs objets d'histoire naturelle* (Paris: Firmin Didot, 1822).

55 Travis Hudson, Thomas Blackburn, Rosario Curletti, and Janice Timbrook, eds., *The Eye of the Flute: Chumash Traditional History and Ritual as Told by Fernando Librado Kitsepawit to John P. Harrington* (Santa Barbara, Calif.: Santa Barbara Museum of Natural History, 1977), 83–85, 89.

56 Ibid., 103n46.

57 Barbara Browning offers vivid descriptions of how the divine in Condomblé only come down in their own choreographies. See *Samba: Resistance in Motion* (Bloomington: Indiana University Press, 1995), 69.

58 See, for example, Zoila Mendoza, *Shaping Society through Dance: Mestizo Ritual Performance in the Peruvian Andes* (Chicago: University of Chicago Press, 2000).

59 See Elliott, "Dictionary," in which he spells it *chéeya-t*.

60 Elliott, interview.

61 See William Bright, *A Luiseño Dictionary*, Linguistics 51 (Berkeley: University of California Press, 1968), 11, 30.

62 Elliott, interview.

63 Stephanie Wood, *Transcending Conquest: Nahua Views of Spanish Colonial Mexico* (Norman: University of Oklahoma Press, 2003), 19. The work of James Lockhart initiated much of this literature; see *The Nahuas after the Conquest: A Social and Cultural History of the Indians of Central Mexico, Sixteenth through Eighteenth Centuries* (Stanford, Calif.: Stanford University Press, 1992).

64 A. L. Kroeber and W. G. Grace, *The Sparkman Grammar of Luiseño* (Berkeley and Los Angeles: University of California, 1960), 35.

65 See Lockhart, *The Nahuas after the Conquest*; and Wood, *Transcending Conquest*. Wood summarizes the literature on indigenous writing and works with

specific documents and genres of writing. For a history written from Nahuatl and Spanish documents, see Rebecca Horn, *Postconquest Coyoacan: Nahua-Spanish Relations in Central Mexico, 1519–1650* (Stanford, Calif.: Stanford University Press, 1997).

66 Serge Gruzinski, *Painting the Conquest*, trans. Deke Dusinberre (Paris: Flammarion, 1992), 12; see also Gruzinski's discussion of mixing of forms on p. 150. For native documents and translation from verbal forms, see Elizabeth Boone and Walter Mignolo, eds., *Writing Without Words: Alternative Literacies in Mesoamerica and the Andes* (Durham, N.C.: Duke University Press, 1994).

67 See, for example, Louise Burkhart, *The Slippery Earth: Nahua-Christian Moral Dialogue in Sixteenth-Century Mexico* (Tucson: University of Arizona Press, 1989); and Vicente Rafael, *Contracting Colonialism: Translation and Christian Conversion in Tagalog Society under Early Spanish Rule* (Durham, N.C.: Duke University Press, 1993).

68 See James Rumford, *Sequoyah: The Cherokee Man Who Gave His People Writing* (Boston: Houghton Mifflin, 2004); and George Everett Foster, *Se-quoyah, the American Cadmus and Modern Moses: A Complete Biography of the Greatest of Redmen, Around Whose Wonderful Life Has Been Woven the Manners, Customs, and Beliefs of the Early Cherokees* (Philadelphia and Tahlequah: Office of the Indian Rights Association and the Cherokee Nation: H. B. Stone, 1885).

69 See Maureen Konkle, *Writing Indian Nations: Native Intellectuals and the Politics of Historiography, 1827–1863* (Chapel Hill: University of North Carolina Press, 2004).

70 See William Apess, *On Our Own Ground: The Complete Writings of William Apess, A Pequot*, ed. Barry O'Connell (Amherst: University of Massachusetts Press, 1992); and David J. Carlson, *Sovereign Selves: American Indian Autobiography and the Law* (Urbana: University of Illinois Press, 2006).

71 For the writings of John Papa Ii from the 1820s, see *Fragments of Hawaiian History, as Recorded by John Papa Ii*, trans. Mary Kawena Pukui, ed. Dorothy B. Barrère (Honolulu: Bishop Museum Press, 1983). Also see the writing of Davida Malo and Samuel Kamakau.

72 See, for example, Frances Karttunen, *Between Worlds: Interpreters, Guides, and Survivors* (New Brunswick, N.J.: Rutgers University Press, 1994).

JAMES A. SANDOS

Identity through Music: Choristers at Missions San Jose and San Juan Bautista

Franciscan missionaries, in seeking to convert California Indians to Catholicism, regarded the adoption of European musical forms as essential. In this essay on the Indian choirs of Missions San Jose and San Juan Bautista, I seek to provide pre- and post-contact contexts for the Indians' adaptation to European musical styles and to illustrate how training as choristers and participating in choirs gave Indian musicians key roles that cohered with their new, mission-based identity. This research is based on data in the mission sacramental registers found in the Early California Population Project (ECPP) database.[1]

Indian Music before Missionization

Prior to European contact, California native peoples performed music in their religious and spiritual rituals. These included world-renewal cycles at the winter and summer solstices, commemorations of the autumnal and vernal equinoxes, mourning ceremonies for the dead, puberty rites for girls and boys, fertility dances, weddings, and burials, all of which called for both individual and collective singing. At the solstices, groups of men and women sang the songs of creation in cycles, using alternating phrases. The music followed melodic forms that were recognizable to Europeans, sometimes with a contrasting section sung in a higher key than the beginning of the song; musicologists call this type of passage the "rise." The music included ancient stories of people and animals speaking to one another, creation cycles, and songs for hunting, dancing, war, and boasting. To the Spanish, the solo singing frequently sounded like sobbing,[2] which may account for the Franciscans' impression that Indian music was inherently sad.

Fathers Juan Sancho and Pedro Cabot, assigned to Mission San Antonio, had high regard for the musical abilities of the Indians. In addition to shaking rattles and whacking sticks together, Indians at the mission played a long flute-like instrument, handled like a recorder and capable of creating eight perfect pitches.[3] Priests at Mission San Jose, however, maintained that the Indians had "no inclination toward music that has any resemblance to ours" and that their songs consisted of "outrageous shouts and the yells of animals." Franciscans at Mission San Juan Bautista thought that pagan (non-Christian) music was varied and interesting, although much of it consisted of the repetition of single words or short phrases.[4]

Native Californians prided themselves on their hereditary and ceremonial songs,[5] and this rich musical background was adapted to the circumstances presented by Spanish colonization and Franciscan evangelization. In short, Spanish occupation offered upward social mobility to Indians who could replicate European sound in European song.

The Role and Importance of Music in the Missions

Music formed the foundation of daily devotional life at the missions, beginning with the *alabado*, or song of praise, followed by the Mass, the Angelus at noontime, and the opening or closing catechism or recitation of the *doctrina*. As musicologist William Summers has pointed out, "One simply cannot begin to understand mission life without a careful understanding of music (all idioms) and the power it exercised in shaping *rite, ritual*, and *spectacle*." He adds that in missions "the celebration and enactment of *the central cultural values* [took] place out in the public through these three celebratory vehicles."[6] In past studies of mission music, there was no systematic attempt to assess the role of music in mission life until I devoted a chapter to the subject in my book *Converting California*.[7] Here I turn to the social composition of that most important of musical pageant producers, the choir.

Early on in the founding of each mission, the entire congregation—men and women, young and old—sang in response to the priest during daily Mass. Women and men also sang together throughout the workday. Singing accompanied the recitation of the doctrina and was central in devotional services such as the exposition of the Blessed Sacrament (displaying the Host that is the body and blood of Jesus Christ).[8]

As congregations grew, missionaries sought ways to vary the singing, so as to introduce more complicated pieces. Simple monophonic Gregorian chants gave way to polyphonic works with multiple parts and several different melody lines, a transition that doubtless dovetailed with native Californians' use of the rise in pre-contact music. Junípero Serra, first father president of the California missions and a notable singer himself, wanted to create specialized male singing groups for devotional music. He met with limited success, as we shall see at Mission San Jose.

Serra's successors encountered challenges when their charges had to sing memorized parts. Father Narciso Durán, cursed with the gift of perfect pitch, found it necessary to save his own ears by employing a new tactic at Mission San Jose. He taught his singers to play instruments and found that, even if a chorister were absent, the Mass would proceed with the help of the other musicians. Durán recorded his thoughts on teaching music in 1812.[9] His influential ideas coincided with the developments at Mission San Juan Bautista, where the noted Franciscan linguist and musician Felipe Arroyo de la Cuesta served.[10]

We know from several contemporary sources that mission choirs had from thirty to forty members, depending on the size of the mission population.[11] Where possible, missionaries dressed choristers in distinctive garb to differentiate them from other Indians, and they assigned them work that kept them close at hand. Choristers spent a great deal of time with each other and with missionaries, since they practiced twice a day and assisted at least once a day during the Mass. They had a specific social geography within the church in which they practiced and performed, a space dedicated to them—usually a loft in the back, overlooking the congregation. An individual's identity as a chorister was based on skill at replicating European musical sounds and playing European instruments, including the flute, violin, mandolin, cello, guitar, clarinet, trumpet, French horn, triangle, drums, tambourine, or barrel organ.[12] Ringing the mission bells was also important.

Indians gained status from being choristers. A woman from a prominent Californio family recalled, "It was thought such an honor to sing in church that Indian families were all very anxious to be represented."[13] In the few surviving Indian accounts of mission life, the memoirists include descriptions of themselves as singers, instrumentalists, or both, indicating that their musical roles and abilities were important to their identity.[14]

Music played an important function within the church, as it gave the congregation an emotional link to the theological ideas the missionaries were attempting to communicate. The same set of skills that prepared an individual to become a chorister also translated into the secular world, where mission Indians were paid to perform secular music and songs at Californio dances and fiestas; this conferred on them a form of status as well.[15] The process of becoming a mission singer and taking on the attendant identity as a musician or chorister, and then as a spiritual guide for godchildren, illustrates Lisbeth Haas's argument in this volume that Indians maintained a sense of equality in defeat under Spanish colonialism.

An Initial Comparison of Musicians at Two Missions

I have chosen to examine the choristers that the Early California Population Project database shows were identified as *músicos* at Mission San Jose, the site where Durán first tried to codify and implement his thinking about training a choir, and at Mission San Juan Bautista, where Father Arroyo de la Cuesta supervised and trained a similarly impressive choir. Both missions were founded in June 1797. Although the term *músico* means "musician," it can also mean "instrumentalist," and it is the latter sense that I primarily use in this essay. Those who played instruments constituted the heart of the choir. Although most of them sang as well, they provided the musical framework and accompaniment to support the voices of other choristers who did not play instruments. The choir, then, generally would have been larger than the sum of its músicos.[16] Two other terms I deploy later are *maestro de la música* and *cantor*, found in the records of San Jose and San Juan Bautista, respectively. Taken together, these terms suggest new ways of thinking about mission choirs.

There are several ways to find músicos in mission records and the ECPP database. To identify godparents (*padrinos*) in baptismal records or witnesses (*testigos*) in marriage records, "músico" can be entered as a search term for "Occupation." One drawback with this type of search is that the priests who wrote the entries in the registers did not always indicate the godparent's or witness's occupation. Matrimonial records sometimes note that the groom was a músico. Death records may mention músicos in what the database categorizes as "Miscellaneous Attributes" or "Notes," but only for Indians who died before 1850. With all types of records, there is also the possibility of accidentally duplicating names: care must be taken to avoid mistaking a músico for someone else at the mission with the same name. The timeframe for the records at the two missions is comparable, from 1797 to 1850. Following secularization in the mid-1830s, spiritual life continued at both mission churches.[17]

Músicos at Mission San Jose

At Mission San Jose, the músicos who served as witnesses and godparents are not usually identified by occupation in the records: only 11 times as witnesses and 11 times as godparents. A search for specific músicos by name (see table 1), however, reveals that musicians actually served as witnesses 759 times, with the músico Narciso witnessing 226 times, Aniceto

Abendaño 209 times, Aniceto's younger brother Silvestre 55 times, and Pedro Alcántara 35 times. These four men served as witnesses at a total of 525 nuptials, or 69 percent of those where musicians served as witnesses. In addition, músicos acted as sponsors for newly baptized Indians on 697 occasions. Aniceto stood 284 times as padrino; followed by Narciso, 176; Pedro Alcántara, 104; and Lucas, 57. Altogether these four participated in 621 baptisms, or 89 percent of the total sponsored by músicos. Thus, in many instances, Indians who were known to be músicos were not identified by occupation in the mission records, just by name.

The above numbers show the importance of the músicos' involvement in building community at the mission. Their appearance as witnesses at marriages suggests that they also sang during those services, reinforcing the meaning and value of the Christian family through sacred song. As padrinos, the musicians agreed to foster the spiritual lives of the individuals receiving baptism. A músico who served as godfather to more than fifty people most likely did not give each individual the close, personal attention that this duty entailed, but that person could serve as a resource to family members of the baptized, answering questions about how to make their way within the mission's social and religious structure. Families of the baptized, seeing the músicos' high status in the eyes of the missionaries, could feel a bond with the Franciscan institution that they otherwise might not have experienced. Musician participation in spiritual life beyond the choir drew Indians closer to the religious core of the Franciscan endeavor and helped them adjust to the new institution.

What do we know about the lives of these prominent músicos, beyond their musical performances? Aniceto Abendaño was brought by his gentile parents to Mission San Jose in his first year and baptized on January 10, 1798. Two years later his parents were christened Chrisanto and Chrisanta and then married. An older brother, Fermín, was baptized on February 10, 1798, but lived only four more years and was buried April 26, 1802. A younger brother, Silvestre, received baptism on February 26, 1800, the day he was born; no burial record for him has been found, and he may have left the mission following secularization. Aniceto remained at the mission for forty-two years and was interred there March 10, 1841, long after secularization.[18] The records show that he began his career at the mission as a page (*paje*), or assistant to the Franciscan priests. He became a musician, then a sacristan, with the responsibilities of maintaining the altar and sacristy and ringing the mission bells. Ultimately he became the music teacher for the entire mission choir, or the maestro de la música.

Aniceto's first wife, Casilda, was an eighteen-year-old neophyte who had joined the mission in 1815. Aniceto's fellow chorister Lucas served as godfather to Casilda's father, Secundo, the following year; the músico Narciso and his cousin Luis Gonzaga witnessed Aniceto and Casilda's wedding in 1817.[19] Though Aniceto and Casilda had no children, they did act as godparents, with Casilda standing as a *madrina* six times from 1819 to 1830, four times with Aniceto.[20] Together they helped integrate the Indian community with the Franciscan-imposed structures.

Other musicians also played key roles in the community, either directly or through their spouses. Fermina, the wife of Bruno (a músico who served only once as a godparent and never as a witness), acted as godmother seventy-seven times from 1818 to 1820. Miqueas acted as godfather only twice, but his wife, Lorenza, acted as madrina twenty times. Bernardino de Sena acted once as godfather, but his wife, Petra, served as godmother eight times. These women, like many men who actively stood as godfathers or witnesses, frequently served several times in one day or over a short period. In these cases, músicos who gave little or no service in the ceremonies of baptism and matrimony, except as instrumentalists and singers, had wives who extended the reach of music through their status and participation in the community's spiritual life.

Ssaches joined the mission in April 1809 at age twelve and was renamed "Narciso." He died at the mission twenty-two years later, after marrying twice and fathering three children with his second wife, Nominanda. Their daughter, also named Nominanda, was born February 6, 1823, and since there is no burial record for her, she must have survived beyond the mission era. Their other two children were not so fortunate: Marcos José lived for a year and a half, and Sabina for only a week. Narciso began his career as a page and then a musician. Later he became an Indian official, or *alcalde*, for the sick, and he served as an interpreter as well. Amid these duties, he found time to participate frequently as a godfather and witness.

The records show that there were two músico families at Mission San Jose. One of them was Aniceto Abendaño and his brother Silvestre. The other consisted of Lucas, native name Jachucoy, baptized at age sixteen on July 31, 1811, and his younger brother Peregrino, no native name given, baptized four days earlier and described by the priest as being four to six years old. Peregrino married but had no children; he is last mentioned in the records twenty years after his baptism, at his wife's burial. How he became a músico cannot be determined. Nor can we derive from the documents how Lucas became a músico, but he contributed to bonding new Indians to the mission by serving as godparent fifty-two times. His wife, Carlota, did so twice. They had a son, baptized as Lucas on December 6, 1819, but the infant died five weeks later.

A gentile couple brought their two-year-old son, Pucules, to be baptized on November 8, 1804; Father Pedro de la Cueva christened him "Pedro Alcántara." Four months later the boy's parents presented themselves for baptism. Father Ramón Abella renamed forty-year-old Quilchocho "Pedro Antonio" and his thirty-six-year-old wife, Yumete, "Petra Antonia."[21] Their son Pedro Alcántara became a musician and chorister. Because he was brought to the mission at an early age, and his later record shows his accomplishments as godparent and witness, we might infer that he was a page in his youth. Since there is no burial data for him, he likely survived beyond 1850.[22]

Pedro Alcántara married twice and fathered four children. His first wife, Escolástica, was a half-sister of Yldefonso, a man who later became an alcalde. Escolástica, herself a twin, bore male twins on October 17, 1823, at a distance some two leagues (over five miles) from the mission; both children died before Christmas. Guida, a daughter, was born on June 27, 1828, and died within a week. Escolástica gave birth to another daughter, this time named for herself, on December 12, 1829. This child lived only a year. In 1831, Escolástica died during childbirth. Two years later Pedro Alcántara remarried, but his new wife, fifteen-year-old Plácida, succumbed on August 4, 1835. They had no children.

The remaining músicos at Mission San Jose had varied backgrounds. Bernardino de Sena (native name Hoyzela) was baptized at age four by Father Durán, on July 9, 1811. Bernardino seems to have left the mission after secularization, for there is no burial record for him; he is last noted on the burial record for his third child in 1836. Silvestre, Aniceto Abendaño's younger brother, married three times and fathered six children, all with Perpetua, his third wife. Their children, Juan José (born February 19, 1832), José Elías (born November 6, 1842), and María Plácida (born May 15, 1848), survived the mission and early American eras and died away from the mission.

Perhaps the most remarkable músico was Yocitaye, an Indian woman baptized as "Gaudiosa" at age three, on June 27, 1811. At age fifteen she married Cayetano, a widower, on July 17, 1823. She lived until age seventeen and apparently had no children. Gaudiosa is the only woman musician I have found identified in the records for San Jose or San Juan Bautista; I have found no other women from my research of ten other missions. How Gaudiosa came to be an instrumentalist and choir member

Table 1. Musicians at Mission San Jose (SJS), 1797–1850

Spanish Name[a]	Native Name	Baptism Number	Baptism Date	Age at Baptism	Date of Death[b]
Juan	Moychol	00006	09/07/1797	2 yrs	12/28/1840
Aniceto Abendaño (older brother of Silvestre)		00037	02/10/1798	1 mo	03/10/1841
Pedro Juan	Jimas	00056	04/13/1798	3 yrs	11/02/1817
Bruno	Chaucsacsi	00201	07/27/1799	3 yrs	02/26/1823
Quintín	Vegess	00264	02/09/1800	4 yrs	08/03/1817
Silvestre (younger brother of Aniceto)		00292	02/26/1800	0 days	no burial record (05/15/1848)
Pedro	Chuinus	00913	05/29/1803	8 mos	09/22/1844
Yñigo/Ynigo	Ssoyocsse	00942	08/24/1803	4 yrs	05/27/1821
Miqueas	Yruss	01000	10/08/1803	10 yrs	03/18/1829
José Antonio	Sacnecse	01249	10/09/1804	14 yrs	no burial record (04/04/1835)
Pedro Alcántara	Pucules	01292	11/08/1804	2 yrs	no burial record
Obtato/Optato	Chanoas	01316	01/10/1805	1 yr	05/08/1829
Fausto	Ttugue	01362	02/14/1805	2 yrs	01/12/1828
Miguel Francisco		01499	09/29/1805	1 day	02/12/1823
Lucas (older brother of Peregrino)	Yecpac	SFD 03419	08/12/1807	12 yrs	05/06/1829
Narciso	Ssaches	01663	04/??/1809	12 yrs	12/20/1831
Henrrique/Enrique	Septepe	SFD 04022	07/16/1810	15 mos	no burial record (8/23/1833)
Gaudiosa (female)	Yocitaye	02033	06/27/1811	3 yrs	06/24/1825
Bernardino Sena	Hoyzela	02046	07/09/1811	4 yrs	no burial record (02/28/1843)
Manuel		02243	10/20/1811	3 yrs	02/25/1829
Urcino	Lumna	03026	01/03/1816	8 yrs	11/25/1824
Peregrino (younger brother of Lucas)		03822	07/27/1818	46 days	no burial record (09/21/1838)
Patricio	(listed as musico in his marriage record)	no confirmed record			no burial record (03/29/1832)
[Hurso] (name derived from mostly illegible entry)	(listed as musico in spouse's burial record)	no record found			no burial record (04/23/1843)
Felíx	(listed as musico in spouse's burial record)	no record found			no burial record (11/29/1842)

a Listed chronologically in order of baptism.
b For those choristers with no death record, I have entered the last date the priest noted his presence in the mission.

Choristers at Missions San Jose and San Juan Bautista   119

Spanish Name[a]	Age at Death	Marriage Date(s)	Number of Children	Number of Baptisms Sponsored	Number of Weddings Witnessed	Years Recorded in Mission
Juan	43 yrs	10/17/1813 05/18/1818 05/29/1827	0	16 (19?)	42 (45?)	41
Aniceto Abendaño (older brother of Silvestre)	43 yrs	06/06/1817 07/17/1838	0	284	209	43
Pedro Juan	22 yrs	10/17/1813	0	2	15	19
Bruno	27 yrs	04/29/1816	3	1	0	24
Quintín	21 yrs	02/07/1815	2	21	22	17
Silvestre (younger brother of Aniceto)		12/15/1817 07/13/1821 11/04/1825	6	12	55	48
Pedro		02/09/1824	7	1 (3?)	0	41
Yñigo/Ynigo	22 yrs	08/25/1818	1	11	4	18
Miqueas	36 yrs	02/07/1815 08/16/1825	2	2	27	26
José Antonio		07/28/1811 12/07/1820	2	8 (9?)	9	30
Pedro Alcántara		01/07/1823 03/12/1833	4	104	35	29
Obtato/Optato	25 yrs	n/a	0	1	12	24
Fausto	15 yrs	n/a	0	0	0	13
Miguel Francisco	18 yrs	n/a	0	0	0	18
Lucas (older brother of Peregrino)	34 yrs	12/15/1817	1	57	81	32
Narciso	34 yrs	04/29/1816 01/07/1822	3	176	226	22
Henrrique/Enrique		08/14/1829	1	0	12	23
Gaudiosa (female)	17 yrs	07/17/1823	0	0	0	14
Bernardino Sena		03/11/1828	3	1 (3?)	5	32
Manuel	21 yrs	n/a	0	0	0	18
Urcino	16 yrs	n/a	0	0	5	8
Peregrino (younger brother of Lucas)		05/02/1836	0	0	0	20
Patricio		03/29/1832		0	(11?)	?
[Hurso] (name derived from mostly illegible entry)		n/a	?	0	0	?
Felíx		02/13/1834	?	(2?)	(8?)	?

is a mystery requiring further investigation. Summers has pointed out that local conditions could have prompted priests to deviate from the Serra-prescribed norm by permitting women to be choristers. In the instance of Gaudiosa, he writes, "I wonder if the exceptional woman in this case is the tip of an iceberg?"[23]

This brief overview of nine of the twenty-five musicians identified by occupation at Mission San Jose reveals much about their standing within the mission. For twenty-two of the musicians, Franciscans also recorded the age of their incorporation into the church. Seventeen of them joined the church as children (*párvulos*), those age four and under; two as boys under thirteen (*muchachos*); and the remaining three as adults (*adultos*) who were fourteen (in one instance, twelve) years of age and older. Priests buried sixteen, or 64 percent, of the twenty-five musicians at the mission, leaving nine who moved into the non-mission world after secularization. The músicos' occupation was not noted in the records by priests until the nineteenth century, beginning in the 1810s and running past 1836.

The músicos at Mission San Jose, the most populous mission in northern California, lived relatively long lives. Out of the twenty-five músicos identified, records for twenty-two chronicle repeated involvement in mission life over a significant span of years. Their tenures range from thirteen years for Fausto to forty-eight years for Silvestre, with twenty-five years as the average length of service. Four of the músicos were active in the mission more than forty years. On average, a priest could count on a músico to provide a generation of continuity and training for new musicians and to help develop complex musical programs for the Mass and for Holy Days. We can compare this twenty-five-year contribution with the appallingly low life expectancy of about eleven years for a child born at a mission.[24]

The marital status of mission choristers is also revealing. Nineteen of the twenty-five músicos, or 76 percent of them, married a total of twenty-eight women. They fathered thirty-five children, a few of whom survived beyond secularization. Living with the daily specter of death surrounding them, a fact made all the more poignant when the dying included their own children and wives, these men, instead of fleeing the mission, nonetheless persevered in making music and sustaining church ritual.

By acting as godparents, witnesses, and role models, the choristers contributed significantly to building an Indian community within the mission. As mentioned above, their wives also participated in this process. Even members of the choristers' extended families contributed to the web of society. For instance, Luis Gonzaga, mentioned above as a cousin of chorister Pedro Alcántara, witnessed 362 weddings and acted as godfather 364 times. Gonzaga is identified in the records as a sacristan, interpreter, and alcalde. In the baptism records, however, he is only identified twice by occupation: once as a page and once as an interpreter. In the marriage records, the priests listed Gonzaga seven times as alcalde, four times as interpreter, and twice as sacristan. In most cases, his occupation was not listed.

Músicos at Mission San Juan Bautista

Nine músicos can be identified in the records of Mission San Juan Bautista (see table 2). The four most prominent músicos were Telesforo/Thelesforo, Gavino/Gabino, Valentín/Balentín,[25] and Rodrigo. They served as witnesses 100 times from 1813 to 1841, with Telesforo serving at 45 weddings, Gavino at 42, Valentín at 9, and Rodrigo at 4. They participated in 95 percent of the 105 weddings witnessed by músicos. Likewise, musicians at the mission acted as godfathers 103 times: Telesforo served in 57 instances, Gavino in 17, Luis Antonio in 15, and Rodrigo in 7. Together they accounted for 96 baptisms, or 93 percent of those sponsored by músicos. Among the other musicians, only Dativo apparently never served as a godparent or witness.

Seven of the nine músicos married a total of ten women and produced twenty-three children. Of the nine musicians, only three—Valentín, Epifanio, and Juan Capistrano—are not found in the burial records, suggesting that they lived outside the mission following secularization. The rest, or 67 percent of the total, were interred in the cemetery. All of these men were baptized before age four, which means that they were párvulos at the time of their incorporation.

Liquithe was two years old when he received baptism on March 3, 1800, and was renamed "Telesforo." His father, Llomoi, headman (*capitán*) of the village of Ausaima (Jupagtac), joined the mission more than three years later; José María Estudillo of the Santa Barbara presidio stood as his godfather. Llomoi was given his padrino's name.[26] Telesforo married Cecilia in 1815 and had one child, Eulalia, baptized on December 6, 1816. Eulalia lived another twelve years, but her mother succumbed ten days after giving birth.

The músico Valentín married three times and fathered a son, baptized Julio, with his first wife, Marta. Julio received baptism on January 16, 1817, and lived four years. Valentín's second child, fathered with his third

Table 2. Musicians at Mission San Juan Bautista (SJB), 1800–1850

Spanish Name[1]	Native Name	Baptism Number	Date	Age	Death Date
Valentin/Balentin	Licaxte	00402	03/03/1800	1 yr	no death record (2/04/1844)
Telesforo/Thelesforo	Liquithe	00414	03/03/1800	2 yrs	03/13/1824
Luis Antonio		00751	11/25/1801	2 yrs	12/26/1842
Manuel Esteban/Estavan		00813	12/26/1801	1 yr	09/23/1835
Rodrigo		00971	09/05/1802	3 mos	02/08/1838
Gabino/Gavino		01302	11/14/1802	2 yrs	07/12/1835
Epifanio		01742	04/19/1807	0 days	no death record (02/03/1842)
Dativo/Datibo		01765	06/04/1807	0 days	01/02/1828
Juan Capistrano	(listed as Musico once as Godparent)	no confirmed record			no death record (10/13/1850?)

1 Listed chronologically in order of Baptism
2 For those choristers who left no death record, I have used the last date a priest noted his presence in the mission.

wife, Abenodia, was baptized Pedro Bautista in 1844. Valentín and his family do not appear in the records after this date.

The músico Luis Antonio married only once, and his wife, Pudenciana, bore seven children between 1824 and 1838. Simón, their firstborn, was just over three-and-a-half years old when measles (*sarampión*) struck him down. Five more children died as infants, living for thirteen months at most. Only the last child, Francisco Antonio—born in 1838, after the mission had been secularized—does not appear in the death records. Perhaps he lived well into the American period. These músicos, like their counterparts at San Jose, found themselves surrounded by death but continued to perform sacred Christian music.

Unlike the spouses of músicos at San Jose, few wives served as godmothers at San Juan Bautista. Valentín's first wife, Marta, did so once, and his second wife, María de los Santos, served four times.

Of the nine músicos who worked in the mission, two stayed for twenty-one and twenty-four years, five for thirty-three to thirty-eight years, and one for forty-one years. The average number of years spent in the mission was thirty-three, eight years longer than for the musicians of San Jose. The San Juan Bautista músicos served the Franciscans for nearly a generation and a half, in a mission where the average life expectancy was five years.[27]

Spanish Name[1]	Age	Marriage Date/s	Number of Children	Godparent	Witness	Years Recorded in Mission[2]
Valentin/Balentin		11/30/1815, 07/16/1833, 04/02/1838	2	0	9	38
Telesforo/Thelesforo	26 yrs	08/16/1815	1	57	45	24
Luis Antonio	43 yrs	09/23/1823	7	15	1	41
Manuel Esteban/Estavan	35 yrs	04/29/1818, 08/27/1829	4	2	4	34
Rodrigo	36 yrs	07/15/1824	4	7	4	36
Gabino/Gavino	35 yrs	07/15/1824	0	17	42	33
Epifanio		12/19/1828	5	4	0	35
Dativo/Datibo	21 yrs		0	0	0	21
Juan Capistrano			0	1(7?)	(3?)	?

Conclusion

What does this preliminary inquiry about the musicians and choristers at Missions San Jose and San Juan Bautista reveal? First, we can see the developing institutionalization of music over thirty-five years, from the mid-1810s to California statehood in 1850. The number of músicos designated in the records is smaller than the figure that has been given traditionally—that is, twenty to thirty choristers per mission. At San Jose, with its large population, the missionaries only identified twenty-five músicos, and at San Juan Bautista, only nine. Either mission choirs were smaller than previously thought, which seems unlikely, or the mission records do not give a full listing of mission músicos. If we posit that pages and sacristans provided a larger pool of singers who could participate in the Mass, the likely size of the choir corresponds to levels noted by contemporary observers. A hint of this larger number of choristers is suggested by the hierarchy of musicians that developed. For instance, Aniceto Abendaño at San Jose became maestro de la música for the entire mission, meaning that he selected the musical pieces to be performed and rehearsed with the musicians and singers. He did this in consultation with the missionary, but there may not have been a need for his title if he didn't have a large group to manage. The same may be true of the role of cantor, which Gavino fulfilled at San Juan Bautista. Such responsibilities required organizational skills to manage groups of more than ten to fifteen people. Given the increasing evidence for sophisticated and intricate musical performances in California missions,[28] even the larger figures for choirs might be too small.

One possible explanation for this observed difference relates to Durán's desire to develop the choirs by teaching the choristers to play musical instruments. Perhaps the instrumentalists are listed in the mission registers as músicos, while the other singers who were used to augment the choir for Sundays, Holy Days, and other important services were not recorded as such. In the registry of deaths at Mission San Jose, Durán and his fellow Franciscan Buenaventura Fortuny mentioned the other occupations of Narciso—who was also a page and an *alcalde* of the infirmary—and Miguel Francisco, who was a page. In other missions, many músicos doubtless went unidentified in the records.

The ECCP database also offers insight into the differences between those who entered the missions as adults and became músicos as opposed to those who were born at the mission or indoctrinated as young children. Fourteen percent of the músicos recorded at San Jose were baptized as adults, meaning that older Indians had the option to join the choir if they could carry a European tune. In contrast, all músicos recorded at San Juan Bautista were baptized as children. By examining the occupations of all of the witnesses and godparents in the database, we can see that músicos entered a privileged social and spiritual world of Indians who were closely linked to the missionaries. Here we find Indians assisting in the sacraments of baptism and matrimony and fulfilling the roles of pages, alcaldes, sacristans, and interpreters. In short, the músicos, cantors, and maestros de la música, along with other choristers, constituted an elite group within a tier that surrounded the missionaries in daily interaction. Through their playing, singing, and often through their service as witnesses, godparents, and exemplars of the new order, músicos affected the lives of hundreds of Indians at each mission.

Finally, there is the unfortunate case of Mission San Antonio de Padua, whose records are silent about the identity of músicos, just as they are silent about the occupations of nearly all the Indians who served as godparents and marriage witnesses. At this mission, two Mallorcan Franciscans, Juan Sancho and his co-father, Pedro Cabot, both music zealots, together presided over what was doubtless the finest and most intricate European music heard in Alta California. In 1814 they wrote to their superiors concerning Indian music performance in their mission. The Franciscans thought that the Indians had "a lot of musical talent" and noted that they played "violins, cello, flutes, horn, drum, and other instruments that the Mission has given them." The priests wrote that the Indians sang "Spanish lyrics perfectly, and they easily learn every kind of singing that is taught to them." Indians could "successfully perform as a choir, or even pull off the singing of a polyphonic Mass with separate, independent melodic lines... In all this they are aided by a clear voice and good ear that they all have, both men and women alike."[29] Musicologist Craig Russell has deduced from this report that Mission San Antonio had "a full Classical Period orchestra that could handle anything in the modern style (*estilo moderno*) of Haydn or Mozart and their equivalents in the Spanish Empire of Francisco Corselli, Ignacio de Jerusalem, and Francisco Delgado."[30] As more and more musical materials in Sancho's handwriting are being discovered in diverse places, it becomes clear that the musical performances at Mission San Antonio rivaled the best ones in Spain.[31]

Remarkably, Sancho and Cabot may have used women in their choir, recalling the instance of Gaudiosa from San Jose. In their 1814 report they said that "men and women alike" possessed good ears and clear voices. Although an enigma, the Mission San Antonio orchestra and choir represented the apex of classical and modern Spanish music, performed not in Seville, or Barcelona, or Palma de Mallorca, but on New Spain's North American frontier. Considering the rich musical tradition that developed at San Antonio, what a loss it is that the priests failed to identify their músicos, leaving us without insight into their life stories.

Throughout the mission system, choristers and instrumentalists took their musical knowledge and abilities and applied them beyond the mission walls. In her memoir published in 1890, Guadalupe Vallejo, niece of the celebrated Mariano Guadalupe Vallejo, recalled her experiences from the 1840s: "One of the dearest of my childish memories is the family expedition from the great thick-walled adobe, under the olive and fig trees of the Mission [San Jose], to the *agua caliente* [hot spring] in early dawn and the late return at twilight, when the younger children were all asleep in the slow *carreta* [cart], and the Indians were singing hymns as they drove the linen-laden horses down the dusky ravines." Guadalupe Vallejo had heard California singing,[32] and the mission compound proved the primary source for the production of that music.

Notes

This essay is primarily based on my work with the Early California Population Project (ECPP) database. I thank Roy Ritchie for making this database a reality; John R. Johnson, Randall Milliken, and others who have contributed to its formation; and Steven W. Hackel, its general editor, for critical assistance in getting started and insightful comments during revisions. I also thank Johnson and Milliken for sharing information with me from their respective California mission databases. I especially thank my wife, Tish Sandos, for her invaluable consultation in optimizing use of the ECPP database.

1. The Huntington Library's Early California Population Project database, http://missions.huntington.org, provides data on more than 101,000 baptisms, 27,000 marriages, and 71,000 burials performed by Franciscans in California, from the beginning of the mission system in 1769 through 1850.

2. Richard Keeling, "Music and Culture Areas of Native California," *Journal of California and Great Basin Anthropology* 14, no. 2 (1992): 146–58.

3. Craig H. Russell, "Juan Bautista Sancho: Tracing the Origins of California's First Composer and the Early Mission Style," in *J. B. Sancho, Pioneer Composer of California*, ed. Antoni Pizà (Palma, Spain: Universitat de les Illes Balears, 2007), 183. This is Russell's translation of the original Spanish contained in a series of questions sent by the Spanish Crown to California missionaries in October 1812 and answered during the years 1813–15. Earlier translators were insufficiently familiar with eighteenth- and nineteenth-century musical conventions to satisfy Russell's demand for musical accuracy.

4. *As the Padres Saw Them: California Indian Life and Customs as Reported by the Franciscan Missionaries, 1813–1815*, ed. Maynard Geiger and Clement W. Meighan (Santa Barbara: Santa Barbara Mission Archive-Library, 1976), 135–37. This is the best-known translation of the questions and responses referred to in the previous note.

5. See the essay by Lisbeth Haas in this volume.

6. William Summers, "Comments on *Converting California*," *Boletín: The Journal of the California Mission Studies Association* 21, no. 2 (2004): 66, emphasis in the original.

7. James A. Sandos, *Converting California: Indians and Franciscans in the Missions* (New Haven, Conn.: Yale University Press, 2004): 128–53. Summers, "Comments on *Converting California*," 65–66, situates my work in context.

8. Personal communication from William Summers.

9. Narciso Durán, "Prólogo ad Lectorum," Catholic Church, Liturgy, Ritual, 1812, Bancroft Library, Berkeley, Calif.

10. Guadalupe Vallejo, "Ranch and Mission Days in Alta California," *The Century Magazine* 41, no. 2 (1890): 183–92; Sister Mary Dominic Ray and Joseph H. Engbeck Jr., *Gloria Dei: The Story of California Mission Music* ([Sacramento, Calif.]: State of California, Department of Parks and Recreation, 1974): 8–19; Sandos, *Converting California*, 128–53; and Maynard J. Geiger, *Franciscan*

Missionaries in Hispanic California, 1769–1848: A Biographical Dictionary (San Marino, Calif.: Huntington Library, 1969), 19–24.

11   Sandos, *Converting California*, 128–53.

12   William Summers, "Spanish Music in California, 1769–1840: A Reassessment," in *International Musicological Society Report of the Twelfth Congress, Berkeley 1977*, ed. Daniel Heartz and Bonnie Wade (Basel: American Musicological Society, 1981): 360–80, especially appendices II and III. Owen da Silva, *Mission Music of California* (Los Angeles: W. F. Lewis, 1941), 8, presents an incomplete list of instruments used in California missions.

13   Vallejo, "Ranch and Mission Days in Alta California," 186.

14   Lorenzo Asisara, a former neophyte from Mission Santa Cruz, described being sent to Monterey, where he was taught the clarinet, and later returned to Santa Cruz to serve as sacristan while he sang and played in the choir. See Edward Harrison, *History of Santa Cruz County, California* (San Francisco: Pacific Press Publishing Co., 1892), 45. For other Indians who described themselves as choristers in biographical accounts, see Sandos, *Converting California*, 151–52.

15   Former Mission San Luis Rey Indian Julio César grumbled that for singing at the mission he "received no other pay than my food and clothing." "From the Reminiscences of Julio César," in *Lands of Promise and Despair: Chronicles of Early California, 1535–1846*, ed. Rose Marie Beebe and Robert M. Senkewicz (Berkeley, Calif.: Heyday Books, 2001), 470. See also Sandos, *Converting California*, 140–45.

16   Information derived from my conversation with musicologists William Summers and Craig Russell at the Western History Association annual conference, October 10, 2009, Denver, Colorado.

17   At San Jose witnesses were identified from 1808 to 1843; at San Juan Bautista they were identified from 1813 to 1834. At San Jose godparents were identified from 1811 to 1840, and at San Juan Bautista, from 1811 to 1841.

18   All citations of sacramental records are to ECPP. For Aniceto Abendaño, see San Jose bapt. no. 37 and burial no. 6449. For Fermín, see San Jose bapt. no. 36 and burial no. 185. For Silvestre, see San Jose bapt. no. 292. For their parents' baptisms, see San Jose bapt. nos. 246 and 251.

19   See San Jose marr. no. 1060. For Casilda, see San Jose bapt. no. 2777. For her father, Secundo, see San Jose bapt. no. 3044.

20   See San Jose bapt. nos. 3967, 4881, 5074, 5542, 5997, 6205, and 6206, the last four sponsored jointly with Aniceto.

21   Note that in the case of Pedro Alcántara and in that of Aniceto Abendaño, the priests christened adult Indian couples using male and female forms of the same name—Chrisanto/Chrisanta, and Pedro Antonio/Petra Antonia—perhaps for the sake of convenience. For the imperial power, this common practice was a way to identify and track those whose lives that power sought to alter. Yet in this action there is a hint of the banality of spiritual and cultural imperialism. For most native peoples in California, the name one was given at birth was provisional. One later acquired a special, individual name through the ordeal and knowledge gaining of a vision quest or puberty rite. For the children who

became músicos, the problems of tribal identity and naming may have been mitigated either by diminished exposure to old ways, greater familiarity with the mission system and its rewards, or both.

22   For Pedro Alcántara, see San Jose bapt. no. 1292. There is no burial record. For the parents, see San Jose bapt. no. 1336 for Pedro Antonio and no. 1337 for Petra Antonia. See also San Jose burial no. 978 for Pedro and no. 1083 for Petra.

23   Personal communication from William Summers.

24   Steven W. Hackel, *Children of Coyote, Missionaries of Saint Francis: Indian-Spanish Relations in Colonial California, 1769–1850* (Chapel Hill: University of North Carolina Press, 2005), 107, observed at Mission Carmel that "as with infant mortality, both of the sexes suffered very high childhood mortality rates: 46 percent of boys and 39 percent of girls died between ages one and five. This meant a very low expectation of life at birth: 11.2 years." Hackel uses the most accurate method for determining vital statistics, the family reconstitution model that his data from Carmel provide (96–118). Another technique is inverse projection from residual population, which produces more questionable figures. For example, see Robert H. Jackson, *Indian Population Decline: The Missions of Northwestern New Spain, 1687–1849* (Albuquerque: University of New Mexico Press, 1994), 105, wherein life expectancy for Mission San Jose is given as 1.7 years.

25   Hereafter I use just the first spelling of these names. The músicos primarily known to us as Gavino and Telesforo, based on the frequency of those spellings, on occasion are listed as Gabino and Thelesforo, "v" giving way to "b" in the first instance, and "t" to "th" in the second, hence the father identified as Gavino in a series of baptisms on December 20, 1819, and as Gabino in 1823, 1826, and 1831. For Telesforo, see San Juan Bautista bapt. nos. 2892, 2959–3014, 3016, and 3304. The pattern of using male and female variants of the same name for Indian couples continued, as the examples of Fructuoso/Fructuosa and Justo/Justa illustrate. See San Juan Bautista bapt. nos. 810 and 811, Father Arroyo de la Cuesta officiating.

26   See San Juan Bautista bapt. nos. 414 and 1215. Telesforo's father was identified through his eight-year-old brother, Martín, baptized on the same date as Telesforo. See San Juan Bautista bapt. no. 409.

27   Jackson, *Indian Population Decline*, 55–56, 95–98.

28   Sandos, *Converting California*, 131–42.

29   Sancho and Cabot, translated by and quoted in Russell, "Juan Bautista Sancho," 183.

30   Ibid., 184.

31   Ibid., 186–97. See also William Summers, "Sancho, Alta California's Preeminent Musician," in *J. B. Sancho*, 68–90, especially table 4A–C, enumerating work that Sancho brought with him or wrote while in California.

32   Vallejo, "Ranch and Mission Days in Alta California," 192.

Part 3
Borderland Identities of Soldiers and Settlers

LOUISE PUBOLS

Becoming Californio: Jokes, Broadsides, and a Slap in the Face

On June 14, 1828, three "Spanish" officers captured the Mexican presidio in the town of Santa Barbara, Alta California. Wearing the uniforms and insignia of the royal military, they marched first to the home of resident Spaniard Don José de la Guerra y Noriega. The former presidial commander was away in Mexico City, but his wife, María Antonia Carrillo, rushed to send word to her brother Anastasio Carrillo, who served in the presidio as sergeant. While he ran off to stammer the news to his commander, Lieutenant José Joaquín Maitorena, the Spanish officers strolled past the sentries into the presidio and rang the bell to summon the troops. Panicky presidial officers scrambled to assemble their soldiers in formation and make "reverent demonstrations," as one witness later testified, while artillerymen loaded cannons. At last, the Spanish officers revealed their joke—they were none other than José Antonio de la Guerra, the oldest son of Captain de la Guerra; Raymundo, the son of Sergeant Anastasio Carrillo; and their cousin Joaquín Carrillo. All three, ranging in age from fourteen to twenty-three, served as cadets in that very presidio. The next year, after an official investigation, the governor dismissed the incident as a silly prank perpetrated by boys. But Artillery Captain Don Miguel González wasn't laughing. In a letter to a Mexican newspaper, he warned, "[I]f they call it a joke today, tomorrow it will be for real."[1]

This essay explores the formation of national identities among Spanish-Mexicans in Alta California from the end of the colonial era through the early years of the Mexican Republic. This development was neither simple nor straightforward. As many historians have noted, frontier spaces can foster especially fluid and contingent identities.[2] At one time or another, residents of California felt loyalty to Spain, to Mexico, or to California itself, and the lines between the categories blurred and shifted. Within this particular territory, national identity did not stand apart from a person's race or ethnicity, their interaction with California Indians, their loyalty to the monarchy, the military, or the Church, their economic interests, the books and newspapers they read, their family relationships, their sense of honorable behavior, their shared history, or even their personal appearance. And at the dawn of the Mexican era, one's profession of national identity could have profound consequences, opening or shutting doors to land ownership, access to workers or markets, government office, or even salvation. Three teenagers dressed as Spaniards and had a good laugh in 1828, but as an anxious Captain González knew, identity was no joke.

After Mexico won its independence from Spain in 1821, national unity was hardly a foregone conclusion. For decades, the new state struggled to create both a unified political structure and an integrated culture—what Benedict Anderson has called the "imagined community" of the nation. This was not an easy task. Mexico's population divided along ethnic, class, and corporate lines. It included indigenous people, African slaves, and European-born Spaniards, as well as their Creole descendants. Corporate bodies such as the Catholic Church and the military held special governing privileges. And family, village, and province often demanded more immediate loyalty than the distant capital did.

California posed a unique challenge to the Mexican state. A product of the Bourbon Reforms, Alta California had been settled late—only a generation before the wars for independence began—and it lacked the mature Creole society found in most other provinces. It was also one of New Spain's most isolated outposts: soldiers, missionaries, and settlers began arriving there in 1769, but the territory became in essence an island after 1781, when Quechán Indians retook the Colorado River crossing to Sonora. After independence, the territory continued under central control, which created opportunities for the national state to directly intervene in ways that were not available to it in other regions.

These factors created a distinctly contested space. In the first few decades of the nineteenth century, royalists and Spaniards imagined California as a safe haven, while radical liberals saw a blank slate for experimentation. Each group carried its own political ideologies and loyalties to California in the form of newspapers, books, and private correspondence. New arrivals from Mexico, Latin America, and Europe spoke and demonstrated their allegiances, hoping to rally supporters and marginalize opponents. And Mexican officials created and reinforced national identity with public symbols and spectacles.

As native-born Californians negotiated their place in the world, and as they sketched out the boundaries between "us" and "them," they also learned to challenge these discourses. They absorbed and accepted many of the new ideas and policies that national leaders proposed. But in dressing as Spanish officers, posting satirical broadsides, and making other defiant gestures, they began to manipulate and undermine the symbols of national identity. Eventually, native sons like José Antonio de la Guerra and his cousins began to imagine and then act out their own nation—free California—and to proudly call themselves Californios.[3]

By the time of independence, California had a colonial population of about 3,270 people, living in twenty missions, four presidios, and three civilian towns. Out of a total Indian population of 200,000, about 21,000 lived at the missions.[4] California's non-Indian population retained an unusually strong identification with Spain and Spanishness at all levels, an association that stemmed largely from the colonial project itself. The Bourbon reformers who had planned the settlement of California had also aimed to purge Creole leadership in Spain's colonies. In California, European-born Spaniards could be found at the very top of the fledgling social order, as missionaries and high-ranking officers in the military—men like Father Narciso Durán, Governor Pablo Vicente de Solá, and Captain de la Guerra. Unlike in other areas of New Spain, however, the Church's near-monopoly of arable lands in California suppressed the creation of a landed elite.

Only a few colonizers in California below this top level had actually been born in Spain. Most were from nearby frontier zones such as Sinaloa and Baja California, where the Bourbon Reforms had also encouraged the social mobility of mixed-race soldiers and settlers. This mobility was reflected in racial drift.[5] In 1781, less than 5 percent of Los Angeles's settler population was recorded as "Spanish" in the census. But by 1790, 46 percent of those same settlers were listed as "español."[6] In these records, "español" did not indicate European birth—instead, this racial term sat at the top of a complex system of official castes, or *castas*, with the categories "negro" and "indio" at the bottom, and various mixtures such as "mestizo" and "mulato" in between.

Unique conditions in the colonial era tended to simplify the casta system to just two categories in California: español and Indian. In presidial towns in particular, the military reinforced a unified Spanish identity. A 1762 regulation, for example, required that frontier garrisons be at least two-thirds español. Under pressure to meet this quota, some officers whitened soldiers on reports. The full wardrobes that California recruits and their families received—including hats, shoes, stockings, shawls, and petticoats—minimized the visible differences among the various castas.[7] The language of the soldiers' orders, the uniforms and insignias they wore, the Spanish flags that flew over their presidios—even the soldiers' hair, worn as a long braid—all signaled shared submission to the colonial order and to the Spanish king.[8]

Even more significant, if less official, was the distinction that soldiers and settlers made between themselves and the Indians they had been sent to subdue. In this sense, when they called themselves "español," they identified not just their national origin or race but also a bundle of other elements of identity—religion, dress, speech, and behavior. In the central regions of New Spain, Indian peoples had been absorbed into Spanish society and displayed many of these cultural markers. But the Indians of California were clearly different. For one thing, they were not convincingly Catholic. This meant they were *gente sin razón*, or "people without reason" to understand Catholicism, and should therefore not be punished for heresy. Over time, the opposite term, *gente de razón*, or "people of reason," came to be used interchangeably with "español" to mean simply "non-Indian."[9] Work also created divisions between indio and español. California's soldiers, as poor, mixed-race people, should have expected to engage in hard physical labor such as building construction. Yet most of them saw service in the frontier military as a way to transcend their humble origins, and they complained, refused to do the work assigned, and in some cases deserted.[10] In response, their commanding officers found ways to transfer hard labor to the backs of California's Indians. In so doing, ordinary soldiers claimed another marker of Spanish status. As Father José Francisco Señán observed in 1800, "It is common that the soldiers, and their wives, when they take Indians [as laborers], begin to act like nobles."[11]

By the time New Spain's wars of independence began, the non-Indian inhabitants of California had forged a common identity as Spaniards, despite their disparate origins. Their classification in official documents, their freedom from hard labor, the clothing they wore, the language they spoke, and their participation in the sacraments of the Church outwardly demonstrated who they were.[12] Soldiers lived among even more symbols of the Spanish state, including their own braided hair. Most took great pride in their identity. As Father Ramón Olbés of Mission Santa Barbara noted in 1813, "although it is well known that not all [the inhabitants of Santa Barbara] are genuine Spaniards, if they were told to the contrary they would consider it an affront."[13]

This generation's identification with Spain was greatly complicated by Napoleon's invasion and the collapse of the Spanish monarchy in 1808. In March, the followers of the king's son Fernando forced his father, Carlos IV, to abdicate in Fernando's favor. Soon after, the French emperor Napoleon overran Iberia, kidnapping the royal family and forcing both father and son to cede their rights to the throne. In New Spain, this caused much uncertainty, as the colonial order had been predicated on having a Spanish king as the ultimate source of authority. Quickly, elites all over New Spain organized to support Fernando VII as a symbol of the Spanish nation and as a defender of the Catholic faith against the revolutionary French.

News of the invasion of Spain and the fall of the monarchy there inspired Spanish Americans to plunge into the kind of open political debate that had been suppressed under colonial rule. Elites organized to support the deposed king, Fernando VII, and waves of printed and manuscript text—letters, books, and newspapers—passed from hand to hand, read aloud and endlessly discussed. The news made it to California in the autumn of 1808 in a letter to the Spanish-born officer José de la Guerra from a Creole cousin in Mexico City. "This iniquity has no equal in History," proclaimed the cousin, "I only regret not being in Spain in order to ... seek out the enemy, and be able to die in defense of the King, of the Holy Religion, ... and for the Homeland."[14] This trinity of loyalties became the rallying call of Spanish royalists against the French invasion. In their name de la Guerra sent two hundred pesos and asked his cousin to forward copies of the *Gaceta del Reyno* [Gazette of the Kingdom], which he passed along to local missionaries.[15]

Across Latin America, in the process of all this reading, writing, and debating, a new political idea rose to the surface: America for the Americans. Two years after the fall of the Spanish monarchy, on September 16, 1810, the rural priest Miguel Hidalgo y Costilla issued the famous "Grito de Dolores," a call to rebellion that is now interpreted as the spark of Mexico's independence movement. Hidalgo's movement demanded broad agrarian reform and the abolition of Indian tribute and slavery. But like every other independence movement in Latin America, it also pulled together supporters of all classes and ethnicities by asserting a common native-born identity. Mexican insurgents called for independence from Spain, marched under the banner of the Virgin of Guadalupe, and shouted "Death to the Spaniards!"[16]

On the isolated frontier, Californians did not feel the full force of the wars for independence, but at least one Spaniard, José de la Guerra, got a very personal taste of this nativism shortly after the wars began. Promoted to a bureaucratic post in Mexico City, de la Guerra left California in November 1810 with his native-born wife, María Antonia, their young daughter Rita, and his wife's brother José Antonio. They never reached the capital. Revolutionaries captured the ship at the Pacific port of San Blas and took the Spanish government official and his family captive. María Antonia was slashed with a saber, her daughter died, and her husband and brother were sentenced to be executed.[17] At the last moment Spanish troops retook the town, freeing the two men, and the bedraggled family finally made their way back north.

During the unsettled years of civil unrest and rebellion in Mexico, California was cut off from official supplies and suffered hunger and poverty while its military and religious leaders defended New Spain's frontier as an oasis of Spanish fidelity. And when, in the fall of 1818, insurgent privateer Hipólito Bouchard brought the fight to California, sacking the town of Monterey, his explicit attack on Spanish property only succeeded in hardening Spanish loyalties.[18] Down in San Diego, Father Pedro Muñóz assured the governor, "[H]ave no fear; this country belongs to Fernando!!"[19] The violent rejection of peninsular Spaniards, part of the creation of a common identity across Latin America, failed to unite the population in California, where so many at the highest levels of power were European-born and so many of their subordinates identified with them. California was barren ground for Creole revolution.

Mexico's provisional government was under little illusion that pulling California into the national project would be easy. As the territory made its hesitant and uneven transition from viceregal subject to republican territory, national leaders made sure distant citizens participated in public signs and ceremonies that affirmed their new identity as Mexicans. Because only a minority could read, it was essential for rulers to employ images and rituals to engage the entire population in the creation and reinforcement of political identity.[20] Between 1821 and 1825, Californians received instructions to observe no fewer than three of these national celebrations. And in everyday life, national officials surrounded Californians with symbols of their new nation: new uniforms, new hairstyles, new coins, new flags, new slogans, and even new government stationery. Yet, a royalist Spanish identity stubbornly persisted.

On February 24, 1821, Agustín de Iturbide issued the Plan de Iguala, declaring Mexico independent. Unlike Hidalgo, Iturbide was conservative, a landowner and Creole officer who had served in the royalist armies. His Plan gave citizenship to people of Indian and African ancestry but preserved the privileges and property of the Church, the military, and the oligarchy. Hoping to gather the support of royalists, Iturbide also called for independent Mexico to continue as a constitutional monarchy under Fernando VII or another European head of state. Mexican elites found much to like in this conservative independence, but up in California, Governor Solá was less enthusiastic, ridiculing Iturbide's "absurd views" and calling independence "a dream."[21]

Facing such uncertainty, the provisional government under Iturbide knew it needed to stage spectacular celebrations on the occasion of his triumphant arrival in Mexico City in September 1821. All towns and villages that had not already sworn independence were ordered to do so on that day, and the governing *junta* printed detailed instructions for local authorities, spelling out which elements would go into such ceremonies: the loyalty oaths, the formal Mass, the procession through town. All was to resemble as much as possible the old rituals of allegiance to the king of Spain.[22]

Two sets of these printed instructions were sent to California, but Governor Solá did not in fact officially announce Mexico's independence there until March of the next year. In the meantime, rumors flew around the territory. The common soldiers and settlers who had been born in California showed some support for the idea, "although very discreetly," remembered soldier José María Amador.[23] At last, on April 9, 1822, the religious and military leaders of Alta and Baja California assembled at the governor's house in Monterey and swore their allegiance to the Mexican regency. They regrouped in the plaza two days later and publicly administered the required oath of loyalty to the troops and a crowd of townsfolk. Father Mariano Payeras led prayers, and the soldiers fired into the air, shouting "Viva!" to the new nation. Music and fireworks rounded out the day.[24] With this observance, California became the last province to acknowledge Mexico's independence.

Still unsure of California's loyalty, Iturbide sent a representative from the capital, Canónigo Agustín Fernández de San Vicente of Durango. Upon the canónigo's arrival in September 1822, eight-year-old Juana Machado was struck by his physical presence, designed to inspire awe and respect. "Whenever some woman or girl would be taken aback by the splendor and colors of his outfit, she would ask, 'Who is that man?'"[25] The canónigo found no evidence of open rebellion, but neither did he find much enthusiasm. Bringing the unwelcome news that Iturbide himself had been declared emperor in May 1822 and was now head of state, rather than Fernando VII, Canónigo Fernández insisted on public demonstrations of allegiance. In Monterey, he ordered that the Spanish flag be lowered for the last time over the plaza, to be followed by "feasts...salvos, processions, mock battles, and an oath to support independence, parties, dances, bullfights, and other activities that lasted for three days or more."[26] In San Diego, where there was no flagpole, the military improvised by having a soldier hold a flag in each hand. As Commander Francisco María Ruíz gave the cry, "Long live the Mexican empire!" the soldier lowered the arm holding the Spanish flag and raised the arm with the Mexican flag.[27]

Despite the festivities, Californians felt mixed emotions at these events. When the Spanish flag dropped in Monterey to grim silence, Governor Solá was forced to explain, "They do not cheer, because they are unused to independence."[28] María Inocenta Pico was struck by "the tremendous emotion expressed by the Spaniards, especially the missionary Fathers, because of that event."[29] Amador recalled that the priests refused to participate in the ceremonies at all, "believing that they would be violating the rights of the Spanish King."[30] In San Diego, Juana Machado remembered the day her father was ordered to cut off his long braid: "He gave it to my mother. His face showed such sorrow...She would look at the braid and cry."[31] Captain de la Guerra found an excuse not to be present for the change of flags in Santa Barbara, traveling up to "some rancho," according to his daughter.[32] Years later, Antonio María Osio summed up their feelings: "[W]hen the government changed in 1821, if the Californios had been offered the opportunity to serve the republic or to serve the King in the labors of the conquest, in spite of their advanced age there is no doubt that they would have chosen the King."[33]

In a final ritual of allegiance, Californians were asked to officially recognize the liberal constitution of 1824. This document made Mexico a republic, not an imperial regency, and banished forever the notion that Fernando VII might once again rule over the nation. For this occasion, in March 1825, California's interim governor, Luis Antonio Argüello, administered an oath of loyalty to the territorial assembly and read the constitution to the public in the plaza at Monterey. Three days of musket and cannon fire, "Vivas," and bell ringing followed, but once again the missionaries refused to participate, and there were no public sermons or special masses said. Instructions were sent to each presidio and pueblo to repeat the ceremonies, but in at least one of the towns, there is no record of such events taking place. Four years had passed, filled with the excitement of new flags, fireworks, and solemn oaths of loyalty designed to transform Spanish subjects into Mexican citizens, yet in California, the emergence of a new national identity remained a work in progress.

Although Mexican nationalists made little headway with the older generation in California, they did find willing converts to some aspects of the national program among the younger, native-born generation—those who had whispered their tentative support of the new nation in 1821. In addition to replacing Spain with Mexico on the symbolic level of image and ritual, the Mexican liberals who led the nation sought to build a unified republican state, replacing colonial corporations such as the military and the Church. In theory, their policy was a coherent one, rationalist and secular, that called for a constitutional government, free trade, and individual liberty. In practice, it often fragmented into clusters of ideas and programs.[34] California, still governed as a territory under central control, served as a space for liberal experimentation in the early republic, and newly arrived representatives from Mexico preached their philosophies to the younger generation, calling for mission secularization and local civilian government.[35] Elite native sons, the children of military officers, actively participated in these debates and adopted aspects of liberal ideology that seemed to explain their own perceived economic and political oppression. Yet, in their hands, nation building parted ways with national identity.

Two officials appointed in Mexico were instrumental in introducing liberalism to California's second generation: Governor José María de Echeandía and his aide Lieutenant José María Padrés.[36] Both belonged to the York Rite lodge of Masons. During the years of the early republic, Masonic lodges offered Mexican political elites the space to develop political consensus and discuss legislative agendas. The Scottish Rite lodge, brought to Mexico by Spaniards in the waning years of the empire, tended to be conservative, centralist, and pro-Church. The York Rite lodge, founded in 1825, was generally composed of federalist liberals.

José María de Echeandía, the first centrally appointed governor, arrived shortly after Californians (or most of them, anyway) had sworn allegiance to the new constitution in 1825. "He talked about republican and liberal principles that were stirring in the minds of the Mexicans of that time," remembered Angustias de la Guerra, the daughter of Santa Barbara's presidial commander. "He was sent to California to introduce the new regime and he certainly put these ideas into practice."[37] The governor and Padrés organized study groups for young Californios in San Diego and Monterey, modeled on Masonic lodges, and taught the principles of republican government and the importance of secularizing the missions. Padrés, who was more radical than Echeandía, stressed the universal rights of man and the tyranny of missionaries over Indians.[38] "If I resolved to give liberty to the Indians," disciple Juan Alvarado recalled later, "I did it because my republican education did not permit me to continue to be... insensible to the cry of anguish from the breast of thirty thousand Indians who, deprived of their liberty, were nothing more than puppets in the hands of the priests."[39] Not only would secularization release Indians from oppression and make them full participants in the market economy, they argued, but it would also break the power of the Church in secular affairs, make huge tracts of developed land available to private ranchers and farmers, and give the national economy a needed shot in the arm.[40] "Of course the young men made common cause with the bold preacher of doctrines that were in harmony with our own progressive and philanthropic outlook," Mariano Guadalupe Vallejo said later of his own conversion to the cause.[41]

In addition to the tutelage of Echeandía and Padrés, young men of the Californio elite turned to imported books for lessons in the new liberal ideologies.[42] Works by Baron de Montesquieu, Jean-Jacques Rousseau, Benjamin Constant, and Voltaire had been circulating in Mexico's capital for years. English merchant William Hartnell had brought a stash of these books to California just two months after the territory celebrated independence and used this library to tutor the elite sons of Monterey. In 1823, these "young men of education" formed a secret "Historical Society," to "compile the history of our homeland," as Alvarado later remembered. But only one meeting was held, "at which," Alvarado remarked, "the object of the meeting forgotten, [we] talked about the best means to improve the condition of the territory... and in the end things got quite heated."[43] In 1831, Vallejo bought the entire floating library of German trader Enrique Virmond and shared books like François Fénelon's *Telemachus* with his friends Alvarado and José Castro. The latter read aloud from them to his girlfriend "every night... with great pleasure."[44] For spreading such dangerous ideas, the three were temporarily excommunicated by Father Durán. Vallejo recorded bitterly in his memoirs that "the missionary fathers were adamantly opposed to the circulation of books among us that might inspire liberal ideas and knowledge of the rights of free men in young people."[45]

Mexican officials hoped the young men of California, newly converted to liberalism, would support not only the national project of mission secularization but also the restructuring of local government along republican lines. Prior to independence, the military dominated the administrative and judicial systems of California and held ultimate authority over the town councils of Monterey, Los Angeles, San Jose, and Santa Cruz. But under the new state, the federal government removed this military supervision over towns and encouraged popular suffrage.⁴⁶ Pío Pico, the son of a soldier from San Diego, remembered his first encounter with the defiant mood of republicanism in Los Angeles. Sent there as a scribe in 1827 under military commander Captain Pablo de la Portilla, Pico was taken aback when a witness in a pending court case, a Mexican merchant named Bringas, refused to recognize the authority of the military to conduct the investigation. "I was even more surprised," Pico remembered, "when I heard Bringas tell Portilla that the civilians [*paisanos*] were the sacred core of the nation, and that the military were nothing more than servants of the nation, which was constituted of the people and not of the military." Ever after, he declared, "it always appeared to me, deep in my soul, that the citizens were the nation."⁴⁷

In this heady era, the young men of the territory earnestly debated how a liberal society might overcome the entrenched corporate privilege of the colonial order, manifested in the missions and the military, and create a new nation of free citizens. Mexican liberals had every reason to believe Californians would join them in building the Mexican nation. Unfortunately for the national project in California, however, Mexican representatives did just as much to push native sons away as they did to pull them in. As more and more Mexicans arrived to reshape the territory, native-born Californians felt themselves to be at the mercy of a central authority that looked at their homeland as a dumping ground for undesirables or a prize awarded to sycophantic politicians, and that looked at its citizenry as nothing but disloyal Gachupines and uneducated rubes.⁴⁸ "Given the great distance separating California from the capital of the Republic," noted Alvarado, one of the young men of Monterey, "the sons of that department were considered foreigners."⁴⁹

Despite Mexico's new republican principles, California did not immediately come under civilian rule at the highest levels. Instead, California's governors were still military men, appointed by the central government. They brought with them artillery and infantry units, many of whom were not trained soldiers but conscripts sent north to serve for criminal offenses or vagrancy. Californians called these men "cholos," mixed-race degenerates with no sense of discipline or order—"lost men," one said, "full of vice."[50] The officers who arrived with them seemed little better. During the wars for independence, many lower-class and mixed-race men had risen through the ranks of the insurgent military, and their service earned them high ranks after the war. Governor Echeandía, escorted by many of these new officers in 1825, immediately began to force out the old military men in the presidial companies and "to assign the posts there to the officers who had accompanied him."[51] Artillery Captain Miguel González was one such officer, and as soon as he arrived in California, he began to complain that Californian officers and soldiers refused to obey his orders. They dismissed his authority with insults to his character, calling him ignorant, brutal, and despotic, and they publicly called him by the racial slur El Macaco, or "The Monkey."[52] Using such language, Californians drew a distinction between themselves—white, cultured, civilized—and other Mexicans—dark-skinned, uncivilized, criminal.

So when José Antonio de la Guerra and his cousins, all cadets born in California, rummaged around in their fathers' trunks, dressed as Spanish officers, and tricked their superiors into surrendering the presidio in 1828, the message was clear to González and the other newcomers stationed there: "If they call it a joke today, tomorrow it will be for real." Through playacting and mockery, the young men of California began to draw a clear line between themselves and the outsiders, pointing out their own cleverness and expressing contempt for the Mexicans. And by pretending to be Spanish, these cadets were beginning to create a Californian identity that, unlike the national identity of Mexico, managed to incorporate Spaniards.

They did so in part as a reaction to the continuing Mexican initiative to purge Spaniards from the new nation. Although the Plan de Iguala had guaranteed the rights of European-born Spaniards who continued to live in Mexico, Creoles in most regions continued to distrust and fear them. Local politicians across the nation, hoping to unite supporters against a common enemy, labeled Iberian Spaniards as economic exploiters, tyrants, and slave masters who were planning to rise up at any moment and reconquer Mexico in the name of the king.[53] Governor Echeandía's aide Padrés, a militant Mexican nationalist, actively promoted the expulsion of Spaniards from California, particularly Spanish missionaries. Young cadet José Antonio de la Guerra had already been personally affected by this anti-Spanish sentiment. His Spanish-born father, elected to the national congress as California's representative, had been denied his seat in early 1828 because of his Spanish birth.[54] The threat to California's Spanish-born population became even more intense after the passage of two national expulsion laws in 1827 and 1829. The first spared those who had Creole wives and children, but the second expelled all Iberian Spaniards, regardless of circumstance. In California, popular sentiment ran against these laws; Angustias de la Guerra remembered that, despite her father's misadventures in Mexico City, he "was sure that as soon as he returned, nobody would touch him, because the Californios at that time were a people who were very Spanish, except for a few who were supporters of independence."[55] Governor Echeandía recognized that carrying out these laws would threaten the social order, so he simply asked European-born Spaniards to sign oaths of loyalty to the republic. Even then, he looked the other way when a handful refused. But in late 1829, events pushed him to take more extreme measures.

Californians were just learning the news that over the summer of 1829, Spanish forces had in fact assembled in Cuba and invaded Mexico at Tampico, when on November 12, 1829, destitute soldiers of the Monterey presidio rose up, took possession of the garrison, and imprisoned their officers, demanding back pay and rations. This revolt soon spread to the presidio of San Francisco, and the rebels sent word south encouraging their fellow soldiers to join them. A Mexican convict named Joaquín Solís led this insurrection.[56] At first, Solís encouraged the troops to overthrow the Mexican governor, Echeandía, "with a view to put all the offices in the hands of Californians," but then undermined his attempt by imprisoning most of the young men of Monterey along with the recently arrived Mexican government officials.[57] On his way south to meet the governor's forces at Santa Barbara, Solís stopped at several of the missions and along the way changed his tune, claiming that he was acting to restore Spanish dominion in California.

Solís eventually surrendered, but his appeal to Spaniards had struck a nerve with alarmed Mexican officials. Echeandía declared Solís an accomplice to the Tampico plot to reconquer the republic.[58] He also became convinced that the missionaries, particularly Luis Martínez of San Luis Obispo, were plotting a counter-revolution to restore California to Spain.[59] After all, it was widely known that many missionaries had refused outright to swear loyalty to the new republic. So Governor Echeandía ordered the arrest of Martínez. Two Spanish-born tallow traders operating out of Lima, Juan Ignacio Mancisidor and his partner Antonio José Cot, were forced to leave on the same ship in March 1830.[60]

These expulsions threatened to disrupt California's hide-and-tallow trade and its ties to Pacific commercial networks. Under the new republic's free-trade policies, California's markets had opened to the world, and by 1829, merchants were arriving from South America, the United

States, and Europe to sell manufactured goods in exchange for products of the missions' cattle herds, in the form of hides, tallow, and horns.[61] Mancisidor and Cot in particular connected Californians to the mines and markets of Peru, where they found ready buyers for soap and candles made of California tallow. Martínez, on the other hand, provided Californians with the sacraments essential to their religion. California had no parish priests before 1840, so in the absence of missionaries, babies could not be baptized, young couples could not marry, and the dying could not receive last rites. So, while politicians in other parts of Mexico whipped up support with anti-Spanish proclamations, in California such tactics had the opposite effect. Purging Spaniards there felt less like an attack on foreign oppressors and more like one on the community itself.

The same month that Father Martínez and the two Spanish merchants from Lima were taken to a waiting ship and sent south, the *María Ester* arrived from Mexico, bringing about eighty more convicts. Again, Mexican policy provoked the Californians, who saw little justice in a government that replaced trusted merchants and priests with dangerous criminals and their Mexican guards. The new arrivals provided a flashpoint for national and local identity when a Mexican guard from Acapulco attacked an English sailor from the same ship, shouting, "I am Creole, and I have made my purpose to kill all the Foreigners or Gachupines that I can!" Even more shockingly, Mexican Commander Romualdo Pacheco, another 1825 arrival, set the guard free the next day for his "patriotic" and nationalistic motives. "I don't know if with thanks," the Spanish-born José de la Guerra commented sardonically.[62] Later, rumors circulated in Santa Barbara that the soldiers and convicts were plotting together to rob and kill foreign residents like Alfred Robinson, a hide-and-tallow trader newly arrived from Boston. International traders were further alarmed on Independence Day that year, September 16, 1830, when convicts and Mexican soldiers gathered in the presidio square to set off fireworks, burn the figure of a Gachupín in effigy, and shout "Viva Pacheco!" and "Death to the Spaniard and foreigners!"[63]

Up in Monterey, many of the young Californios had already sent petitions to Echeandía to protest the arrival of the convict ship, but it was not just the events in Santa Barbara that had provoked their alienation. In the territorial capital, young men had been working hard to catch up with the liberal and republican theorists in far-off Europe and Mexico City, but they continued to be acutely sensitive to their isolation from these centers of thinking and debate. Their insecurity had only intensified the year before, in the summer of 1829, when word had come back of the treatment José Joaquín Maitorena had received in Mexico. Maitorena, who had served in California's military since his arrival in 1801 (and was commander at Santa Barbara during the Spanish-officer prank), had been sent as California's congressional representative, replacing Spaniard José de la Guerra. On his arrival in the Pacific port of Tepic, Maitorena eagerly began his political life by buying everyone drinks and talking political theory. Figuring the new deputy for a drunk and a fool, his new acquaintances "persuaded him to undertake [being a] Mason, since if he didn't he wouldn't be received in Congress." They then led him to a fake lodge, where men dressed in drag performed a phony ceremony. "In the end all was laughter," wrote one witness to a friend in California. "If they are sending this Man from California now," he concluded, "in the future they will send a bear."[64]

So on Independence Day, 1830, as Mexicans burned a Spaniard in effigy in Santa Barbara, the younger generation in Monterey reached their breaking point. The trouble started when Lieutenant Rodrigo del Pliego, who had arrived with fellow officer Miguel González in 1825, insulted native-born Californians at a dance held to celebrate the national holiday. Native son Juan Alvarado was just twenty-one that year but had already held the post of secretary to the California *diputación*, or territorial legislature, for three years. He responded with his own toast to those "who may know how to appreciate the frank hospitality with which the Californians are accustomed to treat them . . . I loathe every man who, forgetting his education and good taste, might insult them, as just happened in this room," he added pointedly. According to Alvarado's account, Pliego answered the challenge by throwing his drink at Alvarado, who in turn knocked the Mexican to the ground.[65] Other versions of the event held that Pliego had simply refused to raise his glass to this toast and received a slap in the face in return.[66] Perhaps significantly, all these attacks were to the face and head, making the affront to masculine honor especially grave.

That same year, Alvarado's friend José Castro was arrested for posting *pasquinades*, or satirical broadsides, and otherwise publicly expressing his contempt for Mexicans. Unfortunately, Castro's pasquinade doesn't seem to have survived, but the form had a long history in Mexico for oppositional speech. Posted anonymously in a public place such as a church door or a central plaza, the pasquinade was meant to refute official proclamations with what purported to be the voice of the people. Sometimes the content appeared in verse, or with illustration, and it frequently contained insults and violent threats.[67] If Castro's broadside attacked Pliego in particular, we can imagine what it might have said, based on other assessments of Pliego's character left by Castro's contemporaries. Angustias de la Guerra, for example, called Pliego a "sycophant" and a "blind instrument of despotism."[68] Castro had his own personal run-in with Pliego, slapping him for an insult about the stupidity and poor education of Californio native sons.[69]

As Andrés Reséndez has noted, citizens in Texas and New Mexico enthusiastically embraced the celebration of Independence Day. "Patriotic committees" and town leaders spent months planning elaborate demonstrations of patriotism, such as fandangos, bullfights, and fireworks.[70] Things were different in California. Recent arrivals organized fireworks and dances to celebrate Independence Day in September and the festival of the Virgin of Guadalupe in December, but as young native-born Californians entered public service to carry out the liberal policies of the new state, they also developed feelings of alienation from Mexicanness that holiday parties did little to overcome. They expressed their newly formed identity through pranks, insults, and open mockery, and when they talked about *mi país*, or *mi suelo*, they meant California, not Mexico. The provinces to the south were *estos suelos Republicanos*, "those Republican lands." Some, only partly in jest, called their territory's administration an "island government," a reference to the prize promised to Sancho Panza in the works of Cervantes—a reward given to incompetent toadies, an invented place to play at being ruler.[71] In this, they seemed to have the sympathies of their Spanish-identified fathers, whose loyalty to the new administration was also tenuous.

As a result, even though native sons enthusiastically championed many elements of liberal nation building, such as civilian government and the secularization of the missions, they did not automatically absorb a Mexican national identity with them. In fact, the struggle for local control over these projects pit the territory against the nation for the next five years. In 1831, this pro-reform, nativist sentiment culminated in the ouster of the new Mexican governor, Manuel Victoria, a conservative who had dissolved the territorial assembly and town councils, expelled the radical Padrés, and halted the work of secularization.[72] Victoria's ejection, along with that of the hated Rodrigo Pliego, convinced the native sons that together they could be a potent political force against Mexicans in California.

In 1834, the tables were turned, and it was a liberal plan from Mexico City that prompted native sons to organize an expulsion. That year, Mexican Vice President Valentín Gómez-Farías sent an experimental colony north to take possession of all secularized mission lands; the colonists were headed by José María Híjar, a federalist from Guadalajara, and none other than the previously expelled Padrés. At their farewell ball, Vice President Gómez-Farías had toasted the colonists with the prediction that California would become "a haven for liberals when they could no longer remain in Mexico."[73] Demonstrating how much California's native sons had separated the tools of liberal nation building from the nation itself, the young men of the territory rebuffed the newcomers, even their old mentor Padrés, and expelled the colony directors on suspicion of conspiracy against the government.[74] Afterward, Californios continued to grant former mission lands to themselves.

Finally, in 1836, another new governor arrived, bringing with him President Santa Anna's new centralist constitution. Under the new regime, secularization was repealed.[75] All territories and states in Mexico were transformed into "departments," their governors appointed by the Mexican president, and their popularly elected state assemblies replaced by advisory juntas. The constitutional amendments also abolished most popularly elected town councils; instead, municipalities fell under the authority of prefects and sub-prefects, who would report directly to the governor. Income requirements limited those who could vote and hold office.[76] By the time Governor Mariano Chico landed at Santa Barbara in April 1836, native sons in California had a good idea of what was to come, and eighty of them met the new governor dressed in black, wearing "in the buttonhole of the frock coats a small red rosette which was the distinguishing badge of the federalists," according to one of them.[77]

Confident in their identity as Californios, native-born men moved to protect home rule and keep the distribution of mission lands under their control. If Monterey was the most nativist town in California, then Santa Barbara, under the influence of Captain de la Guerra, was the most Spanish. But the deputies of Monterey knew how to unite native sons and Spanish fathers. With the example of Father Martínez in mind, the deputies tricked Governor Chico into ordering the expulsion of Father Durán of Mission Santa Barbara. To no one's surprise, a (carefully orchestrated) riot broke out in Santa Barbara the day Durán was to leave.[78] Faced with such an ungovernable population, Chico resigned his post less than a week later, vowing to return someday with reinforcements and leaving a subordinate, Nicolás Gutiérrez, in charge.[79]

Gutiérrez did little to improve relations with the native-son deputies. When he tried to dissolve the legislature, California's revolutionaries, including Castro, Alvarado, José Antonio de la Guerra, and Vallejo, sharpened their pens, and on November 6, 1836, signed a *pronunciamiento*, or declaration, that severed all ties with Mexico and declared the territory of California "free and sovereign."[80] A new flag flew over the capital: a large red star on a white ground.[81] These young men of Monterey, Antonio María Osio remembered, "wanted to be called *californios* and not Mexicans. That is why," he explained, "the troops adopted the practice of answering the challenge 'Who goes there?' with the response 'California libre.' The individual who responded 'Mexico' would be punished with sentry duty."[82] Eventually, rebellious Californians managed to score critical concessions from the central state before they rejoined the nation: recognition of a native-son governor, Juan Alvarado, and local control over secularization. Unrest continued to plague the administrations of Alvarado's successors.

As Mexico's new republic struggled to take shape, the remote territory of California became a deeply contested space. Conservative "Spaniards" protected their safe haven against nativist Americans; liberal nationalists saw open ground to remake the social order. Native-born Californians sympathized with nation-building projects and Enlightenment theory but balked at a new national identity that excluded the Spaniards among them. Through the 1820s and 1830s, as they grew to adulthood, the native sons and daughters of California struggled to shape national initiatives to their own desires, endlessly debating what it meant to be Spanish, Mexican, or Californio.

In hindsight, many Americans pointed to the conflicted national identities of Californians as a factor in their easy defeat of the province. Still, when the United States invaded its southern neighbor in 1846, Californians knew where they stood. "I admit," Julio Carrillo later wrote, "that the general government of Mexico was like a very mean stepmother to us... but in my estimation this was no reason why we should have renounced our birthrights."[83] Angustias de la Guerra protested that John Charles Frémont, leader of the Bear Flag Revolt, "had insulted the Mexican nation by raising his flag in our territory."[84] Francisco de la Guerra, her brother, announced "that he had been born a Mexican and would remain one, regardless of the flag he might live under."[85] Their father, the former presidial commander, reapplied for his Spanish citizenship.[86]

Notes

1. Provincial State Papers, vol. 70, Military, 1829, The Bancroft Library, University of California, Berkeley, BANC MSS C-A 19, pp. 35–38. José María de Echeandía, case against José Antonio Noriega, Joaquín Carrillo, and Raimundo Carrillo, April 25, 1829, San Diego. See also Hubert Howe Bancroft, *History of California*, 7 vols. (San Francisco: The History Company, 1884–89), 2:576.

2. See David J. Weber's essay in this volume, as well as, for California: Michael J. González, *This Small City Will Be a Mexican Paradise: Exploring the Origins of Mexican Culture in Los Angeles, 1821–1846* (Albuquerque: University of New Mexico Press, 2005); Lisbeth Haas, *Conquests and Historical Identities in California, 1769–1936* (Berkeley, Los Angeles, and London: University of California Press, 1995); Douglas Monroy, *Thrown Among Strangers: The Making of Mexican Culture in Frontier California* (Berkeley: University of California Press, 1990); Rosaura Sánchez, *Telling Identities: The Californio "Testimonios"* (Minneapolis: University of Minnesota Press, 1995); and Barbara L. Voss, *The Archaeology of Ethnogenesis: Race and Sexuality in Colonial San Francisco* (Berkeley: University of California Press, 2008).

3. The term "Californio," according to Rose Marie Beebe and Robert Senkewicz, was originally used in what is now Baja California in the early eighteenth century, and it was widely adopted in Alta California beginning in the 1820s to describe the gente de razón of the second generation, who were born and raised in the territory. Antonio María Osio, *The History of Alta California: A Memoir of Mexican California*, trans. and ed. Rose Marie Beebe and Robert M. Senkewicz (Madison: University of Wisconsin Press, 1996), 343.

4. Oakah L. Jones, *Los Paisanos: Spanish Settlers on the Northern Frontier of New Spain* (Norman: University of Oklahoma Press, 1996), 240–41; David J. Weber, *The Spanish Frontier in North America* (New Haven, Conn.: Yale University Press, 1992), 263–64.

5. On this phenomenon in the U.S. Southwest, see Gloria E. Miranda, "Racial and Cultural Dimensions of *Gente de Razón* Status in Mexican California," *Southern California Quarterly* 70 (1988): 265–78; Weber, *Spanish Frontier*, 326–28; and Ramón A. Gutiérrez, "Ethnic and Class Boundaries in America's Hispanic Past," in *Social and Gender Boundaries in the United States*, ed. Sucheng Chan (Lewiston, N.Y.: Edwin Mellon Press, 1989), 37–53. On the purchase of legitimacy or whiteness in other regions of Spanish America, see Ann Twinam, *Public Lives, Private Secrets: Gender, Honor, Sexuality, and Illegitimacy in Colonial Spanish America* (Stanford, Calif.: Stanford University Press, 1999), 18, 289, 310.

6. William Marvin Mason, *The Census of 1790: A Demographic History of Colonial California*, Ballena Press Anthropological Papers 45 (Menlo Park, Calif.: Ballena Press, 1998), 53–54.

7. Voss, *The Archaeology of Ethnogenesis*, 265.

8. One disgruntled recruit, José María Amador, complained that a more extreme version of the hairstyle, introduced by Spaniard José de la Guerra at Monterey, "was so ridiculous that no one would voluntarily accept it." The "Monterey haircut" involved shaving the front half of the head and wearing a hairpiece that

curled over the sides of the head. Gregorio Mora-Torres, *Californio Voices: The Oral Memoirs of José María Amador and Lorenzo Asisara* (Denton: University of North Texas Press, 2005), 36–37.

9   Miranda, "Racial and Cultural Dimensions," 268.

10 Steven W. Hackel, *Children of Coyote, Missionaries of Saint Francis: Indian-Spanish Relations in Colonial California, 1769–1850* (Chapel Hill: University of North Carolina Press, 2005), 287–96.

11 Quoted in ibid., 320.

12 Barbara Voss in particular has examined the material practices that indicate the emergence of a collective identity among California settlers "no later than the 1790s." Voss, *Archeology of Ethnogenesis*, 112.

13 Quoted in Weber, *Spanish Frontier*, 328.

14 José Antonio Noriega to José de la Guerra, Mexico City, August 6, 1808, folder 712, de la Guerra Papers, Santa Barbara Mission Archive-Library, Santa Barbara, California. Henceforward, references to the DLG collection are listed by folder number.

15 José Antonio Noriega to José de la Guerra, Mexico City, April 19, 1809, DLG 712; and José Antonio Noriega to José de la Guerra, Mexico City, July 1, 1809, DLG 712.

16 John Charles Chasteen, "Introduction," and François-Xavier Guerra, "Forms of Communication, Political Spaces, and Cultural Identities in the Creation of Spanish American Nations," in *Beyond Imagined Communities: Reading and Writing the Nation in Nineteenth-Century Latin America*, ed. Sara Castro-Klarén and John Charles Chasteen (Baltimore: Johns Hopkins University Press, 2003), ix–xxv, 3–32; Peter Guardino, *The Time of Liberty: Popular Political Culture in Oaxaca, 1750–1850* (Durham, N.C.: Duke University Press, 2005), 122–55. For more on the development of a collective identity among American-born Spaniards, see David A. Brading, *The First America: The Spanish Monarchy, Creole Patriots, and the Liberal State, 1492–1867* (Cambridge: Cambridge University Press, 1991).

17 Joseph A. Thompson, *El Gran Capitán: José de la Guerra* (Los Angeles: Cabrera and Sons, 1961), 17.

18 For accounts of Bouchard and his raid of the California coast, see Thompson, *El Gran Capitan*, 35–51; Patrick O'Dowd, "Pirates and Patriots," *La Campana* (Santa Barbara Trust for Historic Preservation, Winter 1997–98): 2–16; and María de las Angustias de la Guerra de Ord, "Ocurrencias en California," 1878, The Bancroft Library, BANC MSS C-D 134; translation in Rose Marie Beebe and Robert M. Senkewicz, *Testimonios: Early California through the Eyes of Women, 1815–1848* (Berkeley: Heyday Books, 2006), 201–70 at 202–5.

19 Fray Pedro Muñóz to Gov. Pablo Vicente de Solá, San Diego Mission, no date, quoted in Thompson, *El Gran Capitan*, 50. When yet another rumor of insurgent attack swept California in the spring of 1820, Father Antonio Ripoll of Mission Santa Barbara assured Captain de la Guerra, "They are killing themselves to form a company of royalist gente de razón in every presidio." Fr. Antonio Ripoll to José de la Guerra, Mission Santa Barbara, April 26, 1820, DLG 826.

20 Guerra, "Forms of Communication," 7–9. Literacy rates in California are hard to quantify. Forty years before independence, about 30 percent of the soldiers at the presidios of Monterey and San Francisco could read. The rates in civilian settlements and among the wives and daughters of soldiers were no doubt much lower. Real Presidio de Monterey, "Lista de la Compania del Referido Presidio," 31 Julio de 1782, Prov. St. Pa. B. Mil iv 663–94, and R[eal] Presidio de San Francisco, Lista de La Compania, 31 Agosto de 1782, Prov. St. Pa. B. Mil iv 601, The Bancroft Library.

21 Solá to Gov. José Argüello, January 10, 1822; see David J. Weber, *The Mexican Frontier, 1821–1846: The American Southwest under Mexico* (Albuquerque: University of New Mexico Press, 1982), 8.

22 Andrés Reséndez, *Changing National Identities at the Frontier: Texas and New Mexico, 1800–1850* (Cambridge: Cambridge University Press, 2005), 84–85.

23 Mora-Torres, *Californio Voices*, 153–55.

24 Bancroft, *History of California*, 2:451; and Herbert E. Bolton, "The Iturbide Revolution in the Californias," *Hispanic America Historical Review* 2 (1919): 188–242.

25 Juana Machado, "Los tiempos pasados de la Alta California," 1878, The Bancroft Library, BANC MSS C-D 199; translation in Beebe and Senkewicz, *Testimonios*, 122–44 at 127.

26 María Inocenta Pico, "Cosas de California," 1878, The Bancroft Library, BANC MSS C-D 34; translation in Beebe and Senkewicz, *Testimonios*, 301–17 at 313.

27 Machado, "Los tiempos," The Bancroft Library, BANC MSS C-D 199; translation in Beebe and Senkewicz, *Testimonios*, 127.

28 Quoted in Weber, *Mexican Frontier*, 8.

29 María Inocenta Pico, "Cosas," The Bancroft Library, BANC MSS C-D 34; translation in Beebe and Senkewicz, *Testimonios*, 312.

30 Mora-Torres, *Californio Voices*, 113.

31 Machado, "Los tiempos," The Bancroft Library, BANC MSS C-D 119; translation in Beebe and Senkewicz, *Testimonios*, 128.

32 Angustias de la Guerra, "Ocurrencias," The Bancroft Library, BANC MSS C-D 134; translation in Beebe and Senkewicz, *Testimonios*, 209.

33 Osio, *The History of Alta California*, 81.

34 For more on liberalism in Mexico's early national era, see David A. Brading, *The Origins of Mexican Nationalism* (Cambridge: Centre of Latin American Studies, 1985); Charles A. Hale, *Mexican Liberalism in the Age of Mora, 1821–1853* (New Haven, Conn.: Yale University Press, 1968); Peter Guardino, *Peasants, Politics, and the Formation of Mexico's National State: Guerrero, 1800–1857* (Stanford, Calif.: Stanford University Press, 1996), and *The Time of Liberty*; John Lynch, *The Spanish American Revolutions 1808–1826*, 2nd ed. (New York: W. W. Norton & Co., 1986); and Jaime E. Rodríguez O., *The Independence of Spanish America* (New York: Cambridge University Press, 1998).

35 Sánchez, *Telling Identities*, 99. For a discussion of Texas as another haven for Mexican liberalism and liberals, see Reséndez, *Changing National Identities*, 61–74.

36 Sánchez, *Telling Identities*, 110.

37 Angustias de la Guerra, "Ocurrencias," The Bancroft Library, BANC MSS C-D 134; translation in Beebe and Senkewicz, *Testimonios*, 225. Angustias de la Guerra, a literate daughter of an elite family, was married to a high-ranking government official in the Mexican era, and from her home in Monterey, was an astute political observer.

38 Bancroft, *History of California*, 3:184; Sánchez, *Telling Identities*, 116; Angustias de la Guerra, "Ocurrencias," The Bancroft Library, BANC MSS C-D 134; translation in Beebe and Senkewicz, *Testimonios*, 222.

39 Juan Alvarado, "Historia de California," 1876, The Bancroft Library, BANC MSS C-D 1, pp. 208–9.

40 Weber, *Mexican Frontier*, 47–50; Sánchez, *Telling Identities*, 111–13.

41 Mariano Guadalupe Vallejo, "Recuerdos históricos y personales tocante a la Alta California," 1874, The Bancroft Library, BANC MSS C-D 18, p. 261.

42 On the impact of French philosophers in Los Angeles, see González, *This Small City*, 149–52. On liberal works circulating in Mexico, see Hale, *Mexican Liberalism in the Age of Mora*, 39–71.

43 Alvarado, "Historia de California," The Bancroft Library, BANC MSS C-D 2, pp. 42–43. Alvarado claims that the historical society was the inspiration of Joaquín de la Torre, while Dakin credits Hartnell. Susanna Bryant Dakin, *The Lives of William Hartnell* (Stanford, Calif.: Stanford University Press, 1949), 48, 97. See also Alan Rosenus, *General M. G. Vallejo and the Advent of the Americans: A Biography* (Albuquerque: University of New Mexico Press, 1995), 9.

44 Vallejo, "Recuerdos históricos," The Bancroft Library, BANC MSS C-D 19, p. 113. Few young women were literate enough to read such books themselves, and none were invited to attend the study groups that Mexican theorists set up for their brothers. Yet, despite the fact that women were not considered citizens in the early republic, some did eagerly follow the political debates of their era. For later commentary on the ideological and political debates of the era by women, see Beebe and Senkewicz, *Testimonios*. For the impact of liberalism on women's status in Latin America generally, see Arlene J. Díaz, *Female Citizens, Patriarchs, and the Law in Venezuela, 1786–1904* (Lincoln: University of Nebraska Press, 2004), 105–70; Lara Putnam, Sarah C. Chambers, and Sueann Caulfield, "Transformations in Honor, Status, and Law over the Long Nineteenth Century," in *Honor, Status, and Law in Modern Latin America*, ed. Sueann Caulfield, Sarah C. Chambers, and Lara Putnam (Durham, N.C.: Duke University Press, 2005), 1–24; Sarah Chambers, *From Subjects to Citizens: Honor, Gender, and Politics in Arequipa, Peru, 1780–1854* (University Park, Penn.: University of Pennsylvania Press, 1999), 200–215; and Christine Hunefeldt, *Liberalism in the Bedroom: Quarreling Spouses in Nineteenth-Century Lima* (University Park: University of Pennsylvania Press, 2000).

45 Vallejo, "Recuerdos históricos," The Bancroft Library, BANC MSS C-D 19, pp. 109–10; translation in Rosaura Sánchez, *Telling Identities*, 119. Later, they were granted absolution on the condition that they would not loan the books to anyone else.

46 Bancroft, *History of California*, 2:661; Thompson, *El Gran Capitán*, 79; Weber, *Mexican Frontier*, 29–30.

47 Pío Pico, "Narración histórica," 1877, The Bancroft Library, BANC MSS C-D 13; translation in Rose Marie Beebe and Robert M. Senkewicz, eds., *Lands of Promise and Despair: Chronicles of Early California, 1535–1846* (Berkeley, Calif.: Heyday Books, 2001), 346–48.

48 Gachupín was a derogatory term for a European-born Spaniard.

49 Alvarado, "Historia de California," The Bancroft Library, BANC MSS C-D 5, p. 82.

50 Osio, *The History of Alta California*, 87.

51 Ibid., 86.

52 Bancroft, *History of California*, 3:39–40.

53 For more on anti-Spanish discourse in Mexico, see Guardino, *The Time of Liberty*, 134–37, 184–86.

54 Bancroft, *History of California*, 2:570–71.

55 Angustias de la Guerra, "Ocurrencias," The Bancroft Library, BANC MSS C-D 134; translation in Beebe and Senkewicz, *Testimonios*, 210.

56 Solís had committed brutal crimes in Mexico, but because of his service during the wars of independence, had his sentence reduced to banishment to California. Bancroft describes him as a "companion" of Vicente Gómez, a notoriously violent criminal nicknamed El Capador, or "The Castrator." Bancroft, *History of California*, 3:68.

57 Among those imprisoned were Juan Alvarado, then secretary of the territorial legislation, Ensign Mariano Guadalupe Vallejo, acting commander of the presidio, and José Castro, their friend.

58 Bancroft, *History of California*, 3:77.

59 Angustias de la Guerra fingers "Mexican artillerymen Joaquín and Lázaro Piña" as the source for these claims. "Ocurrencias," The Bancroft Library, BANC MSS C-D 134; translation in Beebe and Senkewicz, *Testimonios*, 216.

60 Angustias de la Guerra, "Ocurrencias," The Bancroft Library, BANC MSS C-D 134; translation in Beebe and Senkewicz, *Testimonios*, 218; and José de la Guerra, "Ocurrencias Curiosas, 1830–31," March 20, 1830, The Bancroft Library, BANC MSS C-B 73, pp. 21–34.

61 According to one estimate, at this time the missions possessed 210,000 branded cattle, and perhaps more than 100,000 unbranded; over 60,000 were slaughtered every year just to maintain sustainable stock levels. Thomas Coulter, "Notes on Upper California," ca. July 5 and 7, 1832, p. 66, Huntington Library, San Marino, California. See also Adele Ogden, "Boston Hide Droughers Along California Shores," *California Historical Society Quarterly* 8, no. 4 (1929): 305.

62 José de la Guerra, May 1830, "Ocurrencias Curiosas," The Bancroft Library, BANC MSS C-B 73, p. 22.

63 Alfred Robinson, *Life in California: During a Residence of Several Years in That Territory*, introduction by Andrew Rolle (Santa Barbara, Calif., and Salt Lake City: Peregrine Smith, 1970), 68; Bancroft, *History of California*, 3:576.

64 Manuel Varela to José de la Guerra, Tepic, August 1, 1829, DLG 1001.
65 Robert Ryal Miller, *Juan Alvarado, Governor of California, 1836–1842* (Norman: University of Oklahoma Press, 1998), 27–28.
66 José de la Guerra, "Ocurrencias Curiosas," September 16, 1830, The Bancroft Library, BANC MSS C-B 73, pp. 30–31.
67 Guerra, "Forms of Communication," 28.
68 Angustias de la Guerra, "Ocurrencias," The Bancroft Library, BANC MSS C-D 134; translation in Beebe and Senkewicz, *Testimonios*, 220.
69 Bancroft, *History of California*, 2:49–50.
70 Reséndez, *Changing National Identities*, 83–91.
71 Carlos Carrillo to José de la Guerra, Tepic, April 2, 1831, DLG 137; Angustias de la Guerra, "Ocurrencias," The Bancroft Library, BANC MSS C-D 134; translation in Beebe and Senkewicz, *Testimonios*, 252.
72 Bancroft, *History of California*, 3:187–200. Angustias de la Guerra, "Ocurrencias," The Bancroft Library, BANC MSS C-D 134; translation in Beebe and Senkewicz, *Testimonios*, 220–24.
73 Reséndez, *Changing National Identities*, 68–69; and González, *This Small City*, 44. For more on Gómez-Farías's projects in the north, see Sánchez, *Telling Identities*, 108; Juan Gómez-Quiñones, *Roots of Chicano Politics, 1600–1940* (Albuquerque: University of New Mexico Press, 1994), 115; Weber, *Mexican Frontier*, 185; and C. Alan Hutchinson, *Frontier Settlement in Mexican California: The Híjar-Padres Colony and Its Origins 1769-1835* (New Haven, Conn.: Yale University Press, 1969), 161.
74 Weber, *Mexican Frontier*, 186. See also Francisco Lombardo, Minister of Relations, instructions, April 23, 1834, quoted in Hutchinson, *Frontier Settlement*, 210. Gómez-Quiñones, *Roots of Chicano Politics*, 116; Bancroft, *History of California*, 3:272–78; Hutchinson, *Frontier Settlement*, 197–206; and Robinson, *Life in California*, 110, 112–13.
75 The decree repealing secularization was dated November 7, 1835, although knowledge of it did not reach California until after the first of the year. Bancroft, *History of California*, 3:355.
76 Weber, *Mexican Frontier*, 33–36; Reséndez, *Changing National Identities*, 175–76.
77 Vallejo, "Recuerdos históricos," The Bancroft Library, BANC MSS C-D 19, pp. 80–81; quoted in Weber, *Mexican Frontier*, 256.
78 Bancroft, *History of California*, 3:435; Angustias de la Guerra, "Ocurrencias," The Bancroft Library, BANC MSS C-D 134; translation in Beebe and Senkewicz, *Testimonios*, 243–45; Alvarado, "Historia de California," The Bancroft Library, BANC MSS C-D 3, pp. 79–86; Vallejo, "Recuerdos históricos," The Bancroft Library, BANC MSS C-D 19, pp. 121–24.
79 Bancroft, *History of California*, 3:442; Miller, *Juan Alvarado*, 43.
80 Alta California Diputación Territorial, "La Escelentísima Diputación de la Alta Calif. á sus habitantes," [broadside], Monterey, November 6, 1836. Huntington Library, MS 433152. See also Bancroft, *History of California*, 3:461; Osio, *The*

History of Alta California, 155; and Joseph E. Cassidy, "Life and Times of Pablo de la Guerra" (PhD diss., University of California at Santa Barbara, 1977), 54.

81 This flag is currently in the collections of the Southwest Museum of the American Indian at the Autry National Center, 8.P.1.

82 Osio, *The History of Alta California*, 185.

83 "Narrative of Julio Carrillo," 1875, The Bancroft Library, BANC MSS C-E 67 Docs. 1-11; quoted in Weber, *Mexican Frontier*, 275.

84 Angustias de la Guerra, "Ocurrencias," The Bancroft Library, BANC MSS C-D 134; translation in Beebe and Senkewicz, *Testimonios*, 262.

85 William Streeter, "'Recollections of Historical Events in California, 1843–1878' of William A. Streeter," ed. William H. Ellison, *California Historical Society Quarterly* 18, nos. 1–3 (1939): 64–71, 157–79, 254–78 at 169.

86 Thompson, *El Gran Capitán*, 176; Cesareo Lataillade to José de la Guerra, Santa Barbara, July 13, 1847, DLG 576.

JOHN R. JOHNSON AND

JOSEPH G. LORENZ

Genetics and the *Castas* of Colonial California

Cultural anthropologists have long been interested in the ways in which social groups maintain or lose their identities as they interact with other groups. In recent decades, they have increasingly come to believe that cultural identities are *socially constructed*. In other words, how a group's membership identifies itself and how others distinguish it is more important than a common biological inheritance from a geographically specific population.[1] Colonial society in Alta California had its origins in the multiracial society that had been forged in the northwest frontier of New Spain. While a variety of *castas* (classifications based on degree of miscegenation) were commonly used in colonial Mexico, these terms were often fluid, depending on how individuals identified themselves or how others in society perceived them. Mission sacramental registers of baptisms, marriages, and burials reflect the important distinction that developed between indigenous groups (*indios*) and Spanish Californians, called *gente de razón* no matter what biological ancestry they possessed. Thus, in colonial California, as long as a person could achieve the cultural status of being *de razón*, biological inheritance became unimportant in defining social identity.[2] While we recognize that the social construction of identity was paramount in Spanish California, we nonetheless find it of considerable anthropological and historical interest to understand how far along the process of *mestizaje*, the genetic mixing that occurred during colonization, had proceeded prior to the emigration of the Californio population from northwest Mexico. To pursue this line of inquiry, this study uses emerging techniques of genetic genealogy that have led scholars to return to older foundational debates about the origins of social, cultural, and racial identities in Spanish California.

The subject of genetic genealogy has recently engaged the public's imagination. Bestselling books such as *The Seven Daughters of Eve, Out of Eden*, and *Deep Ancestry* speak to those eager to understand their place in the human family tree.[3] The PBS documentary series *African American Lives*, hosted by Harvard professor Henry Louis Gates Jr., demonstrates how genetics has been used to trace the ancestry of a number of prominent African Americans, including Oprah Winfrey, Whoopi Goldberg, and Chris Tucker.[4] Commercial labs in Britain and the United States vie to capitalize on the desire to determine one's own genetic origins. All of these developments are based on a relatively new field of molecular anthropology that goes beyond studies of comparative craniometrics and geographical patterns of blood groups to explore the ancestry of world populations based on detailed studies of mitochondrial, Y-chromosome, and autosomal DNA.

The interests of anthropologists, historians, and members of the general public converge in discovering what this emerging science can contribute to an understanding of the past of peoples whose ancestry remains clouded by virtue of myth and a partial documentary record. In this study, we take the first steps toward understanding how mitochondrial DNA evidence, used in combination with mission record research, clarifies the origins of Spanish-Mexican families who came to the region before 1790, the year Spanish officials undertook the first census of Alta California. A number of descendants of early California Spanish families participated in this study, as did other Mexican Americans. These two subgroups, the former with relatively well-documented ancestry and the second with ancestry that reflects their more recent immigration, can be compared and contrasted to produce network diagrams illustrating phylogenetic (ancestral) relationships. Our eventual goal is to place the mitochondrial DNA lineages that are of indigenous origin into an ethnohistorical and geographical context, shedding light on peoples of northwest Mexico, especially Sonora and Sinaloa, whose population histories are poorly known.

The Castas *of Colonial California*

In 1813, Spanish officials circulated a questionnaire among the missionaries of Alta California, inquiring about the customs of the native inhabitants of the region. Although the majority of the questions pertained solely to the characteristics of California Indian peoples, the first question in particular elicited responses from many missionaries as to the colonial population of settlers and soldiers that had become established in the new territory since the first expedition of 1769 led by Gaspar de Portolá:

> Question 1. Let them state into how many castes the population is divided: for example, whether they are Americans, Europeans, Indians, Mulattos, Negros, etc., omitting no group whatsoever.[5]

The response from Mission Santa Barbara is illustrative of the nature of cultural identity in the region:

> It cannot be known with certainty into how many castes the inhabitants of the presidio adjoining this mission are divided. Although it is very well known that not all are genuine Spaniards either of European or American origin, yet at least they regard themselves as such. Furthermore if they were told to the contrary they would consider it an affront, so we are unable to state anything further on this particular matter.[6]

The missionaries at San Gabriel made a similar statement about the *pobladores* of Los Angeles and other Spanish-Mexican families under their ecclesiastical jurisdiction:

> The general and distinctive population of this mission are only Indians. However...we have to attend to a town of whites who are known as *gente de razón*. In civil matters it is the headquarters of four ranchos composed of the same class of people. This mission also cares for another rancho belonging to the civil jurisdiction of Presidio San Diego, as well as for the families of the six soldiers who guard this mission. All the individuals who live in these places amount to 526. They are of various castes. How many these castes are and precisely which castes they are we do not know because, as we have said, they are all known as *gente de razón*.[7]

In response to a follow-up question, the San Gabriel missionaries articulated the prevailing myth regarding the homeland of the native Mexican peoples as being in the north and provided further details regarding the gente de razón families of their area:

> In regard to the origin of our [California] Indian people we think that during the migration of the ancient Mexicans, various families in the course of their passage remained behind,... With regard to the people of the other class [gente de razón], it seems to us they have the same origin as those of New Spain, for the first settlers came from the provinces of Sonora, Sinaloa and Nueva Vizcaya. Some of them, however, both Spaniards and men of other castes, have consorted with Indian women of this peninsula.[8]

These responses make it clear that Alta California's colonial population ultimately derived from people of mixed ancestry who came largely from northwest Mexico. The comments of the San Gabriel missionaries in particular indicate that many of the settlers and soldiers were regarded as having considerable indigenous genetic inheritance.

Nearly a quarter of a century before the questionnaire, Spanish officials had undertaken a regionwide census of gente de razón families that recorded the caste designations in use among Alta California's pioneer families. The census of 1790 tabulated each individual and gave his or her occupation, approximate age, and caste designation, as well as the town of origin for the head of each household.[9] This census, combined with the clues found in the various mission registers of baptisms, confirmations, marriages, and burials, provides an excellent beginning for studying the genetic origins of the Alta California colonists and comparing their public identities with what is revealed through DNA analysis.

Some Comments on DNA Analysis

Although DNA analysis has much to contribute to the study of population origins, genetics do not necessarily coincide with the ways in which people identify themselves. For instance, people who speak different languages often do reflect separate population histories, but a group's linguistic affiliation does not necessarily correspond to its genetic origins. Recent studies show that certain DNA lineages can crosscut language groupings in the Pre-Columbian Americas because of prehistoric patterns of intergroup marriage and cultural dominance of one group over another. Of course, examples of these processes can be seen following European contact, when miscegenation certainly occurred and the languages of Spanish, English, French, and Portuguese replaced many of the indigenous ones, even though descendants of the original populations remained. Genetic patterns must be carefully compared to ethnolinguistic groupings in order to sort out what kinds of meanings underlie correlations between genes and languages.

Among the several types of DNA studies of Native American descendants, those based on mitochondrial DNA (mtDNA) have elucidated patterns among indigenous groups in the greater Southwest region, including California and northwest Mexico. Mitochondrial DNA is especially useful because it is extra-nuclear in origin and inherited only from one's mother. Thus it is unaffected by the mixing of chromosomes that results from mestizaje.[10] Mitochondrial DNA exists in abundance, with hundreds of copies present in each cell. Its genome is relatively short, consisting of 16,569 nucleotide base pairs, composed of adenine, guanine, cytosine, and thymine. Each mtDNA molecule contains genes that provide instructions for the energy-producing functions of the cells. Also present are segments that do not code for metabolic activities; these can accumulate occasional random mutations in female lineages, rendering them invaluable for determining phylogenetic relationships among the world's populations. Because of its abundance, its short molecular length, and the variability of certain non-coding segments, mtDNA is relatively easy to extract and amplify, which increases its usefulness for genetic analysis.[11]

Mutations that occurred in the distant past have given rise to broad groups (called *haplogroups* or *clades*) of mtDNA lineages that allow molecular anthropologists to reconstruct the interrelationships and migrations of the world's populations. Haplogroups are divided into daughter groups, herein called *lineages*, that reflect more recent mutations; any specific mtDNA sequence within a lineage is called a *haplotype*. Mitochondrial lineages indigenous to the Americas belong to one of five ancestral haplogroups: A, B, C, D, and X; these are also found in Asia.[12] Haplogroup X is almost entirely absent in the Californias and northwest Mexico and is not considered in this study.

Mitochondrial DNA can be analyzed in several different ways: (1) RFLP (restriction fragment length polymorphism) analysis determines which haplogroup a sample belongs to, (2) nucleotide-sequence analysis determines specific mutations that occur within one or two lengthy hypervariable segments in the mitochondrial DNA molecule's *control region*, and (3) complete genome sequencing detects additional mutations. Most of the analysis of this study uses the first two approaches because complete genome sequencing of mitochondrial DNA is only recently becoming widely reported for Native Americans.

Distributional analyses of mtDNA lineages found among Native American populations began with the work of Douglas Wallace and his associates at Emory University. Their studies demonstrated relationships between mtDNA types found among American Indian peoples and those of northeast Asia, and it determined that a non-random distribution of the four predominant mtDNA haplogroups (A, B, C, and D) existed throughout the Americas.[13] Further studies have built on these findings, showing that specific mtDNA lineages arose among geographically separated tribal groups following the migrations that initially peopled the two continents of the Americas. Those mtDNA lineages that were determined to be ancestral to more specific haplotypes within each haplogroup were more widespread. Among the most ancient haplotypes were those considered to be founding lineages among the original migrants who spread southward from the Bering land bridge around 14,000 years ago or earlier, once pathways became available through previously glaciated areas of Alaska and Canada.[14] The latest evidence suggests that a coastal migration route would have been accessible somewhat earlier than an ice-free interior passage east of the Rocky Mountains.[15]

Some individuals express the hope that DNA will shed light on their genetic heritage so that they can determine with certainty the tribal affiliations of their Native American ancestors. Others worry that DNA evidence will be used to exclude people from membership in particular federally recognized tribes if their DNA sequences do not align with others who are known tribal members. Yet, those who harbor these hopes and concerns attribute more to molecular evidence than it can presently deliver. While particular genetic lineages do appear to correlate with ethnolinguistic groupings to some degree, the reverse is not true. Speakers of a given language are typically not confined to specific genetic lineages. This is because the older, non-distinctive haplotypes within each haplogroup can be found among many widely separated populations, and because prehistoric patterns of migration and intermarriage have resulted in the sharing of mtDNA haplotypes among populations that come from different ethnolinguistic backgrounds.

Genetic Research in Northwest New Spain

Bearing in mind the potential contributions and limitations of genetic research, we can turn to the topic of mtDNA variation among indigenous populations that inhabited the greater American Southwest during the colonial period. Studies of indigenous groups in the Spanish Borderlands have revealed that populations characterized by Haplogroup B and

C lineages dominated much of the region. To the south, in central and southern Mexico, Haplogroup A lineages predominate. The indigenous peoples of the Central Valley of California and portions of the adjacent Great Basin include a considerable component descended from one of the founding types of Haplogroup D, as well as Haplogroup B. The Chumash peoples of south central California are characterized largely by Haplogroup A and a different founding haplotype from Haplogroup D. The Apache and Navajo, who speak an Athabaskan language, demonstrate their northern origins by the widespread presence of Haplogroup A lineages clearly related to the Na-Dene peoples of Alaska and Canada.[16]

These differences in the mtDNA haplogroup distributions among indigenous peoples of northwestern New Spain are derived from separate population histories. Isolated ethnolinguistic groups, such as the Chumash peoples of the Santa Barbara Channel region, the Zuni of New Mexico, and the Seri of the Sonoran coast, harbor distinctive mtDNA lineages that bespeak their longtime presence in those areas. The Yokuts and Miwok peoples of Alta California's Central Valley appear to have expanded across the Sierra Nevada from the Great Basin region many millennia ago, bringing with them genetic lineages characteristic of their homeland. With the exception of the Apache and Navajo, already mentioned, the remainder of the greater American Southwest is dominated by peoples speaking languages in the Uto-Aztecan and Yuman-Cochimí linguistic families.[17] Some researchers have argued that the spread of these two language families within the Greater Southwest correlates with population growth associated with the adoption of agriculture and subsequent budding off of subgroups into adjacent areas.[18] Brian Kemp, a molecular anthropologist who has considered the genetic implications of this hypothesis, discovered a distinctive genetic marker within a major mtDNA Haplogroup B subgroup that appears to be shared among many peoples in the Greater American Southwest. With this clue, he has dated the main spread of Uto-Aztecan and Yuman-Cochimí populations to sometime between 1,300 and 3,800 years ago, using a pedigree-based rate of mtDNA evolution.[19]

Based largely on the genetics of contemporary descendants, mtDNA research has thus revealed some important clues pertaining to the prehistory of population movements within the northwest region of the Spanish Borderlands following the conquest of Mexico in 1521. This picture is incomplete, however, because some groups have not been previously sampled and others are poorly known, having been displaced or absorbed into the expanding colonial state.[20] In northwest and west Mexico, only certain populations have received attention from mtDNA investigative surveys: the aforementioned Seri, the Tarahumara of Sonora, the Cora and Huichol of Jalisco, and inhabitants of Ciudad Juárez and Ojinaga, who live along the Rio Grande.[21] Uto-Aztecan peoples of Sonora and Sinaloa have not yet been studied genetically. Native peoples of certain portions of Sinaloa and Baja California are almost completely lacking with regard to evidence of linguistic affiliation, much less molecular genetics.[22] Sonora and Sinaloa are precisely those regions from which the majority of the colonial families immigrated to the Californias during the seventeenth and eighteenth centuries.[23] Presuming that an underlying layer of indigenous Sonoran and Sinaloan mtDNA existed among these early settlers, a study of the Alta California colonial lineages has the potential to make a significant contribution to our understanding of the native peoples who inhabited the north frontier of New Spain. Our research represents the first effort to tackle this problem and will lay the groundwork for future studies in the region.

Sample Descriptions

Our sampling of Alta California's Spanish-Mexican population began entirely by accident, as a byproduct of research into the genetic lineages of California Indians.[24] One of the women whom we had believed to be descended from a female Native American ancestor baptized at Mission San Gabriel proved otherwise, once we had fully reconstructed her genealogy.[25] Instead, this individual could be traced back through her maternal line to a woman named María Rufina Hernández, who had been born in Sinaloa or Loreto, Baja California, according to different sources.[26] As our study continued, several other individuals who were uncertain as to whether they had California Indian or Spanish-Mexican ancestry provided us with samples. Further genealogical investigations demonstrated that some of these women could be traced back to women who were part of Alta California's colonial population. Soon we began expanding our study to include mtDNA samples from lineages descended from colonial California women.

In January 2005, we presented a lecture about mtDNA research to a gathering of Los Californianos, a group descended from the earliest colonists of Alta California. This resulted in additional volunteers for our study. A larger sample of descendants from northwestern Mexico was desirable, to compare with the accumulating colonial California mtDNA sequences, so we also sought Mexican American volunteers. Many of these were husbands or wives of participants in our California Indian study. Others were acquaintances who agreed to be involved once they learned of our research. Finally, a Southern California organization called Familia Ancestral Research Association twice invited us to lecture about mtDNA research, and many of its members contributed mtDNA samples. This group actively sought information in Mexican archives in order to reconstruct its members' genealogies, thus assisting in the determination of the origin of many female lineages, sometimes tracing them back two centuries or more. Most Familia members were descended from northwestern Mexican immigrants from Sonora, Chihuahua, and Durango.

All who contributed samples were interviewed about their family genealogies. Most could provide the names and birthplaces of their maternal grandmothers; some were able to consult family records or other relatives to trace the lineages further. For about half of those forebears who could be demonstrated to have lived in Alta California prior to 1850, it was possible to use mission records to trace their earliest female ancestors who had immigrated during the colonial period. Most of these were listed in the census of 1790, so their caste descriptions are known, and most had their place of birth mentioned in contemporary documents or ecclesiastical records.[27] If two individuals had the same ancestor through their direct female lines, then only one sample was used in our analysis, to avoid duplication. Figure 1 illustrates the places of origin in Mexico, Central America, and the Spanish Borderlands of 115 female ancestors out of a total of 179 descendants who contributed mtDNA samples for analysis.[28] This total of 115 ancestors includes only those who were determined to possess Native American mtDNAs and for whom origins could be traced. The participants in our study included: (1) those who were "California Spanish" descendants, defined as those whose direct female ancestors were part of the old Californio population, (2) those who were from elsewhere in the Hispanic Southwest (that is, Arizona, New Mexico, or Texas), and (3) those of more recent Mexican or Central American immigrant backgrounds.

Mitochondrial Haplogroup Distributions

Table 1 presents the general categories for 179 samples based on ethnic attributions or regions of origin and provides the numbers for each that were assignable to the four principal mtDNA haplogroups found among Native Americans, as well as those that were European, African, or Asian in origin. Figure 2 illustrates these results in terms of percentages. More than 80 percent of the samples were from mitochondrial haplogroups

Figure 1. mtDNA samples determined to be of Native American derivation traceable to particular regions of the Hispanic Southwest, Mexico, and Central America. This map excludes thirty individuals who were of European or African mtDNA affiliation and thirty-four others whose ancestry in Mexico was unknown.

indigenous to the Americas, illustrating that the process of mestizaje has been predominantly characterized since the advent of the colonial period by men of European, African, or Asian origin fathering children with women of Mexican Indian ancestry. Women from the Old World did not emigrate in great numbers until years after an original *entrada* had taken place, so families produced by non-indigenous men and native wives were commonplace in frontier settings. This pattern is not unique to the Californias and has been documented in many other Latin American genetic studies. Thus, it is twenty times more likely that indigenous mitochondrial lineages will survive over indigenous Y-chromosome lineages in many areas of Hispanic America, especially in regions that were of low population density at the time of initial colonization. Given the small size of many indigenous groups and their lack of immunity to introduced European diseases, children of mixed marriages would be more likely to have genetic resistance to new pathogens, thus increasing their chances of survival. In this way an initial pattern of interracial mating skewed toward native women resulted in a much greater likelihood of continu-

Table 1. Distribution of Mitochondrial DNA Haplogroups according to Regional or Ethnic Affiliation

Regional or Ethnic Affiliation	Haplogroup A	Haplogroup B	Haplogroup C	Haplogroup D	Other Haplogroup	Total
Spanish Californian	16	10	7	9	11	53
Spanish Californian or Mexican American	5	1	2	0	0	8
Mexican American	19	17	25	5	18	84
Hispanic Southwest	9	4	8	1	1	23
Mexican Indian						
Cocopa	1	0	0	0	0	1
Huichol	0	0	1	0	0	1
Nahua	1	0	0	0	0	1
Opata	0	1	0	0	0	1
Tarahumara	0	0	1	0	0	1
Yaqui	2	1	2	0	0	5
Central America	1	0	0	0	0	1
Total	54	34	46	15	30	179

ation of indigenous mitochondrial lineages as compared to indigenous Y-chromosome inheritance.

Among sixty-one probable and suspected California Spanish mtDNAs shown in table 1, Haplogroup A represents about a third of the total, with the remainder split fairly evenly among Haplogroups B, C, D, and Other. It is interesting to note that a higher percentage of samples for colonial California appear to be derived from Haplogroup D than for other regions, a point that we discuss in greater detail below.

Table 2 breaks down the sample according to geographic origin documented for traceable female ancestors, pooling the results of the genealogical investigations of Alta California's colonial population with those derived from more recent Mexican American immigrants. As the data reported simply as "Alta California" show, we thus far have been unable to trace family trees of twenty-six individuals with indigenous Native American mtDNAs who appear to have descended from the early colonial population. Sometimes a female ancestor's birthplace in Mexico could not be determined because of inadequate genealogical clues in surviving documents. For the seventy-two samples traceable to northwestern Mexico, Haplogroups A, B, and C are all present in relatively equal proportions, whereas samples belonging to Haplogroup D are comparatively rare. Even though Haplogroup D appears to be less present in Sonora and Sinaloa than other mitochondrial haplogroups, its almost

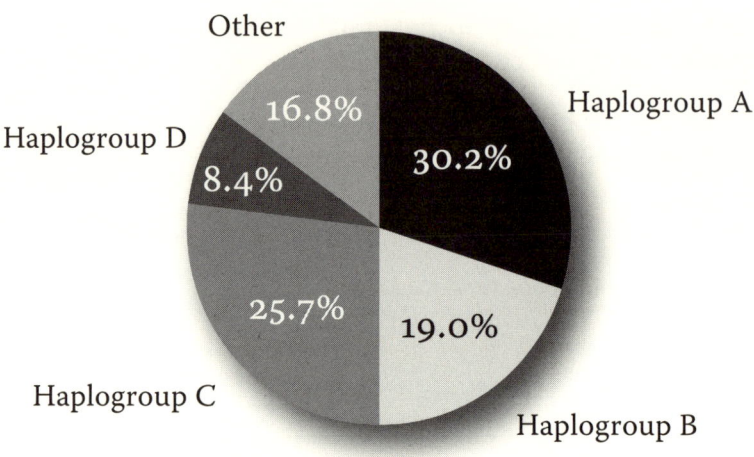

Figure 2. California Spanish and Mexican American Sample (N=179)

total absence elsewhere, except for among Alta California's colonial population, is perhaps significant. The surviving Haplogroup D lineages from northwest Mexico may be informing us about the genetic ancestry of otherwise poorly documented indigenous groups from this region.

Table 3 presents the results of the haplogroup assignments of thirty-five colonial California women listed in the 1790 census or otherwise determined to have resided in Alta California during the late eighteenth century, including five native Californian women who had married soldiers.[29] Table 3 does not include all samples that were classed as "California Spanish" because of problems encountered in tracing some genealogies (as mentioned previously). Nor does inclusion in this table necessarily mean that we have an associated mtDNA sequence reported in tables 4–7 (for reasons cited at the bottom of table 3). Of the thirty Spanish-Mexican women who had immigrated to Alta California, all but four derived from mtDNA lineages indigenous to the Americas. Of the four that came from the Old World, three were European (Haplogroups H, U5, and V) and one was African (Haplogroup L2). The overall predominance of Native American mtDNAs among Alta California's gente de razón population is quite at odds with the proportion of women in table 3 whose castas were reported in the 1790 census as *española* (40 percent), as opposed to such categories as *india* (nine individuals), *coyota* (three), *mestiza* (six), or *mulata* (one).[30]

The overall distribution of mitochondrial haplogroups, as presented in tables 1–3, suggests that Sonora and Sinaloa were transitional areas

Table 2. Geographic Origins of California Spanish and Mexican American Mitochondrial DNA Samples[a]

Origin	Haplogroup A	Haplogroup B	Haplogroup C	Haplogroup D	Total
Spanish Borderlands (Origin in Mexico not established)					
Alta California	11	5	4	6	26
Arizona	3	0	0	0	3
New Mexico	3	4	4	0	11
Texas	3	0	4	1	8
Borderland Totals	20	9	12	7	48
Northwest Mexico					
Sonora	9	7	8	3	27
Sinaloa	6	3	3	2	14
Chihuahua	5	5	6	3	19
Durango	0	4	1	0	5
Baja California Sur	1	1	2	0	4
Baja California (Norte)	2	0	1	0	3
Northwest Mexico Totals	23	20	21	8	72
Other, Mostly of Mexican Origin					
Coahuila	1	0	1	0	2
Zacatecas	2	2	3	0	7
Guanajuato	2	0	3	0	5
Jalisco	0	0	2	0	2
Michoacán	0	1	1	0	2
Other[b] and Unknown	6	2	3	0	11
Other Totals	11	5	13	0	29
Total Mexican American Sample of Indigenous Origin	54	34	46	15	149

[a] This table includes only those samples for which sequences were obtained that belonged to mitochondrial haplogroups indigenous to the Americas, as well as one Polynesian sample belonging to Haplogroup B. Thirty samples listed in Table 1 that were determined to be from European or African mitochondrial haplogroups do not appear here.

[b] Among the samples included as "Other" is one from Guatemala and one originally Hawaiian in origin, provided by an individual of partial Hawaiian descent, whose female ancestor married a California Spanish man during the colonial period.

between the central Mexican pattern of populations characterized by high percentages of Haplogroup A and populations of the American Southwest where Haplogroups B and C predominated. But to what degree were some of these mitochondrial patterns the result of the movement of colonial families of partial indigenous ancestry from central Mexico following the conquest of indigenous tribes in northwestern New Spain?

Certainly there was a dramatic population decline of tribes living in the region due to the depredations of Nuño de Guzmán in 1530–31 and continual, successive epidemics that spread through the province for many decades afterward.[31] Later, the viceroy of New Spain encouraged colonies of Tlaxcaltecans from central Mexico to move into the area to serve as civilized examples for newly conquered peoples.[32] In order to ascertain which mitochondrial DNA lineages might be the result of incoming settlers as opposed to original inhabitants, it is necessary to look deeper than haplogroup affiliations and determine original haplotypes. Those haplotypes present within our sample can be compared to those identified in a larger sample of Mexican and American Southwest mtDNA lineages in order to differentiate which may have been indigenous to Sonora and Sinaloa and which likely came from elsewhere.[33]

Explorations of Deep Ancestry

Within each mitochondrial haplogroup that was indigenous to the Americas, it is useful to depict ancestral relationships among specific haplotypes by means of network diagrams. Given a large enough sample, such diagrams typically exhibit a star-like pattern, with the haplotypes of the American Indian founding mitochondrial lineages in the center of the star. Subsequent mutations define daughter lineages, which in turn spawned additional daughter lineages. If a branching chain of daughter lineages is specific to a particular ethnolinguistic group, an ancient geographic presence of that group in a particular region is implied because it takes time for haplotypes to become fixed within a population. An example of the branching-chain pattern occurs among the Chumash Indians of the Santa Barbara Channel region, who exhibit five haplotypes within Haplogroup A all characterized by a distinctive mutation at nucleotide position (np) 16093 in the mtDNA molecule.[34] A population must be established in a region over many millennia to "age" in this manner.

Detection of related haplotypes among disparate groups can also provide clues regarding ancient connections that have been disrupted by subsequent population migrations. An example of this pattern is observable in a rare haplotype of Haplogroup A—characterized by distinctive mutations at np 16257 and np 16263—that is present here and there among the Zuni and certain prehistoric samples from the American Southwest.[35] Despite being separated by hundreds of miles of desert, another haplotype containing these same two markers existed among the Ventureño Chumash.[36] Because the Chumash language family and the Zuni language each represent linguistic isolates with ancient presence in

Table 3. *Castas* and Mitochondrial Haplogroups of Early Colonial California Women[a]

Name	*Casta* (1790 census)	Place of Birth	mtDNA Haplogroup
Alvarado, María Ignacia	Española	Loreto, Baja California	H
Beltrán, María Nicolasa	Española	Horcasitas, Sonora	B
Bojórquez, María Antonia	Española	Horcasitas, Sonora	L2
Carrillo, María Ignacia	Española	Loreto, Baja California	U5
Carrillo, María Matilde	Española	Loreto, Baja California	V
Domínguez, Ursula	India	Mission Santa Gertrudis, Baja California	C
Espinosa, Gertrudis Gregoria	Española	Villa Sinaloa, Sinaloa	B
Féliz, Marcelina	Española	Cosalá, Sinaloa	C
Gonzales, Ana María	India	Villa Sinaloa, Sinaloa	B
Gutiérrez, María de los Santos	India	Culiacán, Sinaloa	A
Hernández, María Rufina	N/A	Loreto, Baja California	C
López, María Rosa (aka Monreal)	Española	Álamos, Sonora[b]	D
Lugo, María Pascuala	Mestiza	Villa Sinaloa, Sinaloa	C
Lugo, Rosa María	Española	Villa Sinaloa, Sinaloa	A
Martínez, Juana María Rita	N/A	Villa Sinaloa, Sinaloa	A
Noriega, María Ramona	Española	Loreto, Baja California	A
Ochoa, María Manuela	Mestiza	Villa Sinaloa, Sinaloa	B
Parra, Juana Paula	Mestiza	Santa Cruz de Mayo, Sonora[b]	A
Perez, María Guadalupe	Coyota	Rosario, Sinaloa	B
Piñuelas, María Josefa	Coyota	Villa Sinaloa, Sinaloa	C
Ramírez, Potenciana	Coyota	Villa Sinaloa, Sinaloa	A
Redondo, María Antonia	Española	Villa Sinaloa, Sinaloa	A
Rivera, María Ignacia (aka Velarde)	Mestiza	Maquipa, Santa Cruz de Mayo, Sonora[b]	A
Romero, María Francisca	Mestiza	Villa Sinaloa, Sinaloa	D
Rubio, Petra	Mulata	Álamos, Sonora[b]	A
Salgado, Lugarda	Mestiza	Loreto, Baja California	C
Sánchez, María Gertrudis (aka Límon)	Española	Villa Sinaloa, Sinaloa	B
Sotelo, Micaela	Española	Villa Sinaloa, Sinaloa	A
Tapia, María Antonia	India	Culiacán, Sinaloa	C
Valencia, María Dolores	Española	Horcasitas, Sonora	D
Irene, wife of Julián Ríos	India	Tipu (Obispeño Chumash)	D
Juana María, wife of Hilario Jiménez	India	Siujtun (Barbareño Chumash)	D
Margarita, wife of Juan María Ruiz	India	Lamaca (Antoniano Salinan)	A
María Ildefonsa Bergas	India	Lima (Antoniano Salinan)	D
Regina Josefa Toypurina, wife of Manuel Montero	India	Japchivit (Gabrielino)	C

[a] This table includes haplogroup assignments for four samples typed by RFLP analysis that have not been reported in other tables or figures because precise mtDNA sequence information is still pending, as well as two additional samples traced to Alta California ancestors that were typed by Joseph Donohoe, a Californio descendant who has conducted genetic genealogical research.

[b] Álamos and Santa Cruz de Mayo, while currently within the state of Sonora, were formerly included in the province of Sinaloa at the time of the recruitment of settlers for Alta California. Women from these towns have been included in the totals for Sonora in Figure 1 and Table 2.

their respective regions, the occurrence of closely related haplotypes may well represent prehistoric contact predating the development of agriculture and subsequent expansion of mitochondrial lineages in Haplogroups B and C in the American Southwest sometime around 3,000 years ago.

To search for such meaningful patterns of relationships, we produced network diagrams for each mitochondrial haplogroup within 149 samples of indigenous origin analyzed for this study (see figures 3–6). Tables 4–7 present the mtDNA sequence data that were used to generate these diagrams. The designations next to the circles represent the arbitrarily numbered haplotypes listed in tables 4–7. The size of the circles within each network diagram varies according to the number of samples belonging to each haplotype, and the numbers between two circles refer to the molecular markers that distinguish between them. Those samples that were categorized as Spanish Californian are indicated in solid portions of the circles in these diagrams. To explore the indigenous origin of the specific mtDNA haplotypes occurring among the Spanish Californians, we undertook a close investigation for each of those women listed in the 1790 census whose origin in Sonora or Sinaloa was documented.

Haplogroup A Lineages

The Haplogroup A diagram (figure 3) represents the typical Native American pattern of daughter lineages radiating from a central haplotype (here designated as A30) that represents the principal founding lineage for this mtDNA haplogroup. Six additional mutations are present among one particular daughter lineage (A06) of this ancestral haplotype, but most haplotypes are distinguished by only one or two mutations. The network diagram of our Haplogroup A samples contains some reticulation (indicating multiple pathways that may have produced a haplotype) because of the tendency for certain nucleotide positions to be susceptible to frequent mutations. Two of these positions, np 16111 and 16325, are recognized "hot spots" in the mtDNA genome and have mutated more than once within Haplogroup A, accounting for all instances of reticulation apparent in figure 3.[37]

The fifty-four mtDNA samples belonging to Haplogroup A within our study were sorted into thirty-six haplotypes. The two most common were the founding haplotype (A30), indicated by the central node in figure 3, and Haplotype A26 (six instances), which was distinguished from the founding haplotype by having a mutation at np 16092. Haplotype A26 occurred commonly among our Spanish Californian samples and one individual who had descended from a Yaqui woman. One of the Spanish Californian samples was traceable back to Petra Rubio, who was listed

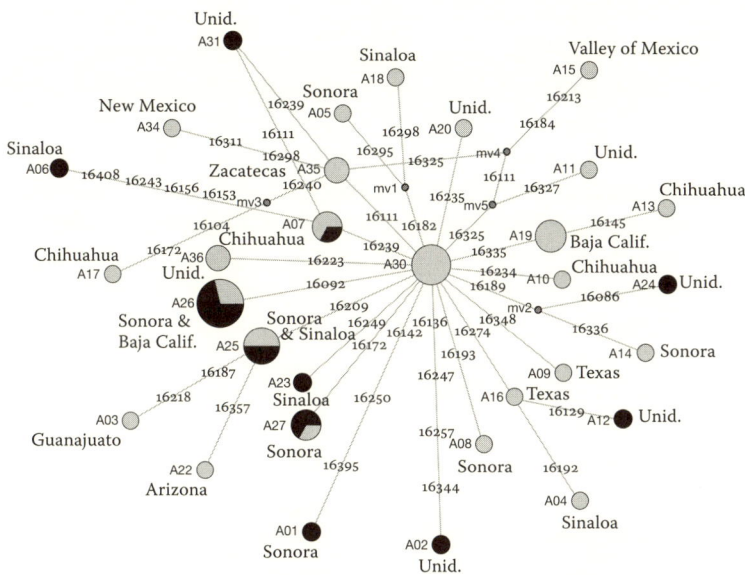

Figure 3. Haplogroup A Network Diagram Showing Ancestral Relationships among Spanish Californians and Mexican Americans

as a mulata from Álamos in the 1790 census. This area, now in the state of Sonora, was inhabited originally by speakers of Cahita, who occupied a considerable portion of the coastal plain and river valleys from the Yaqui River south to the Sinaloa River. Because of its common presence among the Spanish Californian descendants, as well as its occurrence among the Yaqui, this haplotype is hypothesized to have been indigenous to the Cahitan area. Comparisons with Kemp's larger study of mtDNAs show variations on this haplotype to be quite common among the linguistically related Cora Indians further south in Jalisco, but its virtual absence elsewhere supports the hypothesis that this haplotype derives from the original native populations of northwestern and western Mexico.

Two of the Spanish California mestiza women belonging to Haplogroup A were listed as being from Santa Cruz del Mayo, a pueblo formed around a former Jesuit mission in the lower Mayo Valley (see table 3). Indeed, these two women appear to have been the only two listed in the entire 1790 census as having been born at or near this pueblo.[38] One woman was specified as being from Maquipa in the jurisdiction of Santa Cruz del Mayo at the time she was married; but she was associated with the "Pueblo de Guasabe" in an entry in the Santa Barbara presidio's baptismal register.[39] If the identification of these two women as mestizas is accurate, then they were of half-Indian ancestry, which further suggests that their mothers were indigenous to the area. One would have presumed that both women were Mayo, because Santa Cruz is located along the Mayo River; however, the direct statement that one woman, María Ignacia Rivera, was born in the Guasabe pueblo indicates that her maternal origin may have come from the Guasave Indians, a fishing people of undetermined linguistic affiliation who inhabited the coastline to the south of the Mayo.[40] This identification acquires significance because this woman's mitochondrial DNA markers are so distinctive, three mutations removed from the central node of the Haplogroup A diagram (Haplotype A01 in figure 3). Not a single one of these three mutations was found among 100 haplotypes belonging to Haplogroup A in Kemp's larger study of Mexican and American Southwest Indian mitochondrial lineages.[41] Although a single sample cannot be considered representative, it is noteworthy nonetheless that the only Guasave mtDNA sample is so atypical, implying that this linguistically distinct, non-agricultural, maritime-oriented group was of a different origin from their neighbors who spoke Uto-Aztecan languages.

The second woman from Santa Cruz del Mayo, Juana Paula Parra, shared a haplotype (A27) with two other individuals in our sample. One of these was also of California Spanish descent and conceivably could be from the same female ancestor, since full genealogical investigation was not accomplished in this case. The other was from an individual whose mother was born in Texas and therefore had been grouped with the Hispanic Southwest category in our sample; however, the family's oral tradition was that the donor's maternal grandmother might have been of Yaqui ancestry. Kemp's study of Mexican and Southwestern Indian mtDNAs included one Tarahumara sample that matched this haplotype.[42] These data, although too scanty for certain determination, are nonetheless consistent in attributing an indigenous Sonoran ancestry to this mtDNA haplotype, probably associated with groups speaking Uto-Aztecan languages (including the Mayo, Yaqui, and Tarahumara).

Among the California Spanish women who belonged to Haplogroup A is a woman named María de los Santos Gutiérrez from Culiacán, Sinaloa. The 1790 census identifies her casta as india. The original language of Culiacán was Tahue, probably closely related to Cahita, the language of the Mayos and Yaquis, but the dramatic population decline in the sixteenth and seventeenth centuries greatly reduced the original native population. By the 1700s coalescence with immigrants from other Mexican tribes meant that someone described as an Indian from Culiacán could have descended from any number of indigenous groups.⁴³ The mtDNA haplotype (A23) of Gutiérrez is one mutation removed from the central node of the Haplogroup A diagram. This mutation at np 16249 was also present among a Zapotec sample analyzed by Kemp, but other markers in that sample indicate that parallel mutations have occurred at the same molecular location, rather than the two being related phylogenetically.⁴⁴ Thus, it would appear that the haplotype of Gutiérrez represents an indigenous northwestern Mexican mtDNA lineage, although not enough evidence exists for further determination of ethnic affiliation.

The remaining three Haplogroup A samples for California Spanish women listed in table 3 all descend from women from Villa Sinaloa, a small town that contributed more colonists to Alta California than any other town in northwestern Mexico.⁴⁵ Two of these three women were listed as española, and the third was a coyota (table 3). Two samples from these women from Villa Sinaloa represented haplotypes that had no exact matches in our sample nor in Kemp's corpus of 100 Mexican and Southwest Indian mtDNA haplotypes belonging to Haplogroup A. One of these unique haplotypes (A32) belonged to Potenciana Ramírez, the woman described as coyota—that is, a person of three-quarters Indian ancestry. Her haplotype contained genetic markers that were so unusual that further study was deemed necessary. It is possible, however, that the presence of two isolate language groups in the Sinaloa River watershed, known as Ocoroni and Nio, might have harbored distinctive mitochondrial lineages, and women from these groups eventually joined with other mestizo and Indian families who settled in the nearby Villa Sinaloa. The Ocoroni and Nio, if indeed they represent linguistic isolates, are likely to have descended from more ancient groups that were subsequently overwhelmed and isolated after the spread of peoples speaking the Uto-Aztecan Cahita and Tahue languages.⁴⁶

The three española women from Villa Sinaloa who belonged to Haplogroup A may descend from an immigrant population from outside the local region. One of these, Micaela Sotelo, appears to belong to a haplotype (A06) that is derived from a mitochondrial lineage found among the Zapotec.⁴⁷ A second española from Villa Sinaloa, María Antonia Redondo, shared an mtDNA haplotype (A25) with two other participants in our study, one being a Spanish Californian descendant whose ancestry had not been successfully traced and the other coming from a great-grandmother from Sonora, who may have been of Mayo Indian descent, according to family tradition. The marker that characterized this haplotype at np 16209 was also found among Mixtec and Nahua samples analyzed by Kemp, but the Mixtec and Nahua mtDNAs had additional markers that further differentiated them from this ancestral type.[48] In the samples analyzed for the present study, haplotypes A03 and A22, from Guanajuato and Arizona Mexican Americans respectively, were also derived from A25 (see figure 3). The fact that the two women who represented haplotypes possibly from elsewhere in Mexico were also those with enough European admixture to be considered españolas suggests that they could have descended from Indians or mestizos who came with the original Spanish settlers who began settling in the Sinaloa Valley in the late sixteenth century.[49]

Haplogroup B Lineages

A total of twenty-two haplotypes occurred among thirty-four samples belonging to Haplogroup B. Eleven of these represented Haplotype B01, the founding lineage occurring as the central node in the Haplogroup B diagram (figure 4). The difficulty in determining the number of sequential cytosine molecules in the "poly-C" region between np 16180 and np 16193 in the mtDNA sequence introduces some uncertainty in the assignment of haplotypes, so we have eliminated positions np 16182 through 16183.2 from consideration in creating the network diagram in figure 4. This has resulted in combining haplotypes B01 and B06 and haplotypes B02, B08, and B09 in our figures, because the sequence variability reported at these locations appears not to be phylogenetically meaningful in all cases.

The vast majority of the samples belonging to Haplogroup B came from ancestors from Sonora, Chihuahua, and Durango, conforming to the predominance of this haplogroup among groups speaking Uto-Aztecan and Yuman languages in the arid, interior regions of northwestern Mexico and the American Southwest.[50] Although six California Spanish women in table 3 belonged to Haplogroup B, only four of these currently have sequences that can be identified with regard to haplotype. Three of these, an española born in Horcasitas, Sonora, an española from Villa Sinaloa, and a coyota from Rosario, Sinaloa, represent the principal founding lineage within Haplogroup B and therefore cannot be considered distinctive of particular ethnic groups. Similarly, a mestiza from Villa Sinaloa belonging to B08 is only one mutation removed from the founding haplotype.[51] The resettlement of Ópata, Pima, and Tarahumara Indians from interior Sonora and Chihuahua to form enclaves on the Sinaloa River in the eighteenth century may also have introduced Haplogroup B lineages into an area where they may not have been common in precontact times.[52]

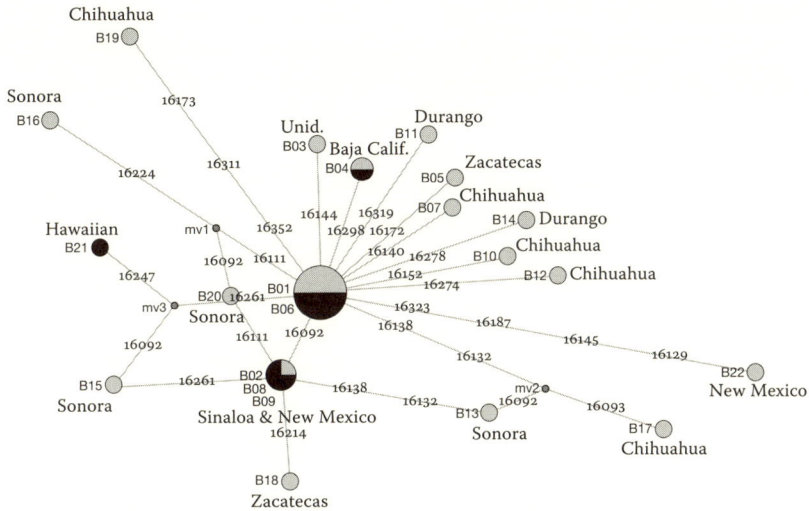

Figure 4. Haplogroup B Network Diagram Showing Ancestral Relationships among Spanish Californians and Mexican Americans

Haplogroup C Lineages

The forty-six samples belonging to Haplogroup C that were analyzed for this study included thirty-four haplotypes. As was the case with Haplogroups A and B, some reticulation is present, obscuring phylogenetic relationships among certain haplotypes because of parallel mutations and reverse mutations at certain molecular "hot spots" in the mitochondrial genome. The founding haplotype, represented by nine samples (here designated as C04), is clearly identifiable at the central node of the network. Although Haplogroup C is extremely common in the American Southwest and northwestern Mexico, it is also frequently encountered in other parts of Mexico, as is indicated in figure 5.

A total of five haplotypes of Haplogroup C have been identified among women listed in the 1790 census. Four of these California Spanish samples in three haplotypes (C31, C33, and C34) share a common marker at np 16295. This marker was present in the mtDNAs from an Indian woman from Culiacán, a coyota from Villa Sinaloa, and two españolas, one from Cosalá, Sinaloa, and the other from Loreto, Baja California (table 3). This particular mutation is also quite common among Akimel O'odham (Pima) and other American Southwest samples belonging to Haplogroup C, even though further mutations differentiate these from those haplotypes occurring among the California Spanish women. This marker also appears among haplotypes present among the

Huichol in Jalisco.[53] At least some of these Haplogroup C haplotypes carried to Alta California by settlers in the late eighteenth century would appear to be derived from people speaking Uto-Aztecan languages in Sonora and Sinaloa. The presence of the np 16295 marker among native groups in Arizona and Jalisco, to either side of Sonora and Sinaloa, suggests an ancestral association with the nearly continuous chain of indigenous Uto-Aztecan groups connecting these regions.

Haplogroup D Lineages

Haplogroup D is quite rare in Mesoamerica and the American Southwest. Kemp's study of 713 mtDNA samples from these regions produced only 22 that belonged to Haplogroup D, representing 12 haplotypes.[54] Another study yielded only one Haplogroup D individual out of 223 samples from towns on the Texas-Chihuahua international border.[55] The current study of 179 samples produced 15 that belonged to Haplogroup D, representing 12 haplotypes. Although our study supports the observation that Haplogroup D lineages are a minority, they would appear to be not quite as rare among people originating in coastal Sonora and Sinaloa as they are elsewhere in Mexico or the American Southwest. Thus, the California Spanish samples in particular acquire some significance in reconstructing the genetic mosaic of the original inhabitants of this subregion of northwestern Mexico.

The reconstructed network diagram based on the twelve haplotypes that characterize Haplogroup D reveals a pattern quite different from what we have come to expect from the diagrams for Haplogroups A, B, and C (figures 3–5). Instead of a star-like configuration of daughter lineages arranged around a central node, Haplogroup D illustrates a double-star pattern (figure 6). Based on a discovery made by a team of researchers led by Olga Rickards, who studied the Cayapa Indians of coastal Ecuador, and supported by additional evidence gathered by Kemp and his colleagues, it is now recognized that there are two substantially different founding lineages of Haplogroup D that occur among Native Americans.[56] In figure 6, these two founding haplotypes are differentiated from each other by a minimum of three genetic markers at np 16342, 16325, and 16241, creating a "left" group of nine samples sorted into seven haplotypes and a "right" group of six samples sorted into five haplotypes. The subgroup on the left represents the central node (D01) and daughter branches of the most widespread of the founding haplotypes, which was recognized first. The subgroup on the right is arranged around the newly discovered founding haplotype, labeled D04 in table 7 and figure 6, but now officially designated as D4h3 in the molecular anthropological

Genetics and the *Castas* of Colonial California 179

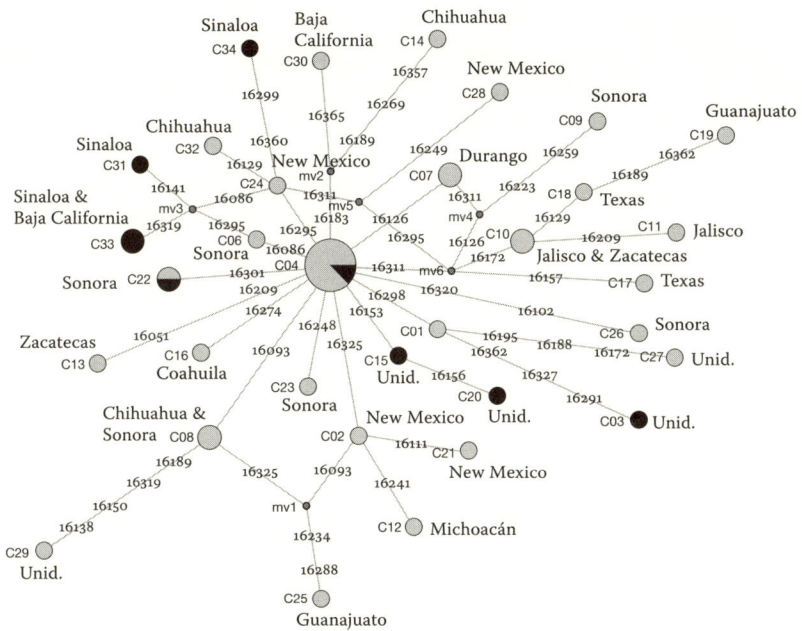

Figure 5. Haplogroup C Network Diagram Showing Ancestral Relationships among Spanish Californians and Mexican Americans

literature.[57] The recognized central node of this rarer subgroup is represented by one sample of presumed California Spanish origin (Sample JJ216), which exactly matches samples documented for the Chumash Indians of coastal California. Because this sample comes from an individual living in Santa Barbara in the central portion of territory inhabited by Chumash peoples and because the female lineage has not been traced further than the participant's grandmother, it cannot be ruled out that this lineage may have come from Chumash ancestors.

The newly discovered founding haplotype (D4h3) and its related haplotypes exhibit an interesting distribution of discontinuous occurrences, geographically separated from one other along the western margin of the American continents.[58] In the view of the authors of this study, this geographic pattern provides some of the best evidence to date in support of the hypothesis, long advanced by some archaeologists, that an ancient coastal migration may have taken place during the initial peopling of the Americas.[59] In view of the significance of this rare subgroup, it would be interesting to know if any of the six samples belonging to this subgroup could be traced to places of origin in coastal Sonora or Sinaloa. Among the haplotypes included in the Haplogroup D subgroup, surrounding haplotype D04 are three that descended from the Spanish Californian population (one containing two samples not obviously related to one another). Unfortunately only one of these has so far been traced to a female ancestor living in northwestern Mexico, María Dolores Valencia, who had been born in Horcasitas, Sonora (table 3). Her casta is listed as española, so it cannot be presumed that she was originally of native ancestors indigenous to the Pimería Bajo, where Horcasitas was founded. She might well have descended from a mestizo contingent of settlers who moved into the area following its pacification in the sixteenth century. None of the other haplotypes in this subgroup were traceable to more than general regions of the Spanish Borderlands (for example, Chihuahua and Texas); however, Kemp reported the presence of Haplotype D04 (D4h3) among one of his Tarahumara samples, and Lance Green and colleagues discovered a closely related haplotype in their genetic study of residents from two Rio Grande border towns.[60] Even though the Tarahumara affiliation is of interest, most Tarahumara samples belonged to Haplogroups B and C, so its presence in the twenty-first century may be an accident of postcolonial intermarriage with people from other parts of Mexico. Clearly not enough evidence yet exists to associate the rare subgroup of Haplogroup D with any particular ethnolinguistic group or with a particular geographic area.

The other, more common subgroup of Haplogroup D included six individuals who were descended from the Spanish Californian colonial population (figure 6). Only two of these were successfully traced through their female ancestry to women listed in the 1790 census. One of these was María Rosa López (also known as Monreal), an española from Álamos, a prominent mining town, once part of Sinaloa but later annexed to Sonora, which drew many settlers from other regions of Mexico. The other individual was María Francisca Romero, a mestiza from Villa Sinaloa. Villa Sinaloa was founded in the area where Cahita was spoken, but there were other nearby local groups reported by early missionaries to be linguistically distinct.[61] Also, enclaves of Ópata, Pima, and Tarahumara later settled on the Sinaloa River during the eighteenth century.[62] So although it might be suspected that Romero's casta hints at an origin indigenous to the Sinaloa region, the ethnolinguistic affiliation of her ancestors cannot be reliably determined. It is interesting to note that her haplotype was shared with an individual whose mother was born in Texas to an immigrant woman from Chihuahua (figure 6). Also, Kemp's larger study of Mexican Indian mtDNA lineages reported three Tarahumara individuals who belonged to this haplotype.[63] These findings collectively support the conclusion that Romero's haplotype was indigenous

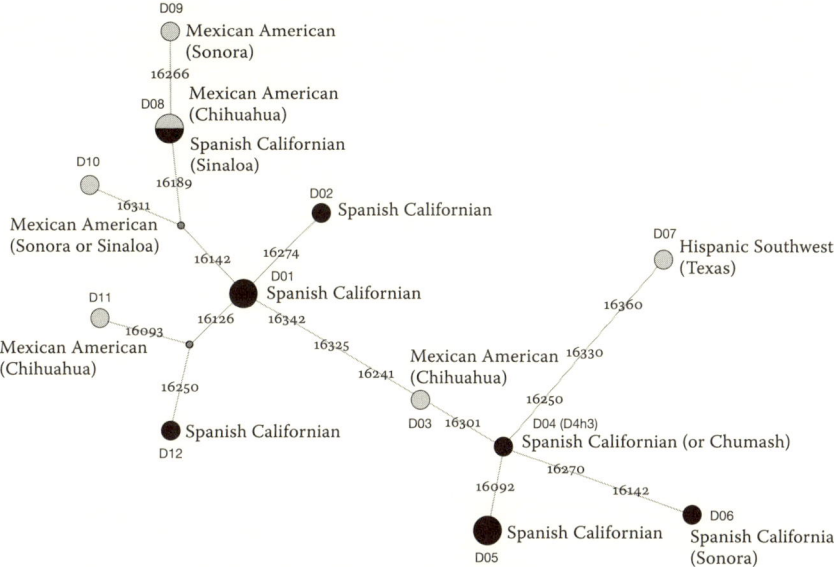

Figure 6. Haplogroup D Network Diagram Showing Ancestral Relationships among Spanish Californians and Mexican Americans

to northwestern Mexico, and we might further hypothesize that this mtDNA lineage type was found in a minority of lineages among several different tribes.

Conclusion

The study of the mitochondrial DNA lineages found among Alta California's colonial population has resulted in substantive new discoveries that supplement the findings based on historical documentary research. No matter what castas were indicated for Spanish California women of the colonial period, part of the descent of the greater majority of female settlers, exceeding 80 percent, was derived from indigenous groups of Mexico. The explanation for this apparent discrepancy has to do with the prevalent pattern of directional mating that occurred following the conquest of Mexico and subsequent spread of colonial control northward. The simple, traditional formula used during colonial times for determining castas illustrates how women with indigenous mitochondrial DNA could have great-granddaughters who were considered españolas:

1. De español é india, produce mestizo,
2. De español y mestiza, castiza.
3. De español y castiza, produce española.[64]

Thus, the casta of a woman who was seven-eighths European would be considered española in colonial times, even though her mitochondrial DNA lineage was of indigenous origin. Genetic data demonstrate that social identity, as expressed by the castas reported in the 1790 census, did not necessarily reflect actual ancestry.

Our ultimate goal was to explore in greater detail whether these mitochondrial lineages might shed light on the original Native American groups that inhabited the region of Sonora and Sinaloa, where most of the Alta California female ancestors had been born. Some progress was made toward this objective, even though it was far from clear in most cases, given the limitations of surviving documentary evidence, which ethnolinguistic group might be the ancestral source of the lineage. Further hope is provided in that many mitochondrial sequences of Spanish Californians harbor unique genetic markers that can be the basis for research regarding their indigenous origin in Mexico.

One of the interesting observations about the native groups that inhabited the coastal plains and foothills of Sonora and Sinaloa (as well as southern Baja California) is that they had a fair amount of linguistic diversity, according to missionary testimony. Unfortunately, little evidence in the form of word lists or texts from these linguistically distinct local groups has survived. In the absence of sufficient linguistic data, some scholars have been inclined to attribute Uto-Aztecan affiliation to some of these groups, but this is clearly unwarranted in some cases.[65] Groups like the Guasave, Huite, Nio, and Ocoroni of Sinaloa, the Seri of Sonora, and the Guaicura and Pericú of Baja California del Sur likely represent survivals of earlier hunter-gatherers and fishermen who inhabited pericoastal areas prior to the arrival of agriculturalists speaking Uto-Aztecan and Yuman-Cochimí languages. Some of these locally distinct peoples of Sinaloa had adopted agriculture by the time of contact, while others, like the Guasave, had not. We can hypothesize that in the prehistoric past, some local Sinaloan groups had shifted to speaking Uto-Aztecan languages, especially Cahita and Tahue, through a process of cultural dominance. These languages spread at the expense of others during a period of demographic expansion resulting from the dependability of food supplies afforded by cultivation. As has been demonstrated in both Europe and North America, the spread of agriculture often did accompany the arrival of a new genetic component; however, older mtDNA lineages from the pre-agricultural population survived as well (or even predominated, such as in northwestern Europe). As Kemp's research has shown, there is a substantive disconnect between mtDNA lineages among the Uto-Aztecan peoples of the American Southwest, where Haplogroups B and C predominate, and those of Central Mexico, where Haplogroup A prevails.[66] Thus, genes and languages do not necessarily coincide. The coastal regions of Sonora and Sinaloa lie directly between these two regions and thus have the potential to inform us regarding the processes of demographic and cultural change that left a genetic signature in native populations.

The preliminary data derived from our analysis of Alta California's Spanish colonial population help answer some of the questions posed regarding the genetic affinities of the original peoples of Sonora and Sinaloa. It appears clear that the predominance of Haplogroups B and C is not likely to extend to the Cahitan peoples (Yaqui, Mayo, and related groups) of Sonora and Sinaloa. Enough information has now been accumulated to suggest that Haplogroup A lineages were likely to have been common in this area, including a distinctive haplotype that may have been present among the Guasave, and Haplogroup D appears to have been more prevalent there than elsewhere in Mexico. The presence of the rare subgroup of Haplogroup D in northwestern Mexico is surely significant, because of its hypothesized ancestral connection with an ancient coastal migration; however, its association with any particular ethnolinguistic group is conjectural at present. At this stage, it is not inappropriate to draw an analogy between the native peoples of Sinaloa and the Chumash population of coastal California, both of whom contrasted with their neighbors by harboring distinctive lineages belonging to Haplogroups A and D. We wonder if both populations might be descended from an ancient maritime-oriented group that established itself early in the settlement of the Americas during a fairly rapid Late Pleistocene coastal migration. To further test this hypothesis, of course, more research is necessary. To gain confidence in the patterns presented here, more sampling is needed among the surviving Yaqui and Mayo peoples, and further genealogical sleuthing should be undertaken in archives containing Sinaloan and Sonoran colonial records.

Certainly many Spanish Californians must have been aware of their partial Indian ancestry; in the new frontier setting in which they found themselves, however, this genetic inheritance became less important. In order to differentiate themselves from the populations indigenous to Alta California, the newly arrived colonists from Sonora and Sinaloa constructed a gente de razón social identity that eclipsed the old casta distinctions of their homeland.

Table 4. Haplogroup A mtDNA Sequence Data for Spanish Californians and Mexican Americans, Part 1

Sample	Ethnicity	Traceable Origin	Haplotype	16086	16092	16104	16111	16129	16136	16142	16145	16153	16156	16172	16182	16183	16184	16187	16189	16192	16193	16209	16213	16218	16223	16224	16234	16235	16239	16240	16243	16247	16249	16250	16257	16270	16274	16290	16295	16298	16311	16319	16325	16327	16335	16336	16344	16348	16352	16357	16362	16395	16408
CRS				T	T	C	C	G	T	C	G	G	T	A	A	C	C	T	C	C	T	C	C	T	C	C	T	C	A	T	C	A	C	T	C	C	G	C	C	T	T	G	T	C	A	G	C	T	T	T	C	C	C
JJ143	California Spanish	Sonora	A01	.	.	.	T	.	T	.	.	.	.	.	.	.	.	.	.	.	.	.	.	.	T	.	.	.	.	.	.	.	.	.	.	.	.	T	.	.	.	A	.	.	.	.	.	.	.	C	.	C	.
JJ096	California Spanish	Unidentified	A02	.	.	.	T	.	C	.	.	.	.	.	.	.	.	.	.	.	.	.	.	.	T	.	.	.	.	.	.	.	.	.	.	.	.	T	.	.	.	A	.	.	.	.	T	.	.	C	.	C	.
JJ242	Mexican American	Guanajuato	A03	.	.	.	T	.	.	.	.	.	.	.	.	.	.	.	T	.	.	.	.	.	T	.	.	.	.	.	.	.	.	.	.	.	.	T	T	.	.	A	.	.	.	.	.	.	.	C	x	C	x
JJ412	Mexican American	Sinaloa	A04	.	.	.	T	.	.	.	.	.	.	.	.	.	.	.	.	T	.	.	.	.	T	.	.	.	.	.	.	.	.	.	.	.	A	T	.	.	.	A	.	.	.	.	.	.	.	C	.	C	.
JJ397	Mexican American	Sonora	A05	.	.	.	T	.	.	.	.	.	.	.	G	.	.	.	.	.	.	.	.	.	T	.	.	.	.	.	.	.	.	.	.	.	.	T	.	.	.	A	.	.	.	.	.	.	.	C	.	C	.
JJ173	California Spanish	Sinaloa	A06	x	x	.	T	.	.	.	.	A	.	A	.	.	.	.	.	.	.	.	.	.	T	.	.	.	.	.	.	.	.	.	.	.	.	T	.	.	.	A	.	.	.	.	.	.	.	C	.	C	x
JJ110	California Spanish?	Unidentified	A07	.	.	.	T	.	.	.	.	.	.	.	.	.	.	.	.	.	.	.	.	.	T	.	.	.	.	T	.	.	.	.	.	.	.	T	.	.	.	A	.	.	.	.	T	.	.	C	.	C	T
JJ249	Apache	Arizona	A07	.	.	.	T	.	.	.	.	.	.	.	.	.	.	.	.	.	.	.	.	.	T	.	.	.	.	T	.	.	.	.	.	.	.	T	.	.	.	A	.	.	.	.	.	.	.	C	.	C	.
JJ438	Mexican American	Chihuahua	A07	.	.	.	T	.	.	.	.	.	.	.	.	.	.	.	.	.	.	.	.	.	T	.	.	.	.	T	.	.	.	.	.	.	.	T	.	.	.	A	.	.	.	.	.	.	.	C	x	C	x
JJ236	Yaqui	Sonora	A08	.	.	.	T	.	.	.	.	.	.	.	.	.	.	.	.	.	T	.	.	.	T	.	.	.	.	.	.	.	.	.	.	.	.	T	.	.	.	A	.	.	.	.	.	.	.	C	.	C	.
JJ315	Hispanic Southwest	Texas	A09	.	.	.	T	.	.	.	.	.	.	.	.	.	.	.	.	.	.	.	.	.	T	.	.	.	.	.	.	.	.	.	.	.	.	T	.	.	.	A	.	.	.	.	.	T	.	C	.	C	.
JJ351	Mexican American	Chihuahua	A10	.	.	.	T	.	.	.	.	.	.	.	.	.	.	.	.	.	.	.	.	.	T	.	T	.	.	.	.	.	.	.	.	.	.	T	.	.	.	A	.	.	.	.	.	.	.	C	.	C	.
JJ353	Mexican American	Unidentified	A11	.	.	.	T	.	.	.	.	.	.	.	.	.	.	.	.	.	.	.	.	.	T	.	.	.	.	.	.	.	.	.	.	.	.	T	.	.	.	A	C	T	.	.	.	.	.	C	.	C	.
JJ207	Calif. Spanish or Mex. American	Unidentified	A12	.	.	.	T	A	.	.	.	.	.	.	.	.	.	.	.	.	.	.	.	.	T	.	.	.	.	.	.	.	.	.	.	.	A	T	.	.	.	A	.	.	.	.	.	.	.	C	.	C	x
JJ333	Mexican American	Chihuahua	A13	.	.	.	T	.	.	A	.	.	.	.	.	.	.	.	.	.	.	.	.	.	T	.	.	.	.	.	.	.	.	.	.	.	.	T	.	.	.	A	.	.	.	.	.	.	.	C	.	C	.
JJ223	Mexican American	Sonora	A14	.	.	.	T	.	.	.	.	.	.	.	.	.	C	.	C	.	.	.	.	.	T	.	.	.	.	.	.	.	.	.	.	.	.	T	.	.	.	A	.	.	G	.	.	.	.	C	.	C	.
JJ292	Nahuatl	Valley of Mexico	A15	.	.	.	.	.	.	.	.	.	.	.	.	.	.	.	.	.	.	A	.	.	T	.	.	.	.	.	.	.	.	.	.	.	.	T	.	.	.	A	.	C	.	A	.	.	.	C	.	C	.
JJ451	Hispanic Southwest	Texas	A16	.	.	.	T	.	.	.	.	.	.	.	.	.	.	.	.	.	.	.	.	.	T	.	.	.	.	.	.	.	.	.	.	.	A	T	.	.	.	A	.	.	.	.	.	.	.	C	.	C	.
JJ226	Mexican American	Chihuahua	A17	.	.	.	T	.	.	.	.	.	.	.	.	.	.	.	.	.	.	.	.	.	T	.	.	.	.	.	G	.	.	.	.	.	.	T	.	.	.	A	.	.	.	.	.	.	.	C	.	C	x
JJ334	Mexican American	Sinaloa	A18	.	.	.	T	.	.	.	.	.	.	.	.	.	.	.	.	.	.	.	.	.	T	.	.	.	.	.	.	.	.	.	.	.	.	T	.	C	.	A	.	.	.	.	.	.	.	C	.	C	.
JJ244	Mexican American	Baja California	A19	.	.	.	T	.	.	.	.	.	.	.	.	.	.	.	.	.	.	.	.	.	T	.	.	.	.	.	.	.	.	.	.	.	.	T	.	.	.	A	.	.	.	.	.	.	.	C	.	C	.
JJ453	Mexican American	Unidentified	A20	.	.	.	T	.	.	.	.	.	.	.	G	.	.	.	.	.	.	.	.	.	T	.	.	G	.	.	.	.	.	.	.	.	.	T	.	.	.	A	.	.	G	.	.	.	.	C	.	C	.
JJ335	Mexican American?	Zacatecas	A21	.	.	.	T	.	.	.	.	.	.	.	.	.	.	.	.	.	.	.	.	.	T	.	.	.	.	.	.	.	.	.	.	.	.	T	.	.	.	A	.	.	G	.	.	.	.	C	.	C	.
JJ440	Hispanic Southwest	New Mexico	A21	.	.	.	T	.	.	.	.	.	.	.	.	.	.	.	.	.	.	.	.	.	T	.	.	.	.	.	.	.	.	.	.	.	.	T	.	.	.	A	.	.	G	.	.	.	.	C	.	C	.
JJ058	Hispanic Southwest	Arizona	A22	.	.	.	T	.	.	.	.	.	.	.	.	.	.	.	.	.	.	C	.	.	T	.	.	.	.	.	.	.	.	.	.	.	.	T	.	.	.	A	.	.	.	.	.	.	C	C	.	C	.
JJ228	California Spanish	Sinaloa	A23	.	.	.	T	.	.	.	.	.	.	.	.	.	.	.	.	.	.	.	.	.	T	.	.	.	.	.	.	.	.	.	.	.	.	T	.	.	.	A	.	.	.	.	.	.	.	C	.	C	x

Table 4. Haplogroup A mtDNA Sequence Data for Spanish Californians and Mexican Americans, Part 2

Sample	Ethnicity	Traceable Origin	Haplotype	16086	16092	16104	16111	16129	16136	16142	16145	16153	16156	16172	16182	16183	16184	16187	16189	16192	16193	16209	16213	16218	16223	16224	16234	16235	16239	16240	16243	16247	16249	16250	16257	16270	16274	16290	16295	16298	16311	16319	16325	16327	16335	16336	16344	16348	16352	16357	16362	16395	16408
CRS				T	T	C	C	G	T	C	G	G	G	T	A	A	C	T	C	C	C	T	G	C	C	T	C	A	C	A	T	C	C	C	G	C	T	G	C	C	T	T	G	C	A	G	C	T	T	T	C	C
J306	California Spanish	Unidentified	A24	.	C	.	.	.	.	.	.	.	.	.	.	.	.	.	.	.	.	.	.	.	T	.	.	.	.	.	.	.	.	.	.	.	.	T	.	.	.	A	.	.	.	.	.	.	.	.	C	.	.
J134	California Spanish	Unidentified	A25	C	x	.	T	.	.	.	.	.	.	.	.	.	.	.	.	.	.	.	.	.	T	.	.	.	.	.	.	.	.	.	.	.	.	T	.	.	.	A	.	.	.	.	.	.	.	.	C	.	.
J383	California Spanish	Sinaloa	A25	.	.	.	T	.	.	.	.	.	.	.	.	.	.	.	.	.	.	.	.	.	T	.	.	.	.	.	.	.	.	.	.	.	.	T	.	.	.	A	.	.	.	.	.	.	.	.	C	.	.
J404	Mexican American	Sonora	A25	.	.	.	T	.	.	.	.	.	.	.	.	.	.	.	.	.	.	.	.	.	T	.	.	.	.	.	.	.	.	.	.	.	.	T	.	.	.	A	.	.	.	.	.	.	.	.	C	.	.
J195	California Spanish	Sonora	A26	.	C	.	T	.	.	.	.	.	.	.	.	.	.	.	.	.	.	.	.	.	T	.	.	.	.	.	.	.	.	.	.	.	.	T	.	.	.	A	.	.	.	.	.	.	.	.	C	.	.
J288	California Spanish	Unidentified	A26	.	C	.	T	.	.	.	.	.	.	.	.	.	.	.	.	.	.	.	.	.	T	.	.	.	.	.	.	.	.	.	.	.	.	T	.	.	.	A	.	.	.	.	.	.	.	.	C	.	.
J319	Calif. Spanish or Mex. American	Unidentified	A26	.	C	.	T	.	.	.	.	.	.	.	.	.	.	.	.	.	.	.	.	.	T	.	.	.	.	.	.	.	.	.	.	.	.	T	.	.	.	A	.	.	.	.	.	.	.	.	C	x	x
J355	Yaqui	Sonora	A26	.	C	.	T	.	.	.	.	.	.	.	.	.	.	.	.	.	.	.	.	.	T	.	.	.	.	.	.	.	.	.	.	.	.	T	.	.	.	A	.	.	.	.	.	.	.	.	C	.	.
J361	California Spanish	Baja California	A26	.	C	.	T	.	.	.	.	.	.	.	.	.	.	.	.	.	.	.	.	.	T	.	.	.	.	.	.	.	.	.	.	.	.	T	.	.	.	A	.	.	.	.	.	.	.	.	C	.	.
J366	Calif. Spanish or Mex. American	Unidentified	A26	.	C	.	T	.	.	.	.	.	.	.	.	.	.	.	.	.	.	.	.	.	T	.	.	.	.	.	.	.	.	.	.	.	.	T	.	.	.	A	.	.	.	.	.	.	.	.	C	x	x
J130	California Spanish	Sonora	A27	.	.	.	.	.	.	.	.	.	.	C	.	.	.	.	.	.	.	.	.	.	T	.	.	.	.	.	.	.	.	.	.	.	.	T	.	.	.	A	.	.	.	.	.	.	.	.	C	x	x
J251	California Spanish	Unidentified	A27	.	.	.	.	.	.	.	.	.	.	C	.	.	.	.	.	.	.	.	.	.	T	.	.	.	.	.	.	.	.	.	.	.	.	T	.	.	.	A	.	.	.	.	.	.	.	.	C	x	x
J252	Hispanic Southwest	Texas	A27	.	.	.	.	.	.	.	.	.	.	C	.	.	.	.	.	.	.	.	.	.	T	.	.	.	.	.	.	.	.	.	.	.	.	T	.	.	.	A	.	.	.	.	.	.	.	.	C	x	x
J332	Mexican American	Sonora	A28	.	.	.	.	.	.	.	.	.	.	.	.	.	.	.	.	.	.	.	.	.	T	.	.	.	.	.	.	.	.	.	.	.	.	T	.	.	.	A	.	.	.	.	.	.	.	.	C	.	.
J415	Mexican American	Unidentified	A29	.	C	.	.	.	.	.	.	.	.	.	.	.	.	.	.	.	.	.	.	.	T	.	.	.	.	.	.	.	.	.	.	.	.	T	.	.	.	A	.	.	.	.	.	.	.	.	C	x	x
J079	Hispanic Southwest	New Mexico	A30	.	.	.	T	.	.	.	.	.	.	.	.	.	.	.	.	.	.	.	.	.	T	.	.	.	.	.	.	.	.	.	.	.	.	T	.	.	.	A	.	.	.	.	.	.	.	.	C	x	x
J224	Cocopa	Baja California	A30	.	.	.	T	.	.	.	.	.	.	.	.	.	.	.	.	.	.	.	.	.	T	.	.	.	.	.	.	.	.	.	.	.	.	T	.	.	.	A	.	.	.	.	.	.	.	.	C	x	x
J254	Mexican American	Guanajuato	A30	.	.	.	T	.	.	.	.	.	.	.	.	.	.	.	.	.	.	.	.	.	T	.	.	.	.	.	.	.	.	.	.	.	.	T	.	.	.	A	.	.	.	.	.	.	.	.	C	.	.
J312	Mexican American	Coahuila	A30	.	.	.	T	.	.	.	.	.	.	.	.	.	.	.	.	.	.	.	.	.	T	.	.	.	.	.	.	.	.	.	.	.	.	T	.	.	.	A	.	.	.	.	.	.	.	.	C	.	.
J354	Mexican American	Chihuahua	A30	.	.	.	T	.	.	.	.	.	.	.	.	.	.	.	.	.	.	.	.	.	T	.	.	.	.	.	.	.	.	.	.	.	.	T	.	.	.	A	.	.	.	.	.	.	.	.	C	.	.
J401	California Spanish?	Unidentified	A31	.	.	.	.	.	.	.	.	.	.	.	.	.	.	.	.	.	.	.	.	.	.	.	.	.	T	.	.	.	.	.	.	T	A	.	.	.	.	.	.	.	.	.	.	.	.	.	.	.	.
J392	California Spanish	Sinaloa	A32	.	.	.	.	.	.	.	.	.	.	.	.	.	.	.	.	.	.	.	.	.	T	C	.	.	.	.	.	.	.	.	.	.	.	T	.	.	.	A	.	.	.	.	.	.	.	.	C	.	.
J103	California Spanish	Unidentified	A33	.	.	.	T	.	.	.	.	.	.	.	.	.	.	.	C	.	.	.	.	.	T	.	.	.	.	.	.	.	.	.	.	.	.	T	.	.	.	A	.	.	.	.	.	.	.	.	C	.	.
J211	Hispanic Southwest	New Mexico	A34	.	.	.	.	.	.	.	.	.	.	.	.	.	.	.	.	.	.	.	.	.	T	.	.	.	.	.	.	.	.	.	.	.	.	T	.	.	C	A	C	.	.	.	.	.	.	.	C	.	.
J089	Hispanic Southwest	Arizona	A35	.	.	.	.	.	.	.	.	.	.	.	.	.	.	.	.	.	.	.	.	.	T	.	.	.	.	.	.	.	.	.	.	.	.	T	.	.	C	A	.	.	.	.	.	.	.	.	C	.	.
J344	Mexican American	Zacatecas	A35	.	.	.	.	.	.	.	.	.	.	.	.	.	.	.	.	.	.	.	.	.	T	.	.	.	.	.	.	.	.	.	.	.	.	T	.	.	C	A	.	.	.	.	.	.	.	.	C	.	.
J441	Central American	Guatemala	A36	.	.	T	T	.	.	.	.	.	.	.	.	.	.	.	.	.	.	.	.	.	T	.	.	.	.	.	.	.	.	.	.	.	.	T	.	.	.	A	.	.	.	.	.	.	.	.	C	.	.
J449	Mexican American	Unidentified	A36	.	.	T	T	.	.	.	.	.	.	.	.	.	.	.	.	.	.	.	.	.	T	.	.	.	.	.	.	.	.	.	.	.	.	T	.	.	.	A	.	.	.	.	.	.	.	.	C	.	.

Table 5. Haplogroup B mtDNA Sequence Data for Spanish Californians and Mexican Americans

Sample	Ethnicity	Traceable Origin	Haplotype	16092	16093	16111	16129	16132	16138	16140	16144	16145	16152	16172	16173	16182	16183	16183.1	16187	16189	16214	16217	16224	16247	16261	16274	16278	16298	16311	16319	16323	16325	16352
CRS				T	T	C	G	A	A	T	T	G	T	T	C	A	A	·	C	T	C	C	T	A	C	G	C	T	T	G	T	T	T
J084	Mexican American	Sonora	B01	.	.	.	.	.	.	.	.	.	.	.	.	.	.	.	.	C	C	C	.	.	.	.	.	.	.	.	.	.	.
J129	California Spanish	Unidentified	B01	.	.	.	.	.	.	.	.	.	.	.	.	.	C	C	.	C	C	C	.	.	.	.	.	.	.	.	.	.	.
J139	California Spanish?	Unidentified	B01	.	.	.	.	.	.	.	.	.	.	.	.	.	C	C	.	C	C	C	.	.	.	.	.	.	.	.	.	.	.
J201	California Spanish	Unidentified	B01	.	.	.	.	.	.	.	.	.	.	.	.	.	C	C	.	C	C	C	.	.	.	.	.	.	.	.	.	.	.
J204	California Spanish	Sinaloa	B01	.	.	.	.	.	.	.	.	.	.	.	.	.	C	C	.	C	C	C	.	.	.	.	.	.	.	.	.	.	.
J208	California Spanish	Sonora	B01	.	.	.	.	.	.	.	.	.	.	.	.	.	C	C	.	C	C	C	.	.	.	.	.	.	.	.	.	.	.
J237	Mexican American	Durango	B01	.	.	.	.	.	.	.	.	.	.	.	.	.	C	C	.	C	C	C	.	.	.	.	.	.	.	.	.	.	.
J296	Mexican American	Michoacán	B01	.	.	.	.	.	.	.	.	.	.	.	.	.	C	C	.	C	C	C	.	.	.	.	.	.	.	.	.	.	.
J320	Hispanic Southwest	New Mexico	B01	.	.	.	.	.	.	.	.	.	.	.	.	.	C	C	.	C	C	C	.	.	.	.	.	.	.	.	.	.	.
J487	California Spanish	Sinaloa	B01	.	.	.	.	.	.	.	.	.	.	.	.	.	C	C	.	C	C	C	.	.	.	.	.	.	.	.	.	.	.
J266	Mexican American	Durango	B01	.	.	.	.	.	.	.	.	.	.	.	.	.	C	C	.	C	C	C	.	.	.	.	.	.	.	.	.	.	.
J181	California Spanish	Unidentified	B02	C	.	.	.	.	.	.	.	.	.	.	.	.	C	C	.	C	C	C	.	.	.	.	.	.	.	.	.	.	.
J203	Mexican American	Unidentified	B03	.	.	.	.	.	.	.	C	.	.	.	.	C	C	C	.	C	C	C	.	.	.	.	.	.	.	.	.	.	.
J262	California Spanish	Baja California	B04	.	.	.	.	.	.	.	.	.	.	.	.	.	C	C	.	C	C	C	.	.	.	.	.	.	.	.	.	.	.
J356	Yaqui?	Sonora	B04	.	.	.	.	.	.	.	.	.	.	.	.	.	C	C	.	C	C	C	.	.	.	.	.	.	.	.	.	.	.
J328	Mexican American	Zacatecas	B05	.	.	.	.	.	.	.	.	.	C	.	.	.	C	C	.	C	C	C	.	.	.	.	.	.	.	.	.	.	.
J362	Hispanic Southwest	New Mexico	B06	.	.	.	.	.	.	.	.	.	.	.	.	.	C	C	.	C	C	C	.	.	.	.	.	C	.	.	.	C	.
J364	Mexican American	Chihuahua	B07	.	.	.	.	.	.	C	.	.	.	.	.	.	C	C	.	C	C	C	.	.	.	.	.	.	.	.	.	.	.
J388	Calif. Spanish or Mex. American	Sinaloa	B08	C	.	.	.	.	.	.	.	.	.	.	.	C	C	C	.	C	C	C	.	.	.	.	.	.	.	.	.	.	.
J410	California Spanish	Unidentified	B08	C	.	.	.	.	.	.	.	.	.	.	.	C	C	C	.	C	C	C	.	.	.	.	.	.	.	.	.	.	.
J188	Hispanic Southwest	New Mexico	B09	C	.	.	.	.	.	.	.	.	C	.	.	.	C	C	.	C	C	C	.	.	.	.	.	.	.	.	.	.	.
J457	Mexican American	Chihuahua	B10	.	.	.	.	.	.	.	.	.	.	.	.	.	C	C	.	C	C	C	.	.	.	.	.	.	.	.	.	.	.
J177	Mexican American	Durango	B11	.	.	.	.	.	.	.	.	.	.	.	.	.	C	C	.	C	C	C	.	.	.	.	.	.	.	.	.	.	.
J341	Mexican American	Chihuahua	B12	.	.	.	.	G	.	.	.	.	.	.	.	C	C	C	.	C	C	C	.	.	.	A	.	.	.	.	.	.	.
J360	Mexican American	Sonora	B13	C	.	.	.	.	.	.	.	.	.	.	.	.	C	C	.	C	C	C	.	.	.	.	.	.	.	.	.	.	.
J337	Mexican American	Durango	B14	C	.	.	.	G	.	.	.	.	.	.	.	C	C	C	.	C	C	C	.	.	.	.	.	.	T	.	.	.	.
J057	Opata	Sonora	B15	C	.	.	.	.	.	.	.	.	.	.	.	.	C	C	.	C	C	C	.	.	T	.	.	.	.	.	.	.	.
J309	Mexican American	Sonora	B16	.	.	T	.	.	.	.	.	.	.	.	.	.	C	C	.	C	C	C	.	.	.	.	.	.	.	.	.	.	.
J342	Mexican American	Chihuahua	B17	.	A	.	.	.	.	.	.	.	.	.	.	.	C	C	.	C	C	C	C	.	.	.	.	.	.	.	.	.	.
J386	Mexican American	Zacatecas	B18	C	.	.	.	.	.	.	.	.	.	.	.	.	C	C	.	C	T	C	.	.	.	.	.	.	.	.	.	.	.
J437	Mexican American	Chihuahua	B19	.	.	.	.	.	.	.	.	.	.	T	.	.	C	C	.	C	C	C	.	.	.	.	.	.	.	.	C	.	.
J444	Mexican American	Sonora	B20	C	.	T	.	.	.	.	.	.	.	.	.	.	C	C	.	C	C	C	.	.	.	.	.	.	.	.	.	.	.
J1176	Calif. Spanish/Nat. Hawaiian	Hawaiian Is.	B21	.	.	.	A	.	.	.	.	A	.	.	.	.	C	C	T	C	C	C	.	G	T	.	.	.	.	.	.	C	.
J339	Hispanic Southwest	New Mexico	B22	.	.	.	.	.	.	.	.	.	.	.	.	.	C	C	.	C	C	C	.	.	.	.	.	.	.	.	.	C	.

Genetics and the *Castas* of Colonial California 187

Table 6. Haplogroup C mtDNA Sequence Data for Spanish Californians and Mexican Americans

Table 7. Haplogroup D mtDNA Sequence Data for Spanish Californians and Mexican Americans

Sample	Ethnicity	Traceable Origin	Haplotype	16092	16093	16126	16142	16183	16183.1	16189	16223	16241	16250	16266	16270	16274	16301	16311	16325	16330	16342	16360	16362
CRS				T	T	T	C	A	-	T	C	A	C	C	C	G	C	T	T	T	T	C	T
JJ255	Spanish Californian	Sonora or Sinaloa	D01	.	.	.	.	.	.	.	.	.	.	.	.	.	.	.	C	.	.	.	C
JJ369	Spanish Californian	Unidentified	D01	.	.	.	.	.	.	.	.	.	.	.	.	.	.	.	C	.	.	.	C
JJ190	Spanish Californian?	Unidentified	D02	.	.	.	.	.	.	.	.	.	.	.	.	A	.	.	C	.	.	.	C
JJ264	Mexican American	Chihuahua	D03	.	.	.	.	.	.	.	T	.	.	.	.	.	.	.	.	.	C	.	C
JJ216	Spanish Californian (or Chumash)	Unidentified	D04	C	.	.	.	.	.	.	T	G	.	.	.	.	T	.	.	.	C	.	C
JJ297	Spanish Californian	Unidentified	D05	C	.	.	.	.	.	.	T	G	.	.	.	.	T	.	.	.	C	.	C
JJ403	Spanish Californian?	Unidentified	D05	.	.	.	.	.	.	.	T	G	.	.	.	.	T	.	.	.	C	.	C
JJ260	Spanish Californian	Sonora	D06	.	.	.	T	.	.	.	T	G	.	.	T	.	.	.	.	.	C	.	C
JJ142	Hispanic Southwest	Texas	D07	.	.	.	.	.	.	.	T	G	T	.	.	.	T	.	.	A	C	G	C
JJ128	Spanish Californian	Sinaloa	D08	.	.	.	T	.	.	C	T	.	.	.	.	.	.	.	C	.	.	.	C
JJ198	Mexican American	Chihuahua	D08	.	.	.	T	C	.	C	T	.	.	.	.	.	.	.	C	.	.	x	x
JJ345	Mexican American	Sonora	D09	.	.	.	T	.	C	C	T	.	.	T	.	.	.	.	C	.	.	.	C
JJ349	Mexican American	Sonora or Sinaloa	D10	.	.	.	T	.	C	.	T	.	.	.	.	.	.	C	.	.	.	.	C
JJ265	Mexican American	Chihuahua	D11	.	C	C	.	.	.	.	.	.	.	.	.	.	.	.	C	.	.	.	C
JJ144	Spanish Californian?	Unidentified	D12	.	.	C	.	.	.	.	T	.	T	.	.	.	.	.	C	.	.	.	C

Notes

1. For theoretical discussions of social identity, see Fredrik Barth, "Introduction," in *Ethnic Groups and Boundaries: The Social Organization of Cultural Difference*, ed. Fredrik Barth (Boston: Little, Brown, 1969), 9–38; Thomas Hylland Eriksen, *Ethnicity and Nationalism: Anthropological Perspectives* (Boulder, Colo.: Pluto Press, 1993).

2. A number of historians and anthropologists have examined changing identities in Alta California. See especially William Marvin Mason, *The Census of 1790: A Demographic History of Colonial California* (Menlo Park, Calif., Ballena Press, 1998); Lisbeth Haas, *Conquests and Historical Identities in California, 1769–1836* (Berkeley: University of California Press, 1995); Brian D. Haley and Larry R. Wilcoxon, "How Spaniards Became Chumash and Other Tales of Ethnogenesis," *American Anthropologist* 107 (2005): 432–45; and John R. Johnson and William M. Williams, "Toypurina's Descendants: Three Generations of an Alta California Family," *Boletín: The Journal of the California Mission Studies Association* 24, no. 2 (2007): 30–55.

3. Bryan Sykes, *The Seven Daughters of Eve* (London and New York: Bantam Press, 2001); Stephen Oppenheimer, *Out of Eden: The Peopling of the World* (London: Constable and Robinson, 2003); Spencer Wells, *Deep Ancestry: Inside the Genographic Project* (Washington, D.C.: National Geographic, 2006).

4. Henry Louis Gates Jr., series host and executive producer, *African American Lives*, DVD (PBS Paramount, 2006).

5. Maynard Geiger and Clement W. Meighan, *As the Padres Saw Them: California Indian Life and Customs as Reported by the Franciscan Missionaries, 1813–1815* (Santa Barbara, Calif.: Santa Barbara Mission Archive-Library, 1976), 11.

6. Ibid., 12.

7. Ibid., 11.

8. Ibid., 15.

9. Mason, *Census of 1790*.

10. Claudio Esteva-Fabregat, *Mestizaje in Ibero-America*, trans. John Wheat (Tucson, Ariz.: University of Arizona Press, 1995).

11. D. Andrew Merriwether, "Mitochondrial DNA," in *Handbook of North American Indians*, vol. 3, *Environment, Origins, and Population*, ed. Dennis Stanford et al. (Washington, D.C.: Smithsonian, 2006), 817–30.

12. Antonio Torroni, "Mitochondrial DNA and the Origin of Native Americans," in *America Past, America Present: Genes and Languages in the Americas and Beyond*, ed. Colin Renfrew (Cambridge: McDonald Institute for Archaeological Research, 2000), 77–87.

13. Ann Gibbons, "Geneticists Trace the DNA Trail of the First Americans," *Science* 259 (1993): 312–13; Antonio Torroni et al., "Asian Affinities and Continental Radiation of the Four Founding Native American mtDNAs," *American Journal of Human Genetics* 53 (1993): 563–90; Douglas C. Wallace and Antonio Torroni, "American Indian Prehistory as Written in the Mitochondrial DNA: A Review," *Human Biology* 64 (1992): 403–16.

14 Peter Forster et al., "Origin and Evolution of Native American mtDNA Variation: A Reappraisal," *American Journal of Human Genetics* 59 (1996): 935–45; Joseph G. Lorenz and David Glenn Smith, "Distribution of Sequence Variation in the mtDNA Control Region of Native North Americans," *Human Biology* 69 (1997): 749–76; Ripan S. Malhi et al., "The Structure of Diversity within New World Mitochondrial DNA Haplogroups: Implications for the Prehistory of North America," *American Journal of Human Genetics* 70 (2002): 905–19.

15 Carol H. Mandryk et al., "Late Quaternary Paleoenvironments of Northwestern North America: Implications for Inland versus Coastal Migration Routes," *Quaternary Science Reviews* 20 (2001): 301–14; John J. Clague et al., "Environments of Northwestern North America before the Last Glacial Maximum," in *Entering America: Northeast Asia and Beringia before the Last Glacial Maximum*, ed. D. B. Madsen (Salt Lake City: University of Utah Press, 2004), 92.

16 John R. Johnson and Joseph G. Lorenz, "Genetics, Linguistics, and Prehistoric Migrations: An Analysis of California Indian Mitochondrial DNA Lineages," *Journal of California and Great Basin Anthropology* 26 (2006): 33–64; Brian M. Kemp, "Mesoamerica and Southwest Prehistory and the Entrance of Humans into the Americas: Mitochondrial DNA Evidence" (PhD diss., University of California, Davis, 2006); Ripan S. Malhi et al., "Native American mtDNA Prehistory in the American Southwest," *American Journal of Physical Anthropology* 120 (2003): 108–24.

17 Ives Goddard, "Native Languages and Language Families of North America," map accompanying *Handbook of North American Indians*, vol. 17, *Languages*, ed. Ives Goddard (Washington, D.C.: Smithsonian, 1996).

18 Jared Diamond and Peter Bellwood, "Farmers and Their Languages: The First Expansions," *Science* 300 (2003): 597–603; Peter Bellwood and Colin Renfrew, eds., *Examining the Farming/Language Dispersal Hypothesis* (Cambridge: McDonald Institute for Archaeological Research, 2002), 331–40.

19 This date range is based upon a 99.5 percent confidence interval (Kemp, "Mesoamerica and Southwest Prehistory," 38–39).

20 Compare Andrés Reséndez and Brian M. Kemp, "Genetics and the History of Latin America," *Hispanic American Historical Review* 85 (2005): 283–98.

21 Lance D. Green, James N. Derr, and Alec Knight, "mtDNA Affinities of the Peoples of North-Central Mexico," *American Journal of Human Genetics* 66 (2000): 989–98; Kemp, "Mesoamerica and Southwest Prehistory"; Malhi et al., "mtDNA Prehistory in the American Southwest"; Karla Sandoval-Mendoza, Leonor Buentello-Malo, and David Comas, "Insights into the Genetic Diversity of Indigenous Mexican Populations" (poster presentation, Languages and Genes: An Interdisciplinary Conference, University of California, Santa Barbara, September 8–10, 2006).

22 Goddard, "Native Languages"; Carl Sauer, *The Distribution of Aboriginal Tribes and Languages in Northwestern Mexico*, Ibero-Americana 5 (Berkeley: University of California, 1934).

23 Mason, *Census of 1790*, 65–72.

24 Johnson and Lorenz, "Genetics, Linguistics, and Prehistoric Migrations."

25 Genealogical research conducted for this study utilized copies of the mission registers available at the Santa Barbara Mission Archive-Library.

26 Marie E. Northrop, *Spanish-Mexican Families of Early California, 1769–1850*, 3 vols. (Burbank, Calif.: Southern California Genealogical Society, 1984–2004), 1:24; Dorothy Mutnick, *Some Alta California Pioneers and Descendants*, 5 vols. (Pleasant Hills, Calif.: Contra Costa County Historical Society), 1:65.

27 Several compilations of genealogical information were consulted for this project, in addition to primary records of baptisms, marriages, burials, and censuses. The most useful were Mason, *Census of 1790*; Mutnick, *Some Early California Pioneers*, vols. 1–5; and Northrop, *Spanish-Mexican Families of Early California*, vols. 1–3. The Huntington Library's Early California Population Project, http://missions.huntington.org, has also facilitated genealogical research.

28 Not included in figure 1 are: (1) thirty samples from mtDNA haplogroups indigenous to Europe and Africa, (2) twenty-five "California Spanish" descendants whose female lineages were not successfully traced to an origin in eighteenth-century Mexico, (3) nine samples from people of more recent Mexican immigrant ancestry who were uncertain of the region in Mexico from where their grandmothers came, and (4) one Polynesian sample descending through the female line from a Native Hawaiian woman who had married a Californio during the Mexican period.

29 This table expands on the information reported previously for twenty women in John R. Johnson, "Identifying the Ancestors of Los Californianos," *Noticias para Los Californianos* 37, no. 4 (2005): 41–43. The samples from four of the Alta California Indian women and one Baja California Indian woman are further discussed in Johnson and Lorenz, "Genetics, Linguistics, and Prehistoric Migrations." The fifth sample, contributed by a descendant from the direct female line from Regina Josefa Toypurina, has only recently been sequenced (see Johnson and Williams, "Toypurina's Descendants," for further information on this family's genealogical background).

30 The proportion of Native American mtDNAs among Spanish Californians (including probable Spanish Californians) is 82.7 percent or 88.6 percent, as calculated from tables 1 and 3 respectively.

31 Daniel T. Reff, *Disease, Depopulation, and Culture Change in Northwestern New Spain* (Salt Lake City: University of Utah Press, 1991); Carl Sauer, *The Aboriginal Population of Northwestern Mexico*, Ibero-Americana 10 (Berkeley: University of California, 1935).

32 Peter Gerhard, *The North Frontier of New Spain*, rev. ed. (Norman, Okla.: University of Oklahoma Press, 1993), 19.

33 Comparisons were made with 330 haplotypes reported by Kemp, "Mesoamerica and Southwest Prehistory"; however, exact matches could not be made with certainty because Kemp's haplotypes were based in part on genetic markers found in the second hypervariable region, which was not sequenced for the present study.

34 Johnson and Lorenz, "Genetics, Linguistics, and Prehistoric Migrations," fig. 5.

35   Kemp, "Mesoamerica and Southwest Prehistory," 38; Meredith Snow, Kathryn Durand, and David Glenn Smith, "Analysis of the Tommy and Mine Canyon Sites" (paper presented at the Society for American Archaeology annual meeting, Austin, Texas, April 28, 2007).

36   Johnson and Lorenz, "Genetics, Linguistics, and Prehistoric Migrations," fig. 5.

37   Certain specific haplotypes from table 4 have not been depicted in figure 3 because "hot spots" in the mtDNA genome have obscured phylogenetic pathways.

38   Mason, *Census of 1790*, 68, 89.

39   Mutnick, *Some Alta California Pioneers*, 1:345; Northrop, *Spanish-Mexican Families*, 2:63.

40   Sauer, *Distribution of Tribes and Languages*, 28–30.

41   Kemp, "Mesoamerica and Southwest Prehistory," 79–87.

42   Ibid., table C-1, HapA075.

43   Gerhard, *North Frontier of New Spain*, 257–61.

44   Kemp, "Mesoamerica and Southwest Prehistory," table C-1, HapA083.

45   Mason, *Census of 1790*, 65, 68, 71.

46   Sauer, "Distribution of Tribes and Languages," 25–26.

47   Kemp, "Mesoamerica and Southwest Prehistory," table C-1, HapA080.

48   Ibid., table C-1, HapA028, HapA051.

49   Gerhard, *North Frontier of New Spain*, 277.

50   See also Green et al., "mtDNA Affinities"; Kemp, "Mesoamerica and Southwest Prehistory."

51   Combined with B02 in figure 4.

52   Gerhard, *North Frontier of New Spain*, 274.

53   Kemp, "Mesoamerica and Southwest Prehistory," 92–95.

54   Ibid., 96.

55   Green et al., "mtDNA Affinities," 994.

56   Olga Rickards et al., "mtDNA History of the Cayapa Amerinds of Ecuador: Detection of Additional Founding Lineages for Native American Populations," *American Journal of Human Genetics* 65 (1999): 519–30; Brian Kemp et al., "Genetic Analysis of Early Holocene Skeletal Remains from Alaska and its Implications for the Settlement of the Americas," *American Journal of Physical Anthropology* 132 (2007): 605–21.

57   Erika Tamm et al., "Beringian Standstill and Spread of Native American Founders," *PLoS ONE* 2, no. 9 (2007): e829 (doi:10.1371/journal.pone.0000829); Ugo Parego et al., "Distinctive Paleo-Indian Migration Routes from Beringia Marked by Two Rare mtDNA Haplogroups," *Human Biology* 19 (2008): 1–8.

58   Kemp et al., "Genetic Analysis," 615.

59   E. James Dixon, *Bone, Boats, & Bison: Archeology and the First Colonization of Western North America* (Albuquerque: University of New Mexico, 1999); K. R. Fladmark, "Routes: Alternate Migration Corridors for Early Man in North America," *American Antiquity* 44 (1979): 55–69; Johnson and Lorenz,

"Genetics, Linguistics, and Prehistoric Migrations," 56; Parego et al, "Distinctive Paleoindian Migration Routes."

60 Green et al., "mtDNA Affinities," 994; Kemp et al., "Genetic Analysis," 214.

61 Wick R. Miller, "Uto-Aztecan Languages," in *Handbook of North American Indians*, vol. 10, *Southwest*, ed. Alfonso Ortiz (Washington, D.C.: Smithsonian, 1983), 122; Sauer, *Distribution of Tribes and Languages*, 25–26, 28–30, 37.

62 Gerhard, *North Frontier of New Spain*, 274.

63 Kemp, "Mesoamerica and Southwest Prehistory," table C-4, HapD009.

64 "1. From Spaniard and Indian, a *mestizo* is born. 2. From Spaniard and *mestiza*, *castiza*. 3. From Spaniard and *castiza*, a Spaniard is born" (Ilona Katzew, *Casta Painting: Images of Race in Eighteenth-Century Mexico* [New Haven, Conn.: Yale University Press, 2004], figs. 163–65 [pp. 130–31]).

65 N. Ross Crumrine, "Mayo," in *Handbook of North American Indians*, 10:264; Miller, "Uto-Aztecan Languages," 122; Sauer, *Distribution of Tribes and Languages*, 15–37.

66 Kemp, "Mesoamerica and Southwestern Prehistory," chap. 2.

Part 4
The Spanish Borderlands: Comparing National Perspectives

ALBERT L. HURTADO

FANTASY HERITAGE: CALIFORNIA'S HISTORICAL IDENTITIES
AND THE PROFESSIONAL EMPIRE OF HERBERT E. BOLTON

Human identity has many sources, but historical experience is one of the most fruitful. In the case of a colonial society, identity may be rooted in a shared sense of heroic accomplishment among the colonizers and of grievance over defeat and dispossession among the colonized. Indeed, historical identities may be defined in the opposition of one group to another. Each group's memory of earlier days—distant homelands for the conqueror and idealized former conditions for the conquered—may also influence its members' sense of self. The past, in sum, may have multiple, incompatible meanings for distinct communities even if they share the same history, the facts of which are not in dispute.

California, whose history traces a series of dispossessions, is a case in point. Before Spanish colonization there were more than 300,000 California Indians, a totality made up of scores of ethnic groups, many speaking different languages. Under the authority and military protection of the Spanish crown, Franciscan priests established Roman Catholic missions for many tribes on the coast and adjacent interior. The priests made these Hispanicized Catholic Indians, called neophytes or *gente sin razón* (people without reason) by Spanish Californians (who called themselves *gente de razón*), into peons of the colony. Mexican independence then brought about the disbandment of missions and distribution of their lands to private citizens (who likewise regarded Indians as a cheap source of labor). The Mexican War and the gold rush led in turn to the marginalization and dispossession of Mexican landholders who had formerly been the lords of the land. So-called Anglo Americans—Anglophone U.S. citizens with various European origins—overwhelmed but did not obliterate Indian and Hispanic Californians. Although the Anglos' social, cultural, economic, and political ways became dominant in California, their triumphal sense of historical identity was countered by Hispanic and Indian versions. To say the least, the California past is contested.[1]

This contested past complicated the task facing early twentieth-century historians of California. Among them was Herbert E. Bolton, who came to California in 1909 to work at Stanford University. He had been a student of Frederick Jackson Turner's at the University of Wisconsin, although he finished his doctorate at the University of Pennsylvania. Bolton had developed his interest in Spanish American history in 1902 when he taught at the University of Texas. After learning Spanish and making many trips to Mexico, Bolton had become the leading authority on colonial Mexican history by the time Stanford hired him. After two years in Palo Alto, Bolton joined the University of California faculty. Eventually he became the director of the Bancroft Library and chairman of the history department.[2] In these positions he sought to establish a California school of history that recognized and valorized the Hispanic past. Yet Anglos who regarded the gold rush as the true foundation of modern California controlled legislative purse strings and sources of private funding. Somehow Bolton had to broaden the perspective on California history without unduly disturbing Anglo sensibilities.

Bolton was the most important California historian of his day.[3] He was not interested merely in revising California history; he also wished to reform the way that American history was taught in the United States. College professors and schoolteachers alike saw U.S. history as Turner described it[4]—beginning with the British colonies on the Atlantic seaboard and proceeding inevitably westward. Rather than view it from an East Coast or even a national perspective, Bolton saw U.S. history as part of a grand hemispheric development led by Spain. No historian worked harder than Bolton to unearth new sources and add them to the documentary record while reinterpreting California and U.S. history in the larger context of the history of the Americas. And within the United States, Bolton drew attention to what he called the Spanish Borderlands, where Anglo and Hispanic culture met and merged in those areas of the United States that had once been part of the Spanish Empire.[5] In trying to accomplish the reorientation of American history, Bolton relied not only on the force of his own formidable scholarship but also on a professional empire populated by his disciples, who taught at all educational levels. He intended to realign American history with the facts that he had unearthed in Mexican and Spanish archives, but he also reinforced the old stereotypes and historical identities known in California as "the fantasy heritage."

Herbert E. Bolton at the St. Francis Hotel in San Francisco, December 28, 1945. The Bancroft Library Portrait Collection, Courtesy of The Bancroft Library, University of California, Berkeley.

The Genealogy of California's Fantasy Heritage

A brief personal reminiscence illustrates how pervasive these myths about California's history continued to be some two generations later. When I was growing up in the 1950s the fantasy heritage worked for me.[6] I was a fifth-generation Californian with a Hispanic surname. When I learned about heroic mission fathers, Spanish soldiers, and rancheros (whose Mexican heritage and racially diverse backgrounds were not worth mentioning in the public schools of Sacramento), I easily identified with them. On the other side of my family, the gold rush supplied a different but equally romanticized past.[7] My mother's side of the family was Anglo. They owned a big hop ranch on the outskirts of Sacramento, and their roots in California extended back to the gold rush (well, almost). My mother's mother married the mayor of Nevada City, a mining town in the mother lode. His family went back to the gold rush too (well, almost). Somehow, I had it all. These associations—Spanish, Anglo, missions, ranchos, gold rush, a landed heritage—deeply impressed on me my identity as a Californian. Even the state of California helped out by buying the hop ranch in 1948 and building a state college for me to attend and to think of as my very own.[8]

There were some troubling inconsistencies in my connections to these California identities. My father, who was born in Cuba and raised in Connecticut, did not come to California until the Great Depression. So despite my infatuation with the Spanish fantasy heritage, my Anglo forbears provided the strongest historic claim to my California identity as well as a connection through generations of land ownership; I still had the gold rush and all of the supposed romance that it entailed. I was nonetheless proud of my Spanish name and continued to identify myself as a Spanish American. As I grew up and learned more about the historical realities of colonial California and the gold rush I came to understand that history is more complicated, ambiguous, and instructive than the imagined past of my childhood. But I have also learned that historians have contributed to these compelling fables and extended their reach and longevity.

California's romanticized past resonated in the academy in Bolton's time and continued to do so for years afterward. These myths did not, after all, emerge from old adobe walls or placer gold mine tailings as a natural excrescence. Californians invented, nurtured, and promoted a vision of the past that was pleasing to tourists and at ease with the Anglo Californian majority. Historians have played an essential role in this process. That is not to say that all historians have fostered an inaccurate version of California history in all of their work. On the contrary, virtually all historians strive for factual accuracy. Yet some historians have found ways to elide disturbing realities while presenting fact-based histories.

Bancroft and the Making of the Myths

In fact, Hubert Howe Bancroft, California's preeminent pioneer historian, deserves much of the credit for creating California's fantasy heritage, although he was ambivalent about California's Hispanic past. When he evaluated Junípero Serra and the other missionaries who founded Spanish California, Bancroft admired their piety, bravery, and dedication to their religious mission; he was less complimentary about their temporal impact on Indians and on the early development of California society. Though Father Serra was a good man and wished only to help the Indians, Bancroft wrote, the priests "with their comforts and their kindness killed as surely as did Cortés and Pizarro with their gunpowder, steel, and piety."[9]

Yet Bancroft regarded the Spanish and Mexican eras of California history as a "Golden Age." And just what, in Bancroft's mind, were the defining attributes that qualified Hispanic California for this appellation? "A golden age," he explained, "must be a time of truth, of right and reason, and universal moderation. Men must be satisfied and women virtuous. Women must be satisfied and men honest." These conditions were met during those halcyon days when California was "half-way between savagism and civilization . . . midst the dreamy reveries of a race half-way between the proud Castilian and the lowly root-digger of the Coast Range vallies." Bancroft envied the Californios, as Mexican Californians called themselves, because they enjoyed an indolent life in the midst of the bounty that California generously poured forth (with an assist from plentiful Indian laborers who were luckily on hand). This happy condition reached its zenith during the Mexican period, when California society seemed to consist of a single cavalier class whose members did nothing that could not be done from horseback. Through the largess of a Mexican government too distant and corrupt to pay much attention to California, a few hundred families came to own vast ranchos, each comprising tens of thousands of acres. California's easily obtained *latifundia* and a servile class of Indian laborers created a near paradise, as far as Bancroft was concerned. Life was easy and life was good. "Never before or since," Bancroft eulogized, "was there a spot in America where life was a long happy holiday, where there was less labor, less care or trouble" than in Mexican California.[10]

The pleasing scenes that Bancroft sketched of Hispanic California created a problem for him to solve as a historian. How was he to explain the Anglo acquisition of this near Eden as anything more or less than a naked conquest? He found the solution in the character of the victims. Happy and self-satisfied, as Bancroft judged them to be, the Californios were an indolent lot living off of California's fat land without toil.[11] With such lazy defenders, the easy-going and virtuous golden age of California was doomed. The Californios became the victims of Yankees in the "Age of Gold," the gold rush that followed the Hispanic "Golden Age." Gone were the grace and ease of earlier days, replaced by personal ambition, the pursuit of mammon, individualism, social chaos, and every other vice of civilization. Bancroft admired the forty-niners' work ethic and single-mindedness, but not their aggressive and sometimes violent greed. They ran roughshod over Californios' land, sensibilities, and pleasant society. As Bancroft put it, the lamb might safely lie down with the lion in the Bible, but "not so with the mild and nerveless inhabitant of southern California, and the wild, tigerish gold-seeker scenting the metal from afar."[12] The life of the Californios resembled the untroubled life "of the ancients," while the gold rush was a time of "avarice . . . wild rudeness and insane revellings." A history of San Francisco published during the gold rush characterized the times:

> [Gold] Dust was plentier than pleasure, pleasure more enticing than virtue. Fortune was the horse, youth in the saddle, dissipation the track, and desire the spur. Let none wonder that the time was the best ever made.[13]

Although the forty-niners themselves naturally took a more cheerful view of their gold rush doings, their version was congruent with Bancroft's ideas about the rough energy of the forty-niners.

So these fantasies about California's Hispanic and Anglo pasts, which at first glance seem to be only tangentially related, are actually complementary pieces of the same imaginary but ideologically useful past. Hispanic indolence and Anglo ambition explain why Anglos won: a superior race overcame and replaced a mythologized inferior one that was ill adapted to defend itself in a newly competitive society. Californios were self-defeating because they were lazy and ignorant of the ways of the modern world—stuck halfway between barbarism and civilization, as Bancroft said. Anglo Americans dispossessed them because they could not do anything else. It was in their nature to replace the Californios so that they could develop California's resources to their fullest potential. Prosperous, modern California was the end result of Anglo aggression. Thus the conquest was a natural and inevitable survival of the fittest. It is worth mentioning that the intended audience for these fantasies was Anglo, not Hispanic. The fantasy validated and valorized Anglo ascendance while acknowledging (even praising) an older Hispanic past in which Anglos had no part.

By the time Bolton arrived in the state, these views of California history were already broadly accepted. Helen Hunt Jackson's popular novel

Ramona had cast the old California missions in a romantic light.[14] Writers like Charles F. Lummis publicized the colorful Spanish heritage of the Southwest.[15] Franciscan missionary and historian Zephyrin Engelhardt had begun his studies that culminated in a multi-volume history of California missions.[16] Add to this the work of early twentieth-century California promoters who saw in the Hispanic and gold rush fantasies a bankable commodity—historical sites on the California coast and Sierra Nevada that attracted automobile tourists, who spent one week on El Camino Real visiting the missions and another on Highway 49 touring gold rush towns.[17]

Bolton and the Native Sons

Though he may not have invented these well-cultivated visions of California's past, Bolton was nonetheless careful not to disturb them. When he arrived in California in 1909 some elderly forty-niners still survived to promote the notion that the gold rush era was "the best ever made." If forty-niners were not here in the flesh, their sons and daughters dutifully maintained the idea that the gold rush marked the true beginning of California. Some of these people sat in the state legislature and on the board of regents and Professor Bolton was ever attentive to the prevailing political winds.[18]

Bolton intended to build a nationally respected school of history at Berkeley. To do that he needed money and allies. He encountered both in the Native Sons of the Golden West, a fraternal organization with an interest in history. At the time of its founding in 1875, membership was limited to white males born in the state after July 7, 1846, the date the American flag was raised in Monterey. The founders were especially interested in memorializing the gold rush era. In time the original membership requirements were amended so that the Californios' descendants were eligible, but the gold rush era continued to be central to the Native Sons' self-image.[19] Beginning in 1910, the Native Sons annually funded fellowships for Berkeley graduate students.[20] Native Sons fellowships were the primary source of graduate research funding during Bolton's long tenure at Berkeley. The officers of the Native Sons were roughly divided into two camps: those who wished to promote excellent research and writing of California history and those who wished to foster the Anglocentric, filiopietistic aims of the Native Sons' original charter.

Bolton was frank about the aims of the Native Sons and the University of California when he spoke to them about fellowship funding. "It seems almost ungracious" to ask for money "but we are all working together," he said. "You are not working for your own glory, nor for the glory of your Native Sons' fellows," Bolton assured them, "you are working for the glory of California, and so are we."[21] Bolton was widely admired by the Native Sons, but some objected to funding any work on Spanish California. From time to time it looked as if dissident Sons would prevail and stop the program, or at least limit it. Whenever these threats arose, Bolton wrote letters to the Native Sons explaining all of the good work that had been done on behalf of Anglo and gold rush history. He usually appended a list of thesis and dissertation titles on topics that would mollify Native Sons. Using these tactics Bolton managed to keep Native Sons funding in place until after World War II.[22] Thus Anglo Californians' prejudices in general, and in particular the expressions of Anglo sentiment from Native Sons, influenced graduate study at Berkeley.

Bolton's Empire

While Bolton is best remembered for his work in Spanish colonial history, most of his students did not write theses and dissertations in that field. In fact, the majority of the topics for these studies were about Anglo history, or at least they were not about Hispanic history. Of 410 thesis and dissertation titles, 234 (57 percent) were on Anglo California, the West, and frontier topics. The remaining 176 (43 percent) were on classic Borderlands and Latin American subjects. Among the studies of California history—of which there were 133 (33 percent)—there were twice as many Anglo as Hispanic subjects.[23] Such things were important when the Native Sons threatened to cut off funds for the fellowships.

Bolton did not challenge the Native Sons' biases in his own writings. On the contrary, Bolton retained much of Bancroft's fantasy heritage in *The Spanish Borderlands*, Bolton's most popular book.[24] Like Bancroft, he lauded the supposed virtues of Californios, but he gave them a racial promotion: they were true Spaniards. Nineteenth-century travelers thought that "Californians were superior to other Spanish colonists in America, including Mexicans," Bolton wrote.[25] Travelers' descriptions did not reflect the racial realities of Hispanic California, which included people of various races and mixtures.[26] Nevertheless, Bolton ascribed Californios' superiority to their greater degree of independence, to "the fact that...the great majority of new colonists were of good Castilian blood; and to...California itself." Thus the generous, easygoing, and gentle Californio appeared to be the inevitable result of unalloyed Spanish racial and cultural traits in combination with the salubrious California climate. Of course, such a careless people could not long withstand the importunities of a more energetic race. "After the inrush of Americans," Bolton duly reported, "this leisurely life inevitably passed away."[27] He approvingly concluded that while "the imprint of Spain" still marked the state, modern Californians commemorated "the day when a people possessed by the energy of labor came to the Golden Gate." *The Spanish Borderlands* found a large popular audience and was widely adopted as a textbook in college classes around the country.

With *The Spanish Borderlands* Bolton gained a national popular audience. He also wished to enhance his authority within California by writing a grade-school history that would be adopted by the state. In 1915, he and his colleague Frederick Teggart submitted a manuscript for consideration.[28] The state did not choose that text, so in 1920 Bolton teamed up with Ephraim D. Adams, a historian at Stanford University, to try again.[29] In 1922 Bolton and Adams published *California's Story*, an elementary-school textbook that would be adopted for classroom instruction by the state of California.[30] It was a standard grade-school textbook for decades and perhaps more important for that reason to Californians at large than *The Spanish Borderlands*, although less well known now.

The textbook was an important part of Bolton's comprehensive influence over history education at all levels in the state. His doctoral students taught in the normal schools, which later became state colleges, in the developing institution now known as UCLA, then called the southern branch of the University of California, and in the Berkeley history department.[31] Although headquartered in California, Bolton's empire was continental in scope. Most of his doctoral students took university positions in western states as well as California, and some of them found professorships east of the Mississippi where they taught courses that reflected Bolton's point of view—the history of the Americas. But there was much more to Bolton's dominion than university professorships. His doctoral students held high positions in the National Park Service, the National Archives, the Rockefeller Foundation, and the State Department. Bolton himself consulted for the State Department and Park Service.[32] Countless history teachers, perhaps numbering in the thousands, took his classes as undergraduates and MA students.[33] More than three hundred MA students studied under Bolton. For twenty years he taught as many as 1,200 undergraduates at a time in his two-semester course, History of the Americas.[34] How many of those students became schoolteachers is impossible to know.

Perhaps the best evidence of Bolton's influence on the teaching of American history at the college level is the popularity of his textbooks and syllabus, which sold well and remained in print for years.[35] Finally,

Bolton's transformation of the teaching of history in California's public schools, though less well understood than his impact on university curriculum, could be seen as the foundation of his professional empire. Bolton's version of California history, fantasy heritage and all, was unavoidable for the state's students in elementary school, high school, community college, state college, and the University of California. It is no fantasy to say that I and other children of California were influenced by Bolton from kindergarten to the PhD. Thus, the Bolton historical industry was horizontally and vertically integrated.

Bolton and the Public Schools

A closer look at Bolton's experience as a schoolteacher suggests something about his comprehensive view of history education. Before attending college Bolton taught elementary grades in a Wisconsin country school. He followed in the footsteps of his older brother Frederick, the first of the large Bolton clan to attend college, and greatly admired by Herbert. Both brothers attended Wisconsin Normal School and then became high school teachers and principals before enrolling in the University of Wisconsin. Herbert eventually took the PhD in history, and Frederick took his doctorate in what we would today call educational psychology. Their correspondence shows that Herbert was reading much of the bibliography that Frederick was studying as well as Frederick's publications. The brothers returned to Wisconsin Normal School as professors, where they taught pedagogy as well as other subjects to aspiring teachers. Both young men turned down presidencies of normal colleges before rising to the top of their respective fields as research scholars. Frederick eventually headed the education programs at the University of Iowa and the University of Washington.[36]

John Bannon, Herbert E. Bolton's first biographer, paid little attention to Bolton's interest in teacher education and school texts. Bannon, who was a doctoral student of Bolton's and an influential historian in his own right, treated Bolton's experience as a teacher as a mere preface to his more important accomplishments as a university professor.[37] Nor did he give any attention to the elementary and high school teachers Bolton taught. Writing a grade-school text was not incidental to Bolton's career aspirations but was part of his larger plan to influence history at all levels. His first history professorship was at the University of Texas where he was a colleague of Eugene C. Barker. The two historians published a source reader of Texas history that was intended for high school and college use.[38] In 1912, after Bolton had gone to California, Barker and two

Herbert Bolton at age sixteen or seventeen in Wisconsin. Courtesy of The Bancroft Library, University of California, Berkeley.

University of Texas colleagues published a textbook of Texas history in an effort to displace the text that then dominated the state's schools,[39] a filiopietistic text first published in 1888 by Mrs. Percy V. Pennybacker, a former schoolteacher who was well connected in the state Democratic party.[40] Pennybacker, who was not about to lose course adoptions to the university upstarts, mounted a political campaign that charged that a "*northern publishing* company" was trying to displace her book.[41] Barker's wife Matilda asked Bolton to solicit letters from out of state, which he was happy to do. Such were the politics of textbook publication in Texas but the game was worth the candle. Ultimately Barker and his friends prevailed and their text supplanted Pennybacker's "sensational clap trap," as Matilda Barker called it.[42]

Professors like Barker and Bolton published school texts because they thought that university professors should be the arbiters of the state's historical narrative. They aimed to replace the texts written by amateurs such as Pennybacker with their own writings because the professors believed that their work was more accurate. This was part of a general movement toward professionalization in the early twentieth century. Leading members of the historical profession worked to see that PhD-holding historians occupied professorial chairs. Replacing unreliable, factually suspect history with scientifically researched "objective" history was a part of that process.[43]

Yet, there were risks in knocking down clay-footed idols, as the Barker-Pennybacker controversy shows. Some people (Californians as well as Texans) preferred history that gave their ancestors unreserved praise.[44] The Bolton and Adams text did not risk political criticism in California. Their preface fulsomely declared that "the authors have emphasized those qualities of courage, self-sacrifice, and service which have been typified in the State's great men. The devotion and heroism of the early [Franciscan] Fathers, the boldness of the Vigilantes, the initiative of the pioneers, the generosity of men prominent in later years—all contribute to that type of citizenship toward which it is hoped all users of this book will strive as an ideal." This encouragement of child vigilantism aside, one must acknowledge the forthright manner in which the authors promoted the worship of California's heroes. As it turned out, California's modern heroes, as identified in *California's Story*, included people like Bancroft as well as David Starr Jordan and Benjamin Ide Wheeler, the presidents of Stanford and the University of California who had hired Bolton and Adams, along with industrialists, entrepreneurs, scientists, artists, and contemporary public figures like Hiram Johnson and Herbert Hoover.

The fantasy heritage survived intact in the Bolton-Adams text. Missionaries, especially Father Serra, were explorer heroes. During the Mexican era, "Spanish ranchers had the finest ranches and country houses," where they lived "in ease and abundance."[45] The Mexican-American War came and went without apparent cause, but with a good effect—the United States' acquisition of California. There were a few interesting twists in the gold rush story. So many men went to California that some people feared that the eastern seaboard would have insufficient workers to staff its industries. Happily, failed revolutions and famine drove German and Irish immigrants out of Europe and into America. "Thus, the east got these new immigrants," the authors explained, "while California got the pick of the energetic, daring, young Americans."[46] There was no question about who got the best end of that deal.

As promised in the preface, the book portrayed the San Francisco vigilantes in the best possible light. The leaders of the first and second vigilance committees were presented as disinterested men who wanted only to restore good government to the chaotic San Francisco scene. After they hanged several bad men and whipped and banished others, "San Francisco was a quiet, orderly city."[47] As Bolton and Adams explained, the only way to "have good government all the time was to be on the watch all the time against evil doers."[48] A few salutary hangings and floggings were merely an illustrative lesson in American civics for the children of California.

As might be expected, authorial responsibilities were divided neatly in half. Bolton contributed the story of the Spanish and Mexican eras while Adams wrote about everything that followed. Nevertheless, Bolton took editorial responsibility for the entire text. Noticing that their writing styles were decidedly different, Bolton "took the bull by the horns" and, without Adams's consent, rewrote his manuscript "with the aim of adjusting the style and form a little bit more closely to the part which I had written."[49] The short history of the San Francisco vigilance committees conformed to the analysis in Mary Floyd Williams's book, which Bolton had edited for publication by the University of California Press.[50]

One of Bolton and Adams's goals in writing *California's Story* was to make some money, a common if seldom-realized object of history professors. Bolton was well paid by the professional standards of the day, but he had seven children and always needed to supplement his university salary. In addition to their pecuniary aims, they sought to establish themselves as the accepted authorities on California history among the state's teachers, students, and their parents. If they shaded their history a little on the side of promoting the dearly held beliefs of Anglo Californians, perhaps the result would be stronger support for the universities that employed them. Bolton had a higher goal than money and fame. He intended to instruct children in the fundamental facts of California's Hispanic history to counter Bancroft's description of a half-civilized society. Over one hundred highly illustrated pages tell the story of the Spanish and Mexican influence on California, from the time of Cortés to the coming of Frémont. Watered down it may have been, but Bolton gave the children of California a positive history of the state's Hispanic past.

Legacy

Upon his arrival in California Bolton found a fantasy heritage with favorable images of Hispanic and Anglo pioneers in place. He gently modified the existing stereotypes to complement his own contributions to Spanish colonial history. His teaching and texts established his commanding authority while promoting a more positive (but partly fanciful) version of the Hispanic past while leaving Anglo fantasies untouched. Fantasy was not Bolton's aim, but a means to an end. He sought material and professional success and attained it. Bolton's professional empire consisting of ideas, texts, and disciples in schools, universities, and public service survived as an artifact of his professional ambition. So passed the fantasy heritage from generation to generation.

Now we are left with an irony. The romantic views of early California that Bolton purveyed in order to buttress his claims to scholarly authority have long since been called into question and now serve to indict the professional reputation that he so assiduously cultivated. Was it necessary for Bolton to pander to popular prejudices about California history in order to do big things in California? Bolton thought so and he was not alone. In his day it was common for university presidents and professors alike to cater to their institutions' constituencies.[51] And with public support Bolton accomplished a great deal for himself, the University of California, his students, the public schools, and the profession of history. Bolton's important and lasting ideas about hemispheric history and the Borderlands as a cultural meeting place speak strongly to today's generation of historians who seek to explain the past in multicultural and transnational terms. We may fairly criticize Bolton for his shortcomings, but at least he left us with an enviable record of scholarship that sits alongside some of his now questionable methods of achieving it. Bolton's career holds lessons for today's historians. Like Bolton, we live in a world of competing historical identities. We should consider how those identities impinge on our work and what that might mean for the future of California's past.

Notes

1   Lisbeth Haas, *Conquests and Historical Identities in California, 1769–1936* (Berkeley, Calif.: University of California Press, 1995), 1–12. On Indian identity and adjustment to mission life, see Steven W. Hackel, *Children of Coyote, Missionaries of Saint Francis: Indian-Spanish Relations in Colonial California, 1769–1850* (Chapel Hill: University of North Carolina Press, 2005), 1–12. For a

hemispheric perspective on Indian history and new identities, see David J. Weber, *Bárbaros: Spaniards and Their Savages in the Age of Enlightenment* (New Haven, Conn.: Yale University Press, 2005).

2   John Francis Bannon, *Herbert Eugene Bolton: The Historian and the Man, 1870–1953* (Tucson, Ariz.: University of Arizona Press, 1978), 12–86.

3   For appraisals of Bolton's work, see Bannon, *Herbert Eugene Bolton*, 255–58; John Francis Bannon, "Herbert Eugene Bolton—Western Historian," *Western Historical Quarterly* 2 (1971): 261–82; David J. Weber, "Turner, the Boltonians, and the Borderlands," *American Historical Review* 91 (1986): 66–81; Donald E. Worcester, "Herbert Eugene Bolton: The Making of a Western Historian," in *Writing Western History: Essays on Major Western Historians*, ed. Richard W. Etulain (Albuquerque: University of New Mexico Press, 1991), 193–213; David J. Langum, "Herbert E. Bolton," in *Historians of the American Frontier: A Bio-bibliographical Sourcebook*, ed. John R. Wunder (New York: Greenwood Press, 1988), 130–46; John W. Caughey, "Herbert Eugene Bolton," in Wilbur R. Jacobs, John W. Caughey, and Joe B. Frantz, *Turner, Bolton, and Webb: Three Historians of the American Frontier* (Seattle: University of Washington Press, 1965): 41–67; David J. Weber, "Blood of Martyrs, Blood of Indians: Toward a More Balanced View of Spanish Missions in Seventeenth-Century North America," in *Archaeological and Historical Perspectives on the Spanish Borderlands East*, vol. 2, *Columbian Consequences*, ed. David Hurst Thomas (Washington, D.C.: Smithsonian Institution Press, 1990), 429–48; David J. Weber, "The Idea of the Spanish Borderlands," in *The Spanish Borderlands in Pan-American Perspective*, vol. 3, *Columbian Consequences*, ed. David Hurst Thomas (Washington, D.C.: Smithsonian Institution Press, 1991), 3–20; James A. Sandos, "Junípero Serra's Canonization and the Historical Record," *American Historical Review* 93 (1988): 1253–69; Albert L. Hurtado, "Herbert E. Bolton, Racism and American History," *Pacific Historical Review* 62 (1993): 127–42; "Parkmanizing the Spanish Borderlands: Bolton, Turner, and the Historians' World," *Western Historical Quarterly* 26 (1995): 149–67; and "Romancing the West in the Twentieth Century: The Politics of History in a Contested Region," *Western Historical Quarterly* 32 (2001): 417–35.

4   Frederick Jackson Turner, "The Significance of the Frontier in American History," in *The Frontier in American History* (New York: H. Holt and Company, 1920), chap. 1.

5   Herbert Eugene Bolton, "Defensive Spanish Expansion and the Significance of the Borderlands," and "The Epic of Greater America," in *Bolton and the Spanish Borderlands*, ed. John Francis Bannon (Norman: University of Oklahoma Press, 1964), 32–64, 301–32; Hubert Eugene Bolton, *The Spanish Borderlands: A Chronicle of Old Florida and the Southwest* (New Haven, Conn.: Yale University Press, 1921). On Bolton's ideas about the Americas, see Russell M. Magnaghi, *Herbert E. Bolton and the Historiography of the Americas* (Westport, Conn.: Greenwood Press, 1998).

6   Carey McWilliams deserves credit for exposing California's "fantasy heritage"; *North from Mexico: The Spanish-Speaking People of the United States* (Philadelphia, 1949; reprint, New York: Greenwood Press, 1968): 35–47 (page citations

are to the reprint edition). Negative stereotypes of Hispanic people coexist with the positive fantasy heritage. See David J. Weber, "'Scarce More than Apes': Historical Roots of Anglo-American Stereotypes of Mexicans," in *New Spain's Far Northern Frontier: Essays on Spain in the American West, 1540–1821*, ed. David J. Weber (Albuquerque: University of New Mexico Press, 1979): 293–307; David J. Weber, "Here Rests Juan Espinosa: Toward a Clearer Look at the Image of the 'Indolent' Californios," *Western Historical Quarterly* 10 (1979): 61–68. See also William Deverell, *Whitewashed Adobe: The Rise of Los Angeles and the Remaking of Its Mexican Past* (Berkeley: University of California Press, 2004): 49–90.

7   Albert L. Hurtado, *Intimate Frontiers: Sex, Gender, and Culture in Old California* (Albuquerque: University of New Mexico Press, 1999): 133–41; Kenneth N. Owens, introduction to *Riches for All: The California Gold Rush and the World*, ed. Owens (Lincoln: University of Nebraska Press, 2002): 1–3.

8   George S. Craft, *California State University, Sacramento, The First Forty Years: 1947–1987* ([Sacramento, Calif.]: Hornet Foundation, 1987), 17.

9   Hubert Howe Bancroft, *California Pastoral*, vol. 34, *The Works of Hubert Howe Bancroft* (San Francisco: The History Company, 1888), 168. Sherburne F. Cook published his pioneering history of the bleak demography of California missions in the 1940s; his study was reprinted as *The Conflict between California Indians and White Civilization*, with a foreword by Woodrow Borah and Robert F. Heizer (Berkeley: University of California Press, 1976). Recent studies have revised Cook in important ways without challenging the basic premise of demographic decline: Hackel, *Children of Coyote*, 65–125; James A. Sandos, *Converting California: Indians and Franciscans in the Missions* (New Haven, Conn.: Yale University Press, 2004), 111–27; Randall Milliken, *A Time of Little Choice: The Disintegration of Tribal Culture in the San Francisco Bay Area, 1769–1810* (Menlo Park, Calif.: Ballena Press, 1995), 4, 67n1.

10 Bancroft, *California Pastoral*, 179, 180, 179.

11 Weber, "Here Rests Juan Espinosa"; Weber, "'Scarce More than Apes.'"

12 Bancroft, *California Pastoral*, 179.

13 Frank Soulé, John H. Gihon, and James Nisbet, *Annals of San Francisco* (New York: Appleton, 1854), 666.

14 Helen Hunt Jackson, *Ramona: A Story* (Boston: Roberts Bros., 1884).

15 Charles F. Lummis, *Land of Poco Tiempo* (New York: Charles Scribner's Sons, 1893); Lummis, *Spanish Pioneers and the California Missions* (Chicago: A. C. McClurg & Co., 1929).

16 Engelhardt, *The Franciscans in California* (Harbor Springs, Mich.: Holy Childhood Indian School, 1897); Engelhardt, *Missions and Missionaries of California*, 4 vols. (San Francisco: James H. Barry Co., 1908–15).

17 Mass tourism in California began with the railroad. See Earl Pomeroy, *In Search of the Golden West: The Tourist in Western America* (New York: Knopf, 1957); and Richard J. Orsi, *Sunset Limited: The Southern Pacific Railroad and the Development of the American West* (Berkeley: University of California Press, 2005), 157–59.

18 Hurtado, "Romancing the West."
19 Peter Thomas Conmy, *The Origins and Purposes of the Native Sons and Native Daughters of the Golden West* (San Francisco: n.p., 1956), 9–10.
20 John F. Davis, "University Fellowships in Pacific Coast History," *The California Outlook*, April 19, 1913, 7.
21 Bolton's papers are found in the Herbert Eugene Bolton Papers, BANC MSS C-B 840, Bancroft Library, Berkeley, California. His letters are in part 2 of the collection, under incoming correspondence (organized alphabetically by correspondents' last names or the name of the organization; cited below as BP In) and outgoing correspondence (organized chronologically; cited below as BP Out). Transcript of meeting of the Native Sons of the Golden West, otherwise unidentified, [1922], BP In, Native Sons of the Golden West.
22 John F. Davis to Bolton, May 11, 1927; John F. Davis to Bolton, January 12, 1929; John F. Davis to Bolton, March 28, 1929; John F. Davis to Bolton, April 15, 1929; John F. Davis to John T. Regan, [filed with Davis] October 28, 1929, all in BP In. See also Bolton's report to the Native Sons in Bolton to Davis, April 12, 1929, BP Out.
23 These figures are derived from "A Bibliography of the Historical Writings of the Students of Herbert Eugene Bolton," in *Greater America: Essays in Honor of Herbert Eugene Bolton*, ed. Adele Ogden, Engel Sluiter, and Gregory Crampton (Berkeley: University of California Press, 1945), 549–672. The figures are as follows: Borderlands (not California) 132 (32 percent); Spanish and Mexican California 44 (11 percent); Anglo California 89 (22 percent); and American West/Frontier/Other 145 (35 percent).
24 For a critique of Bolton's sentimental version of Spanish colonial history, see David J. Weber, *The Spanish Frontier in North America* (New Haven, Conn.: Yale University Press, 1992): 7–9, 353–59.
25 Bolton, *The Spanish Borderlands*, 294; Albert L. Hurtado, introduction to Herbert Eugene Bolton, *The Spanish Borderlands: A Chronicle of Old Florida and the Southwest* (1921; reprint, Albuquerque: University of New Mexico Press, 1996), ix–xxix; Hurtado, "Parkmanizing the Spanish Borderlands," 149–67.
26 Hurtado, *Intimate Frontiers*, 1–44.
27 Bolton, *Spanish Borderlands* (1921), 295.
28 Bolton to Edward Hyatt, February 27, 1915, BP Out.
29 Bolton to Adams, March 16, 1920, BP Out.
30 Boston, 1922.
31 Ogden, Sluiter, and Crampton, *Greater America*, 549–672, contains a list of Bolton's graduate students with employers and bibliographies.
32 Bannon, *Bolton*, 208. The careers of Bolton's students may be glimpsed in their vitas that are included in Ogden, Sluiter, and Crampton, *Greater America*, 549–672. Bolton's connection with the National Park Service began in 1917 with his friendship with Horace Albright, who eventually became Director of the National Park Service; see Albright to Bolton, June 4, 1917, BP In.
33 Ibid.

34 Magnaghi, *Bolton and the Historiography of the Americas*, 55–56.

35 Herbert Eugene Bolton and Thomas Maitland Marshall, *The Colonization of North America, 1492–1783* (New York: Macmillan, 1920); Bolton, *The Spanish Borderlands*; Herbert Eugene Bolton, *History of the Americas: A Syllabus with Maps* (Boston: Ginn, 1928; 2nd ed., 1935).

36 Details of Bolton's career as a teacher and principal are found in correspondence with his brother Frederick, Bolton Family Papers, BANC MSS C-B 841, Bancroft Library (hereafter cited as BFP). For examples of their letters about normal school education, teaching, and education in general, see Bolton to Frederick, November 24, 1889, December 4, 1889, April 17, 1891, October 18, 1891, and passim BFP.

37 John Francis Bannon, *The Spanish Borderlands Frontier, 1513–1821* (New York: Holt, Rinehart, and Winston, 1970).

38 Herbert Eugene Bolton and Eugene C. Barker, *With the Makers of Texas: A Source Reader in Texas History* (Austin, Tex.: Gammel-Statesman Publishing, 1904).

39 Eugene C. Barker, Charles Shirley Potts, and Charles W. Ramsdell, *A School History of Texas* (Chicago: Row, Peterson & Company, 1912).

40 Mrs. Percy V. Pennybacker, *A New History of Texas for Schools, also for General Reading and for Teachers Preparing themselves for Examination* (Tyler, Tex.: Published for the author, 1888); The Handbook of Texas Online, s.v. "Pennybacker, Anna J. Hardwicke" (by Stacy A. Cordery), http://www.tshaonline.org/handbook/online/articles/PP/fpe30.html.

41 Matilda Barker to Bolton, August 5, 1912, BP In, emphasis in original.

42 Matilda Barker to Bolton, August 5, 1912, and August 17, 1912, BP In.

43 Peter Novick, *That Noble Dream: The "Objectivity Question" and the American Historical Profession* (Cambridge: Cambridge University Press, 1988): 198–200.

44 Ibid., 198.

45 Bolton and Adams, *California's Story*, 81.

46 Ibid., 119.

47 Ibid., 135.

48 Ibid., 137.

49 Bolton to Adams, March 16, 1920, BP Out.

50 Mary Floyd Williams, *History of the San Francisco Committee of Vigilance of 1851: A Study of Social Control on the California Frontier in the Days of the Gold Rush* (Berkeley: University of California Press, 1921). Bolton did the editorial work on Williams's manuscript in 1919. Bolton to John F. Davis, September 22, 1919, BP Out.

51 Hurtado, "Romancing the West."

DAVID J. WEBER

A New Borderlands Historiography: Constructing and Negotiating the Boundaries of Identity

Historians in Latin America occasionally preface the titles of their essays with words that suggest their tentative nature. Titles might begin with the phrase "toward a history" (*hacia una historia*), suggesting that a full-fledged history is on the horizon and they are still groping their way toward it, or "notes for the history" (*notas para la historia*), signaling that their essay is so tentative that it does not add up to a history. A similarly modest prelude to the title of this essay would be entirely appropriate, for it is tentative and decidedly not comprehensive. My focus is on the ways in which American historians have treated the subject of identity in the Spanish-Mexican Borderlands in the years before 1848. Since other contributors to this book examine California, my assignment was to look at the other southwestern borderlands in the Spanish and Mexican periods, and I've concentrated on New Mexico, where the literature is richest.

My subject is new historiography, but we must understand the old to recognize what is new. The first generations of Borderlands historians, from the first decade of the twentieth century through the 1960s, seldom used forms of the word "identity." When they did, it was not in the existential sense that we use the word today but rather to associate an individual with a name, as in, "the culprit was identified as José," or to link an individual with a group, as in, "the culprit was identified as José, an Apache." This is not to say, however, that earlier historians of the Spanish-Mexican Borderlands failed to discuss the characteristics of groups or individuals. They did, but rather than the word identity they used expressions like regional or national character, character traits, or the word culture. This is clear in the work of Herbert Eugene Bolton, who founded the field of Borderlands history in the United States. In much the same way that Frederick Jackson Turner, the great historian of the Anglo-American frontier, sought to explain the forces that shaped *American* character, Bolton tried to explain *Spanish* character. In his seminal survey, *The Spanish Borderlands: A Chronicle of Old Florida and the Southwest* (1921), Bolton never used identity or identities to refer to the characteristics of a group or an individual. Instead, he used character and culture.[1]

Character, culture, and identity may not be synonyms, but they can do much of the same work if we define identity as "the set of behavioral or personal characteristics by which an individual is recognizable as a member of a group," and if we define character as "the combination of qualities or features that distinguishes one person, group, or thing from another," and if we define culture as "those patterns, traits, and products considered as the expression of a particular period, class, community, or population."[2] I know this is dangerous ground. The words culture and character are so freighted with meaning that some anthropologists have used them with caution, just as some historians of the West once avoided the word frontier.

One can infer from Bolton's book that he believed, as did Frederick Jackson Turner, that a group's place of origin shaped its character and that national character might be modified by occupational or environmental influences. Bolton's Spanish explorers arrived in America driven by what he called the "ideals" of "adventure, conquest, piety, wealth" (2). Over time Spaniards brought their civilization to the northern reaches of New Spain, a region, Bolton said, that Spain "maintained chiefly to hold the country against foreign intruders and against the inroads of savage tribes" (xii). As with Turner, then, Bolton imagined a line between civilization and savagery.

When Bolton stood back and took a broad view of his line between civilization and savagery, he found positive character traits on the Spanish side and negative traits on the Indian side. When Bolton looked closer at the Spanish side of the line, he divided Spaniards into different groups, such as devout clergy, brave conquistadors, and "nobles and gentry," whom he described as scorning "all labor and trade" (2). Bolton also detected regional influences on Spaniards, beginning in Iberia. The Spanish kingdom of Asturias, he noted approvingly, was a place where "the earth and sky bear men who are honest, not tricksters, truthful, not babblers, most faithful to the King, generous, friendly, light-hearted, and merry, daring and warlike" (140).[3]

Wherever they came from in Iberia, however, Bolton's Spaniards, like Turner's Anglo Americans, underwent changes induced by physical and social conditions on American frontiers. Bolton concluded, for example, that California, with its benign climate, productive soil, and abundant Indian labor, discouraged the Californios from hard work, and that an absence of books left them intellectually impoverished (200–201). Although they lived aimless lives on horseback, Bolton tells us, the Californios were skillful *caballeros*, gracious, and hospitable. "The beauties and graces of the Spanish character flowered there [in California]; and the harsher traits were modified" (294). In offering this interpretation, Bolton reflected a viewpoint that had come into full flower in California a generation before. As historian Hubert Howe Bancroft had expressed it in 1888: "never before or since was there a spot in America where life was a long happy holiday, where there was less labor, less care or trouble."[4]

Like scholars before and after him, Bolton recognized that the character traits he ascribed to the Californios could have social and economic consequences in his own day and immediate consequences for Bolton's own work (an idea that Albert Hurtado develops in his essay in this volume). Bolton hoped to broaden the scope of U.S. history to include the Spanish Borderlands, but to do that he needed to present his readers with Spaniards who lacked the "harsher traits" of their countrymen. He also believed that he needed to present to his readers Spanish explorers and missionaries who could serve as credible "heroes" and take their place alongside Anglo-American "heroes."[5] Heroes need villains, of course, to render them heroic, so Bolton provided them with "savages"— an unsurprising foil for a historian of his generation. Since Bolton was writing for an Anglo-American audience, he also drew comparisons between the Spanish character and the Anglo-American character. Anglos, he said, were "possessed by the energy of labor." His "mellower" Spaniards were not (205, 204).

Bolton's student John Francis Bannon took up that same comparative question and made it more explicit in his overview of *The Spanish Borderlands Frontier: 1513–1821* (1970).[6] Like Bolton, Bannon used the words culture or character rather than identity or identities. Similarly, Oakah Jones, writing in the late 1970s in *Los Paisanos: Spanish Settlers on the Northern Frontier of New Spain*, explained how the northern frontier of New Spain influenced Hispanics who came north from Mexico without using the word identity.[7] Jones suggested that, as a result of isolation and threats from Indians and foreigners, Spanish frontiersmen "developed personal characteristics and an entire culture that differed markedly from those elsewhere in the viceroyalty . . . they became more self-reliant, more individualistic, less class conscious, and more conservative in their political outlook than the people of central New Spain."[8]

In explaining how the northern frontier of New Spain influenced Mexican character, Jones addressed a question that had engaged other historians of his generation, including various historians of Mexico such as Vito Alessio Robles, Woodrow Borah, François Chevalier, Enrique Florescano, Philip Wayne Powell, and Silvio Zavala, along with historians who focused quite specifically on the Borderlands, such as C. Alan Hutchinson, Jack Forbes, and Alicia Tjarks.[9] All of these writers saw character as a fluid state that changes or adapts to physical and social environments. In the 1960s, for example, historians like Jack Forbes and Alicia Tjarks described racial categories in the Borderlands as so fluid that a person could begin life as a black, then become a mulatto, a *mestizo*, or even an *español*, but neither Forbes nor Tjarks used the word identity. Rather, they employed race and ethnicity to describe the transformations that Tjarks termed "ethnic 'migration.'"[10] Historians also understood that specific individuals took on multiple identities or moved back and forth across cultures. We have, for example, one Diego Romero, who journeyed to the Great Plains from New Mexico in 1660 and took an Apache wife, as his father had before him—a story that John Kessell told in 1978 without using the word identity.[11]

Changing Identities

Borderlands historians, then, have long described "identities in formation" (the subject of this volume), without using the word identity. By the 1970s, however, when Kessell was writing about Diego Romero and Jones was writing about *los paisanos*, Borderlands historians had begun to use identity along with character and culture. I find it, for example, in my *Foreigners in Their Native Land: Historical Roots of the Mexican Americans* (1973), and in Elizabeth John's broad survey of the New Mexico, Texas, and Louisiana Borderlands, *Storms Brewed in Other Men's Worlds: The Confrontation of Indians, Spanish, and French in the Southwest, 1540–1795* (1975).[12] Indeed, beginning in the 1970s, if not before, historians of the Spanish-Mexican Borderlands gradually joined other historians in using identity in a variety of forms: political identity, religious identity, social identity, cultural identity, ethnic identity, class identity, racial identity, local identity, regional identity, national identity, collective identity, historical identity, gender identity, legal identity, partial identity, contradictory identity, overlapping identity, strategic identity, alternative identities, elusive identities, and no doubt others that have escaped my attention.

There are doubtless many reasons why we began to embrace the word identity, but much stemmed from the "delayed impact" of the social sciences and popular culture, where it had gained currency,[13] and from historians' growing interest in examining the past from the perspectives of different ethnic groups and subgroups.¹⁴ Elizabeth John, for example, had sought to tell the story of the Borderlands from Indian viewpoints—from "other men's worlds"—while the generation that preceded her, as represented by her mentor, Max Moorhead, tended to devote more of its attention to Spaniards. In his book *The Presidio: Bastion of the Spanish Borderlands*, published in 1975, the same year as John's *Storms*, Moorhead used the word identity only once, and then merely to explain how military officers needed experience to discern "the whereabouts of water holes, the distance from one place to another, the identity of tracks, and the sites most suitable for an ambush."¹⁵ John, on the other hand, used the word with some frequency, and in passages like this: "Attrition by war, starvation, or disease drove dwindling groups to merge for survival. Cherished identities blurred and vanished."¹⁶ Where Moorhead employed the word to describe something elusive or hidden, John used it to characterize something internal to a people.

Well before historians began to use identity to refer to the characteristics of an individual or group, the word had found its way into Borderlands literature in the work of anthropologists. In his influential *Cycles of Conquest: The Impact of Spain, Mexico, and the United States on the Indians of the Southwest, 1533–1960* (1962), Edward Spicer employed identity in one of the ways we use it today, to reflect a group's belief that its members are a distinct people, and he drew a distinction between culture and identity. Some native peoples, he argued, had lost their customs and beliefs as a result of the "cycles of conquest" carried out by Spain, Mexico, and the United States, yet their "sense of identity was not at all proportional to the number of aboriginal traditions persisting. The processes of cultural assimilation were in fact distinct from the processes of group identification."¹⁷

Anthropologist William Merrill once noted with admirable clarity: "Identity is one of the few concepts to have made the transition from the social sciences to popular culture with its technical definitions largely intact. Academic and popular views of the concept of identity agree that identity is, in essence . . . who we think we are and who others think we are . . . identity is the product of the interplay between these insider and outsider perspectives, and that is subject to change as the circumstances change with which an individual or group operates."¹⁸

Merrill's and Spicer's definitions reveal some of what is new about the way that Borderlands historians have come to consider identity. First, as noted, historians now pay more attention to the perspectives of insiders. Where an earlier generation of historians attributed character traits or cultural traits to people in the past, the present generation seems more interested in how people in the past understood their own character or culture and why. Historians try, then, to see historical peoples' worlds as they saw them, to understand their *mentalité*. Indeed, this volume's editor, Steven W. Hackel, has called on us to do more of this: "I hope that at the heart of the next generation of scholarship on early California is a study of individual identity—how Indians, Franciscans, soldiers, and settlers in California understood themselves, not how they were understood by others."[19] (Lisbeth Haas's essay on the Luiseño Pablo Tac, in this volume, suggests that gaining access to Indians' understanding of themselves in early California is likely to remain extraordinarily challenging.)

Second, historians have come to look more closely at the ways in which identity has been formed, maintained, or transformed through interaction between groups. Here, directly or indirectly, historians have fallen under the influence of anthropologist Fredrik Barth and his assertion in 1969 of the importance of boundaries in establishing ethnic identities. As he put it, it is "the ethnic *boundary* that defines the group, not the cultural stuff that it encloses" (italics in original).[20] To put it another way, ethnic identity is constructed and negotiated as groups interact with one another and thus is determined by difference. Often that means ethnocentrically exalting one's own group by diminishing another. As sociologist Pablo Vila has explained succinctly, ethnic identities "all too often depend precisely on a devalued 'other.'"[21] Indeed, the importance of the "other" to the concept of dependency is suggested powerfully by the title of a recent book on identity: *To Exclude in Order to Be* (2005).[22]

Although Borderlands historians pay more attention to insiders' perspectives and look more closely at identity formation than did their predecessors, it could be argued that they have not so much departed from previous scholarship as elaborated on it. Going back to Turner, who defined the frontier as a social space where civilization met savagery, contact with the "other" has been a key to understanding the formation of what he called character and what scholars now call group identity. Nonetheless, recent scholarship on the Borderlands has deepened our understanding of how contact with the "other" shapes identity and has shown us that identity is even more mutable and variable than earlier historians had supposed. This seems clear from a sample of recent books.[23]

First, Ramón Gutiérrez's widely acclaimed *When Jesus Came, the Corn Mothers Went Away: Marriage, Sexuality, and Power in New Mexico, 1500–1846* (1991)[24] brought the sophisticated scholarship of colonial Latin America and the theoretical tools of the social sciences to the Borderlands province of New Mexico and asked new questions about who had honor and who lacked it.²⁵ How did one obtain honor, or lose it? How did race and class confer or deny honor? If, as William Merrill defined it, identity is "the product of the interplay between . . . insider and outsider perspectives," Gutiérrez provided us with plentiful examples. He reminded us, for example, that a group's or an individual's honor required someone else's dishonor. New Mexico's españoles measured their purity of blood against the impurity of others. Conveniently, they had among them the detribalized Indians, or *genízaros*, whom they defined as impure and lacking in honor. Where Bolton and Bannon sought to explain occupational groups—soldiers, missionaries, settlers—Gutiérrez exposed deep divisions within these groups. Where Bolton and Bannon put a gloss on Spaniards to make them palatable to Anglo-American tastes, Gutiérrez revealed status-seeking and hypocrisy.

In *Thread of Blood: Colonialism, Revolution, and Gender on Mexico's Northern Frontier*, which appeared in 1995, anthropologist Ana Alonso similarly argued that the "other" shaped Spaniards' identities, but in her case study, Apaches rather than genízaros constituted the "other." Alonso focused on the Chihuahuan village of Namiquipa, where she found that peons received arms and land in exchange for keeping Apaches at bay in the late eighteenth and early nineteenth centuries. The males in the village became farmer-warriors, developing a sense of ethnic identity that equated honor with land and autonomy and a pride that had less to do with material wealth than with their sense of themselves as the "civilized" opposites of "barbarous" Indians.²⁶

In his examination of community formation in Spanish San Antonio, published in 1995, Frank de la Teja gave us a fresh, nuanced look at divisions *within* this Hispanic community where subgroups of Hispanics constituted the "other." San Antonio consisted of three discrete groups through much of the 1700s—the founding settler-soldiers, neighboring missionaries, and late-arriving Canary Islanders—each with its own identity and each defining itself against the other. De la Teja explored the circumstances that brought the three groups together by the end of the eighteenth century to form a single community with a common identity.²⁷

Ross Frank's book *From Settler to Citizen: New Mexican Economic Development and the Creation of a Vecino Society, 1750–1820* (2000) similarly explained how Hispanics in New Mexico closed ranks as an economic boom in the late 1700s allowed them to rise from the status of struggling settlers to prosperous citizens. As their wealth increased and their numbers grew, they began to appropriate Pueblo lands and take over Pueblo pottery and textile production. At the same time, the racially based caste system that had divided the Hispanic community began to flatten out and Hispanics came to redefine themselves "in contradistinction to the Pueblo Indians." Pueblo Indians, then, took the place of lower-strata Hispanics to become the economically and socially subordinate "other."[28]

Changing identities also characterized Native American societies, as vividly described in Gary Clayton Anderson's *The Indian Southwest, 1580–1830: Ethnogenesis and Reinvention* (1999). Anderson explained, for example, how Apaches came to the south plains as small bands, augmented their numbers by absorbing members of other tribes, and coalesced into larger and more powerful social and political units that could take the offensive against other Indian peoples and against Spaniards. Anderson gives the San Antonio missions a new twist by portraying them as sanctuaries that gave Indians space to refashion their identity and then "return to a more mobile life in the countryside."[29] Missionaries, of course, saw missions as instruments of change that would convert Indians from heathens to Christians. Anderson, in contrast, sees missions as the crucible of a different type of identity transformation. He describes the missions as loci of ethnogenesis.[30] Herded into missions by force or due to the debilitating effects of disease or warfare, Indians from different cultural or linguistic groups came together in the closed mission environment to form new ethnic groups—that is, people who forged a new, shared identity.

James Brooks, in his rich *Captives and Cousins: Slavery, Kinship, and Community in the Southwest Borderlands*, published in 2002, applied the process of identity transformation to Indians and Hispanics alike. "Identities," he wrote, "like Comanche, Kiowa, Apache, Navajo, Ute, Pueblo, Spanish American, and Hispano seem timeless and unquestioned in much historical literature." These identities, however, changed in the crucible of Borderlands dynamics: "ethnicities in the Southwest were often a matter of biological interchange, strategic reconstruction, and political invention, as sexual enslavement, market penetration, and state pacification policies closed some avenues of identity while fostering others."[31] In Brooks's formulation, Spanish and Native American identities intersected, overlapped, and mimicked one another, blurring the lines between Indians and Spaniards. The same person might abandon one identity for another and cross seemingly unbridgeable chasms of culture.

Of course, scholars have long known that no clear line separated Spaniard and Indian or colonizer and colonized. Most Spaniards in the Borderlands had Indian and African blood and were products of colonization as well as instruments of colonization. But Brooks heightened our awareness of blurred ethnic and racial lines, and he was not alone. Indeed, an Argentine ethnohistorian recently suggested that our growing understanding of the many varieties of people along the continuum between Indians and Spaniards needed a new vocabulary. The term "interethnic relations," he said, was no longer commodious enough to cover relationships on the frontiers of Argentina; he suggested that "social relations" would be more descriptive of historical reality.[32]

Our deeper understanding of cross-cultural and cross-racial social relations has resulted, in part, from work on smaller scales, right down to the family level, where identities can also be multiple and fluid. Consider, for example, the way we understand the Pueblo Revolt. For an earlier generation of historians the Revolt was a struggle between Pueblos and Spaniards and those Pueblos who allied themselves with Spaniards. If one looks closer, however, as has historian José Antonio Esquibel, we are reminded not only that Spaniards had Pueblo allies but also that some of the Pueblo rebels were related by marriage and blood to Spaniards. Esquibel noted that some of the Spanish soldiers who returned with Diego de Vargas to reconquer New Mexico in 1692 and 1693 spoke Tewa and had relatives in the pueblos of San Juan and Picurís. When rebel leader Luis Tupatu of Picurís entered into an agreement with Vargas in 1692 that helped pave the way for the Spaniards' return, family ties were apparently on his mind and the reuniting of relatives helped smooth the way for reconciliation.[33] In 2003, on the heels of Brooks's examination of the shifting identities of native peoples in New Mexico, Susan Deeds looked at persisting as well as changing identities.[34] Why, she asked, did some Indian groups vanish after the Spanish conquest of Nueva Vizcaya while others not only endured but also maintained their distinctive ethnic identities? Sedentary groups, she found, were the first to disappear in the face of warfare and disease, with survivors and their descendants blending into the *mestizo* population. At the other end of the spectrum, mobile Indians who lived in greatest isolation from Spaniards—or those who were mobile enough to put distance between themselves and Spaniards—tended to hold on to their ethnic identities.

In his study of the early nineteenth-century Borderlands, *Changing National Identities at the Frontier: Texas and New Mexico, 1800–1850* (2005), Andrés Reséndez looked beyond Hispanics and Indians to another putative binary—Mexicans and Anglo Americans, which also proved illusory on close inspection.[35] On the question of national identity alone, which stands at the heart of his book, Reséndez's Mexicans in Texas and New Mexico were caught in the years before the U.S.-Mexico War between the weak pull of an incipient nationalism in Mexico and the more powerful force of the United States economy that reached into Mexican Texas and Mexican New Mexico. At the same time, Anglo Americans who settled in the Mexican provinces of Texas and New Mexico found themselves torn between two national identities, that of the nation they left and that of the nation they had adopted. In terms of political identity, at least, some Mexicans thus became more Anglo-Americanized and some Anglo Americans became more Mexicanized.

Finally, a word about Juliana Barr's *Peace Came in the Form of a Woman: Indians and Spaniards in the Texas Borderlands* (2007), which takes us into a realm that Spaniards never fully controlled and where, she argues, a Native American kin-based political and social order prevailed. In this world, gender operated "as a system of identity," serving "as a communication tool" that crossed cultures—often without words. Gendered gestures could convey peace or hostility, weakness or strength. Or, as Barr puts it, "the participation of women ... in rituals of respect, hospitality, and intermarriage or in hostage-taking, ransom, and violence—gave expression to amity and enmity in gendered terms."[36]

Recent writers, then, have brought us new ways of thinking about identities and found them more variable and mutable than Bolton's generation had suggested. Identities were not simply shaped by one's origins and slowly modified by one's new physical and social environments. Instead, they were situational, fluid, and multiple. A single person might hold several identities simultaneously, depending on particular circumstances. In this sense, scholarship on identity in the pre-1848 Spanish-Mexican Borderlands resonates with scholarship on identity in the modern-day Borderlands, which reveals that today's border residents' sense of identity emerges from a constellation of overlapping factors that include region, nation, ethnicity, race, gender, and the very stories or narratives that they construct about themselves and about others.[37]

Language and the Construction of Identity

If Borderlands historians' understanding of identity has deepened as they have looked at the ways that groups interacted with one another to invent and re-invent themselves and others, that understanding grew more nuanced after the linguistic turn and cultural studies began to inform their work in the mid-1980s. Historians began to think harder about how language itself defines or constructs identity and how language often becomes its own reality.[38] The following passage, drawn from my own work, exemplifies this. It explains how military officers used language to ascribe identities positively or negatively, as it suited their purposes.

> Whether Spanish soldiers perceived Indians as warlike or peaceful depended as much on Spaniards' designs on Indians as on Indians' behavior. Like philosophes who romanticized Indian society in order to reproach fellow Europeans and like missionaries who portrayed Indians as eager for the gospel in order to justify their ministries, military strategists often drew the Indians they wished to see. When [José de] Gálvez planned to crush the Seris with military force, he described them as rebels and enemies. When [Domingo] Elizondo wanted to firm up a peace with Seris, he characterized them as victims of Spanish oppression who fought to defend their interests. Officers like Lieutenant Colonel Hugo O'Conor who were eager to make war on Apaches described them as perpetrators of "inhuman cruelties" who tore infants from their mothers' wombs. Officers who wanted to make peace with Apaches described them as reasonable and peaceable, more sinned against than sinners.[39]

Again, the idea behind this mode of discourse analysis is not new (although earlier generations of historians would not have used the word discourse any more than they would have used identity). Historians have long understood that contemporaneous descriptions of historical phenomena are mirrors as well as windows and that the words of contemporary observers need to be contextualized and analyzed. That view is old hat to the best practitioners of our craft. One thinks back to a number of works that antedated the linguistic turn but that have informed those of us who write about borderlands: Robert Berkhofer's *The White Man's Indian: Images of the American Indian from Columbus to the Present* (1978), Benjamin Keen's *The Aztec Image in Western Thought* (1971), and Roy Harvey Pearce's *Savagism and Civilization: A Study of the American Mind* (1953).[40] What is new is that Borderlands scholars are beginning to pay more attention to construction of texts, the contexts in which texts were produced, and the phenomenon of intertextuality—how texts borrow from one another and influence one another quite apart from the realities that they purport to describe. My sense, however, is that historians of the Spanish-Mexican Borderlands have left the domain of signs, signifiers, and the signified to specialists in literature, like Maureen Ahern and José Rabasa,[41] and anthropologists like Daniel Reff.[42]

Identity Matters

Borderlands historians have had good reason to be interested in identities. They matter in the real world in ways both positive and negative. Certainly identity mattered in the time and places we write about. Right from the outset, Spaniards labeled all of the indigenous inhabitants of the New World as Indians, and thus, in the words of one scholar, "imposed upon them a new identity that obliterated the great diversity that existed among the many groups native to the New World."[43] Words like *gentiles* and *neófitos* divided Indians into two categories, the heathen and the baptized neophytes, creating identities that "masked the enormous ethnic, cultural, and social differences among the New World's indigenous inhabitants."[44] Identity mattered throughout the colonial period, as when putatively "pure-blooded" Spanish males justified their exploitation and oppression of women, Indians, and mixed-race peoples by ascribing to them a natural inferiority.

Historical identity continued to matter in the last half of the nineteenth century, after the United States wrested from Mexico the area from California to Texas. The region's Spanish-speaking inhabitants were Mexicans when the United States formally annexed the region in 1848, but over time many found it advantageous to identify themselves as of Spanish descent in order to distinguish themselves from the Mexican-American lower class and from new immigrants from Mexico. Our knowledge of this phenomenon goes back at least to the publication of Carey McWilliams's *North from Mexico: The Spanish-Speaking People of the United States* (1948), which famously dismissed as a "fantasy heritage" the *mexicano* elite's effort to turn its back on its Mexican past and repackage itself as Spanish. Today we might call McWilliams's "fantasy heritage" a "fantasy identity."[45]

In New Mexico, three books describe how Hispanos and Anglos constructed a fantasy heritage that turned Mexican Americans into Spanish Americans—this at a time when the state was *not* experiencing a large influx of newcomers from Mexico. Chris Wilson explored this theme in *The Myth of Santa Fe: Creating a Modern Regional Tradition* (1997), Charles Montgomery fleshed the argument out in a deeply satisfying book, *The Spanish Redemption: Heritage, Power, and Loss on New Mexico's Upper Rio Grande* (2002), and John Nieto-Phillips revisited the same subject in *The Language of Blood: The Making of Spanish-American Identity in New Mexico, 1880s–1930s* (2004).[46]

Nieto-Phillips puts the origins of Spanish-American identity in New Mexico in the 1880s, a generation earlier than Montgomery does, but both see Anglo Americans benefiting from this transformation and thus contributing to it. First, Anglos understood that the more their fellow

Americans perceived New Mexicans as Spanish rather than Mexican, the less Congress would object to bringing New Mexico into the union as a state. Second, a Spanish-American identity, with its overtones of arts and crafts and a romanticized pastoral past, would attract tourists (who had begun to arrive by train in the 1880s). Both Nieto-Phillips and Montgomery see the *nuevomexicano* elite cooperating with Anglo Americans to sell this refashioned image of their identity. A Spanish-American identity would give the nuevomexicanos a "white" racial status and the political and economic benefits that would flow from that, yet allow maintenance of language, religion, and other essentials of local culture. In short, nuevomexicano leaders believed that a new Spanish identity would become a source of empowerment.

Freezing nuevomexicanos in time as a pre-industrial tourist commodity also had negative consequences that remain a source of concern in present-day New Mexico. Andrew Lovato's book *Santa Fe Hispanic Culture: Preserving Identity in a Tourist Town* (2004) raised the question of who shapes Hispanic cultural identity in a city overwhelmed by cultural tourism: tourists or Hispanic residents themselves? His answer, not surprisingly, is both: interactions between outsiders and insiders, observers and observed, have shaped modern Santa Fe.[47]

Challenges to nuevomexicanos' alleged Spanish identity have come from several directions over the years, most intensely in the 1970s and 1980s. In those decades young Mexican-American intellectuals tried to construct a Chicano identity that would celebrate the very Indian and Mexican heritage that New Mexico's Spanish Americans sought to erase. Again, much was at stake. The Chicano generation hoped to fashion a broad, regional identity that would transcend individual southwestern states and locales and bring Mexican Americans together in a formidable voting block. To the dismay of many Chicanos, New Mexico's Hispanos largely resisted the lure of a region-wide homeland.[48]

Identity also continues to have political and economic consequences for southwestern Indians, even when the roots of that identity reach into the prehistoric era. Today, for example, Hopis and Zunis occupy tracts of reservation land much smaller than the so-called "aboriginal lands" that they occupied at the time of first contact with Europeans. Federal adjudicators have been willing to recognize "aboriginal lands," but Hopis and Zunis, often working with archaeologists, have identified still larger "cultural landscapes," their boundaries marked by ancient sites of historic and religious significance to particular tribes. The extent to which the dominant society respects Indian religious places and recognizes Indians' use of water and land depends on its recognition of these prehistoric boundaries of ethnic identity.[49]

Just as recognition of the boundaries of Indians' prehistoric identity is a key to protecting land and water, blood quantum has been essential to proving tribal identity, gaining a place on tribal rolls, and receiving material benefits that come from tribal affiliation.[50] Since 1988, when Congress passed the Indian Regulatory Gaming Act that legalized gambling on tribal lands, tribal identity has become especially lucrative for some Indians. Identity is the key to a share of the casino bonanza, or what some Indians have called "the new buffalo." Beneficiaries of the bonanza, however, must belong to tribes, and tribes must enjoy federal recognition or they are not legally tribes. In California, Kent Lightfoot has opened up an important discussion about the ways that Indians' experiences with *some* of the California missions reshaped identities, apparently turning Indians into Hispanics and making it difficult for anthropologists or the federal government to recognize them as Indians, much less tribal people.[51]

An earlier generation of Borderlands historians also understood that identity mattered. Bolton made that clear when he contrasted the supposedly laid-back, easygoing nature of the Californios with the allegedly hardworking Anglo Americans. Bolton's message was unmistakable and resonated with the conventional wisdom of his day: Californios were worthy of memory, but industrious Anglo Americans deserved to prevail over them. What appears new, however, is that Borderlands historians talk more openly about the role that they play in constructing and negotiating identities.

Paradoxically, this greater self-awareness might lead us to abandon the use of the fashionable word identity when we talk about the past, for it is anachronistic and, like many other categories, inherently unstable.[52] Historian Peter Kastor, in a recent book on the Louisiana Purchase and its role in nation building, notes that he avoided using the word identity—"a word that seems almost inseparable from considerations of nationalism." Rather than talk of national identity, Kastor prefers the word "attachment." "Identity," he explains, "rests on fundamentally recent conceptions of self and society ... [whereas] attachment was the word people used at the time."[53]

Is this the beginning of the end of the use of the word identity for historians? Probably not. Anachronism may well be necessary to talk about realities for which contemporaries had no useful vocabulary. Kastor's attachment, though, may point us toward the future even as it illuminates the past. If it is true that identities are continuously constructed and negotiated, is that not also true of the language we employ to signify identities? It seems likely that we will continue to find new vocabulary to analyze still more deeply the multiple forces that have shaped, and continue to shape, the construction and negotiation of identities.

NOTES

    I am grateful to Andrés Reséndez and Todd Meyers for their close readings of the manuscript of this essay and their good advice.

1. Herbert E. Bolton, *The Spanish Borderlands: A Chronicle of Old Florida and the Southwest* (New Haven, Conn.: Yale University Press, 1921). Further citations to this work are given in the text. An electronic version of this book, made by NetLibrary, is available at libraries affiliated with NetLibrary. That is also the case with titles by Bannon, Jones, Moorhead, John, and Sánchez, which I have consulted in electronic editions, as noted in this essay. A keyword search of the electronic edition of Bolton's *Spanish Borderlands* reveals no use of the word *identity*. A keyword search of his collected essays (John Francis Bannon, ed., *Bolton and the Spanish Borderlands* [Norman: University of Oklahoma Press, 1964)] reveals that Bolton used the word just twice, each time meaning "to identify": "Writers hitherto have generally approached the problem of the identity of the Barranca Grande backward," 91, and "For the identity of the Westoes see," 144n13.

2. *American Heritage Dictionary of the English Language*, 3rd ed., s.vv. "identity," "character," "culture."

3. Bolton is quoting someone approvingly at this point, but just who is not clear.

4. Hubert Howe Bancroft, *California Pastoral, 1769–1848* (San Francisco: History Company, 1888), 179.

5. He mentions this in an essay first published in 1930. Herbert Eugene Bolton, "Defensive Spanish Expansion and the Significance of the Borderlands"; reprinted in *Bolton and the Spanish Borderlands*, 32–64 at 63.

6. John Francis Bannon, *The Spanish Borderlands Frontier: 1513–1821* (New York: Holt, Rinehart, and Winston, 1970), 3–7. So, too, did Arthur L. Campa in "Contrasts in Hispanic and Anglo-American Cultures," *Hispanic Culture in the Southwest* (Norman: University of Oklahoma Press, 1979), 282–90.

7. Again, an electronic version of this book has allowed me to search for specific words.

8. Oakah L. Jones Jr., *Los Paisanos: Spanish Settlers on the Northern Frontier of New Spain* (Norman: University of Oklahoma Press, 1979), 238. A search of an electronic version of this book for the keywords "identity" and "identities" reveals no use of either.

9. I elaborate on this in David J. Weber, *The Mexican Frontier, 1821–1846: The American Southwest under Mexico* (Albuquerque: University of New Mexico Press, 1982), 273–85; and David J. Weber, "Turner, the Boltonians, and the Borderlands," *American Historical Review* 91 (1986): 66–81.

10   Alicia V. Tjarks, "Demographic, Ethnic, and Occupational Structure of New Mexico, 1790," *The Americas* 35 (1978): 45–88 at 82. See, too, Alicia Vidaurreta Tjarks, "Comparative Demographic Analysis of Texas, 1777–1793," *Southwestern Historical Quarterly* 77 (1974): 291–338; Jack D. Forbes, "Black Pioneers: The Spanish-Speaking Afro Americans of the Southwest," *Minorities in California History*, ed. George E. Frakes and Curtis B. Solberg (New York: Random House, 1971), 22 (this article first appeared in 1966).

11   John L. Kessell, "Diego Romero, the Plains Apaches, and the Inquisition," *American West* 15 (1978): 12–16.

12   *Foreigners in Their Native Land: Historical Roots of the Mexican Americans*, ed. David J. Weber (orig. pub. 1973; 30th anniversary edition, Albuquerque: University of New Mexico Press, 2003); Elizabeth A. H. John, *Storms Brewed in Other Men's Worlds: The Confrontation of Indians, Spanish, and French in the Southwest, 1540–1795* (College Station: Texas A & M University Press, 1975).

13   Keith Thomas, in "New Ways Revisited: How History's Borders Have Expanded in the Past Forty Years," *TLS* (13 October 2006): 3, noted this "delayed impact," observing that "what happens in one generation in economics, psychology, sociology, philosophy, or anthropology will usually be reflected in the history-writing of the next, even if its authors have never read a word by the theorists concerned."

14   E. P. Thompson's highly influential *The Making of the English Working Class* (London: V. Gollancz, 1963) exemplifies the adoption by historians of the idea of identity as the shared values of a group, or group consciousness, as he explored the evolution of a working-class identity in England between 1790 and 1830.

15   Max L. Moorhead, *The Presidio: Bastion of the Spanish Borderlands* (Norman: University of Oklahoma Press, 1975), 104.

16   John, *Storms*, 153.

17   Edward H. Spicer, *Cycles of Conquest: The Impact of Spain, Mexico, and the United States on the Indians of the Southwest, 1533–1960* (Tucson: University of Arizona Press, 1962). In introducing the concept of identity, Spicer was ahead of his time among anthropologists of the Borderlands. See, for example, Paul H. Ezell, *The Hispanic Acculturation of the Gila River Pimas*, American Anthropologist Memoir 90 (Menasha, Wis.: American Anthropological Association, 1961), 131–46; and Edward P. Dozier, *The Pueblo Indians of North America* (New York: Holt, Rinehart, and Winston, 1970), who rely heavily on the word *culture*. The latter also writes about Pueblos' "world view" and universes (203, 209). Interestingly, George M. Foster, *Culture and Conquest: America's Spanish Heritage* (Chicago: Wenner-Gren Foundation, 1960), a celebrated work published just two years before Spicer's book, also looked at culture change, including beliefs, attitudes, and ethos, without using the word *identity*. A work by a social scientist concerned with the identity of contemporary New Mexicans (George I. Sánchez, *Forgotten People: A Study of New Mexicans* [Albuquerque: University of New Mexico Press, 1940]), also did not; but the work of an anthropologist published in the mid-1960s did use the word: Nancie L. González, *The Spanish Americans of New Mexico: A Heritage of Pride* (Albuquerque: University of New Mexico Press, 1967).

18   William L. Merrill, "Identity Transformation in Colonial Northern Mexico," *Anthro Notes* 19 (1997): 1–8 at 2.

19   "Reply to Commentators," in *Boletín: The Journal of the California Mission Studies Association* 22, no. 2 (2005): 70–75 at 75.

20   Fredrik Barth, introduction, *Ethnic Groups and Boundaries: The Social Organization of Culture Difference*, ed. Barth (Boston: Little, Brown, 1969), 15.

21   Pablo Vila, *Crossing Borders, Reinforcing Borders: Social Categories, Metaphors, and Narrative Identities on the U.S.-Mexico Frontier* (Austin: University of Texas Press, 2000), 225.

22   *Excluir para ser: Procesos identitarios y fronteras sociales en la América hispánica (XVII–XVIII)*, ed. Christian Büschges and Frédérique Langue (Madrid: AHILA Iberoamericana, 2005), a collection of essays on identity formation on the frontiers of Spanish America.

23   The books that follow are a sample of Anglophone works; I do not intend this list to be comprehensive and, indeed, there are many other books on the Borderlands that deal with questions of identity, implicitly or explicitly, such as Stanley M. Hordes, *To the End of the Earth: A History of the Crypto-Jews of New Mexico* (New York: Columbia University Press, 2005), and Cynthia Radding, *Landscapes of Power and Identity: Comparative Histories in the Sonoran Desert and the Forests of Amazonia from Colony to Republic* (Durham, N.C.: Duke University Press, 2005). A thorough study of the recent use of *identity* would also require study of a large periodical literature.

24   Ramón A. Gutiérrez, *When Jesus Came, the Corn Mothers Went Away: Marriage, Sexuality, and Power in New Mexico, 1500–1846* (Albuquerque: University of New Mexico Press, 1991).

25   The question of "honor" was new to the Borderlands but not to colonial Latin Americanists. See, for example, Patricia Seed, *To Love, Honor, and Obey in Colonial Mexico: Conflicts over Marriage Choice, 1574–1821* (Stanford, Calif: Stanford University Press, 1988).

26   Ana María Alonso, *Thread of Blood: Colonialism, Revolution, and Gender on Mexico's Northern Frontier* (Tucson: University of Arizona Press, 1995).

27   Jesús F. de la Teja, *San Antonio de Béxar: A Community on New Spain's Northern Frontier* (Albuquerque: University of New Mexico Press, 1995).

28   Ross Frank, *From Settler to Citizen: New Mexican Economic Development and the Creation of a Vecino Society, 1750–1820* (Berkeley: University of California Press, 2000); quotation on p. 3. Frank did not explore how the various communities of Pueblo Indians constructed or negotiated *their* identities. For an insightful introduction to that topic, see Tracy L. Brown, "Tradition and Change in Eighteenth-Century Pueblo Indian Communities," *Journal of the Southwest* 46 (2004): 463–500.

29   Gary Clayton Anderson, *The Indian Southwest, 1580–1830: Ethnogenesis and Reinvention* (Norman: University of Oklahoma Press, 1999), 67.

30 Borderlands specialists are increasingly using ethnogenesis to describe the formation of new ethnic identities. For example, William L. Merrill, in "La identidad ralámuli, una perspectiva histórica," *Identidad y cultura en la Sierra Tarahumara*, ed. Claudia Molinari and Eugeni Porras (Mexico City: Instituto Nacional Indigenista: Consejo Nacional para la Cultura y las Artes, Instituto Nacional de Antropología e Historia, 2001), 71–103, suggests that Tarahumaras did not become *rarámuri* until the nineteenth century (they identified more with their village than with a larger people; today they prefer the name *ralámuli*). Barbara L. Voss, in "From *Casta* to *Californio*: Social Identity and the Archaeology of Culture Contact," *American Anthropologist* 107 (2005): 461–64, argues that Hispanics in late eighteenth- and early nineteenth-century California underwent ethnogenesis as they ceased to identify themselves within the traditional casta system and turned themselves into Californios.

31 James F. Brooks, *Captives and Cousins: Slavery, Kinship, and Community in the Southwest Borderlands* (Chapel Hill: Published for the Omohundro Institute by the University of North Carolina Press, 2002), 37.

32 Raúl Mandrini, "Presentación," in *Vivir entre dos mundos: Las fronteras del sur de la Argentina, siglos XVIII y XIX*, ed. Mandrini (Buenos Aires: Taurus, 2006), 11–12.

33 José Antonio Esquibel, "The Tupatú and Vargas Accords, 1692–1696," *El Palacio* 111 (2006): 16–19.

34 Susan M. Deeds, *Defiance and Deference in Mexico's Colonial North: Indians under Spanish Rule in Nueva Vizcaya* (Austin: University of Texas Press, 2003).

35 Andrés Reséndez, *Changing National Identities at the Frontier: Texas and New Mexico, 1800–1850* (Cambridge: Cambridge University Press, 2005).

36 Juliana Barr, *Peace Came in the Form of a Woman: Indians and Spaniards in the Texas Borderlands* (Chapel Hill: University of North Carolina Press, 2007), 11, 12.

37 Vila, *Crossing Borders*.

38 For an introduction to this large subject, see Elizabeth A. Clark, *History, Theory, Text: Historians and the Linguistic Turn* (Cambridge, Mass.: Harvard University Press, 2004).

39 David J. Weber, *Bárbaros: Spaniards and Their Savages in the Age of Enlightenment* (New Haven, Conn.: Yale University Press, 2005), 147.

40 Robert F. Berkhofer Jr., *The White Man's Indian: Images of the American Indian from Columbus to the Present* (New York: Knopf, 1978); Benjamin Keen, *The Aztec Image in Western Thought* (New Brunswick, N.J.: Rutgers University Press, 1971); Roy Harvey Pearce, *Savagism and Civilization: A Study of the American Mind* (orig. pub. 1953; Baltimore: Johns Hopkins University Press, 1965).

41 See, for example, Maureen Ahern, "Visual and Verbal Sites: The Construction of Jesuit Martyrdom in Northwest New Spain in Andrés Pérez de Ribas' *Historia de los Triumphos de nuestra Santa Fee* (1675)," *Colonial Latin American Review* 8 (1999): 8–33; and José Rabasa, *Writing Violence on the Northern Frontier: The Historiography of Sixteenth-Century New Mexico and Florida and the Legacy of Conquest* (Durham, N.C.: Duke University Press, 2000).

42 See Daniel T. Reff, "Contextualizing Missionary Discourse: The Benavides Memorials of 1630 and 1634," *Journal of Anthropological Research* 50 (1994): 51–67, and "Text and Context: Cures, Miracles, and Fear in the Relación of Alvar Núñez Cabeza de Vaca," *Journal of the Southwest* 38 (1996): 115–38. Most of this work, however, appears to center on the twentieth-century Borderlands rather than on the colonial period, with which we are concerned in this volume; see, for example, Carl Gutiérrez-Jones, *Rethinking the Borderlands: Between Chicano Culture and Legal Discourse* (Berkeley: University of California Press, 1995).

43 Virginia Bouvier, *Women and the Conquest of California, 1542–1840* (Tucson: University of Arizona Press, 2001), 13.

44 Ibid., 19.

45 Carey McWilliams, *North from Mexico: The Spanish-Speaking People of the United States* (orig. pub. 1948; facsimile ed., New York: Greenwood Press, 1968), 35.

46 Chris Wilson, *The Myth of Santa Fe: Creating a Modern Regional Tradition* (Albuquerque: University of New Mexico Press, 1997); Charles H. Montgomery, *The Spanish Redemption: Heritage, Power, and Loss on New Mexico's Upper Rio Grande* (Berkeley: University of California Press, 2002); and John M. Nieto-Phillips, *The Language of Blood: The Making of Spanish-American Identity in New Mexico, 1880s–1930s* (Albuquerque: University of New Mexico Press, 2004).

47 Andrew Leo Lovato, *Santa Fe Hispanic Culture: Preserving Identity in a Tourist Town* (Albuquerque: University of New Mexico Press, 2004).

48 John R. Chávez, *The Lost Land: The Chicano Image of the Southwest* (Albuquerque: University of New Mexico Press, 1984).

49 T. J. Ferguson and Roger Anyon, "Hopi and Zuni Cultural Landscapes: Implications of History and Scale for Cultural Resources Management," *Native Peoples of the Southwest: Negotiating Land, Water, and Ethnicities*, ed. Laurie Weinstein (Westport, Conn.: Bergin & Garvey, 2001). The extent to which modern-day peoples can be traced into the prehistoric era remains the subject of much contention. Anthropologists and historians alike have been accused of "upstreaming" native societies into distant pasts where they did not rightly belong. Chantal Cramaussel, in *Poblar la frontera: La provincia de Santa Bárbara en Nueva Vizcaya durante los siglos XVI y XVIII* (Zamora, Mexico: El Colegio de Michoacán, 2006), 27–28, finds North American Borderlands historians particularly guilty of this. For a superb study of the way that U.S. courts came to define Indian property rights on the basis of historical occupancy, see Christian W. McMillen, *Making Indian Law: The Hualapai Land Case and the Birth of Ethnohistory* (New Haven, Conn.: Yale University Press, 2007).

50 This has led some non-Indians to pass themselves off as descendants of Indians. See, for example, Brian D. Haley and Larry R. Wilcoxon, "How Spaniards Became Chumash and Other Tales of Ethnogenesis," *American Anthropologist* 107 (2005): 432–45; and Renée Ann Cramer, *Cash, Color, and Colonialism: The Politics of Tribal Acknowledgment* (Norman: University of Oklahoma Press, 2005).

51 Kent G. Lightfoot, in *Indians, Missionaries, and Merchants: The Legacy of Colonial Encounters on the California Frontiers* (Berkeley: University of California Press, 2004), suggests that Indians in the southern missions of San Diego and San Luis Rey won federal recognition because they had remained connected to their homelands and had a land base; Indians at other California missions, he says, had been brought to missions from some distance as local populations died off. Those Indians forged new identities that tied them more to missions than to their lost aboriginal homelands and thus did not fit twentieth-century standards of "Indianness." For commentaries on his argument, see the symposium in *Boletín: The Journal of the California Mission Studies Association* 22, no. 1 (2005): 62–86.

52 Such as the categories of whiteness, or race, or gender; see Daniel Wickberg, "Heterosexual White Male: Some Recent Inversions in American Cultural History," *Journal of American History* 92 (2005): 136–57.

53 Peter J. Kastor, *The Nation's Crucible: The Louisiana Purchase and the Creation of America* (New Haven, Conn.: Yale University Press, 2004), 4–5.

SYLVIA L. HILTON

IDENTITIES AND THE USABLE PASTS OF COLONIAL
BORDERLANDS: SPANISH HISTORIANS AND THE
NORTH PACIFIC FRONTIERS OF THE SPANISH EMPIRE

The links between historiography and nationalism adopt many forms. Their scholarly discussion has generated a considerable body of critical and philosophical analysis.[1] Political and cultural leaders of nation-states have often sought to include the study of history in schools as a way of building "the symbolic capital" of the nation.[2] It is often taken for granted that nationalism is among the major ideological tools and emotional commitments of historians, especially when their specific topics are perceived to lie at the heart of the nation-state itself. But when a modern nation-state has also been a great empire, how do its historians deal with the diversity and unfamiliarity of far-flung frontier lands and peoples? What role do lost imperial peripheries play in "national" identities and historiographies? This case study will discuss historiography published in Spain regarding Spanish activities on the Pacific coasts of North America between the sixteenth century and the early nineteenth century. It illustrates the different ways that the Spanish historical record regarding the North Pacific frontiers of Spain's American empire reflects Spanish national perspectives as well as the collective memories of other, equally significant groups.

Many would argue that, since the Spanish nation-state has provided the main political and cultural context within which nineteenth- and twentieth-century Spanish historiography has developed, Spanish nationalism must necessarily be its chief ideological engine.[3] This may be true in a general sense, and the first section of this analysis will examine some aspects of Spanish national perspectives as illustrated by historical works published in Spain about the Californias and Pacific coasts further north. However, the second section shows that Spanish historians have also been influenced by their own personal circumstances and interests within their diverse social contexts. I specifically argue that professional identities and other birthplace or ethnic identities have been at least as visible as Spanish national identity in inspiring the work of historians publishing in Spain on the chosen topic. Historians, like all human beings, belong to various social groups, defined by various criteria, among which nationality is only one.[4] Consequently, only by accepting certain initial caveats can one imagine that the sum total of historical publications in any one country represents a "national" historiography. In fact, this essay will argue that individual authors do not necessarily always or only represent the nation-state (much less *the* "nation"), but often serve the intellectual and ideological interests of particular institutions and diverse other social groups or communities, as well as their own personal interests.[5]

This analysis is based on approximately six hundred separate bibliographical items published in Spain between 1757 and 2008.[6] Taken as a body, these publications allow us to trace general profiles of Spanish historiography. Since limited space precludes any detailed descriptive and critical evaluation of the content of so many individual publications, the first section will present a general thematic overview, highlighting the specific subjects that have interested Spanish authors and publishers and, at the same time, suggesting their relationship with the overall evolution of Spanish history. Such an overview could be said to reflect a Spanish national perspective, although some might argue that it actually represents little more than a composite picture of choices made by individual historians. The second section will focus on other interpretive aspects of the interplay between different identities and historiography.[7]

On the Margins of Empire and Memory

The study of Spain's North Pacific frontier, extending from Baja California to Alaska, represents only a marginal thematic interest within the larger body of Spanish historiography. Four main factors have contributed to this situation. First, Spanish historians studying the early modern era (from the late fifteenth to the early nineteenth centuries) have tended to use the Hispanic monarchy as their chief historical reference or framework. Within that framework, the Pacific coasts of North America represented the far northwestern periphery of the vast Spanish American empire. The geographical remoteness of that frontier region meant that, in its own time as well as in Spanish historical consciousness, it has seemed to be of little significance for the construction of a Spanish national identity, except as marking the limits of tardy imperial expansion. A second reason for the relative indifference toward the territories and peoples of the Pacific rim of North America is the perception that Spain not only obtained nothing of appreciable economic or political value from them, but also dangerously and unnecessarily overstretched itself, wasting precious resources on a costly and futile (not to say foolhardy) imperial venture. Third, demographic and cultural factors were also clearly unfavorable. The essence of any national community lies in its people's sense of shared cultural identity. The creation of a Hispanic identity on North America's Pacific coasts required the immigration of settlers who carried Hispanic culture with them, and/or the Hispanicization of the indigenous population. On that far-flung frontier, immigration was barely a trickle, and efforts to Hispanicize the native peoples faced the myriad problems encountered everywhere by the frontier agents deployed by the Spanish empire. Finally, chronology has also played a negative role. Spain occupied Alta California and explored the coasts from Oregon to Alaska between 1769 and 1821. Fifty years was hardly a long enough period for the natives and newcomers living in that region to develop a strong sense of a shared Spanish identity. Even if such a consciousness had developed, those years coincided with the age of the democratic revolutions that overturned the existing social and political order in the Atlantic world. Such epoch-making events and processes were bound to dominate the attention of Spanish historians seeking to understand the historical origins of the Spanish nation-state.

In short, the North Pacific coasts from Cabo San Lucas to Alaska not only lay on a remote geographical and cultural periphery of the Spanish American empire but occupied an equally peripheral position in the historical memory of the nineteenth- and twentieth-century Spanish nation-state. Consequently, Spanish historiography concerning that frontier region is understandably less voluminous than that published in the United States or Mexico. It is not, however, in any sense insignificant.[8] Four main subject areas have dominated historical studies published in Spain: missions; maritime expeditions; international rivalry and diplomacy; and science, scientific artwork, and ethnology. Each subject will be discussed with references to the evolution of historical contexts in Spain itself. Relative silence on other subjects will also be noted.

California Missions

There can be no doubt that the religious conversion of Native American peoples was a major concern of the Hispanic monarchy during most of the colonial period. However, before the mid-1980s, Spanish historians other than members of missionary orders rarely dedicated much effort to the scholarly study of the California missions.[9] Eighteenth-century

Spanish political and intellectual leaders saw the need to rewrite the history of Hispanic America, partly as a project of enlightened scholarship and understanding of the world, and partly to counter the latest phase in the European denigration of Spain's culture and colonial system.¹⁰ Several individual attempts failed, as did the collective effort of the Royal Academy of History that had been commissioned in 1764.¹¹ In 1779, having undertaken this historiographical endeavor, Juan Bautista Muñoz defined his overarching theme as Spain's effort to integrate the indigenous peoples of America into Western, Christian, Catholic, and Hispanic civilization. Muñoz had significant government backing, but he died in 1799 before carrying out his plan.¹² In the nineteenth century, multivolume collections of primary sources for Spanish history included a few documents, such as Father Antonio de la Ascensión's diary on Vizcaíno's maritime expedition of 1602–3 ([*CODOINAO*], 1864–84, vol. 8 [1867]), and a short paper by Cesáreo Fernández Duro (1894) focused on Francisco Garcés, but generally speaking, nineteenth- and early twentieth-century secular historians were not drawn to write monographs about California missions and missionaries. The last remnants of Spain's overseas empire were lost in the war of 1895–98, which was widely perceived among Spain's ruling elites as a national disaster. In the aftermath of this colonial crisis, the anticlerical and sometimes even anti-Catholic attitudes of progressive liberal and republican intellectuals became more pronounced in the clamor for national "regeneration."¹³ Neither the Second Republic (1931–36) nor the Civil War years (1936–39) were propitious times for secular historians to take an interest in remote colonial missions.

By contrast, the religious orders of the Catholic Church have always understood the political value of writing their own histories. Four major primary sources for the history of the Californias were published in the late eighteenth century: the diary of a 1751 exploration written by Fernando Consag, published in 1754 by Francisco Xavier Fluviá; Andrés Marcos Burriel's 1757 edition of Miguel Venegas's history of Jesuit travails in Baja California; Francisco Palóu's eyewitness account of the life of Junípero Serra, which came off a Mexican press in 1787; and Father Luis de Sales's firsthand report on California, published in 1794. Following the trend of the nineteenth century, Catholic institutions undertook ambitious projects to produce general histories of and reference works on the Catholic Church and the religious orders. The lives and labors of missionaries in Spanish America (including the Californias) formed part of this larger Catholic history. Junípero Serra, however, was a case apart. Beginning in 1876, Francisco Torréns popularized Serra's story in a series of newspaper articles and conferences, and finally published a biography in 1913 marking the bicentennial anniversary of Serra's birth.[14] In the early twentieth century, a historiographical study by Fidel Fita (1908) of the Venegas-Burriel source on the Jesuit missions of Baja California appeared, and a few other authors focused on individual missionaries who served in the Californias, presenting biographical data on Pablo de Mugártegui (Larriñaga 1915), Magín Catalá (Engelhardt 1924), and Fermín Francisco de Lasuén (García 1932). In the 1930s, two general works were produced, one by Constantino Bayle (1933) on the Jesuits in Baja California, and a compilation of articles by Buenaventura Salazar (1935) that included several on the Franciscans in Alta California.

The consolidation of General Francisco Franco's dictatorial regime in Spain led to an almost immediate surge of academic activity focusing on Hispanic America. Spain was to suffer a long period of international isolation, but Franco had a strong political interest in strengthening Spain's cultural and diplomatic relations with Latin America.[15] This political goal was immediately reflected in Spanish historiography thanks to official policies in support of research and publication on the Americas.[16] In this context, the history of the role of the missions on the frontiers of Spanish America became slightly more substantial. Between 1940 and 1975, a few general works came off Spanish presses. A brief descriptive history of the Alta California missions written by U.S. author James M. Keys was published in Madrid,[17] while the much more valuable study of the foundation of these missions written by Spanish-born Lino Gómez Canedo (1969) was published in Mexico City. However, the main emphasis of mission historiography in this period fell on the activities of individual missionaries. A considerable number of editions of primary sources were published, as well as biographical studies focusing on specific episodes or aspects of the lives of missionaries who were considered outstanding. Among the Jesuits connected with Baja California, Juan María de Salvatierra (Bayle 1946), Francisco María Píccolo (Burrus 1962), and Eusebio Francisco Kino (Burrus 1964) received special attention, while a new edition of the report from California written by Dominican Luis de Sales also appeared (Sales 1960). Among the Franciscans, Junípero Serra inevitably inspired both popular biographies (Sabater 1944, Casas 1949, Majó 1956, Igual 1958, Ramis 1959) and more scholarly studies (Vidal Isern 1949, Sanz y Díaz 1956, Sintes 1961, Font 1969), as well as editions of sources (Lejarza 1949, Palma 1949). Attention was also devoted to Juan Antonio Joaquín de Barreneche (Pazos 1941), Francisco Palóu (Riber 1944), Pablo de Mugártegui (Omaechevarría 1950, 1959),

Pedro Pérez de Mezquía (Omaechevarría 1956, 1958, 1963, and 1964a), Francisco Ajofrín (Castellanos 1958), Fermín Francisco de Lasuén (Lamadrid 1963), Jerónimo Boscana (Font 1966), Mariano Payeras (Font 1968), Francisco Garcés (Bardavío 1971), and Antonio de la Ascensión (Zdenek 1974).

On the whole, the focus of the scholarship and the rhythm of publications on the California missions seem to have been less affected by historical events in Spain than was other subject-specific historiography. Nonetheless, slight signs of change have become visible in the past thirty years. Since the advent of democracy in Spain in 1976 after Franco's death, the near monopoly exercised by members of the clergy on the historiography of missions and missionaries' lives has been dented by work contributed by a few secular historians who have taken a limited scholarly interest in certain aspects of these subjects. This trend is undoubtedly connected with the modernization of professional Spanish historiography. Increasing participation in broader, international debates promises to bring different attitudes, concepts, methods, sources, and thematic interests into the field of mission history. It means, in effect, that the history of missions, Church affairs, and religion is fortunately no longer the exclusive domain of authors who are certainly too close to the ideology and the professional interests of the missionaries to give a full picture of the history of Catholicism in colonial California.[18] This comment is not meant to suggest that all their historiographical achievements are irremediably flawed or without value—far from it—but simply to state the obvious need for professional Spanish historians to come to grips with this subject from new perspectives.

Since the late 1980s, then, a few studies have appeared on the Jesuits (Río 1992; León Portilla 1998; Bernabeu 2000, 2001–3, 2008, 2009; Hausberger 2009) and the Dominicans in Baja California (Fernández Galiano 1987, 1988, 1989; Gómez 1988; Bernabeu and Romero 1988; Serrera and Fuentes 1988; Ribes 1989; Esponera 1994). A general history of the Franciscan period in Baja California (1768–73) published in La Paz was written by Spanish-born Lino Gómez Canedo (1983). More recently, a number of editions of key primary sources for the history of Baja California have appeared. Piña (1992) offers a testament referring to the Pious Fund for the Jesuit missions. A work published in Spain by Mexican scholar Eligio M. Coronado (1996) presents Segismundo Taraval's report on the native rebellion of 1734 together with other important primary sources for the history of Baja California. An edition of missionary reports on Baja California from 1777 was published in La Paz by Salvador

Bernabeu (1992d) thanks to the support of the Spanish Embassy in Mexico City, and this Spanish scholar also published in Mexico a new edition of the testimony penned by Luis de Sales (2003). Innovative historiographical approaches are as yet barely perceptible, but certainly not absent, mainly thanks to Salvador Bernabeu's analyses of Jesuit discourse and historiography concerning the Baja California missions (Bernabeu 2000, 2001–3, 2009). The politics of identity are especially visible in Bernard Hausberger (2009), a work that underscores the tensions between nationalistic perspectives and the more global project of the Jesuits through its examination of the mythologizing of Father Kino in both American and European historiography.

On Franciscans in Alta California, works of a general nature have not been much in evidence and the approaches adopted in the few existing studies have varied greatly (Weber 1979; Castilla 1986; Anta 1988; Guest 1988; Piña 1988, 1991; Toschi 1991; Brandes 1992; Arrieta 1993, 2004a, 2004b; Tóth 1998). On the other hand, a crop of biographies and other studies closely connected with Junípero Serra appeared around the bicentennial anniversary of his death in 1984 and the Catholic Church's subsequent inquiry into his merits for possible canonization. Publishing houses scrambled to exploit the opportunity, producing works by both clergymen (Gómez Canedo 1982, 1989; Vicedo 1984, 1989, 1991; Alcina 1985; Mesquida 1985; Rosselló 1985; Rubí 1985; Xavier 1986; Geiger 1987; Galmés 1988; Oltra 1988, 2004; Corredor 1989; López Bonet 1989; Borges 1991) and secular historians (Bowden 1976; Piquer 1984; Piña 1985; Garriga 1986; Hilton 1987; Font 1985, 1988a, 1988b, 1989a, 1989b, 1991, ca. 1992, 1998; Font and Neuerberg 1992). However, the controversy that flared up in the United States in the years 1985–88 over Serra's proposed canonization was not greatly bruited in Spain.[19] As in the earlier period, some attention has been given to other individual missionaries such as Francisco Palóu (Font 1976, Anta, ed. 1988; Vicedo, ed. 1989, 1992; Pérez Baltasar 1995, Lens Tuero 1998, Soto Pérez 2008); Buenaventura Sitjar (Vicedo 1977); Francisco Hermenegildo Garcés (Bardavío 1988, 1990; Oltra and Martínez 1994, Galvin 1996); Juan González Vizcaíno (Bernabeu [1992]b); Juan Crespí (Font 1994, ed. [1994]; Vicedo 1994); Miguel de la Campa Cos (Bernabeu, ed. 1995); Fermín Francisco de Lasuén (Arrieta 1996b); the first bishop of Sonora, Sinaloa, and the Californias, Antonio de los Reyes (Miguélez 1999); and Vicente de Sarriá (Arrieta, forthcoming).

To summarize, in any single study pertaining to the missions, historians publishing in Spain have mostly focused on the work of one of the missionary orders: Jesuit, Franciscan, or Dominican, and, within each order, on the life and labors of individual missionaries. Generally speaking, Spanish mission historiography has been written from the point of view of the missionaries and their respective orders, and by extension, of the Catholic Church and the Hispanic monarchy. Since the 1980s, some slight change has been visible, as a few professional historians and other secular authors have begun to take an interest in the religious and mission history of the Spanish Californias. However, no historical work published in Spain has attempted to meld the story of all the missions in the Spanish Californias into one narrative or comparative analysis.[20] In short, professional Spanish historians have yet to write a scholarly history of religious and cultural expansion that would take into account not only the interests and contributions of the metropolitan government and the agents of empire (including missionaries) coming from Spain itself but also the cultural characteristics of the different Pacific coast indigenous peoples, the circumstances of the mainly mixed-blood Mexican soldiers and settlers of the Californias, and the specific details of the interaction among these groups. The signs of change are encouraging, but a new ethnohistory of religious proselytism and cultural interaction in and around the California missions is still pending in Spain.

Maritime Horizons

Maritime expeditions of exploration represent without a doubt the most common theme in Spanish historiography about the Pacific coast of colonial North America. Iñigo Abbad y Lasierra's 1783 manuscript is representative of late eighteenth-century interest in this subject. As a product of the Spanish Enlightenment, it was based on good primary and secondary sources, but it remained unpublished until the twentieth century (Abbad 1981).[21] The first substantial historiographical work to be printed in Spain was the introduction written by Martín Fernández de Navarrete to José Espinosa's 1802 edition of a major primary source pertaining to the expedition of the *Sutil* and the *Mexicana* that had taken place ten years earlier (Fernández de Navarrete 1802).[22] Both Abbad and Navarrete presented general histories of Spanish explorations in search of the much-coveted Northwest Passage, together with geographical descriptions and information about the international context of the expeditions. In 1805 and 1809, José Espinosa y Tello published two other important studies of nautical science and cartography on the Northwest Coast, but these would be the last historiographical products of the Spanish Enlightenment connected with that region.[23]

Instead, the destruction of the Spanish naval fleet at the battle of Trafalgar, the desperate Spanish war of independence against Napoleon's invading forces, and the subsequent emancipation of continental Latin America riveted the attention of Spanish intellectuals and other elites. Consequently, during the later revolutionary years and the reign of the infamously absolutist Fernando VII, the Pacific coasts of North America were far removed from Spanish political or historiographical interest, and nothing more of note was to be produced until the 1840s. Like many of their colleagues in other European and American countries, Spanish historians working in the middle to late nineteenth century dedicated their main effort to the production of general national histories, at the same time attending to the publication and/or discussion of primary sources.[24] By this means, a significant number of important documents referring to maritime expeditions of exploration along the Pacific coasts of North America were printed ([*CODOIN España*] 1842–95; [*CODOINAO*] 1864–84; Bodega y Cuadra 1865a, 1865b, 1865c; Bustamante y Guerra 1868; Velázquez de León 1874; Carrasco 1882–83; Novo 1885). Interest in the sixteenth-century claims of Juan de Fuca and Lorenzo Ferrer Maldonado was especially notable (Fernández de Navarrete and Fernández de Navarrete 1849, Fernández de Navarrete 1881; Malaspina 1849a; Novo 1881, 1882–83). The publication of a short biography of Francisco Antonio Mourelle (Mourelle 1856) reflected family pride quite as much as Spanish nationalism.

The 1887 Philippines Exhibition no doubt was the high point of cultural interest in the Pacific in the nineteenth-century,[25] but from the 1890s to 1913, study of Spanish activities in the North Pacific seems to have drifted into the doldrums. The commemoration of the four hundredth anniversary of Columbus's fateful voyage of 1492 was less than inspiring but, in any case, was dominated by discussions of Columbus, of pre-Hispanic indigenous cultures, and of the perceived continuing need to combat the anti-Spanish Black Legend.[26] The lectures offered in Madrid's Ateneo in 1892, which were collected in a published volume that same year, included an overview of Spain's activities in California and the Northwest Coast by geographer-archaeologist Rafael Torres Campos, but nothing else of significance appeared at this time. The colonial crisis of 1895–99, which led to the loss of the Philippines and Spain's other Pacific possessions, may well account for the disappearance of Pacific horizons from Spanish historiography at the turn of the century and during the decade following.[27]

Nonetheless, in reaction to the colonial "disaster," Spanish intellectuals and political leaders were impressed with the need for national regeneration, which among other things required a new look at Spanish history. Ramón de Manjarrés published studies in 1913 and 1914, focusing on early Spanish projects to improve Atlantic-Pacific communications, while a paper by Rafael Altamira (1924) at the 1915 Panama-Pacific Historical Congress tried to call attention to Spain's historical presence in the Pacific in general terms. Both authors were inspired by the desire to recall Spain's role in Pacific exploration, particularly in the search for an interoceanic route, as the world celebrated the culmination of the Panama Canal project and its inauguration in 1914. The account of Francisco de Ulloa's 1539 exploratory expedition to California was published in 1916 (Serrano y Sanz), and new archival material on Sebastián Vizcaíno came to light in 1926 (Ariza). In the early 1930s, a catalogue of primary sources held in the Naval Museum compiled by Fernando Guillén (1932) helped to maintain the interest in naval expeditions connected with the Californias, while the opportunity to mark the four hundredth anniversary of the Spanish discovery of Baja California by Diego de Becerra's rebellious pilot, Fortún Jiménez, occasioned several studies by Constantino Bayle (1932–33, 1933). However, perhaps more significant in the context of the Second Spanish Republic was a study of the Malaspina expedition by Rafael Estrada (1930). This work, in addition to underscoring that great sailor's place in maritime history and reclaiming his scientific legacy, perhaps revealed an ideological and political interest in the rehabilitation of an Enlightenment liberal whose work had been shelved for generations after he was accused of conspiring against the Crown and imprisoned.

The Spanish Civil War (1936–39) put historiographical projects on hold, but as soon as it was over, the (by then) traditional attention to the history of maritime explorations continued throughout the Franco years (1940–75). Many more primary sources made their way into print, and a considerable number of general and monographic studies as well as biographies were published (Lefán 1942; Pereyra 1942; Cebreiro 1943–44; Sanfeliú 1944; Barras 1944, 1949–50, 1951, 1953, 1956; Ybarra 1945, 1964; Martínez-Valverde 1946; Melón 1946; Arco 1947; Portillo 1947; Lejarza 1948; Dotor 1948; Lafarga 1949; Gascón 1950; Pérez Embid 1951; Hernández Sánchez-Barba 1953; Soler Vidal 1953; Ramos 1956; Díaz-Trechuelo 1956; Cutter 1958a, 1958b; Lorenzana 1958; Bolin 1959; *Noticias y documentos* 1959; Quadra-Salcedo 1960; Hidalgo 1961; Barreiro-Meiro 1962, ed. 1964, ed. 1975; Mathes 1965, 1969, 1970–71, 1974; Omaechevarría 1966;

Mourelle-Lema 1967; Landín 1968, 1970, 1971; Pérez Miguel 1973a, 1973b; Albarracín 1975; Sariego 1975; Hernández Aparicio 1975).

Since General Franco's death in 1975, the historiography of Spanish maritime expeditions has not only increased greatly in volume but has also undergone a substantial qualitative change. In order to avoid repetition, some aspects of this evolution will be outlined later, in my discussion of the historiography of international relations and of science, art, and ethnology. At this point, suffice it to say that anniversaries relevant to various events have played a significant role in the recent surge of historiographical interest in Spain regarding maritime expeditions in the Pacific.[28] Of remarkable importance was the bicentennial anniversary of Alejandro Malaspina's expedition, a major project of the Spanish Enlightenment spanning the years 1789–94. For political reasons, Charles IV's government silenced Malaspina's achievements, which were then largely ignored by historians. Consequently, the massive amount of first-class primary sources generated by this expedition has proved to be a trove for historians seeking new materials and those wanting to develop new approaches. Public financing made available from the late 1980s to the mid-1990s in connection with the five hundredth anniversary of Columbus's first voyage to America provided abundant funds for research grants, commemorative conferences, and publications concerning the history of Spanish America. Within this peak period of Americanist activity, study of the Malaspina voyage offered unparalleled opportunities to produce high-quality catalogues and editions of primary sources, as well as original monographs that modernized the study of Spanish maritime expeditions and activities on the west coasts of North America. Thus, the Malaspina expedition's multiple artistic, scientific, and technical activities and achievements have inspired a general broadening of the range of themes and approaches in the more recent Spanish historiography dealing with such expeditions.[29] At the same time, these developments have encouraged contributions from North American scholars based not only in the United States but also in Mexico (González Rodríguez 1985; Léon Portilla 1985, 1998; Coronado 1987; González Claverán 1987, 1989; Vilchis 1992; Jiménez Pelayo 1997) and Canada (Bartroli 1992, 1994; Chartrand 1994; Crosse 1994; Inglis 1994, 1995, 1997, 1998, [2006]; Crosse and Sprätz 1998; [Palau Baquero and] Sprätz 1998; Tovell 1998a, 1998b).[30]

Many post-1975 studies of Spanish maritime expeditions in North Pacific waters deal in general terms with explorations to the Californias and coasts further north to Alaska in various historical periods

(Hilton 1981; Sotos 1984a; Morales 1986; Palau Baquero 1986, 1988; Guirao 1989; Bernabeu 1988b, 1989b, 1989g, 1991c, 1991d, 1998a; Beerman 1990; Pérez Miguel 1991; Landín 1992a, 1992b; San Pío 1992; Cuesta 1993; Beals 1994; Fúster 1997; Palau Baquero and Alcina 1998; Rey 2003). In addition, studies abound that focus on the contributions of individual protagonists. In 1985, on the occasion of the five hundredth anniversary of Hernán Cortés's birth, several studies recalled his activities in the Pacific and in particular his 1535 expedition to California (León Portilla 1985, González Rodríguez 1985, Carreño 1990). Among other sixteenth- and seventeenth-century expeditionaries, Spanish historians have chosen to write about Francisco de Ulloa (Navarro 1994); Juan de Fuca (Martín-Merás 1991); Sebastián Vizcaíno (Landín 1991); Tomás and Nicolás Cardona, the Cardona company and other business ventures in connection with the pearl fisheries of Baja California (Hernández Aparicio 1975, 1976, 1989); Francisco Ortega (Hernández Aparicio 1979); Pedro Porter Casanate (Armillas 1988; Bernabeu 1988a; Gracia 1988, 1989); and Isidro Atondo y Antillón (Hernández Aparicio 1980). The chief interest, however, has been generated by late eighteenth-century maritime expeditionaries such as Father Juan González Vizcaíno, who participated in the expedition to found San Diego in 1769 (Bernabeu [1992]b), Juan Pérez (Bernabeu 1989f; Landín 1992a), Bruno de Heceta (Landín 1992a, Bernabeu, ed. 1995),[31] Juan Francisco de la Bodega y Cuadra (Sota 1985; Menchaca 1989, 1998; San Pío 1989; Bernabeu 1990, 1998b; Hernández de López 1991; Landín 1992a, 1992b; Beerman 1998b), Francisco Antonio Mourelle (Landín 1988, 1992b; Landín and Sánchez 1992; Kendrick 1995; Monge and Olmo 1991), Ignacio de Arteaga (Albarracín 1975; Landín 1992b), Esteban José Martínez (Borrego 1988), José Tobar y Tamariz (Sales 1960), Antonio Tova Arredondo (1988 and 1990 reprints of Sanfeliú 1944; Pimentel 1993), Juan Gutiérrez de la Concha (Pimentel 1993), Salvador Fidalgo (Inglis 1998), Manuel Quimper (Beerman 1998b), Francisco de Eliza (Crosse 1994), José de Bustamante y Guerra (Beerman 1994; Higueras 1999), Dionisio Alcalá Galiano (Higueras and Martín-Merás, eds. 1991; Kendrick 1994a, 1998), Jacinto Caamaño (Barreiro-Meiro, ed. 1975; Inglis 1998), Cayetano Valdés (Higueras and Martín-Merás, eds. 1991; Kendrick 1998), and José Longinos (Bernabeu, ed. 1994a). It would be impossible to mention all the historiography relating to the expedition led by Alejandro Malaspina, much of which is only tangentially relevant for California and Northwest Coast history.[32] However, we may include here a few studies that refer specifically to activities on the Pacific seaboard of North America (Sotos 1982, 1991;

Sota 1989, Malaspina 1990, Cutter 1994, Chartrand 1994, Inglis 1997, Higueras 1998).

International Contexts

A third identifiable theme of Spanish historiography referring to the northern Pacific coast of America is the context of international rivalry and diplomacy in which the northwestern expansion of the Spanish American empire took place. As already noted, late eighteenth-century interest was manifest in the works of Iñigo Abbad y Lasierra and Martín Fernández de Navarrete, as well as the Spanish translations of Kippis's biography of James Cook and French geographer Jean-Nicolas Buache's memorial on the discoveries of Lorenzo Ferrer Maldonado. Both Abbad and Navarrete were well aware of the diplomatic concerns of their day, and none of these works was politically innocent. Abbad, writing during the U.S. Revolutionary War, echoed contemporary and earlier concerns regarding Russian and Anglo-American activities in the North Pacific.[33] Fernández de Navarrete's excellent study was published just in time to bolster the historical foundation of Spanish claims to sovereignty on the west coasts of North America, before the U.S. acquisition of the Louisiana Territory in 1803 vastly complicated the intersection of imperial frontiers and international relations for Spain's beleaguered government. Nothing further of note appeared for a long time. The Nootka incident of 1789, when both Spain and America claimed the island, was the subject of two early twentieth century studies, by Fernández Duro (1903) and Jordán de Urríes (1907), but until 1950 no monographic studies focused specifically on issues connected with international relations. One finds only marginal references to this subject in general works on Spain's diplomatic history, which tend to concentrate on relations with European countries. Perhaps the long periods of relative international isolation of Spain itself, during much of the nineteenth century and Franco's dictatorship, translated into a disinclination of diplomatic historians to undertake monographic studies of Spain's historical connections with remote areas of the world that were perceived to conserve only tenuous links to the greater Hispanic cultural community.

Be that as it may, solid Spanish Catholicism and Franco's strong anticommunist stance after the Second World War made Spain a useful ally of the United States in Cold War diplomacy. In 1953 Franco allowed the United States to establish military bases and accepted substantial U.S. scientific, technical, and economic aid. But for years he resisted U.S. cultural diplomacy, which was making headway in other western European countries at that time.[34] Consequently, the Fulbright Program was introduced relatively late, and only gradually did U.S. intellectual and academic influences begin to make themselves felt in Spain.[35] In the 1950s and 1960s, studies of the North Pacific in early modern Spanish diplomacy and the international aspects of New Spain's northwestern expansion started to appear. Several authors examined the general international context of the late eighteenth century (Rodríguez Casado 1950, Hernández Sánchez-Barba 1953, Sánchez Diana 1965, Landín 1968), while others focused on such specific topics as the Russian threat (Barras 1956, Barreiro-Meiro 1962, Vila 1965), the Nootka incident (Mariñas 1967), and the ceremonial aspects of claiming territories for Spain (Morales Padrón 1955). By the late 1960s, a change was clearly on the way. Although many Spaniards were still emigrating every year in search of seasonal farm work and other jobs, the Spanish economy was taking off, borne aloft in particular by fast expansion in the tourist industry.[36] Tourists flocked to Spain, including a fair number of American "academic tourists" such as university students and scholars participating in conferences and other professional activities. Economic growth, better educational opportunities, and increasing exposure to foreign influences would eventually contribute to create a very different social and cultural environment for the development of Spanish historiography.

The year 1976 was most encouraging for historians interested in Spain's North American colonies and early Spanish-U.S. relations. King Juan Carlos I inaugurated his reign by visiting the United States in that year. At the same time, the Spanish government, through the agency of the Ministry of Foreign Affairs, sponsored an ambitious archival project to celebrate the bicentennial anniversary of U.S. independence by initiating the publication of a series of new catalogues. These excellent research tools guide scholars toward important primary sources held in Spanish archives, which are useful for the international dimensions of Spanish connections with North America from the mid-eighteenth century to the 1820s.[37]

In the 1980s and 1990s, as the development of democracy broadened Spain's international outlook, there was a visible increase in scholarly attention to the international implications of Spanish activities along the Pacific rim of North America. A number of authors have adopted a general approach to this theme, noting Russian, British, French, American, and even Chinese connections with the area (Batista 1985, Vaughan and Crownhart-Vaughan 1986, Hilton 1987b, Sota 1988, Force and Force 1989, Frost 1988, Pérez Miguel 1989, Bernabeu 1989e, Piqueras 1992–93,

Kai 1994, Villar [1995], Kendrick 1995). Another handful of studies has focused specifically on the Russian advance south from the Aleutian-Alaskan coasts (Mandelstamm 1978, Pérez Miguel 1988, Ortega Soto 1989, Voltes 1989). British intentions were nearly always a threatening factor in early modern Spanish international relations, so British explorations and commercial activities in the Pacific Ocean were a source of some concern to eighteenth-century Spanish governments. Consequently, Captain James Cook's last voyage has commanded attention in his time and in our own, although the few studies more recently published in Spain have been penned mainly by foreign authors (Cook 1982, Price 1985, Kendrick 1995, Collingridge 2003, Torres Santo Domingo 2003). However, the subject that has generated most scholarly interest is undoubtedly the incident at Nootka. Since the 1980s a little flurry of studies on the diplomatic contest arising out of the Anglo-Spanish encounter at Nootka has served to revitalize Spanish historiographical work on the international aspects of late-eighteenth century North Pacific history (Sota 1986; Soler Pascual 1996, 1997, 1998; Bernabeu 1995, 1998b; Palau Baquero, Calés, and Sánchez 1998; Beerman 1998a; Tovell 1998a; Rey 2003; Gough [2006]; Novi [2006]).

Science, Scientific Artwork, and Ethnology

A fourth clearly distinguishable and significant branch of Spanish historical scholarship on the Californias and Northwest Coast of America concerns the history of science, scientific artwork, and ethnology. In fairness, nineteenth- and early twentieth-century naval historians of maritime expeditions, already noted, must be considered the precursors of this line of inquiry. The early twentieth-century climate of cultural "regeneration" and scholarly revisionism encouraged the study of modern scientific topics, and progressive republicans were especially sympathetic to this kind of research.[38] At the turn of the century, brief pieces by Cesáreo Fernández Duro (1894, 1901) appeared, the first on ethnological work done by Francisco Garcés, and the second on the naturalist Tadeo Haenke, who did important work on the Northwest Coast during the Malaspina expedition.[39] In the 1930s, a study by Rafael Estrada (1930) focused on the artists who accompanied the Malaspina expedition, while science formed the central focus of a biographical study by Juan Llabrés Bernal (1934) of naval officer and technical draughtsman Felipe Bauzá.

The Civil War and the Franco years effectively strangled this interest in the history of science.[40] Nevertheless, despite the tight rein on intellectual and scientific activities, we have already noted that political interest in Latin America encouraged Americanist scholarship. Through the 1940s, 1950s, and 1960s, the history of scientific endeavors in the Californias and Northwest Coast was kept alive mainly by the efforts of Francisco de las Barras, and a few historians who researched naturalist Tadeo Haenke and other scientific aspects of Spanish maritime expeditions (Barras 1944, 1949, 1949–50, 1951, 1953; Melón 1946; Salva 1950; Henckel 1956; Ramos 1956; Gicklhorn 1966; Arias 1968). For their part, the Naval Museum in Madrid and the Casa de Colón in Las Palmas de Gran Canaria offered exhibitions of drawings and engravings by artists who traveled with the Malaspina expedition (Estrada 1951; Guillén 1952). In addition, a number of studies published in Spain between the late 1950s and the mid-1970s by U.S. scholars could be considered to be contributions to this phase of scientific historiography, since they focused mainly on overland expeditions, historical cartography, and the expansion of geographical knowledge (Cutter 1958a, 1958b; Burrus 1967a, 1967b; Mathes 1965, 1969, 1970–71; Zdenek 1974).[41]

The demise of General Franco in 1975 brought profound change to every aspect of Spanish life and culture as the constitutional monarchy of Juan Carlos I was consolidated. Democratic ideas and practices stimulated historiographical modernization and revisionism. By this time, scholars had acquired much better language skills, and they traveled abroad more easily and frequently, while libraries began to improve their collections, both in Spanish and (more slowly and unevenly) in foreign languages. The number of universities in Spain has increased from fifteen in 1970 to seventy-two today. At the same time, despite the rigid institutional structures of the Spanish higher education system, student training has improved, and both the student body and teaching staff have undergone a rapid process of democratization. Consequently, Spanish historiography has expanded in purely quantitative terms, at the same time as it has become modernized and internationalized in every sense. The relatively young "new" professional historians are not only more numerous than at any previous time in Spanish history, but thanks to the improving economy and access to opportunities in higher education and research, they come from many different social backgrounds. Up until the late 1970s, Spanish historians had rarely engaged in critical and interpretive debates as defined by Anglo-American scholarship, but the younger scholars would produce a very different kind of historiography. The publications record shows that professional Spanish historians have developed thematic, conceptual, and methodological approaches much more attuned to the general historiographical trends and scholarly practices of our times.

This new generation of Spanish historians have ventured into hitherto little-explored thematic terrains, or redefined the study of more traditional ones, as they have begun to revise the general imperial, international, and cultural contexts of Spanish expeditions, including those that touched on the Pacific seaboard of North America. The strong surge of interest in the history of science, scientific artwork, and ethnology, in particular, seems to be a distinguishing characteristic of more recent Spanish scholarship.[42] This flowering of scientific historiography is focused on diverse Spanish contributions to scientific observation and description of the planet and its inhabitants. Bernabeu (2006) provides a general analysis of Spanish perceptions of the California frontier in the light of eighteenth-century scientific activities, while a new article examines the scientific work of Joaquín Velázquez de León in Baja California in the late 1760s and early 1770s (Bernabeu 2010). Hydrographical work and astronomy related to the Pacific coasts of North America have generated a little interest. Hernández Aparicio (1989) published Nicolás Cardona's 1632 hydrographical and geographical descriptions of Baja California, while Bernabeu (1988c, 1988d, 1989a, 1989b, 1991a, 2010) devoted a number of studies to the Franco-Spanish astronomical expedition led by Chappe d'Auteroche to observe the transit of Venus.[43] Cartography and geography are, of course, traditionally well represented as subjects of Spanish historiography, but new studies have kept these scientific activities in view. Among studies of the overland explorations connected with the North Pacific, Picazo (1999) looked at Hennepin's attempt to find a passage to the ocean from the river Mississippi, and Bernabeu (2003) presented the diary written by Cañizares during the expedition from Velicatá to San Diego in 1769, while Bardavío (1990) and Salafranca (Garcés 1996) recorded the efforts of Francisco Garcés to connect Sonora and Monterey by way of the river Colorado. Several authors have pondered the considerable contributions to cartographic work, geographical description, and scientific questionnaires and artwork made by eighteenth-century Spanish naval pilots, and in particular by the expeditionaries who accompanied Malaspina (Higueras and Martín-Merás 1986, González Claverán 1987, Higueras 1988b, Cano Trigo 1991, Martín-Merás 1998, Crosse and Sprätz 1998, López y Sebastián 2000), while Bartroli (1992) compiled and discussed Catalonian toponyms.

Natural history and botany were introduced as historiographical subjects (Galera 1987; *La Botánica en la Expedición Malaspina* 1989; Ibáñez

1994; Engstrand 1998; San Pío and Higueras [2001]), and a few studies focused specifically on the work and testimony of naturalists José Mariano Moziño (or Mociño) (Grunfeld 1986; Vilchis 1992; Higueras, Pimentel, and Fernández 1993; Monge and Olmo 1999; Engstrand 2000; Cabello, Escalera and Carreras 2000), José Longinos Martínez (Bernabeu 1987b, Bernabeu, ed. 1994a), and Tadeo Haenke (Ibáñez and Sanz 1992, Ibáñez 1994). The late eighteenth-century interest in valuable woods and forest resources was discussed by Bernabeu (1991b) and Pimentel (1991), while issues concerning the impact of human activities on the natural world are at the heart of innovative studies by Pérez Miguel (1993), who studied ecological change resulting from European activities on the Northwest Coast, and Carretero (1995), who looked at Indian subsistence in connection with local environments. The application of scientific knowledge and technical expertise to the improvement of living conditions or the greater efficacy of human activities must also be considered as another facet of the new historiographical interest in science and technology, and their uses for human purposes. Medicine and public hygiene have attracted some attention (Sureda 1986, on the influence of Balearic medicine in California), as have scientific aspects of certain economic activities like mining and agriculture (Bernabeu 1987a; Cutter 1987, on agricultural experiments at Nootka). We might also include here some interest in the technical work of Miguel Costansó and other military engineers in New Spain and California (Mañá 1992, Moncada 1995).

In the new Spanish historiography of science and scientific artwork, one field in particular merits special attention. Ethnohistory, or the scholarly study of the native peoples and cultures of the west coasts of North America in the eighteenth century, represents a different way of looking at the historical relations between Spaniards and Native Americans. Traditionally, the Hispanicization of California natives by missionaries in the service of the Catholic Church and the Hispanic monarchy has been the dominant historiographical approach. A few missionaries working among California Indians produced vocabularies and other works that are highly esteemed as valuable sources for the study of indigenous languages and culture, but secular Spanish historians of the nineteenth century and most of the twentieth century showed very little interest in developing ethnohistorical approaches.[44] One of the indicators of the change in Spanish historiography is a more deliberate focus on early Spanish ethnology and its contributions to the understanding of native cultures. Perhaps the U.S. scholars participating in the international conference of Americanists held in Seville and Barcelona in 1964 deserve a special mention as harbingers of this change. Since the beginning of the series in 1875, that academic forum had maintained a strong emphasis on Latin America, but in 1964 the U.S. speakers introduced a number of papers dealing with the ethnohistory of North America.[45] It was symptomatic, if not causal, of a shift in perspective in the field: from that point onward there gradually developed in Spain a new anthropological awareness among historians of the Americas generally.[46] Soon afterward, a modern, if brief, ethnohistorical study by the Spanish anthropologist Alfredo Jiménez Núñez (1969) described the North Pacific coastal peoples encountered by Spanish explorers.

Nothing more of note appeared until the 1980s, when Spanish ethnohistorical scholarship regarding the natives of North America's Pacific coasts suddenly took off. Most of the catalogues, exhibitions, and studies of the scientific artwork generated by the Spanish maritime expeditions to the North Pacific are of ethnohistorical interest. The artists and other participants produced drawings, watercolors, and paintings for technical, scientific, and ethnological purposes, and most of this artwork is useful for the study of the native cultures (Palau de Iglesias 1980; Sotos 1981, 1982, 1984b; Sánchez Montañés 1989; Higueras 1991; Crosse and Sprätz 1998; Palau Baquero and Sprätz 1998; López y Sebastián 2000). Valencian artist Tomás de Suria, in particular, has had a significant impact on the field (Poupeney 1986; Sotos 1989; Monge and Olmo 1991; Rey 1991, 1995; Jiménez Pelayo 1997), as has naturalist José Mariano Moziño (Grunfeld 1986, 1988; Higueras, Pimentel, and Fernández 1993; Monge and Olmo 1999; Engstrand 2000). There are numerous general and miscellaneous studies focusing on the West Coast peoples and cultures of North America (Verde 1980; Alcina 1986, 1988; Navarro 1989; Ortega Soto 1989; Pérez Miguel 1989; Cabello 1989, 1999; Peset 1989; Haberland 1989; Suttles 1989; Alcina 1989; Olmo 1989; Carretero 1989, 1990, 1995, 1999; Sota 1989; Lenz 1989; Wright 1989; Olson and Porrúa 2002; Carlsson 1994; Inglis 1994, [2006]; Bartroli 1994; Sánchez Montañés 1998, 1999, 2008, 2009). The cultural sources most analyzed so far have been portraiture and landscapes, as well as native artistic productions and other artifacts (*El Ojo del Tótem* 1988; Grunfeld 1988; Jonaitis 1989; Sánchez Montañés 1989, 1991; Holm 1989, 1999; Basso, Bello, and Sauquet 1999), with some attention to vocabularies and language (Martín-Merás 1984; Bustamante 1989; Martinell and Martínez 1998). The contributions of the Malaspina expedition to anthropological and ethnographical understanding of the coast peoples have been pointed out in a number of studies (Sotos 1989; Higueras, Pimentel, and Fernández

1993; Pino 1982; Monge and Olmo 1991; Monge 1989, 1994, 2002; González Montero de Espinosa 1990, 1991; Pimentel 1993). The ethnographical value of the primary sources concerning the natives of Nootka has encouraged a special interest in that particular group (Grunfeld 1986; Jewitt 1990; Mociño 1999; Carretero 1989; Inglis 1995; Monge 1999; Palau Baquero, Calés, and Sánchez 1998; Cabello, Escalera, and Carreras 2000).

Adopting anthropological approaches but working mostly with historical documentary sources, Spanish ethnohistorians have tended to use information and perceptions gleaned from first or early contacts narrated by late eighteenth-century seafaring explorers. Consequently, they have focused almost exclusively on the indigenous peoples living along the coasts north of San Francisco as far as Alaska and the Aleutian islands. By contrast, they have shown no interest at all in the ethnohistory of the California mission Indians, for which many other kinds of valuable documentary, material, and archaeological information abound. No modern ethnohistorical study has been published in Spain about the California Indians before the arrival of the missionaries or, indeed, about the natives who, without accepting residence in the missions, maintained close economic relationships with the civilian settlers of Spanish California. Even more strikingly, very few studies have appeared that attempt to examine, from the Indian point of view, the experiences of the neophytes who lived under the mission regime.[47]

One hopes that this apparent thematic preference is a mere temporary coincidence, resulting perhaps from the general enthusiasm for revising the historiography of the maritime expeditions. There would be cause for concern if it actually revealed a certain intellectual prejudice against missionized Indians, considering them to be less worthy of study because of their supposed cultural degradation by virtue of prolonged exposure to Christian influences. As is well known, missionaries sometimes became demoralized or disenchanted with Indians whose own culture was significantly changed as a result of sustained contact with Europeans and their American-born offspring. There is not a little irony in the thought that some ethnohistorians might actually share the attitude that the "uncontaminated" Indian is more worthy of attention. This would leave the California Indians (and of course, *mestizos*) who were "infected" by "alien" cultural influences haplessly inhabiting a no-man's land of historiographical indifference. Certainly, the attention afforded to expeditionary texts can be justified on the grounds that they are indeed major sources for a historical period illuminated by scarce alternative sources of information. Nonetheless, much of the work done by Spanish ethnohistorians to date seems to indicate a greater interest in the early Spanish ethnologists than in the natives themselves. Only Emma Sánchez Montañés and Leoncio Carretero have undertaken anthropological work among native peoples of Canada's Pacific coast, whom they visit regularly, making sustained efforts to combine the results of their fieldwork with historiographical analysis. More recently, José Andrés Alonso has begun producing work on the Aleutian and other northern natives.

Historiographical Fields Untended: Thematic Absences and Silences

Having reviewed the main themes of Spanish historiography on the Californias and Pacific coasts further north, one is struck, too, by the relative scarcity (even total absence, in some cases) of work on other aspects. Relatively few Spanish authors have shown an interest in economic history. In the 1960s and 1970s, a series of volumes of primary sources edited by the U.S. scholar Michael Mathes (1969, 1970–71, 1974) documented early Spanish maritime and missionary expansion toward the North Pacific and, more generally, pointed the way toward economic topics. The fruits of Hernández Aparicio's doctoral research (1975, 1976, 1979) straddled the traditional history of maritime expeditions and a more modern focus on the Baja California pearl fisheries as an economic enterprise. This was followed by other studies looking at various economic activities, such as mining (Serrera 1980, Bernabeu 1987a), agriculture (Cutter 1987), vine cultivation and wine production (Borrego 2002), general commerce (Pérez Miguel 1988, Carretero 1999), and the sea otter trade (Bernabeu 1989c, Gibson 1994). Bernabeu and Romero (1988) looked into diverse economic aspects of mission change in Baja California in 1773, while Serrera and Fuentes (1988) examined statistical material for the Dominican missions of Baja California. An interest in natural environments and resources has encouraged historiographical approaches that explore how forms of economic exploitation, technological innovation, and scientific study have together shaped people's relationship to their environment. In this way, the new emphasis on scientific history has also led naturally to ecological history with strong economic implications, particularly regarding forms of Indian subsistence, or forests and other natural resources (Bernabeu 1991b, Pimentel 1991, Pérez Miguel 1993, Carretero 1995).

Similarly, Spanish historians have given little attention to the military officers who represented and defended Spanish sovereignty along the northwestern perimeter of the empire, or to political aspects of imperial expansion. A few documents and studies have been published on the best-known pioneer of colonizing expeditions to California, Hernán Cortés ([*CODOIN España*] 1842–95, vol. 4 [1844]; [*CODOINAO*] 1864–84, vol. 22 [1874], vol. 23 [1975]; Lorenzana 1958; González Rodríguez 1985; Léon Portilla 1985; Carreño 1990), as has the diary of lieutenant Blas Fernández y Somera, who accompanied Father Linck on a long overland expedition in 1766 (*Noticias y documentos* 1959). However, the names that most often appear as the main subjects of historical works belong to the protagonists of the founding expeditions of 1769–76—Juan Bautista de Anza (*Noticias y documentos* 1959; Hernández Sánchez-Barba 1962), Domingo de Elizondo (*Noticias y documentos* 1959), Miguel Costansó (*Noticias y documentos* 1959; Mañá 1992), Pedro Fages (Soler 1953, 1980; Cugat 1970; Serrera 1978; Beerman 1980; Boneu 1991), Fernando Rivera y Moncada (Burrus 1967a), and of course Gaspar de Portolá (Eldredge 1910; Sanahuja 1945a, 1945b; Carner-Ribalta 1947, 1966, 1971; *Noticias y documentos* 1959; Rodeja 1960; Boneu 1970a, 1970b, 1973, 1983, 1986a, 1986b; Cano, Escandell, and Mampel 1984; Cruz 1984; Infiesta 1985, 1986; Garriga 1986; Bernabeu 1992c; Piqueras 1992–93)—as well as a few key figures of later years, such as governors Felipe de Neve (1777–82) (Mathes 1981; Bernabeu, ed. 1994b), José Joaquín de Arrillaga (1792–94, 1800–14) and Diego Borica (1794–1800) (Martínez Salazar 1991, 1992), Pedro Alberni, who commanded the Spanish forces stationed at Nootka (Cutter 1987; Beerman 1998a), and the explorer of the Sacramento Valley in 1808, Gabriel Moraga (Cutter 1958a). Apart from such biographically oriented studies, government, political, and military matters have inspired only a little historiographical interest. This essay cannot cover the entire biography of José de Gálvez, but the political context of his crucial role in promoting Spanish imperial expansion into Alta California was highlighted by Claret (1963) and Navarro (1964). Boneu (1973) documented the adversarial relations between the protagonists of the founding expeditions of 1769–70, which were analyzed by Hilton (1994). Portolá's problems in establishing government authority were examined by Bernabeu (1992c), who also published (ed. 1994b) Felipe de Neve's *reglamento* of 1781. Galán (1988) studied conflicts between military and ecclesiastical authorities in the 1780s, while López Urrutia (2000) made a general appraisal of the Spanish army in California. Continuities and conflicts in the Mexican period (1821–48) are almost a historiographical desert in Spain, mitigated only recently by a study of the California missions under Mexican rule by Ruiz de Gordejuela (2007).

Likewise, there is practically nothing from Spain that addresses issues that might come under the thematic headings of demographic or social history of the Hispanic communities. Virtually no studies specifically address any issues connected with immigration, social structure, customs, Hispanic families and daily life, or gender. Under this category we can cite only articles by Manuel de Aranegui (1976) on the Argüello family in the eighteenth and nineteenth centuries; by Ramón Serrera (1980), on the difficulties of establishing civil communities around Baja California's silver mines; by Salvador Bernabeu (1994b, 2007), on the case of a bigamist and on the social role of rumors, respectively; and by Teresa Meade (1995), on marriage, class and identity in Alta California. Neither has the development of secular Hispanic culture in California communities attracted much historiographical attention. The enduring importance of the Spanish language seems to be the subject that most interests Spaniards today, judging by the articles dedicated to this subject from time to time in Spain's mass media. It has not, however, generated any great interest among historians, there being only one historical study of early Spanish linguistic influence in California (Blanco 1971).[48] Finally, practically no Spanish authors have attempted to write works of general synthesis about the history of the far northwestern expansion of the Spanish empire.[49]

Now, if the foregoing discussion reflects the general trends of Spanish historiography, and thus might be said to represent national perspectives, the next section of this essay will reveal that many of these historians share certain other discernible identities that have influenced their work.

Of Historians and Heroes: Other Collective Memories

One characteristic of Spanish historiography is the marked tendency of authors to broach the subjects we have mentioned from the perspective of individual protagonists or specific groups of individuals. This approach might be said to reflect old-fashioned historiographical models centered on the exaltation of Spanish national heroes.[50] This is not, however, always the case, or at least it is not the only possible interpretation. Indeed, it is clear that many of the protagonists discussed here have been portrayed as heroes representing collective identities other than Spanish national identity.

Of course, protagonists (whether presented as heroes or villains) have been at the center of historiography since it was invented, although the narrative style might vary from the romantic to the "scientific," from the hagiographic to the positivist, or from the nuts-and-bolts, blow-by-blow daily grind to the spiritual and psychological journey of self-discovery. The attraction of biographical or personal approaches, for the scholar and the general public, resides in how individual lives can encapsulate, for good or ill, the social and cultural values shared by authors and their readers. Individual travails, virtues, and ideas, whether these include heroic triumphs over adversity or not, can inspire emotional involvement as well as intellectual admiration. Historians can achieve effective persuasiveness either by rational discussion or by turning the historical narrative into romantic drama, but the greatest success accompanies a seamless discourse that appeals to a combination of reason and emotion, interest and passion. When historical protagonists are identified as members of particular social groups or communities, all the members of those groups and communities are invited to appropriate and celebrate the finer human qualities displayed in those single lives. Moreover, according to one theorist, the heart of every biographical work is the relation established between the biographer and his subject.[51] It seems reasonable to suppose that this personal connection becomes especially relevant when the bond between authors and the individuals they study is seen to gain strength and meaning from a shared interest or identity, in this case other than (or as well as) the "Spanish national" label. A closer look at these relationships reveals that professional interests and diverse ethnic or national identities have exerted powerful influences on the thematic choices and interpretive frameworks of many Spanish historians who have studied the North Pacific rim of the Spanish American empire.

Professional Identities

Easily discernible in Spanish historiography is the special attention paid to the role of missionaries, naval officers, and scientists. This predilection might go unnoticed or prove to be meaningless, except for the fact that it often reveals professional identities shared by historians and their subjects.

We have already noted that a considerable number of studies of the California missions focus on group biographies of religious orders and on individual missionaries.[52] Furthermore, one of the most striking characteristics of this historiographical field is that it has been dominated by members of religious orders. Here we have the clearest possible case of a close connection between authors and their historical subjects, based on shared professional and ideological identities. Eyewitness chroniclers Francisco María Píccolo, Juan María de Salvatierra, Fernando Consag, and Miguel Venegas, and editors or historians Andrés Marcos Burriel,

Francisco Xavier Fluviá, Fidel Fita, Constantino Bayle, and Alejandro Rey-Stolle (writing under the pseudonym of Adro Xavier) were all Jesuits. The first Franciscan chronicler of Alta California, Francisco Palóu, has had able successors in historians Fidel de Lejarza, Zephyrin Engelhardt, Pedro Sanahuja, Ignacio Omaechevarría,[53] Andrés de Palma, Juan R[uiz de] Larriñaga, Bonifacio Castellanos, Manuel Pazos, Lázaro Lamadrid, Lino Gómez Canedo, Enrique Oltra, Valentín Martínez Grácia, Pedro Borges, Salustiano Vicedo, and José Luis Soto Pérez, all of whom were or are Franciscans. Other authors professionally connected with the Catholic Church who have written about the California missionaries and their work are Fathers Francisco Torréns and Miguel López Bonet,[54] the Augustines Casiano García and Antonio Corredor, the Pauline Sebastián Rubí Darder, and the Dominican Lorenzo Galmés Más. Likewise, Dominicans Luis de Sales, Alfonso Esponera, and Vito T. Gómez wrote about the contribution of their own order to California history. These Spanish scholars have been well supported by their U.S. colleagues, Jesuit Ernest Burrus, and Franciscans Zephyrin Engelhardt, Francis J. Weber, Francis F. Guest, and Maynard J. Geiger, who have also been published in Spain.[55]

These religious historians have all displayed strong loyalties grounded in their own professional and ideological identities. Their heroes are members of their faith and usually of their own religious order. In other words, the "nation" to which they and their historical subjects belong is the Catholic Church. Arguably, then, their work is more representative of a transnational historiography of Catholicism and, within that, of their respective religious orders, than of "Spanish national" historiography.

Naval officers who participated in maritime expeditions along the Pacific coast of North America have also frequently been singled out by historians publishing in Spain.[56] Shared professional interests hold strong here too. Throughout the nineteenth and twentieth centuries, many historical works about maritime expeditions, their protagonists, and their international contexts have been compiled, edited, or written by naval officers: José Espinosa,[57] Martín Fernández de Navarrete,[58] Lieutenant Pedro de Novo, Lieutenant Cesáreo Fernández Duro, naval surgeon Cristóbal Ariza, Junior Captain (or Commander) Julio Fernando Guillén,[59] Luis Cebreiro,[60] Junior Captain (or Commander) Lorenz Sanfeliú, Rear Admiral Carlos Martínez-Valverde, Roberto Barreiro-Meiro,[61] Captain Agustín Albarracín, Amancio Landín, Luis Sánchez Masiá, Senior Lieutenant (or Lieutenant Commander) Antonio Menchaca, and Ricardo Cerezo.[62] Clearly, Spanish naval officers with scholarly inclinations have found effective motivation in the professional identity that they have had in common with the protagonists of their historical research. In addition, other contributions have been published by qualified personnel professionally affiliated (or otherwise closely associated) with naval institutions. Authors and editors María Dolores Higueras and María Luisa Martín-Merás, for example, are research librarians and curators who work in the Naval Museum.[63]

By contrast, military officers who are also scholars of history have found little in the Spanish Californias to inspire their particular professional interests or to reinforce their esprit de corps. None of the studies of Cortés, Anza, Rivera, Costansó, Fages, Portolá, Neve, Arrillaga, Borica, Alberni, and Moraga have been written by professional soldiers. A minor professional link is afforded by a study of strategic defense by artillery officer Juan Batista González. A different collective identity linking those historical protagonists with their historians will be discussed in the next part of this essay.

Dramatic and compelling aspects of Spain's historical connections with North America have inspired a significant number of Spanish diplomats, particularly those who have served at some point in the United States, to pen historiographical works; but curiously enough, the international contexts of the Spanish North Pacific expeditions and colonial expansion have not attracted much attention from members of this professional body. Only one very early study of the international conflict at Nootka may be described as reflecting the professional interests of its author, Jordán de Urríes, Marqués de Ayerbe, who was a high-level diplomat.[64] Editors and authors who are in some way connected with the Spanish Ministry of Foreign Affairs are Antonio Orozco, the director of the Real Academia Hispano-Americana in Cadiz; Mercedes Palau Baquero, who is now retired from the civil service in the ministry but remains active in historiographical endeavors;[65] and Palau Baquero's assistants Aránzazu Zabala and Blanca Saiz.[66]

Among the men who contributed to the increase of scientific knowledge in California and the Northwest, Spanish historiography has dedicated considerable attention to natural scientists José Mariano Mociño and José Longinos Martínez, naval hydrographer José Espinosa y Tello, technical naval draughtsman Felipe Bauzá, and artist Tomás de Suria, as well as the Czech naturalist Tadeo Haenke. Historians writing before 1975 who can themselves be considered professional scientists or technical experts include naval officers Cesáreo Fernández Duro and Rafael Estrada Arnaiz; industrial engineer Ramón Manjarrés, whose special expertise was in chemistry and experimental physics; geographer Amando Melón; and naturalists Francisco de las Barras y de Aragón and Carlos Henckel. More recent authors of scientific history, Marisa González Montero de Espinosa,[67] María Victoria Ibáñez Montoya,[68] Luis Rafael Martínez-Cañavate,[69] and Félix Muñoz Garmendía,[70] are formally trained scientists. We might further broaden the group of historians who could identify with such subjects by considering scientific intellectual perspectives as well as formal training. We have already noted that the post-Franco generation of professional historians has shown a remarkable interest in the history of science, scientific artwork (technical drawing, botanical drawings, landscape, portraiture), and ethnography. One might say that they have found their own heroes in the scientists and artists of Spain's maritime explorations of the Enlightenment. Perhaps a case might be made for another kind of shared "professional" identity based on similar intellectual attitudes. We could argue that historians and ethnologists in Spain today share with the scientists of the late-eighteenth century a sense of modernity, of connectedness with other scientists and intellectuals of the Western world, of being (then and now) actively involved in a progressive intellectual endeavor to know and understand the world.

Natural Patriotisms: Identities of Birthplace and Ethnicity

There is no doubt that Spanish nationalism has influenced the development of historiography in Spain. Nonetheless, since the formation of this nation-state in the early modern era, "nationalism" as a category has defied easy definition or application.[71] Contested "national" identities with deep historic roots and territorial heartlands have always had a place in Spanish consciousness and historiography, and, since the advent of democracy in 1976, they have gained increasing social, cultural, and political visibility. Today, *within* the Spanish nation-state, other identities based on birthplace, family lineage, or perceived ethnicity are flourishing, as individuals and groups claim the right to define their own national identities as they (or the politicians who represent them) see fit.[72] Consequently, it is of historiographical interest to inquire whether these diverse patriotisms and national identities have played any part in Spanish publications concerning the Pacific rim of North America.

The colonial Spanish borderlands of North America have in fact offered plenty of opportunities to construct and exploit "usable" pasts for the purposes of showcasing, promoting, or reinforcing natural patriotisms and contested nationalisms. The approach which lends itself most readily to such representations is, once again, the focus on historical protagonists, either individually or in groups, but in this case defined by their local birthplace or ethnic nationality. Nineteenth-century Spanish erudites published many reference works compiling biographical information about the "illustrious sons" of cities and regions.[73] This tradition fell out of favor during most of the twentieth century, but since Franco's death in 1975, a new kind of attention to native sons and local heroes has been developing apace, as the political and cultural leaders of regional ethnic nationalities have increasingly sought to reinforce their own present communities' sense of their separate historical identities. These leaders may or may not believe that the "narrativity" of a nation's history can satisfy the human longing for immortality, or that linking historical heroes with present members of the community promotes a sense of "deep, horizontal comradeship," but most would no doubt recognize the political value of such a proposition.[74]

The examples given in this section show that a considerable number of historians and their subjects do indeed have birthplace or ethnic identities in common. In many cases this coincidence seems to have been a motivational factor. General interpretive comments will follow the examples, but it must be stressed that, while local patriotism must be recognized as a motivating ideology, this essay is not trying to argue that all the historiography produced in these circumstances has necessarily been inspired by political agendas of Andalusian, Aragonese, Basque, Catalonian, Galician, Mallorcan (or Balearic), and Valencian nationalisms.[75]

Andalusia does not provide the strongest case, but historical protagonists explicitly identified as being from this region by historians who are also Andalusians are silver miner Manuel de Ocio (Serrera 1980) and naval officer Esteban José Martínez (Borrego 1988).[76] Aragon offers several examples. Admiral Pedro Porter and missionary Francisco Garcés are claimed as representatives of this region by a number of authors who are themselves Aragonese or who have formed strong attachments to Aragon. Ricardo del Arco (1947) was born in Granada but settled in Huesca, where he worked in the state department of archives and libraries and was an active promoter of local erudition.[77] Anselmo Gascón (1950) and professional historian José Antonio Armillas Vicente (1988)[78] are both Aragonese, as is naval officer Manuel Gracia Rivas (1988, 1989), who thus shares both professional and national identities with his subject, Pedro Porter.[79] The treatment of Garcés by José María Bardavío (1971, 1988, 1990) leaves no doubt about the reason for his historiographical interest in this Aragonese missionary-explorer.

Basque Franciscans Pedro Pérez de Mezquía, Fermín Francisco de Lasuén, Pablo de Mugártegui, and Vicente de Sarriá formed a strong contingent among the missionaries connected with Alta California, giving ample scope to Basque authors Buenaventura Salazar (1935), Ignacio Omaechevarría (1950, 1956, 1958, 1959, 1963, 1964a), Juan Ruiz de Larriñaga (1915), and Idoia Arrieta (1996b, 2004a, 2004b, forthcoming) to underscore the Basque national identity of these men.[80] Arrieta has made her point of view quite clear in several other publications (and unpublished studies) on the Basque contribution to California history. In addition, several Basques were among the noteworthy military officers in California. Diego de Borica, Joaquín Arrillaga and Pablo Vicente Sola Arrizabalaga provided Basque journalist Ángel Martínez Salazar (1991, 1992, 1994) with good subjects for several of his forays into Basque history, while Arrieta has initiated a research project on Arrillaga. Basque genealogist Manuel de Aranegui (1976) contributed a study of the Argüello family, several of whose members served in the California military.[81] Basque authors have been most diligent in popularizing and exalting the role of Basque sailors who participated in the North Pacific explorations, possibly because seamanship and seafaring enterprise have been useful as distinguishing historical traits for those promoting traditional Basque national consciousness. Author Antonio Menchaca is not only Basque but also a naval officer, as well as being a successful entrepreneur and a novelist. In his work on naval expeditions to the North Pacific, another Basque businessman, politician, and historian, Javier de Ybarra y Bergé (1945, 1946, 1964), especially emphasized Bodega y Cuadra's role.[82] Even though this naval officer was born in Lima, he is presented by Basque genealogist Adolfo Lafarga (1949), Ana De la Quadra-Salcedo (1960), and Ybarra (1964) as being Basque by virtue of his Biscayan ancestry.[83] This is consistent with tendencies visible in most historiography on ethnic groups and nations that have developed a strong sense of their people's historical diaspora. They often claim as their own individuals who emigrated and adopted other national identities, sometimes, as in this case, including later generations.

Magín Catalá and Pedro (Pere) Sanahuja, who translated Zephyrin Engelhardt's biography of the California missionary, were also compatriots of the closest kind, both having been born in the town of Montblanc, in the Catalonian province of Tarragona. However, Catalonian historians have been most inspired by the Catalonian soldiers who served in California and the expeditions further north. Coupled in representation of Catalonia are, on the one hand, military engineer Miguel Costansó and author Tibisay Mañá and, on the other, Pedro Fages and his biographers Joseph Soler Vidal,[84] Josep M. Cugat, and Fernando Boneu. The most frequent case of shared ethnic identity is that of the plethora of Catalonian authors who have chosen to write about explorer and military leader Gaspar de Portolá: Pedro Sanahuja, Joseph Carner-Ribalta,[85] Eduardo Rodeja,[86] Fernando Boneu,[87] Angela Cano, Neus Escandell and Elena Mampel,[88] José Luis Infiesta,[89] Ernesto Beya,[90] and Ricardo Piqueras.[91] Of these, perhaps among the more interesting cases are two Catalonian exiles living in Mexico after the Spanish Civil War: Joseph Carner-Ribalta and Joseph Soler Vidal. These two authors published works about the Catalonian protagonists of the occupation of Alta California, Portolá and Pedro Fages, respectively, not only writing in the Catalan language but also actually translating documents from their original Spanish into Catalan.

For his part, Amancio Landín surely chose to pay special attention to the exploits of Francisco Antonio Mourelle de la Rúa in part because, as well as being a great sailor, he was a Galician, a strong ethnic identity that he and Landín also had in common. Naval officer and editor Roberto Barreiro-Meiro and one of his subjects, Jacinto Caamaño Moraleja, were also both natives of Galicia.

Many of the Alta California missionaries hailed from the island of Mallorca. Francisco Palóu, Juan Crespí, Mariano Payeras, Jerónimo Boscana, Buenaventura Sitjar, Junípero Serra himself, and others were among that Balearic island's most famous native sons. In this case, too, the number of authors who shared the Mallorcan (or Balear) national identity is significant. Lorenzo (Llorenç) Riber was an eminent Latinist and Spain's foremost translator of classical texts into Spanish.[92] Andrés de Palma was born in the Mallorcan capital, Palma, and therefore had both professional and national identities in common with the California Franciscans.[93] Salustiano Vicedo settled at the convent in Petra, Serra's hometown, in 1969, when the Franciscan province was reestablished there. José Vidal Isern published several biographies and many other works on Mallorcan history and culture. Francisco Sintes was a Minorcan.[94] The Dominican historian Lorenzo Galmés was born in Manacor, near Petra.[95] Mallorcan historian Bartolomé (Bartomeu) Font dedicated the greater part of his professional life to the story of Serra and his companions in the California missions, and their links to Mallorca.[96] Several other authors of mission historiography, whose exact birthplaces I have not been able to ascertain, certainly have strong ties to Mallorca or one of the other Balearic Islands.[97] Mallorca also claims as a native son one of the outstanding scientific artists of the Malaspina expedition, Felipe Bauzá,[98] whose name is paired with that of a Balearic historian who specialized in naval and maritime subjects, Juan Llabrés.[99]

Finally, Dominican Luis de Sales, whose first-hand accounts are a key source for the history of his coreligionaries in Baja California, was from Valencia, as is historian Vicente Ribes, who has published several other studies about the historical links between Valencians and America.

In summary, diverse patriotisms have clearly played a significant role in Spanish historiography on the Californias and Pacific coasts of North America. Missionaries and soldiers in particular are portrayed as representatives of ethnic nationalities by virtue of their birthplaces. By contrast, the ethnic identities of the maritime expeditionaries in the North Pacific seem to have been less "usable" for historians than their professional naval-scientific identities and their Spanish national identities. Sailors are arguably less easily portrayed as representatives of their places of birth because they are stereotypically rootless wanderers, serving for long periods at sea, or stationed on ships or at ports away from home. Nonetheless, the examples of naval officers that we have identified reflect the historical importance of the maritime dimensions of Basque and Galician national identities. We have also seen that many authors share local or ethnic identities with their subjects. Indeed, this factor may often explain why some historians have chosen to write about certain historical protagonists. The composite list of authors contributing to this kind of local patriotic historiography includes Borrego and Serrera for Andalusia; Armillas, Bardavío, Arco, Gracia Rivas, Gascón, and Vito T. Gómez for Aragon; Arrieta, Quadra-Salcedo, Lafarga, Larriñaga, Martínez Salazar, Menchaca, Omaechevarría, Salazar, and Ybarra, for the Basque Country; Infiesta, Bartroli, Boneu, Cano, Escandell and Mampel, Carner-Ribalta, Cugat, Garriga, Mañá, Piqueras, Rodeja, Sanahuja, and Soler Vidal, for Cataluña; Barreiro-Meiro and Landín for Galicia; Palma, Font, Galmés, Llabrés Bernal, Palóu, Riber, Sintes, Torréns, and Vidal, and also probably Llabrés Martorell, López Bonet, Piña, Ramis, Rubí, and Sabater for Mallorca (or the Balearic Islands generally); Ribes and Sales for Valencia. Clearly, for some, the recognition of a shared birthplace ethnicity has been an issue, although it is obviously impossible to make any generalizations about the extent to which this circumstance has affected the results of their historiographical work. At the very least, then, diverse local birthplace and ethnic patriotisms have influenced the choices of subject made by a considerable number of historians, as well as the sympathetic if not hagiographic treatment of their chosen heroes. Such natural patriotic affinities may sometimes reflect political ideologies and agendas, but one cannot rule out the possibility that authors and readers alike may consider such identities to be compatible with Spanish nationalism.

While one should not exaggerate the significance of these professional and birthplace or ethnic identities shared by authors and their subjects, being aware of them may serve as a counterweight or corrective to the notion that historical studies published in Spain (or for that matter, any other European nation-state) necessarily or predominantly reflect a single national perspective. At the very least, these findings suggest that historiography, like many other human endeavors, may simultaneously reflect and serve multiple individual as well as collective interests and identities. They also lend support for the idea that the development of Spanish nationalism has been relatively weak and has struggled historically with other ethnic and national identities within the nation-state.[100]

Some Political and Commercial Uses of Collective Identities

Apart from considering the shared interests and identities of historical protagonists and their historians, we should note the importance of the role of sponsors, promoters, and publishers. Even a cursory glance at the bibliography shows that diverse agents actively support certain professional groups (whether they are religious orders or the armed forces) as well as nationalisms (inspired by either the Spanish nation-state or regional and local patriotisms). In effect, sponsors and publishers are often not commercial publishing houses, but institutions that represent professional interests, local and regional cultural and political interests, or the Spanish national government, through public funding and other support of diverse academic activities.[101] Some agencies are cultural institutions, publicly or privately financed, that produce books and/or periodical publications on specific themes. Some reinforce the identities of professional bodies while others reinforce the identities of local and perceived ethnic communities.

Most remarkably, perhaps, the newly created autonomous regional governments and numerous local institutions seek to encourage all kinds of historiography, amateur and professional, in the service of regional and ethnic historical consciousness and patriotic pride.[102] They promote and finance conferences, expositions, prizes, and the publication of works that stress the origins and historical importance of protagonists and emigrants who were born in (or otherwise represent) their respective regions and municipalities. The spectacular growth of these governments has led to the efficient convergence of two new phenomena: the political will to promote stronger ethnic national consciousness (and a hopefully concomitant political loyalty) within autonomous regions and the availability of funds to finance research and publication. Most actively supportive of publications focusing on their respective historical regional or ethnic "nations" (at least in this particular thematic case study) have been the autonomous governments of the Basque Country and Catalonia.[103] These programs are purportedly part of a general policy of encouraging academic activities in whatever field, with no favored subjects or approaches. The reality may not be so innocent, but even when authors, patrons, and publishers freely announce that their aim is to strengthen and celebrate collective identities, it is impossible to measure the actual result. The scholar, the popularizer, the patron, and the publisher doubtless know what they aim to achieve, but they could be preaching to the converted while broader public opinion (and deeper private sentiment) may or may not respond as hoped. Moreover, even if it were possible to affirm the effectiveness of such politically oriented historiography, regional and ethnic national identities are not necessarily incompatible with Spanish nationalism.

An underlying ideological persuasion or personal conviction may lead some authors to identify with the political and cultural agendas of local and regional governments, but in many cases a more neutral explanation can probably be found in mere academic opportunism in the face of institutional and government sponsorship. In short, it is a question of scholars taking advantage of chances to participate in conferences and to publish papers and monographs thanks to the availability of local or autonomous government funds. In such circumstances, expediency rather than local patriotism might recommend the identification of the historical protagonists by their birthplace or regional nationalities. Examples of this practice include two of Salvador Bernabeu's papers, one explicitly identifying Father Juan González Vizcaíno as being from Palencia for a conference about people from Castile and León in America ([1992]b), and another about Galicians in Alta California for a conference held in Galicia (1989g); Arsenio Rey's studies on the Valencian artist Tomás de Suria; Armando Miguélez's article for a journal published in Alicante; and even more obviously John Kendrick's paper highlighting Dionisio Alcalá's origins in Cabra, for a conference held in Andalusia. These authors opportunistically stressed the birthplace identity of their subjects, but clearly had no personal attachment to the birthplace or ethnicity of their respective biographees.

It is difficult to make any generalizations about the relative weight of the factors that have moved historians in Spain to write about particular historical protagonists or groups of individuals. Apart from the perennial attraction of the personal or biographical approach to historiography, this essay points to possible motivations such as shared professional identities and patriotism inspired by birthplace or perceived ethnicity, as well as uncomplicated opportunistic responses to institutional and government sponsorship, all of which the authors themselves may not have bothered to rationalize even briefly. In any case, while it is useful to be aware of ideological and circumstantial factors that influence historians' choices, in the end, the historiographical value of their work must rest on the merits of the scholarship.

One last thought concerns the impact of modern tourism on museums, monuments, and other attractions. This trend is still in its infancy in Spain, where massive tourism has been organized almost exclusively around the beaches and leisure resorts. But the commercial promotion of Spain's rich cultural heritage will no doubt lead the custodians of naval, military, and ecclesiastical museums, monuments, sites, buildings, and even cemeteries, increasingly to promote touristic consumption of popular historical works destined for the general reader. This is likely to give a fresh boost to historiography focusing on professional, local, regional, and ethnic identities. The combined force of the mass media, the Internet, touristic historiography, special interest sponsors, promoters and publishers, politicians, and other cultural brokers poses a stiff challenge to professional historians based at universities for control of the interpretive narratives of Spain's past.[104] In such a struggle, who can tell if Spanish historical connections with the West Coast of North America will become even more "usable"?

Conclusion

North America's western seaboard lay on the remote periphery of the early modern Spanish empire. Its active political connection with Spain lasted only a few generations, in times of severe crisis for successive metropolitan governments. Most of the inhabitants were only faintly Hispanicized in culture. Consequently, that region and its peoples have existed only tenuously in Spanish historical consciousness, as once forming part of Spain's imperial frontiers but having little if any impact on the formation of Spanish national identity in Spain itself.

Spanish nationalism may appear to explain the historiographical tendency to focus on the exploits of historical protagonists, whether individually or in groups. However, without disputing that interpretation, this study shows that the heroes of Spain's colonial expansion into the Californias and further north may just as easily be seen to represent other collective identities. A great many of those historical protagonists and their historians have in common professional interests, or identities based on birthplace, lineage, or perceived ethnicity. Indeed, in some cases, historians and their heroes share both professional and birthplace or ethnic identities. Members of religious orders and priests have edited sources or written about the lives and labors of missionaries, naval officers have written about naval officers, and scientists (including perhaps the current generation of professional historians) have written about scientists. At the same time, Aragonese historians write about Aragonese heroes, Basques write about Basques, Catalonians about Catalonians, and so on. These other collective identities may be more or less compatible with Spanish national identity, but there is no doubt that they represent powerful and enduring interests and attachments that have also functioned as ideological motives of historiography.

An appraisal of the subjects most frequently appearing in Spanish historiography since the late eighteenth century reveals a constant predominant interest in maritime expeditions and Catholic missions. Both are redolent of national-imperial expansionist perspectives, but this study suggests another (again, not incompatible) interpretation. The historiography on maritime expeditions has clearly been influenced by the professional interests and loyalties of authors belonging to the Spanish navy and naval institutions, while mission history has been written almost exclusively by members of religious orders and other Catholic institutions.

The development of democracy in Spain since 1976 and Spain's growing presence in world affairs has encouraged the professional modernization and gradual internationalization of Spanish historical scholarship. Increasingly influenced by the general theoretical and methodological trends of Western historiography, the new generation of professional historians and anthropologists have successfully claimed their place as members of a global community of historians, following the same criteria and applying the same standards regarding sources and methods, and conversant with the same interpretive theories and practices. Meanwhile, greater optimism about Spain's place in the modern world has led Spanish scholars to focus on Spain's historical contributions to that modernity. Whereas mission historiography has as yet barely been touched by modern ethnohistorical approaches, the traditionally predominant attention to maritime expeditions has not only increased but has also been linked to broader studies of international contexts, as well as to the history of science, scientific and technical artwork, and ethnology on the Pacific coasts of North America. In fact, the remarkable enthusiasm for studying the work of scientists, artists, and ethnologists seems to suggest that these may be the new heroes of today's historians. This trend is undoubtedly motivated in part by a desire to seek due recognition, at home and abroad, of Spain's scientific contributions and role in the intellectual progress of the early modern world. On the other hand, and stretching the idea of professional identities, it might be interpreted as a case of scientists studying scientists, reflecting the existence of intellectual affinities between the new Spanish historians and their chosen heroes of the Spanish Enlightenment.

NOTES

I wish to thank Amancio Labandeira, Salvador Bernabeu, María Luisa Martín-Merás, and Miguel Luque for their help, and the Spanish Ministry of Education and Science for financial aid awarded to research projects HUM2006-11365/HIST and HAR2009-13284.

1   For overviews of the Spanish case, see, for example, Paloma Cirujano, Teresa Elorriaga, and Juan S. Pérez Garzón, *Historiografía y nacionalismo español, 1834–1868* (Madrid: C.S.I.C., 1985); Gonzalo Pasamar, "La historiografía franquista y los tópicos del nacionalismo historiográfico español," *Studium* 5 (1993): 7–31; Carolyn P. Boyd, *Historia patria: History and National Identity in Spain, 1875–1975* (Princeton, N.J.: Princeton University Press, 1997); Juan S. Pérez Garzón, "El debate nacional en España: ataduras y ataderos del romanticismo medievalizante," *Ayer* 36 (1999): 159–76, and, with others, *La gestión de la memoria: la historia de España al servicio del poder* (Barcelona: Crítica, 2000); Carlos Serrano, *El nacimiento de Carmen: símbolos, mitos y nación* (Madrid: Taurus, 1999); Jorge Cañizares-Esguerra, "Historiography and Patriotism in Spain," in *How to Write the History of the New World* (Stanford: Stanford University Press, 2001), 130–203; Juan Pro Ruiz, "La crítica al estado liberal y la perspectiva americanista: los ingredientes ideológicos del nacionalismo español, 1890–1940," in *Redes intelectuales y formación de naciones en España y América Latina (1890–1940)*, ed. Marta E. Casaús and Manuel Pérez Ledesma (Madrid: Universidad Autónoma, 2005), 329–54; Antonio Feros, "'Spain and America: All Is One': Historiography of the Conquest and Colonization of the Americas and National Mythology in Spain c.1892–c.1992," in *Interpreting Spanish Colonialism: Empires, Nations, and Legends*, ed. Christopher Schmidt-Nowara and John M. Nieto-Phillips (Albuquerque: University of New Mexico Press, 2005), 87–134.

2   See Peter Mandler, "What Is 'National Identity'? Definitions and Applications in Modern British Historiography," *Modern Intellectual History* 3 (2006): 271–97 at 286.

3   Feros argues that, for more than a century, historians in Spain have maintained "only one view about the identity of Spain as a global empire," constructing a "master imperial narrative" in which the history of Spanish America has been celebrated as "part of a shared concept of 'nation', or better still, a fundamental part of Spanish nationalism" ("'Spain and America: All Is One,'" 112, 126). His interpretation is debatable on more than one count, but in this essay I aim only to suggest that historiography (whether scholarly or popular) can actually work on several levels, reflecting and serving not one but several identities.

4   Useful introductions to social scientific theory on collective identities are Sheldon Stryker and Peter J. Burke, "The Past, Present and Future of an Identity Theory," *Social Psychology Quarterly* 63 (2000): 284–97; and Richard D. Ashmore, Kay Deaux, and Tracy McLaughlin-Volpe, "An Organizing Framework for Collective Identity: Articulation and Significance of Multidimensionality," *Psychological Bulletin* 130 (2004): 80–114.

5   As Peter Mandler concludes: "We certainly cannot assume that 'national identity' trumps other identities, or indeed that one 'national identity' must trump others" ("What is 'National Identity'?" 297).

6   The survey is based on works published in Spain, including books, articles, individual contributions in collective works, and a few PhD theses; and covers historiographical works as well as editions or printed transcriptions of primary sources. It includes a few titles contributed by non-Spanish authors (whether resident or not in Spain), and (with a few exceptions) excludes works published elsewhere by Spanish authors.

7   Many items fit two or more thematic or other descriptions. The bibliography that follows the endnotes contains the complete citations of references, which, for the sake of economy, are given only in author-date form in the main text. Other historiographical references and discursive comments will appear in the endnotes.

8   For earlier surveys, see for example, Salvador Bernabeu, "Las Californias en la historiografía española (1940–1989)," *Revista de Indias* 49 (1989): 817–28; and Sylvia L. Hilton, "Spanish Colonies in North America: Recent Historical Scholarship from Spain," *American Studies International* 32 (1994): 70–95.

9   The lack of studies on the post-Serra period, in particular, was "simply disconsolating" before 1989, according to Bernabeu, "Las Californias," 824, 822.

10 On this well-worn topic, see, for example, Charles Gibson, *The Black Legend: Anti-Spanish Attitudes in the Old World and the New* (New York: Knopf, 1971); Miguel Molina, *La leyenda negra* (Madrid: Nerea, 1991).

11 On late eighteenth-century Spanish historiography, see, for example, María Teresa Nava, "En torno a la historiografía oficial indiana (1764–1768): la bibliografía americanista y la primera Comisión de Indias," *Revista de Indias* 49 (1989): 111–33, and *Reformismo ilustrado y americanismo: la Real Academia de la Historia, 1735–1792* (Madrid: Universidad Complutense, 1989); Victor Peralta, "Patriotismo y reinos integrados. La historiografía americanista a fines del siglo XVIII," in *Relaciones sociales e identidades en América: IX Encuentro-Debate América Latina ayer y hoy*, ed. G. Dalla Corte et al. (Barcelona: Universitat de Barcelona, 2004), 301–14; Palmira Vélez, *La historiografía americanista en*

España, 1755–1936 (Madrid: Iberoamericana, 2007), 19–28. See also M. Dolores González-Ripoll, "La expedición del Atlas de la América Septentrional (1792–1819): orígenes y recursos," *Revista de Indias*, 50 (1990): 767–88, on the project to produce a maritime atlas of North America.

12 Munoz was appointed chief cosmographer of the Indies in 1770. See Nicolás Bas Martín, *Juan Bautista Muñoz (1745–1799) y la fundación del Archivo General de Indias* (Valencia: Generalitat Valenciana, 2000).

13 See note 38 on Spain's intellectual "Age of Silver."

14 See Sabater 1944, 183.

15 See Silvia Enrich, *Historia diplomática entre España e Iberoamérica en el contexto de las relaciones internacionales (1955–1985)* (Madrid: Cultura Hispánica, 1989); Lorenzo Delgado, *Imperio de papel: acción cultural y política exterior durante el primer franquismo* (Madrid: C.S.I.C., 1992); and Rosa Pardo, *Con Franco hacia el Imperio: la política española en América Latina (1939–1945)* (Madrid: Universidad Nacional de Educación a Distancia, 1995).

16 See Manuel Ballesteros Gaibrois, "La moderna ciencia, americanista española (1938–1950)," *Revista de Indias* (Madrid) 9 (1949): 579–95; Fernando de Armas et al., *Bibliografía americanista española, 1935–1963*. (Seville: C.S.I.C., 1964); Francisco Morales, *Historiadores españoles de América* (Seville: E.E.H.A., 1967); José A. Calderón, *El Americanismo en Sevilla, 1900–1980* (Seville: E.E.H.A., 1987); Sandra Rebok, "Americanismo, ciencia e ideología: la actividad americanista española a través de la historia," *Anales del Museo de América* 4 (1996): 79–105; and Jesús R. Navarro, "La Escuela de Estudios Hispanoamericanos: Sesenta Años de Americanismo en Sevilla (1942–2005)," *Anuario Americanista Europeo* 2 (2004): 35–54.

17 Keys 1950. This had been presented at the University of Madrid as a PhD thesis. Introducing the published version, Amando Melón contrived to remark that the thesis was given the highest grade, "it is fair to say, without recourse to the exceptionally benevolent rules that exist in Spain for the concession of Ph.D. degrees to foreigners" (Keys 1950, 8).

18 James A. Sandos, "Junipero Serra's Canonization and the Historical Record," *American Historical Review* 93 (1988): 1253–69, argued that historians' personal biases (both ethnocentric and religious) subvert objectivity, implying that this adversely affected the versions of Serra's life and work written by Catholic historians in the United States.

19 On May 9, 1985, the Pope declared Serra to be venerable, and on December 11, 1987, he accepted the Congregation of Sacred Rites' recommendation for Serra's beatification (that is, the Church recognized that his intercession produced one miracle). Sainthood requires recognition of another miracle. See Sandos, "Junipero Serra's Canonization."

20 One recent comparative study of all the frontier missions of northern New Spain by a Mexican scholar concludes that local conditions and other variables mean that it is not appropriate to apply a single preconceived idea or model of mission. See José Refugio De la Torre Curiel, "La frontera misional novohispana a fines del siglo XVIII: Un caso para reflexionar sobre el concepto de mis-

ión," in *El Gran Norte Mexicano. Indios, misioneros y pobladores entre el mito y la historia*, ed. Salvador Bernabeu Albert (Madrid: C.S.I.C., 2009), 285–330.

21 Abbad is best known for his history of Puerto Rico, but he gathered documentary sources for a more ambitious work. His *Relación de La Florida* (1785) also remained unpublished until recently, when it was edited by José María Sánchez and Juan José Nieto (Madrid: Iberoamericana, 2003).

22 The *Relación del viaje* was long attributed to José Espinosa y Tello, and several authors believe pilot-artist José Cardero could have been the author, but a greater consensus supports the authorship of the ships' captains Dionisio Alcalá Galiano and Cayetano Valdés. Previously, the Royal Press had printed a Spanish translation of Andrew Kippis's *Life* of Captain Cook (1795). A Spanish translation and refutation of Buache's memorial of 1790, which supported the veracity of Ferrer Maldonado's discoveries of 1588, was published in 1798.

23 On this naval officer, see Cuesta 1993.

24 On nineteenth-century Spanish historical and Americanist scholarship, see, for example, Manuel Moreno, *Historiografía romántica española: introducción al estudio de la historia en el siglo XIX* (Seville: Universidad de Sevilla, 1979); Leoncio López-Ocón, *De viajero naturalista a historiador: las actividades americanistas del científico español Marcos Jiménez de la Espada (1831–1898)* (Madrid: Universidad Complutense, 1991); Ignacio Peiró, "La historiografía académica en la España del siglo XIX," *Memoria y Civilización* 1 (1998): 164–96; *Los americanistas del siglo XIX: La construcción de una comunidad científica internacional*, ed. Leoncio López-Ocón, Jean-Pierre Chaumeil, and Ana Verde (Madrid: Iberoamericana, 2005); Vélez, *La historiografía americanista*; and Christopher Schmidt-Nowara, *The Conquest of History: Spanish Colonialism and National Histories in the Nineteenth Century* (Pittsburgh, Pa.: University of Pittsburgh Press, 2006).

25 See Luis Á. Sánchez Gómez, *Un imperio en la vitrina. El colonialismo español en el Pacífico y la Exposición de Filipinas de 1887* (Madrid: C.S.I.C., 2003).

26 See Salvador Bernabeu, *1892. El IV Centenario del Descubrimiento de América en España: coyuntura y conmemoraciónes* (Madrid: C.S.I.C., 1987), esp. pp. 107–50. See also José A. Calderón Quijano, "El IV Centenario del Descubrimiento de América," *Boletín de Bellas Artes* 18 (1990): 91–166.

27 Only two brief pieces by Cesáreo Fernández Duro (1901, 1903) appeared in this period.

28 We have already noted the appearance of publications commemorating other anniversaries: Serra's birth (1913, 1963), the discovery of California (1933), and Serra's death (1984).

29 Blanca Saiz 1992 is the indispensable starting point for historiography on the Malaspina expedition, although many new titles have appeared since the publication of that reference work. Here we shall refer only to titles dealing specifically or significantly with that expedition's activities on the coasts of California and the far northwest.

30 Bartroli i Nogué is a Spanish Civil War exile teaching Hispanic philology at the University of British Columbia in Vancouver.

31　The latter includes not only Hezeta's diaries but the one written by Father Miguel de la Campa Cos.

32　For general studies and context, see, for example, Higueras 1985–93, 1988a, 1999; González Claverán 1989; Alvariño 2000; Cerezo 1987–99.

33　The alarm regarding these threats had already been sounded. See for example, José Torrubia, *I moscoviti nella California, o sia dimostrazione della veritá del passo all'America Settentrionale nuovamente scoperto dei Russi* (Rome: Generoso Salomoni, 1759).

34　See, for example, *The Fulbright Difference, 1948–1992*, ed. Richard T. Arndt and David Lee Rubin (New Brunswick, N.J.: Transaction Publishers, 1993); *American Foundations in Europe: Grant-Giving Policies, Cultural Diplomacy, and Trans-Atlantic Relations, 1920–1980*, ed. Giuliana Gemelli and Roy MacLeod (Brussels: P.I.E.-Peter Lang, 2003; and Nicholas Cull, *The Cold War and the United States Information Agency: American Propaganda and Public Diplomacy, 1945–1989* (Cambridge: Cambridge University Press, 2008).

35　On Spanish-U.S. relations in this period, see for example, Boris N. Liedtke, "Spain and the United States, 1945–1975," in *Spain and the Great Powers in the Twentieth Century*, ed. Sebastian Balfour, and Paul Preston (New York: Routledge, 1999), 229–44; Lorenzo Delgado, "Las relaciones culturales entre España y Estados Unidos. De la Guerra Mundial a los Pactos de 1953," *Cuadernos de Historia Contemporánea* 25 (2003): 35–59, "Cooperación cultural y científica en clave política. Crear un clima de opinión favorable para las bases U.S.A. en España," in *España y Estados Unidos en el siglo XX*, ed. Lorenzo Delgado and M. Dolores Elizalde (Madrid: C.S.I.C., 2005), 207–45, and *Viento de poniente: El programa Fulbright en España* (Madrid: LID, Fulbright España, M.A.E., A.E.C.I., 2009); and Francisco J. Rodríguez, "'Haciendo amigos': intercambios educativos hispano-estadounidenses en clave política, 1959–1969," *Studia Historica. Historia Contemporánea* 25 (2007): 339–62.

36　See Neal M. Rosendorf, "Be El Caudillo's Guest: The Franco Regime's Quest for Rehabilitation and Dollars after World War II via the Promotion of U.S. Tourism to Spain," *Diplomatic History* 30 (2006): 367–407; and Sasha D. Pack, *Tourism and Dictatorship: Europe's Peaceful Invasion of Franco's Spain* (New York: Palgrave Macmillan, 2006).

37　*Documentos relativos a la Independencia de Norteamérica existentes en archivos españoles*, 11 vols. (Madrid: Ministerio de Asuntos Exteriores, 1976–86).

38　The period from the late nineteenth century to 1936 has been characterized as an intellectual and cultural "Age of Silver." On that generation of Spanish intellectuals and scholars, see for example, José Carlos Mainer, *La edad de plata (1902–1931): Ensayo de interpretación de un proceso cultural* (Barcelona: Asenet, 1975); *1907–1987: La Junta para Ampliación de Estudios e Investigaciones Científicas 80 años después*, ed. José M. Sánchez Ron, 2 vols. (Madrid: C.S.I.C., 1988); José M. López Sánchez, *Heterodoxos españoles: El Centro de Estudios Históricos, 1910–1936*. (Madrid: Marcial Pons, C.S.I.C., 2006); Salvador Bernabeu, "El Americanismo en el Centro de Estudios Históricos: Américo Castro y la creación de la Revista Tierra Firme (1935–1937)," in *De las Independencias al Bicentenario*, ed. Ariadna Lluís, Gabriela Dalla Corte, and Ferrán Camps

(Barcelona: Casa Amèrica Catalunya, 2006), 47–70, and "Los americanistas y el pasado de América: tendencias e instituciones en vísperas de la Guerra Civil," *Revista de Indias* 57 (2007): 251–82; and Álvaro Ribagorda, *Caminos de la modernidad. Espacios e instituciones culturales de la Edad de Plata (1898–1936)* (Madrid: Biblioteca Nueva, Fundación José Ortega y Gasset, 2010).

39 On this historian, see Salvador Bernabeu, "Cesáreo Fernández Duro, americanista," *Cuadernos del Instituto de Historia y Cultura Naval* 6 (1990): 49–56.

40 The historiography on the persecution and exile of scientists and other intellectuals during Franco's regime is too large a subject to broach here, but see, for example, Juan J. Carreras and Miguel Á. Ruiz, *La universidad española bajo el régimen de Franco (1939–1975)* (Saragossa, Spain: Institución Fernando el Católico, 1991); Luis E. Otero et al., *La destrucción de la ciencia en España: Depuración universitaria en el franquismo* (Madrid: Universidad Complutense, 2006).

41 Iris Higbie Wilson [Engstrand], "El Coronel Antonio Pineda y su viaje mundial," *Revista de Historia Militar* 8 (1964): 49–64, may also be mentioned here. Although Pineda's work is not especially relevant for California and Northwest Coast history, this U.S. scholar was one of the first modern historians to call attention to the value of Spanish contributions to the history of science in these late-eighteenth century expeditions. See, for example, Iris H. Wilson [Engstrand], "Scientists in New Spain: The Eighteenth Century Expeditions," *Journal of the West* 1 (1962): 24–44, and *Spanish Scientists in the New World: The Eighteenth Century Expedition* (Seattle: University of Washington Press, 1981).

42 The former president of Spain's Higher Council for Scientific Research, Alejandro Nieto, remarked in his preface to María de los Ángeles Calatayud, *Catálogo de las expediciones y viajes científicos españoles a América y Filipinas (siglos XVIII y XIX). Fondos del Archivo del Museo Nacional de Ciencias Naturales* (Madrid: C.S.I.C., Museo Nacional de Ciencias Naturales, 1984): "Now not only warriors and friars travel: there are scientists. Science is once again being written in Spanish (p. 12)."

43 See Martínez-Cañavate 1994 for hydrographical, astronomical, and geodesical work accomplished by the Malaspina expedition.

44 We have already mentioned the brief paper transcribing the work of Francisco Garcés on two Indian languages by Fernández Duro (1894).

45 See *XXXVI Congreso Internacional de Americanistas. España 1964. Actas y Memorias*, 4 vols. (Seville: Editorial Católica Española, 1966 [1967]). The proceedings also included a paper on eighteenth-century California Indians by Spanish author María Asunción Medel Valpuesta, who had just obtained her degree in history from the University of Seville.

46 José Alcina, "La antropología americanista en España, 1950–1970," *Revista Española de Antropología Americana* 7 (1972): 17–58, gives a long list of Spanish ethnohistorical publications for the years 1950–70, but on the Californias he mentions only the 1958 edition of Ajofrín's journey.

47 Only the contributions already mentioned in the discussion of mission historiography, by Fernández Galiano, Río, Serrera and Fuentes, and especially

Bernabeu (including one article in co-authorship with Fuentes), have tackled this subject using modern approaches. The other two contributions on mission Indians (Brandes 1992, Tóth 1998) are by non-Spanish scholars.

48 I hasten to clarify that linguists may have produced historiographical work that is not known to me. Rosenberg 1933 and Omaechevarría 1964b made only minor contributions.

49 Only Hilton 1992 has produced a general history of Spanish Alta California that takes into account imperial defense and expansion strategies, the international context, missions, presidios and civilian settlement, and the impact of Spanish colonization on the indigenous peoples.

50 See, for example, *La construcción del héroe en España y México, 1789–1847*, ed. Manuel Chust and Víctor Mínguez (Valencia: Universitat de Valencia, 2003), especially "Presentación" (pp. 9–15), Manuel Chust, "Héroes para la nacion" (pp. 91–112), and Francesc-Andreu Martínez, "El rescate del héroe: el panteón sincopado del liberalismo español (1808–1936)" (pp. 253–79).

51 Leon Edel, *Writing Lives: Principia Biographica* (New York: W. W. Norton, 1984), 14.

52 Among the Jesuits connected with Spanish expansion into Baja California, those receiving most historiographical attention are: Eusebio Francisco Kino, Juan María de Salvatierra, Francisco María Píccolo, and Sigismundo Taraval. Among the Franciscans, those most studied are: Junípero Serra, Francisco Palóu, Francisco Garcés, Juan Crespí, Fermín de Lasuén, Pedro Pérez de Mezquía, Pablo de Mugártegui, Juan Antonio Joaquín de Barreneche, Francisco Ajofrín, Miguel de la Campa Cos, Magín Catalá, Jerónimo Boscana, and Mariano Payeras. Other religious protagonists who appear in Spanish historiography are Father Antonio de la Ascensión; the Dominicans Luis de Sales and Francisco Galisteo; and the first bishop of Sonora, Sinaloa and the Californias, Antonio de los Reyes.

53 On this author, see Paulo Agirrebaltzategi, "Ignacio Omaechevarría: Historiador de misiones y biógrafo de misioneros," *Verdad y Vida* 61 (2003): 191–208.

54 Miguel López Bonet is possibly also a Franciscan, but I have not been able to verify this.

55 Two other works fall outside the chronological framework of this study. One was written by an American Jesuit about the first archbishop of California: John Bernard McGloin, *El primer arzobispo de California: La vida de José Sadoc Alemany, O.P., 1814–1888* (Vich: Claret, 1974). The other is Claudio Vilá Palá, S.P., *Escolapios en California, datos para su historia* (Salamanca: Calatrava, 1975).

56 Sixteenth and seventeenth century expeditionaries most often studied are Juan Rodríguez Cabrillo, Francisco de Ulloa, Lorenzo Ferrer Maldonado, Sebastián Vizcaíno, Pedro Porter, and Isidro Atondo y Antillón. Eighteenth-century expeditionaries are Juan Pérez, Bruno de Heceta, Juan Francisco de la Bodega, Francisco Antonio Mourelle, Ignacio de Arteaga, Esteban José Martínez, José Tobar, Antonio Tova, Juan Gutiérrez de la Concha, Salvador Fidalgo, Manuel Quimper, Francisco de Eliza, José María Narváez, Alejandro Malaspina, Dionisio Alcalá, Jacinto Caamaño, Cayetano Valdés, and José Longinos.

57 First director of the Hydrographical Deposit in Madrid.
58 Appointed director of the Hydrographical Deposit in 1797. See Miguel Salvá and Pedro Sainz de Baranda, "Nota biografica de don Martín Fernández de Navarrete, y Catálogo de sus obras, 15 marzo 1845," in [*CODOIN España*] 6 (1845):5–22.
59 Also director of the Naval Museum in Madrid.
60 Director of the Naval Museum and commander of the marine guard's training ship *Juan Sebastián Elcano*, 1950–52.
61 Secretary of the Historical Marine Institute and subdirector of the Naval Museum.
62 Director of the Naval Museum.
63 Martín-Merás is currently the technical director at the Naval Museum. Alicia Fernández González, who transcribed texts for Higueras, Pimentel, and Fernández 1993 is an administrative staffer in the civil service. María Pilar San Pío is a curator of the archive at the Botanical Garden in Madrid.
64 L. A. Bolín might also be included in this diplomatic category. I believe that this author is Luis Antonio Bolín, a medical doctor who, at different times, served as the London correspondent of the daily newspaper *ABC*, as the general director of tourism (in the late 1930s), and as information consultant in the Spanish embassy in Washington.
65 Mercedes Palau Baquero served as director of exhibitions for the commemoration of the fifth centennial of Spain's discovery of America.
66 Both Zabala and Saiz had university degrees when employed as research assistants to Mercedes Palau.
67 Marisa González Montero de Espinosa is a trained biologist with a strong research interest in physical anthropology.
68 María Victoria Ibáñez Montoya received her PhD degree in science from the Complutense University of Madrid in 1992.
69 Rear Admiral Martínez-Cañavate is a hydrographer.
70 Muñoz Garmendía works at the Royal Botanical Garden in Madrid. Also, María Vigón Tobar, who was an assistant in the preparation of the nine-volume work directed by Ricardo Cerezo Martínez (1987–99), holds a degree in biology.
71 See *Nationalism and the Nation in the Iberian Peninsula: Competing and Conflicting Identities*, ed. Clare Mar-Molinero, and Angel Smith (Oxford: Berg, 1996); Juan Pablo Fusi, España. *La evolución de la identidad nacional* (Madrid: Temas de Hoy, 2000); José Álvarez Junco, "España y su laberinto identitario," and Juan S. Pérez Garzón, "Memoria, historia y poder. La construcción de la identidad nacional española," both in Francisco Colom González, ed., *Relatos de nación. La construcción de las identidades nacionales en el mundo hispánico*, 2 vols. (Madrid: Iberoamericana; Frankfurt: Vervuert, 2006), 1:463–76 and 2:697–728; and Sebastian Balfour and Alejandro Quiroga, *The Reinvention of Spain: Nation and Identity since Democracy* (Oxford: Oxford University Press, 2007).

72 On love of birthplace and homeland among different groups of Spaniards, see, for example, Boyd, *Historia patria*, 264.

73 See, for example, Amancio Labandeira, *Repertorios por lugar de nacimiento*, vol. 1, *Biblioteca Bibliográfica Hispánica*, series editor Pedro Sainz Rodríguez (Madrid: Fundación Universitaria Española, 1975).

74 In his discussion of Benedict Anderson's *Imagined Communities: Reflections on the Origin and Spread of Nationalism* (London: Verso, 1991), 6–36, Peter Mandler remarks that "the nation can appear plausibly to give individuals a role, both time- and place- marked, in a long (even eternal) and continuous plot" ("What is 'National Identity'?" 279–80).

75 The temptation arises to find significance in the fact that all of these peninsular nationalities are peripheral in relation to Castile, and it leads toward reflection on the theme of "national peripheries" looking at "imperial peripheries," but enough is enough, so we shall concentrate on the task in hand.

76 Other historical protagonistas explicitly identified as Andalusians are naval officer Dionisio Alcalá Galiano (Kendrick 1994a), Dominican missionary Francisco Galisteo (Esponera 1994), and Franciscan bishop Antonio de los Reyes (Miguélez 1999).

77 He was a founder of the Instituto de Estudios Oscenses in Huesca.

78 Armillas holds a chair in History of the Americas at the University of Saragossa, in Aragon.

79 Born in Borja (Saragossa) in 1947, Gracia Rivas has served as medical doctor aboard the training ship *Juan Sebastián Elcano*. He studies maritime history and is the president of the Centro de Estudios Borjanos and of the "Fernando el Católico" Institution in Borja.

80 Franciscans Salazar, Omaechevarría, and Larriñaga thus share both professional and Basque national identities with their subjects.

81 Aranegui was an industrial engineer, but he published many articles on genealogy and heraldry in *Hidalguía*. Although born in Barcelona, his Basque ancestry led him to serve as president of the provincial government of Álava (Diputación Foral de Álava) from 1957 to 1966.

82 Ybarra y Bergé was the author of *Catálogo de monumentos de Vizcaya* and a member of the Royal Academy of History. He was president of the daily newspaper *Informaciones* and of the publishing house Bilbao Editorial. He served as president of the provincial government of Vizcaya between 1947 and 1950, and mayor of Bilbao from 1963 to 1969. He was considered to belong to the right-wing Biscayan oligarchy, and criticized for supporting Franco. He was assassinated by the Basque terrorist group ETA in 1977.

83 De la Quadra-Salcedo (1960) describes Bodega as "a sailor of Biscayan origin" (p. 465), and makes a point of saying that he habitually signed as "Francisco de la Quadra." Menchaca's book title, too (1989), makes a hyphenated surname Bodega-Quadra, suggesting an attempt to underscore the Basque family lineage. By contrast, one of the most outstanding Basque sailors who took part in the North Pacific expeditions, Ignacio de Arteaga, has so far not received much attention.

84 Soler Vidal was born in 1908 in Barcelona. His family was known for its strong socialist and Catalonian nationalist politics, and in 1940 he went into exile in Mexico, where he earned his living as a journalist. In 1965 he returned to Spain, working for the Catalonian publisher Montaner i Simon and settling in Gavà, where he died in 1999.

85 Carner-Ribalta abandoned Spain after the Civil War and earned his living as a translator in Mexico.

86 Rodeja Galter (1896–1963) was an assistant teacher at the secondary school in Figueras in 1940, and he was active in the Institut d'Estudis Empordaneses and in the Instituto de Estudios Gerundenses. He published works on the local history of Figueras.

87 There is no secret about the origin of Boneu's interest in Portolá. They were both born in Balaguer.

88 Escandell is a secondary school teacher, and co-author with Mampel of a work on colonial Spanish American literature.

89 Historian José Luis Infiesta Pérez resides in Barcelona and is the author of many works on the Spanish Civil War, particularly foreign participation and interventions. He wrote his Portolá book under the pseudonym of Josep Lluis Alcofar.

90 Beya's paper is about Portolá's last direct descendant, Buenaventura Portolá, who died in 1944.

91 Piqueras is a professional historian based in the Department of Social Anthropology and History of America and Africa at the University of Barcelona.

92 Lorenzo (Llorenç) Riber (1882–1958) was a well-known poet and humanist who wrote a number of works about classical-era Romans and possibly published more translations from Latin than any other Spanish translator. See Francisco Calero, "Traducir a Vives: elogio crítico de Lorenzo Riber," *Cuadernos de Filología Clásica. Estudios Latinos* 15 (1998): 529–39.

93 Palma was born in 1889 and died in Sarriá in 1963. During his early years he was called Manuel de Lete y Triay.

94 Sintes Obrador (1912–1982) was born in Mahón. He was a military officer and the author of many works on military history and Spanish culture and for a time in the early 1950s he was director general of archives and libraries.

95 Born in 1925, Galmés Más held a PhD degree in history from the University of Valencia. He was a professor of church history at the San Vicente Ferrer Theology Faculty in Valencia. He died in 2006.

96 Font Obrador (1932–2005) earned his first degree in Philosophy and Letters (general arts) in 1959 at the University of Barcelona, soon specializing in Mallorcan archaeology and prehistory. In 1966 he was appointed official historian of the city of Lluchmajor (not far from Petra on the island of Mallorca), and in 1968 he obtained his PhD. He was a member of Spain's Royal Academy of History. California missionary Gerónimo Boscana and Font shared their birthplace since both men were born in Lluchmajor.

97 These are Gaspar Sabater (the author of a history of the Balearic Islands), Miguel Ramis (director of the Fray Junípero Serra Museum), Pere Llabrés

Martorell (member of the editorial staff of the Mallorcan theological journal *Comunicació*), Father Sebastián Rubí Darder, and Father Miguel López Bonet. Román Piña Homs is a professional historian based at the university of the Balearic Islands.

98 Bauzá was born in Palma de Mallorca in 1764. Before being recruited for Malaspina's expedition in 1789, he was a professor of fortifications and technical drawing at the Academy of Marine Guards on the island of León, Cádiz. He died in London in 1834.

99 Llabrés Bernal (1900–1975) was involved in archaeological work, and was the compiler of the first five volumes of a local history entitled *Noticias y relaciones históricas de Mallorca, siglo XIX* (1958–1971); vols. 6–9 (1985–98) were compiled by Pou Muntaner.

100 See, for example, Borja de Riquer, "La débil nacionalización española del siglo XIX," *Historia Social* 20 (1994): 97–114; Boyd, *Historia patria*; José Álvarez Junco, *Mater Dolorosa: la idea de España en el siglo XIX* (Madrid: Taurus, 2001); Clare Mar-Molinero and Angel Smith, "The Myths and Realities of Nation-Building in the Iberian Peninsula," in Mar-Molinero and Smith, *Nationalism and the Nation in the Iberian Peninsula*, 3–9.

101 Spain is not the only European country in which government funding has encouraged the study of national consciousness since the 1970s. British politicians, journalists and academics have engaged in their own discussion of the four-nation approach to Britishness, which recognizes English, Scottish, Welsh, and Irish identities. See Mandler, "What is 'National Identity'?" 282.

102 As Mandler says: "it is the politicians who have the greatest vested interest in 'national identity' itself" ("What is 'National Identity'?" 295).

103 On these two nationalisms, see, for example Antonio Elorza, *Ideologías del nacionalismo vasco, 1876–1937* (San Sebastian: L. Haranburu, 1978); Antoni Simón, "Els mites històrics i el nacionalisme català: La història moderna de Catalunya en el pensament històric i politic català contemporani, 1840–1939," *Manuscrits* 12 (1994): 195–211; Josep R. Llobera, "The Role of Commemorations in (Ethno) Nation-Building: The Case of Catalonia," in Mar-Molinero and Smith, *Nationalism and the Nation in the Iberian Peninsula*, 191–206; Josetxo Beriain, "Los ídolos de la tribu en el nacionalismo vasco," and Agustí Colomines, "Cataluña en la España contemporánea. Interpretaciones sobre la identidad nacional," both in Colom González, *Relatos de nación*, 1:477–506 and 507–32.

104 See the discussion in Jörn Rüsen, ed., *Western Historical Thinking: An Intercultural Debate* (New York: Berghahn Books, 2002), especially Peter Burke (15–30, 189–98) and Hayden White (111–18).

Spanish Colonial Californias and Pacific Coasts of North America: Historiography Published in Spain

This list excludes general studies of the Spanish Pacific, and is selective regarding biographies, publications on the Malaspina expedition, and separate entries for published primary sources. Several publishers' names are given in abbreviated form: Consejo Superior de Investigaciones Científicas (given as C.S.I.C), Ministerio de Asuntos Exteriores (M.A.E.), Agencia Española de Cooperación Internacional (A.E.C.I.), and Escuela de Estudios Hispano-Americanos (E.E.H.-A.).

Abbad y Lasierra, Iñigo. 1981. *Descripción de las costas de California*. Ed. Sylvia Lyn Hilton. Madrid: C.S.I.C., Instituto Gonzalo Fernández de Oviedo.

[Ajofrín, Fr. Francisco]. 1958. *Breve descripción de las Californias, por Fray Francisco de Ajofrín*. Ed. Bonifacio Castellanos. Madrid: José Porrúa Turanzas. Also in *Noticias y documentos* 1959, 13–48.

Albarracín, Agustín. 1975. "El teniente de navío don Ignacio de Arteaga y Bazán." In *Colección de diarios y relaciones* 1943–75, 7:11–16.

[Alcalá Galiano, Dionisio, and Cayetano Valdés]. 1802. *Relación del viage hecho por las goletas "Sutil" y "Mexicana" en el año de 1792 para reconocer el estrecho de Fuca, con una introducción* [by M. Fernández de Navarrete] *en que se da noticia de las expediciones executadas anteriormente por los españoles en busca del paso del noroeste de la América*. Madrid: Imprenta Real. Reprint, Col. Chimalistac 1. Madrid: José Porrúa Turanzas, 1958. Facsimile of 1802 edition, *Relación del viaje hecho por las goletas Sutil y Mexicana en el año 1792 para reconocer el Estrecho de Juan de Fuca*, ed. María Dolores Higueras and María Luisa Martín-Merás. Madrid: Museo Naval, 1991. Digital facsimile of 1802 edition in *Las Raíces Hispánicas del Oeste de Norteamérica: Textos Históricos*. Ed. Sylvia L. Hilton. Biblioteca Digital Clásicos Tavera, ser. 2: Temáticas para la historia de Iberoamérica CT021, CD-ROM. Madrid: Fundación Mapfre-Tavera, Digibis, 1999.

Alcina, Llorenç. 1985. "L'espiritualitat missionera de Fra Juníper Serra, O.F.M." *Comunicació. Revista del Centre d'Estudis Teològics de Mallorca* 37–38 (March–June): 33–41.

Alcina Franch, José. 1986. "The Culture of the Indians of the Northwest Coast." In *To the Totem Shore* 1986, 120–57.

———. 1988. "La cultura de los indios de la Costa Noroeste." In *El Ojo del Tótem* 1988, 48–85.

———. 1989. "El problema de las 'jefaturas' de la Costa Noroeste a la luz de los primeros informes españoles del siglo XVIII." In *Culturas de la costa noroeste de América* 1989, 33–50.

Alcofar Nassaes, Josep Lluis. See Infiesta, José Luis.

Alonso de la Fuente, José Andrés. 2004. "Sobre el origen y significado de las palabras *esquimal* y *aleutiano*." *Revista Española de Antropología Americana* 34:237–44.

———. 2006. "Los inuksuit. Otra forma de ver el mundo." *Revista Española de Antropología Americana* 36, no. 1:205–15.

———. 2008a. "Terminología cromática aleuta." *Revista Española de Antropología Americana* 38, no. 1:75–89.

———. 2008b. "Farewell Marie Smith Jones... Farewell Eyak." *Revista Española de Antropología Americana* 38, no. 2:274–79.

Altamira y Crevea, Rafael. 1924. "La huella de España en el Pacífico." In *La huella de España en América*, 107–36. Biblioteca histórica 1. Madrid: Reus. First published as "The Share of Spain in the History of the Pacific Ocean." In *The Pacific Ocean in History: Papers and Addresses Presented at the Panama-Pacific Historical Congress, 1915*, ed. H. Morse Stephens and Herbert E. Bolton, 34–54. New York: Macmillan.

Alvariño, Ángeles. [2000]. *España y la primera expedición científica oceánica, 1789–1794: Malaspina y Bustamante con las corbetas "Descubierta" y "Atrevida."* [Santiago de Compostela]: Xunta de Galicia. Reprint, [2002].

Anta Félez, José Luis. 1988. "Motivos e ideales en la expansión hacia la Alta California." *Quinto Centenario* 14:271–82.

———, ed. 1988. See Palóu 1988.

Anza, Juan Bautista de. 1959. "Descubrimiento de Sonora a Californias en el año de 1774. Ruta del primer viaje." In *Noticias y documentos* 1959, 137–57.

Aranegui y Coll, Manuel de. 1976. "Una familia española en California." *Hidalguía* 24, no. 138 (September–October): 729–40.

Arco, Ricardo del. 1947. "El almirante Pedro Porter y Casanate, explorador del golfo de California. Noticias inéditas." *Revista de Indias* 8, no. 30 (October–December): 783–844.

Arias Divito, Juan Carlos. 1968. *Las expediciones científicas españolas durante el siglo XVIII. Expedición botánica de Nueva España*. Madrid: Ediciones de Cultura Hispánica.

Ariza Torres, Cristóbal. 1926. *Datos históricos sobre Don Rodrigo de Vivero y el General Sebastián Vizcaíno encontrados en el Archivo de Indias por el Comandante Médico de la Armada D. Cristóbal Ariza Torres: investigación llevada a cabo en cumplimiento de la real orden*. Madrid: [Ministerio de Marina].

Armillas Vicente, José Antonio. 1988. "Pedro Porter y Casanate, explorador de California (1611–1662)." In *Aragón en el mundo*, 249–58. Saragossa: Caja de Ahorros de la Inmaculada.

Arrieta Elizalde, Idoia. 1993. "La RSBAP y su influencia en las misiones de California." In vol. 1 of *La RSBAP y Méjico. IV Seminario de la Real Sociedad Bascongada de los Amigos del País*, 485–516. San Sebastián-Donostia: Real Sociedad Bascongada de los Amigos del País.

———. 1996a. *Transculturación y civilización en la formación de California: la RSBAP y el aporte vasco (1769–1834)*. PhD diss., Universidad del País Vasco.

———. 1996b. "El alavés Fray Fermín Francisco de Lasuén." In *Álava y América*, ed. Ronald Escobedo, Ana de Zaballa, and Oscar Álvarez, 205–20. Vitoria: Diputación Foral de Álava.

———. 2004a. "Euskal erlijiosoak Kaliforniako Misioetan: Ikuspegi orokor bat (1697–1834) [Basque missionaries in California: a general assessment (1697–1834)]." In *Euskal Herriko Erlijiosoen Historia: Familia eta Institutu Erlijiosoen Euskal Herriko Historiaren, 1. Kongresuko Aktak/Historia de los Religiosos en el País Vasco-Navarra: Actas del Primer Congreso de Historia de las Familias e Institutos Religiosos en el País Vasco y Navarra*, ed. Joseba Intxausti, 833–39. 2 vols. Oñati: Arantzazu Edizio Frantziskotarrak/Ediciones Franciscanas.

———. 2004b. *Ilustración y utopía: los frailes vascos y la RSBAP en California, 1769–1834*. Col. Ilustración Vasca 13. San Sebastián: Real Sociedad Bascongada de los Amigos del País.

———. Forthcoming. "Franciscanos vascos en las misiones de California (siglos XVIII–XIX), Fray Vicente de Sarriá." In vol. 2 of *Las huellas de América. I Congreso Internacional Arantzazu y los franciscanos vascos en América. Oñate (Guipúzcoa), 11–15 diciembre 2001*, ed. Óscar Álvarez Gila and Idoia Arrieta Elizalde. Cola. Alea 28. Donostia: Eusko Ikaskuntza.

Arteaga y Bazán, Ignacio de. 1975. "Diario de la navegación que con el favor de Dios y de la Virgen de Regla, espera hacer el teniente de navío don Ignacio de Arteaga, mandando la fragata de S.M. Nuestra Señora del Rosario (alias) la Princesa, desde el puerto de San Blas, que está en los 27 grados, 30 minutos de latitud norte, hasta los 70 grados de la misma especie, a exploraciones de las costas septentrionales de la California, llevando a sus órdenes a la fragata Favorita, mandada por el de la misma clase don Juan Francisco de la Bodega y Quadra" (1779). In *Colección de diarios y relaciones* 1943–75, 7:17–162.

Ascensión, Fr. Antonio de la. 1867. "Relación breve en que se da noticia del descubrimiento que se hizo en la Nueva España, en la mar del Sur, desde el puerto de Acapulco hasta más adelante del cabo Mendocino... de Californias, octubre 12, 1620." In [*CODOINAO*] 1864–84, 8:537–74.

Bardavío Gracia, José María. 1971. "Localización de copias manuscritas y ediciones del 'Diario de 1775' original de Fray Francisco Hermenegildo Garcés, O.F.M." *Revista Zaragoza* (Saragossa) 34:29–34.

———. 1988. *California empieza en Aragón*. [Saragossa]: Comisión Aragonesa V Centenario, Diputación General de Aragón.

———. 1990. "Exploraciones de Fray Francisco Garcés en el suroeste de los Estados Unidos." In *Los aragoneses en la empresa de Indias*, 85–96. Saragossa: Institución Fernando el Católico.

Barras y de Aragón, Francisco de las. 1944. "Viaje del astrónomo francés Abate Chappe a California en 1769 y Noticias de José Antonio Alzate sobre la historia natural de Nueva España." *Anuario de Estudios Americanos* 1:741–81.

———. 1949. "Paso de Venus por el disco del sol." *Anales de la Universidad Hispalense* 1, no. 2:25–53.

———. 1949–50. "D. Juan Pérez y don Esteban José Martínez, grandes marinos y también etnógrafos." In vol. 2 of *Homenaje a D. Luis de Hoyos y Sainz*, ed. José Rogerio Sánchez, Francisco Caso, Pablo Martínez Strong, Manuel Cardenal Iracheta, and Juan Zaragüeta, 45–51. 2 vols. Madrid: Valera.

———. 1951. "Un gran marino español del siglo XVIII: don Francisco Antonio Maurelle." *Anales de la Asociación Española para el Progreso de las Ciencias* (Madrid) 26, no. 1:161–211.

———. 1953. *Don Esteban José Martínez, alumno del Colegio de San Telmo de Sevilla*. Série B, no. 312. Madrid: Real Sociedad Geográfica.

———. 1956. "Los rusos en el noroeste de América." *Anales de la Asociación Española para el Progreso de las Ciencias* (Madrid) 31, no. 1:111–26.

Barreiro-Meiro, Roberto. 1962. "El primer encuentro entre españoles y rusos en América." *Revista General de Marina* 162 (April): 229–34.

———. 1964. "Esteban José Martínez." In *Colección de diarios y relaciones 1943–75*, 6:7–17.

———, ed. 1964. See *Colección de diarios y relaciones 1943–75*, 6:19–148.

———. 1975. "El Teniente de Navío Jacinto Caamaño Moraleja." In *Colección de diarios y relaciones*, 7:163–72.

———, ed. 1975. See *Colección de diarios y relaciones 1943–75*, 7:173–238.

Bartroli i Nogué, Tomás. 1992. "Topónims catalans de la costa del nord-oest d'Amèrica." In *IV Jornades d'Estudis Catalano-Americans, Octubre 1990*, 335–44. Barcelona: Generalitat de Catalunya.

———. 1994. "Dos homicidios en Nootka, 1789–1790." In Palau Baquero and Orozco 1994, 402–13.

Basso, Mercedes, Ariadna Bello, and Silvia Sauquet, eds. 1999. *Espíritus del agua. Arte de Alaska y la Columbia Británica*. Barcelona: Fundación "La Caixa."

Batista González, Juan. 1985. "Significación político-estratégica de la ruta juniperiana." *Revista de Historia Militar* (Madrid) 29, no. 59:72–106.

Bauzá, Felipe. 1987. "Descripcion física de las costas de la California." In vol. 1 of *Californiana IV. Aportación a la historiografía de California en el siglo XVIII*, ed. W. Michael Mathes, 127–232. Madrid: José Porrúa Turanzas.

Bayle, Constantino, S.J. 1932–33. "El IV Centenario del Descubrimiento de California." *Razón y Fe* 100, nos. 11 and 12 (November and December 1932): 340–61 and 487–510, and 101, no. 2 (February): 167–81.

———. 1933. *Historia de los descubrimientos y colonización de los padres de la Compañía de Jesús en la Baja California*. Madrid: Librería General de Victoriano Suárez.

———, ed. 1946. See Salvatierra 1946.

Beals, Herbert K. 1994. "Malaspina's Precursors: New Light on Spanish Voyages to the Northwest Coast of America, 1774–1779." In Palau Baquero and Orozco 1994, 161–66.

Beerman, Eric. 1980. "Bosquejo biográfico del gobernador de California: Pedro Fages." *Issauna* (Guisona, Lérida) 3, nos. 18–19 (March and April).

———. 1990. "Pizarro. Extractos de providencias para el descubrimiento del Mar del Sur y Californias desde la conquista de Indias, y para la exclusión impuesta a todas las naciones extranjeras de navegar aquellos mares. Formados de orden de S.M. por los Sres. D. Joseph García de León y Pizarro, and D. Fernando Joseph Mangino, del Consejo Real y Supremo de las Indias." *Revista de Historia Naval* 8, no. 31: 43–56.

———. 1994. "José de Bustamante, capitán de la *Atrevida*." In Palau Baquero and Orozco 1994, 199–204.

———. 1998a. "Pedro Alberni y los Voluntarios de Cataluña en Nutka, 1790–1792." In Palau Baquero, Calés, and Sánchez 1998, 33–36.

———. 1998b. "Manuel Quimper y Bodega y Quadra: dos limeños al servicio de la Real Armada," and "Testamento de Tomás de la Bodega y Quadra." In *Nutka 1792* 1998, 32–43 and 44–46.

Bernabeu Albert, Salvador. 1987a. "Ciencia y minería en Baja California: el informe de Joaquín Velázquez de León (1771)." *Asclepio. Revista de Historia de la Medicina y de la Ciencia* 39, no. 2:103–22.

———. 1987b. "1792. La expedición botánica en el noroeste de América. Los viajes a California y Nutka." In *La Real Expedición Botánica a Nueva España, 1787–1803*, 173–92. Madrid: Real Jardín Botánico, C.S.I.C., and Comisión Nacional V Centenario.

———. 1988a. "El Almirante Pedro Porter y los errores de la navegación en el siglo XVII." In vol. 2 of *Estudios sobre Historia de la Ciencia y de la Técnica. IV Congreso de la Sociedad Española de Historia de las Ciencias y de las Técnicas. Valladolid, 22–27 de septiembre de 1986*, ed. Mariano Esteban Piñeiro, 651–64. Valladolid: Junta de Castilla y León.

———. 1988b. "El Noroeste, entre la geografía y la ficción." In *El Ojo del Tótem* 1988, 10–25.

———. 1988c. "La expedición hispano-francesa a medir el Paso de Venus." In *Carlos III y la ciencia de la Ilustración*, ed. Manuel A. Selles, José Luis Peset, and Antonio Lafuente, 313–30. Madrid: Alianza.

———. 1988d. "Astronomía en la América de Carlos III: la expedición hispano-francesa a medir el Paso de Venus." *Cuadernos Hispanoamericanos, Los complementarios, vol. 2: Carlos III y la América* (December): 175–86.

———. 1989a. "La Comisión española en la expedición de Chappe d'Auteroche." In vol. 3 of *Ciencia, vida y espacio en Iberoamérica*, ed. José Luis Peset, 15–35. Madrid: C.S.I.C.

———. 1989b. *Viajes marítimos y expediciones científicas españolas en el Pacífico septentrional (1767–1788)*. 3 vols. PhD diss., Universidad Complutense de Madrid.

———. 1989c. "Sobre intercambios comerciales entre China y California en el último tercio del siglo XVIII: el oro suave." In *Extremo Oriente Ibérico. (Actas del primer simposio internacional: El Extremo Oriente Ibérico, Madrid, 7–10 noviembre 1988). Investigaciones históricas, metodología y estado de la cuestión*, ed. Francisco de Solano, Florentino Rodao, and Luis E. Togores, 471–84. Madrid: C.S.I.C., A.E.C.I.

———. 1989d. "Las Californias en la historiografía española (1940–1989)." *Revista de Indias* 49, no. 187:817–28.

———. 1989e. "El océano Pacífico en el reinado de Carlos III: respuestas españolas a las agresiones foráneas." In *Estudios sobre Filipinas y las islas del Pacífico*, ed. Florentino Rodao García, foreword by Manuel Alvar, 23–30. Madrid: Asociación Española de Estudios del Pacífico (AEEP).

———. 1989f. "Juan Pérez, navegante y descubridor de las Californias (1768–1775)." In *Culturas de la costa noroeste de América* 1989, 277–290.

———. 1989g. "Los gallegos en la Alta California." In *Jornadas Presencia de España en América, I: Aportación gallega. Pazo de Mariñán, 28 de septiembre–3 de octubre de 1987*, 65–76. Madrid and La Coruña: Deimos and Excma. Diputación Provincial de A Coruña.

———, ed. 1990. See Bodega y Cuadra 1990.

———. 1991a. "Los científicos del desierto: ciencia y técnica en Baja California durante la centuria ilustrada." *Revista de Indias* (Madrid) 51, no. 192 (May–August): 419–31.

———. 1991b. "Los bosques del fin del mundo." In *El bosque ilustrado. Estudios sobre la política forestal española en América*, ed. Manuel Lucena Giraldo, 93–105. Madrid: Instituto Nacional para la Conservación de la Naturaleza, Instituto de la Ingeniería de España.

———. 1991c. "La frontera califórnica: de las expediciones cortesianas a la presencia convulsiva de Gálvez (1534–1767)." In *Estudios (Nuevos y Viejos) sobre la frontera*, ed. Francisco de Solano and Salvador Bernabeu, 85–118. Madrid: C.S.I.C.

———. 1991d. "Ya les vino el Plus Ultra: las expediciones al Noroeste de América durante el reinado de Carlos III." In *La ciencia española en Ultramar. Actas de las I Jornadas sobre España y las expediciones científicas en América y Filipinas*, ed. Alejandro R. Díez Torre and others, 287–99. Aranjuez: Doce Calles.

———. 1992a. *El Pacífico ilustrado: del lago español a las grandes expediciones*. Madrid: Mapfre.

———. [1992]b. "La Santa Expedición en el mar: el diario del palentino fray Juan González Vizcaíno (1769)." In vol. 3 of *Castilla y León en América. III: Los castellanos en la Iglesia y en la cultura indianas. Actas del IV Congreso de Americanistas Españoles*, 59–77. Valladolid: Junta de Castilla y León, Caja España.

———. 1992c. "El 'virrey de California' Gaspar de Portolá y la problemática de la primera gobernación californiana (1767–1769)." *Revista de Indias* 52, nos. 195–96 (May–December): 271–95.

———. 1992d. *"Edificar en desiertos": los informes de fray Vicente de Mora sobre Baja California en 1777*. Mexico: Embajada de España.

———. 1994a. "'La religión ofendida': Resistencia y rebeliones indígenas en la Baja California colonial." *Revista Complutense de Historia de América* 20:169–80.

———. 1994b. "Pesquisas inquisitoriales en la frontera californiana: el caso del bígamo José Antonio Cortés." *Revista de Indias* (Madrid) 54, no. 201 (May–August): 465–78.

———, ed. 1994a. See Longinos 1994.

———, ed. 1994b. See Neve 1994.

———, ed. 1995. *Trillar los mares. (La expedición descubridora de Bruno de Hezeta al Noroeste de América, 1775)*. Foreword by Francisco de Solano. Madrid: C.S.I.C.-Fundación Banco Bilbao-Vizcaya.

———. 1995. "El Tratado de Límites de 1792. Repercusiones del tratado de Tordesillas en el Pacífico Septentrional." In *El Tratado de Tordesillas y su época*, 1701–13. Vallodolid: Comisión del V Centenario del Tratado de Tordesillas.

———. 1996. See Taraval 1996.

———. 1998a. "España en el Noroeste. Navegantes y proyectistas en el siglo XVIII." In Palau Baquero, Calés, and Sánchez 1998, 15–25.

———. 1998b. "Bodega y Quadra o el instante frágil en el Noroeste. Un retrato inacabado" and "El Tratado de Tordesillas y su repercusión en el Tratado de Límites de 1792." In *Nutka 1792* 1998, 20–31 and 47–59. "Bodega y Quadra o el instante frágil en el Noroeste. Un retrato inacabado" was also published in *Científicos criollos e Ilustración*, ed. Diana Soto, Miguel Ángel Puig-Samper, and Dolores González-Ripoll, 199–211. Aranjuez [Madrid]: Doce Calles, 1999.

———. 2000. "El diablo en California. Recepción y decadencia del maligno en el discurso misional jesuita." In *El septentrión novohispano: ecohistoria, sociedades e imágenes de frontera*, ed. Salvador Bernabeu Albert, 139–76. Col. Tierra nueva e cielo nuevo 39. Madrid: C.S.I.C.

———. 2001–3. "California, o el poder de las imágenes en el discurso y las misiones jesuitas." *Contrastes. Revista de Historia Moderna* (Murcia) 12:159–85.

———. 2003. "Por tierra nada conocida. El diario inédito de José Cañizares en la Alta California." *Anuario de Estudios Americanos* (Seville) 60, no. 1 (January–June): 235–76.

———, ed. 2003. See Sales 2003.

———. 2006. "Una mirada científica a la frontera: California en la centuria ilustrada." *Brócar* (Logroño) 30:15–36.

———. 2007. "Voces furtivas en la frontera californiana (1533–1767)." In *Sensibilidades na história: memórias singulares e identidades sociais*, ed. Sandra Jatahy Pesavento and Frédérique Langue, 43–90. Porto Alegre, Brazil: Universidade Federal do Río Grande do Sul.

———. 2008. *Expulsados del infierno: el exilio de los misioneros Jesuitas de la península californiana, 1767–1768*. Madrid: C.S.I.C.

———. 2009. "La invención del Gran Norte Ignaciano; la historiografía sobre la Compañía de Jesús entre dos centenarios (1992–2006)." In *El Gran Norte Mexicano. Indios, misioneros y pobladores entre el mito y la historia*, ed. Salvador Bernabeu Albert, 165–211. Madrid: C.S.I.C.

———. 2010. "Velázquez en el Purgatorio: los días y los trabajos de un científico en California." *Revista de Indias* 70, no. 248 (January–April): 211–36.

——— and Catalina Romero. 1988. "El cambio misional en la Baja California (1773), aspectos socioeconómicos y culturales." In *Actas del I Congreso Internacional sobre "Los Dominicos y el Nuevo Mundo." Sevilla, 21–25 de abril de 1987*, 557–94. Madrid: Deimos.

Beya Alonso, Ernesto. 1985. El último descendiente del colonizador de California." In vol. 1 of *IV Congreso d' Historia de la Medicina Catalana. Poblet, 7–9 de juny de 1985. Actes*, 36–40. Full text available online at RACO (Revistes Catalanes amb Accés Obert): http://www.raco.cat/index.php/Gimbernat/article/view/ 43201/53810.

Blanco S., Antonio. 1971. *La lengua española en la historia de California. Contribución a su estudio*. Madrid: Ediciones de Cultura Hispánica.

Bodega y Cuadra, Juan Francisco de la. 1865a. "Viajes de exploración: Primer viaje de D. Juan Francisco de la Bodega y Quadra hasta la altura de 58 grados en una goleta de 18 codos de quilla y 6 de manga, tripulada con un piloto, un contramaestre, un guardián, diez marineros, un paje y un criado. Año de 1775." *Anuario de la Dirección de Hidrografía* (Madrid) 3:279–93.

———. 1865b. "Segunda salida hasta los 61 grados en la fragata 'Nuestra Señora de los Remedios,' alias 'Favorita,' de 39 codos de quilla y 13 de manga, calada de popa en 14 pies y de proa en 13. Año de 1779." *Anuario de la Dirección de Hidrografía* (Madrid) 3:294–331.

———. 1865c. "Método de la navegación que conjeturo convendrá se observe para seguir los descubrimientos de la costa septentrional de la California." *Anuario de la Dirección de Hidrografía* (Madrid) 3:331–34.

———. 1943. "Navegación hecha por D. Juan Francisco de la Bodega y Quadra, teniente de fragata de la Real Armada y comandante de la goleta *Sonora* a los descubrimientos de los mares y costa septentrional de California" (1775). In *Colección de diarios y relaciones* 1943–75, 2:97–143.

———. 1959. "Navegaciones y descubrimientos hechos . . . hasta los 61 grados por el teniente de navío de la Real Armada don Juan Francisco de la Bodega y Quadra, comandante de la fragata de S.M. Nuestra Señora de los Remedios, alias la Favorita . . . 1779." In *Noticias y documentos* 1959, 167–213.

———. 1990. *El descubrimiento del fin del mundo (1775–1792)*. Ed. Salvador Bernabeu Albert. Madrid: Alianza. Contains: "Primer viaje. Diario 1775," 55–110; "Segundo viaje. Diario 1779," 111–58; "Tercer viaje. Diario 1792," 159–221; "Catálogo de los animales y plantas que han reconocido . . . José Mociño y don José Maldonado," 222–27; "Breve diccionario . . . del idioma de los naturales de Nutca," 228–40; "Método de navegación," 241–45; "Derrota que deberán seguir . . . 1778," 246–49; and other documents.

———. 1998. "Diario del 'Viaje a la Costa Noroeste de la América Septentrional por Juan Francisco de la Bodega y Quadra . . . 1792.'" In *Nutka 1792* 1998, 137–85.

Bolin, L[uis?] A[ntonio?]. 1959. "Nombres españoles en las costas de Alaska." *Revista General de Marina* 156 (May): 608–21.

Boneu Companys, Fernando. 1970a. *Don Gaspar de Portolá, el noble militar leridano, descubridor y primer gobernador de California*. Madrid: Publicaciones Españolas.

———. 1970b. *Don Gaspar de Portolá, descubridor y primer gobernador de California*. Lérida: Instituto de Estudios Ilerdenses. This work was translated into English and revised by Alan K. Brown, and published as *Gaspar de Portolá: Explorer and Founder of California*. Lérida: Instituto de Estudios Ilerdenses, 1983.

———, ed. 1973. *Documentos secretos de la expedición de Portolá a California. Juntas de Guerra*. Lérida: C.S.I.C., Instituto de Estudios Ilerdenses. New ed., Lleida: Amics de Gaspar de Portolá, Milenio, 1999.

———. 1983. "Documentació de la presa de possessió de California a Monterrei pel Lleidatà Gaspar de Portolà." *Ilerda* 44:207–33.

———. 1986a. *Don Gaspar de Portolá, descubridor y primer gobernador de California*. New ed., revised and enlarged. Lérida: Excma. Diputació Provincial de Lleida.

———. 1986b. *De Catalunya a California: Gaspar de Portolá*. Lleida: Excma. Diputació de Lleida.

———. 1991. *Pere Fages: un català molt singular a California*. Lleida: Diputació de Lleida.

Borges Moran, Pedro, O.F.M. 1991. "Fray Junípero Serra, apóstol de California." In *La América de los virreyes. En torno al virreinato de Nueva España*. Cádiz: Delegación Diocesana de Cádiz-Ceuta, 2:9–28.

Borrego Plá, María del Carmen. 1988. "El piloto sevillano Esteban José Martínez, explorador de Alaska." *Archivo Hispalense* 521, no. 217 (May–August): 71–94.

———. 2002. "El vino, peregrino de vida: su enclave en las Californias." In vol. 1 of *IX Congreso Internacional de Historia de América*, ed. Fernando Serrano Mangas, Joaquín Álvaro Rubio, Rocío Sánchez Rubio, Isabel Testón Núñez, 357–64. Mérida: Editora Regional de Extremadura.

Botánica en la expedición Malaspina, 1789–1794, La. Catálogo de la exposición celebrada en el Pabellón Villanueva del Real Jardín Botánico de Madrid, octubre–noviembre 1989. 1989. Madrid: Real Jardín Botánico, Quinto Centenario-Turner.

Bowden, Dina Moore. 1976. *Junípero Serra in His Native Isle (1713–1749)*. Palma de Mallorca: Dina Moore Bowden, Miramar.

Brandes, Stanley. 1992. "Las misiones de Alta California, como instrumentos de conquista." In *De palabra y obra en el Nuevo Mundo. 2. Encuentros interétnicos. Interpretaciones contemporáneas*, ed. Manuel Gutiérrez Estévez, Miguel León-Portilla, Gary H. Gossen, and J. Jorge Klor de Alva, 153–72. Madrid: Siglo XXI de España, Extremadura En-Clave.

Buache de Neuville, Jean-Nicolas. 1798. *Memoria sobre el descubrimiento antiguo [por Lorenzo Ferrer Maldonado el año 1588] del Paso del Norte, o del NorOceano al del Sur por la parte septentrional de la América*. Trans. Martín Fernández de Navarrete, and refutation by Ciriaco Cevallos. Isla de León

(Cádiz): n.p. Also appears, with slightly different titles, in Novo 1881, 84–102, and Malaspina 1885, 144–49.

Burman, Conchita. 1998. "Relación de las embarcaciones citadas en el Diario del 'Viaje,' Catálogo de dibujos y mapas del Album del 'Viaje.' Ms. 146 del Archivo del Ministerio de Asuntos Exteriores." In *Nutka 1792* 1998, 214–17.

Burriel, Andrés Marcos, S.J. 1757. See [Venegas and Burriel] 1757.

Burrus, Ernest J., S.I., ed. 1962. See Píccolo 1962.

———, ed. 1964. *Kino escribe a la Duquesa: Correspondencia del P. Eusebio Francisco Kino con la Duquesa de Aveiro y otros documentos*. Col. Chimalistac 18. Madrid: José Porrúa Turanzas.

———, ed. 1967a. *Diario del capitán comandante Fernando de Rivera y Moncada. Con un apéndice documental*. 2 vols. Col. Chimalistac 24 and 25. Madrid: Porrúa Turanzas.

———, ed. 1967b. *La obra cartográfica de la provincia mexicana de la Compañía de Jesús (1567–1967)*. 1 vol. + 1 folder with folded maps. Col. Chimalistac, Serie José Porrúa Turanzas 1. Madrid: José Porrúa Turanzas.

——— and Félix Zubillaga, eds. 1982. *Misiones mexicanas de la Compañía de Jesús, 1618–1745: cartas e informes conservados en la "Colección Mateu."* Madrid: José Porrúa Turanzas.

Bustamante, Jesús. 1989. "Los vocabularios mexicanos, Malaspina y la Costa Noroeste. Un modelo clasificatorio." In *Culturas de la costa noroeste de América* 1989, 81–92.

Bustamante y Guerra, José. 1868. "Relación de las navegaciones que executó separadamente la corbeta de S.M. 'Atrevida' en el viaje verificado unida a la 'Descubierta' en los años 1789, 1790, 1791, 1792, 1793 y 1794, ordenada por su comandante D. José Bustamante y Guerra, de la Real Armada." *Anuario de la Dirección de Hidrografía* (Madrid) 6:240–364.

———. 1999. "Diario." See Higueras 1999.

Caamaño Moraleja, Jacinto. 1849. "Expedición de la corbeta 'Aránzazu,' 1792." In [*CODOIN España*] 1849–95, 15:323–63.

———. 1975. "Extracto del Diario de las navegaciones, exploraciones y descubrimientos hechos en la América Septentrional por D. Jacinto Caamaño, teniente de navío de la Real Armada y comandante de la fragata de Su Majestad nombrada 'Nuestra Señora de Aránzazu,' desde el puerto de San Blas, de donde salió en 20 de marzo del año de 1792." In *Colección de diarios y relaciones* 1943–75, 7:173–238.

Cabello Carro, Paz. 1989. "Materiales etnográficos de la Costa Noroeste recogidos en el siglo XVIII por viajeros españoles." In *Culturas de la costa noroeste de América* 1989, 61–79.

———. 1999. "Expediciones, descubrimientos y colecciones españolas en el siglo XVIII en la costa noroeste americana y en Alaska." In Basso, Bello, and Sauquet 1999, 29–43.

———, Andrés Escalera Ureña, and Raquel Carreras Rivery. 2000. "La conjunción de noticias de Mociño sobre Nutka y los análisis de laboratorio. Nuevos aportes sobre la composición de algunos objetos del siglo XVIII de la costa noroeste." *Anales del Museo de América* 8:293–302.

Campa Cos, Fr. Miguel de la, O.F.M. 1995. "Diario del viaje de exploración de 1775." In Bernabeu, ed. 1995, 189–232.

Cano Sánchez, Angela; Neus Escandell Tur; and Elena Mampel González, eds. 1984. *Gaspar de Portolá: Crónicas del descubrimiento de la Alta California, 1769*. Barcelona: Publicacions i Edicions de la Universitat de Barcelona. Contains: "Extracto de noticias" (1770), 25–27; Miguel Costansó. "Diario histórico" (1770), 29–50, and "Diario del viaje de tierra hecho al norte de la California" (7 February 1770), 55–37; Pedro Fages. "Continuación y suplemento" (1775), 145–93; Gaspar de Portolá. "Diario del viaje" (1769–70), 201–13; Vicente Vila. "Diario de navegación" (1769–70), 219–59; Juan Manuel de Viniegra, "Apuntamiento instructivo" (1771), 263–87; "Entrada en la California de los Religiosos Franciscanos" (post-1794), 289–307.

Cano Trigo, José María. 1991. "Cartografía grabada de la expedición Malaspina." In *La Expedición Malaspina, 1789–1794. Bicentenario de la salida de Cádiz*, 97–110. Cádiz: Comisión Nacional V Centenario, Real Academia Hispanoamericana de Cádiz.

Cardona, Nicolás de. 1868a. "Relación del descubrimiento del reino de la California por el capitán y cabo Nicolás de Cardona." In [*CODOINAO*] 1864–84, 9:30–42.

———. 1868b. "Memorial del Capitán Nicolás de Cardona al Rey sobre sus descubrimientos y servicios en la California." In [*CODOINAO*] 1864–84, 9:42–57.

———. 1989. *Descripciones geográficas e hidrográficas de muchas tierras y mares del norte y sur en las Indias, en especial del descubrimiento del Reino de California*. Ed. Pilar Hernández Aparicio. Facsimile edition. Madrid: Turner.

Carlsson, Roy L. 1994. "Before Malaspina: the Archaeology of Northwest Coast Indian Cultures." In Palau Baquero and Orozco 1994, 34–42.

Carner-Ribalta, Joseph. 1947. *Els catalans en la descoberta i colonització de California seguit del "Diari historic" de Gaspar de Portolá, amba catorze gravats i quatre cartes geografiques*. Mexico: Biblioteca Catalana.

———. 1966 [1967]. *Contribució a una biografía de Gaspar de Portolá*. Barcelona: Rafael Dalmau.

———. 1971. *Gaspar de Portolá, conqueridor de California*. Barcelona: Selecta.

Carrasco y Guisasola, Francisco, ed. 1882–83. *Documentos referentes al reconocimiento de las costas de las Californias desde el cabo de San Lucas hasta el cabo Mendocino; recopilados en el Archivo de Indias*. 2 vols. Madrid: Dirección de Hidrografía.

Carreño Pérez, José A. 1990. "La hueste de Cortés en la expedición de 1535 a California." In *Hernán Cortés, hombre de empresa. Primer congreso de americanistas, Badajoz, 1985*, foreword by Demetrio Ramos Pérez, 113–24. Valladolid: Gráficas 66.

Carretero Collado, Leoncio. 1989. "La evolución del sistema de estratificación social en la Costa Noroeste desde el período del precontacto." In *Culturas de la costa noroeste de América* 1989, 15–32.

———. 1990. "El sistema de estratificación social en la Costa Noroeste norteamericana a través del proceso de aculturación, 1774–1921." *Revista Española de Antropología Americana* 20:161–82.

———, ed. 1990. See Jewitt 1990.

———. 1995. "Environment, Food Availability, and Nutrition in the Northwest Coast: Hazards in Native Traditional Subsistence." *Revista Española de Antropología Americana* 25:119–34.

———. 1998a. "De Yuquot a Tsaxana: la historia reciente de los mowachaht (Columbia británica)." In *VII Congreso Internacional de Historia de América. II: España en América del Norte*, ed. José A. Armillas Vicente, 1003–16. Saragossa: Diputación General de Aragón, Dept. de Educación y Cultura/Ministerio de Educación y Cultura.

———. 1998b. "Yoquot, Ahaminaquus, Tsaxana: el largo camino de los Mowachaht hacia el futuro." In Palau Baquero, Calés, and Sánchez 1998, 55–66.

———. 1999. "Mamajlni: política, comercio y coleccionismo en la costa noroeste americana durante los siglos XVIII y XIX." In Basso, Bello, and Sauquet 1999, 45–51.

Casas, Augusto. 1949. *Fray Junípero Serra, el apóstol de California*. Barcelona: Luis Miracle [Agustín Núñez].

Castellanos, Bonifacio, O.F.M., ed. 1958. See [Ajofrín] 1958.

Castilla, Alberto. 1986. "Una emigración de misioneros: franciscanos españoles en Alta California." In *Emigración española en USA*, ed. David Cardús, 31–48. Monografías de ALDEEU (Asociación de Licenciados y Doctores Españoles en Estados Unidos), Literatura 2. [Spain]: Beramar, Instituto Español de Emigración.

Cebreiro Blanco, Luis, ed. 1943–44. See *Colección de diarios y relaciones* 1943–75, vols. 1, 2, and 4.

Cerezo Martínez, Ricardo, series editor, 1987–99. *La Expedición Malaspina, 1789–1794*. 9 vols. Madrid: Ministerio de Defensa, Museo Naval; Barcelona: Lunwerg. For each volume see: 1. Cerezo 1987; 2. Cerezo 1991; 3. Muñoz and Sanz 1992; 4. Ibáñez 1992; 5. Higueras, Pimentel, and Fernández 1993; 6. Martínez-Cañavate 1994; 7. Pimentel 1995; 8. Estrella 1996; 9. Higueras 1999.

———. 1987. *La expedición Malaspina, 1789–1794. I: Circunstancias históricas del viaje. Presentación de la obra*. Madrid: Ministerio de Defensa, Museo Naval; Barcelona: Lunwerg.

———, ed. 1991. *La expedición Malaspina. II: Diario general del viaje*. 2 vols. Madrid: Ministerio de Defensa, Museo Naval; Barcelona: Lunwerg.

Chartrand, René. 1994. "Malaspina and the Spanish Explorations: A Contribution to the Geostrategic History of Canada's West Coast." In Palau Baquero and Orozco 1994, 319–28.

Claret, Pompeyo. 1963. *José de Gálvez, marqués de Sonora, visitador general de la Nueva España y fundador de las Californias, ministro de Indias con Carlos III*. Barcelona: [Casulleras].

[*CODOINAO*]. 1864–84. *Colección de documentos inéditos relativos al descubrimiento, conquista y organización de las antiguas posesiones españolas de América y Oceanía*. Series ed. Joaquín Pacheco, Francisco Cárdenas, and Luis Torres de Mendoza. 42 vols. Madrid: Manuel B. Quirós, Frías y Cía., José María Pérez, etc. Reprint, Vaduz and Nendeln, Liechtenstein: Kraus Reprint, 1964–66. Vol. 5 (1866) contains: Lorenzo Ferrer Maldonado. "Relación del descubrimiento del Estrecho de Anián...1588," 420–47. Vol. 8 (1867) contains: Fr. Antonio de la Ascensión. "Relación breve, 1620," 537–74. Vol. 9 (1868) contains: Pedro Porter Casanate. "Carta relación...desde que salió de España el año 1643 para el descubrimiento del Golfo de la California, hasta 24 enero 1649, " 5–18; "Memorial del Almirante D. Pedro Porter Casanate al Rey, recomendando una nueva expedición a la California," 19–29; "Relación del descubrimiento del reino de la California por el capitán y cabo Nicolás de Cardona," 30–42; and "Memorial del Capitán Nicolás de Cardona al Rey sobre sus descubrimientos y servicios en la California," 42–57. Vol. 12 (1869) contains: "Cuenta...del armada que salió a descubrir en el Mar del Sur...de que fue por capitán Diego Becerra. (Año de 1533)," 298–313; and "Traslado de una Real Cédula por la que se concede a Hernán Cortés pueda descubrir y poblar en el Mar del Sur y Tierra Firme...5 de noviembre de 1529" (read by order of Hernán Cortés at Puerto de Santa Cruz, 10 May 1535), 490–510. Vol. 14 (1870) contains: "Relación y derrotero de una armada...mandada por el capitán Hernando de Grijalva...a descubrir en el Mar del Sur. Año 1533," 128–42; and [Juan Páez]. "Viaje por las costas de las Californias de Juan Rodríguez Cabrillo, y piloto Bartolomé Ferrelo, descubriendo Cabo Mendocino y rebasando 42°N, en 1542," 165–91. Vol. 22 (1874) contains: "Capitulación que se tomó con el Marqués del Valle de 27 octubre 1529," 285–95. Vol. 23 (1875) contains: "Real Orden de Valladolid, 26 junio 1523, a Hernán Cortés," 353–68.

[*CODOIN España*]. 1842–95. *Colección de documentos inéditos para la Historia de España*. Ed. Martín Fernández de Navarrete, Miguel Salvá y Munar, Pedro Sainz de Baranda, and others. 112 vols. Madrid: Viuda de Calero. Nendeln, Liechtenstein: Kraus Reprint, 1964–75. Vol. 4 (1844) contains: "Instrucción que dio el Marqués del Valle [Hernán Cortés] el año de 1532 a Diego Hurtado de Mendoza, su lugarteniente de capitán general, para el viaje que debía hacer el armada del propio Marqués, al descubrimiento del Mar del Sur," 167–75; and "Auto de posesión que de las tierras que había descubierto en el Mar del Sur, tomo el Marqués don Fernando Cortés, en el puerto y bahía de Santa Cruz, en mil quinientos treinta y cinco años, conforme a las capitulaciones hechas con S.M., 3 mayo 1535," 190–92. Vol. 15 (1849) contains: Martín Fernández de Navarrete and Eustaquio Fernández de Navarrete. "Examen histórico-crítico de los viajes y descubrimientos apócrifos del Capitán Lorenzo Ferrer Maldonado, de Juan de Fuca, y del Almirante Bartolomé de Fonte," 5–214; and documentary appendices: "1. Año de 1636. Declaración que hicieron en 17 septiembre 1636 don Alonso Botello y Serrano y don Pedro Porter Casanate de las conveniencias del servicio de S.M., y públicas que se seguirían, de descubrir cómo se comunica por la California el mar del

Sur con el del Norte, de las varias tentativas hechas hasta entonces por todas las naciones para su hallazgo, con expresión de los navegantes que lo hicieron y de los daños que resultarían de que se fortificasen los extranjeros en cualquiera parte de aquellas costas, y al fin una Memoria muy particular de los autores que tratan de las Californias y su ensenada, e igualmente del paso del Mar del Sur al del Norte," 215–27; "2. Disertación escrita por don Alejandro Malaspina sobre la legitimidad de la navegación hecha en 1588 por Ferrer Maldonado desde las inmediaciones de Terranova al mar Pacífico, y al contrario: se examinan en esta ocasión las reflexiones del Sr. Buache, presentadas a la Real Academia de Ciencias en 13 noviembre 1590 [sic: 1790] los rastros engañosos de otras navegaciones semejantes y la utilidad verdadera para la navegación al Asia de una comunicación cualquiera entre los dos mares," 228–50; "3. Lorenzo Ferrer Maldonado. De la *Gaceta* de Madrid, martes 18 de febrero de 1812, núm. 49, pág. 149, col. 2ª. Inserta dos artículos publicados en Biblioteca Británica, núms. 431 y 457–58," 251–61; "4. Correspondencia entre Juan de Fuca y Miguel Lok sobre una nueva expedición al estrecho," (1596), 262–63; "5. Carta de don Antonio de Ulloa a don Martín Fernández de Navarrete. Isla de León, y enero 10 de 1792," 264–67; "6. Viaje de Malaspina," 268–320; "7. Nota sin título sobre el viaje de las goletas 'Sutil' y 'Mexicana,' que no se incluye por estar publicado," 321–22; and "8. Expedición de la corbeta 'Aránzazu' al mando del teniente de navío don Juan Caamaño, a comprobar la relación de Fonte . . . 1792," 323–63.

Colección de diarios y relaciones para la historia de los viajes y descubrimientos. 1943–75. 5 vols. Madrid: Instituto Histórico de Marina. Of interest for California-Northwest Coast history: vol. 1 (1943) includes "Rodríguez Cabrillo 1542." Ed. Luis Cebreiro Blanco, 27–42; vol. 2 (1943): includes "Bodega y Quadra 1775." Ed. Luis Cebreiro Blanco, 97–133; vol. 4 (1944) includes "Sebastián Vizcaíno, Costa W. de California, 1602–3," 39–68, and "Francisco de Ortega, Golfo de California, 1631–36." Ed. Luis Cebreiro Blanco, 69–110; vol. 6 (1964) includes "Esteban José Martínez (1742–1798)." Ed. Roberto Barreiro-Meiro, 19–148; vol. 7 (1975) includes "Arteaga 1779." Ed. Agustín Albarracín, 17–162, and "Caamaño 1792." Ed. Roberto Barreiro-Meiro, 173–238.

Collingridge, Vanesa. 2003. *El Capitán Cook*. Barcelona: Martínez Roca.

Consag, Fernando. 1754. "Diario [del viaje que hizo el padre Fernando Consag de la Compañía de Jesús en la California desde 27 grados y 2 tercios hacia el norte, entre la Sierra Madre y el océano, 22 mayo–8 julio 1751]." In [José de Ortega]. *Apostólicos afanes de la Compañía de Jesús, escritos por un padre de la misma sagrada religión de su provincia de México*, ed. Francisco Xavier Fluviá, 391–429. Barcelona: Pablo Nadal.

"Convenio de San Lorenzo el Real de 1790." 1998. In *Nutka 1792* 1998, 218–19.

Cook, James. 1982. *Los tres viajes alrededor del mundo*. 3 vols. Barcelona: Olañeta.

Cook, James. 1985. See Price 1985.

Coronado, Eligio M[oisés], ed. 1987. *Descripción e inventarios de las misiones de Baja California, 1773*. Preface by Bartolomé Font Obrador, foreword by W. Michael Mathes. Palma de Mallorca: Institut d'Estudis Baleàrics.

———, ed. 1996. See Taraval 1996.

Corredor García, Fr. Antonio, O.S.A. 1989. *Fray Junípero Serra*. Barcelona: Antalbe.

———. 1994. *Beato Junípero Serra: apóstol de Sierra Gorda y las Californias*. Seville: Apostolado Mariano.

Cortés, Hernán. 1523. "Real Orden de Valladolid, 26 junio 1523." In [*CODOINAO*] 1864–84, 23:353–68.

———. 1529. "Capitulación... de 27 octubre 1529." In [*CODOINAO*] 1864–84, 22:285–95.

———. 1532. "Instrucción que dio el Marqués del Valle el año de 1532 a Diego Hurtado de Mendoza, su lugarteniente de capitán general, para el viaje que debía hacer con el armada del propio Marqués, al descubrimiento del Mar del Sur." In [*CODOIN España*] 1842–95, 4:167–75.

———. 1535. "Auto de posesión que de las tierras que había descubierto en el Mar del Sur, tomo el Marqués don Fernando Cortés, en el puerto y bahía de Santa Cruz, en mil quinientos treinta y cinco años, conforme a las capitulaciones hechas con S.M. 3 mayo 1535." In [*CODOIN España*] 1842–95, 4:190–92.

Costansó, Miguel. 1771. *Diario histórico de los viajes de mar y tierra hechos al Norte de la California, escrito por Miguel Costanzó en el año 1770*. Madrid: Tomás López.

———. 1950. *Diario histórico de los viajes de mar y tierra hechos al Norte de la California, escrito por Miguel Costanzó en el año 1770*. Col. Chimalistac 5. Madrid: Porrúa.

———. 1959. "Diario histórico" (1770); "Informe sobre proyecto fortificar presidios Alta California" (1794); and "Informe sobre proyecto enviar auxilios a Alta California" (13 July 1795). In *Noticias y documentos* 1959, 77–124 and 223–44.

Crosse, John. 1994. "Malaspina and the Eliza Expedition of 1791." In Palau Baquero and Orozco 1994, 329–34.

——— and Pamela Sprätz. 1998. "Catálogo de dibujos y mapas del Ms. 10 y del Ms. 11 del Archivo del Ministerio de Asuntos Exteriores." In *Nutka 1792* 1998, 206–13.

Cruz Hermosilla, Emilio de la. 1984. "Don Gaspar de Portolá, conquistador y primer gobernador de California." In *Huella de España en América II*, 29–42. Cádiz: Aula Militar de Cultura, Gobierno Militar de Cádiz.

———. 1989. "El apoyo logístico de la armada en la conquista y evangelización de California." *Revista General de Marina* 216 (June): 735–40.

Cuesta Domingo, María del Pilar. 1993. *José Espinosa y Tello y su aportación a la historia de la hidrografía*. PhD diss., Universidad Complutense de Madrid.

Cugat Bonet, Josep María. 1970. *Don Pedro Fages en el bicentenario de la fundación de California*. Lérida: Instituto de Estudios Ilerdenses.

Culturas de la costa noroeste de América. 1989. Ed. José Luis Peset. Madrid: Turner, Comisión del V Centenario.

Cutter, Donald C. 1958a. "Una expedición militar española en California en 1808." *Revista de Historia Militar* 2, no. 2: 41–58.

———. 1958b. "Fr. Blas Ordaz: La última exploración española en América." *Revista de Indias* 18, no. 72 (April–June): 227–41.

———. 1987. "Pedro Alberni y los primeros experimentos de agricultura científica en la costa noroeste del Pacífico." *Revista de Historia Naval* 5, no. 18:41–56.

———. 1994. "The Two Visits of Malaspina to California." In Palau Baquero and Orozco 1994, 335–39.

Díaz-Trechuelo, María Lourdes. 1956. "Dos nuevos derroteros del galeón de Manila (1730 y 1773)." *Anuario de Estudios Americanos* 13:1–83.

Dotor, Ángel. 1948. "Las expediciones marítimas cortesianas." *Revista General de Marina* 134 (June): 787–93.

Ducrue, Benno Francisco. 2008. "Relación de la expulsión de la Compañía de Jesús de la Provincia Mexicana, y particularmente de California, en el año 1767, con otras noticias dignas de saberse." In Bernabeu 2008, 153–83.

Eldredge, Zoeth S. 1910. "La marxa de Portolá y'l descobriment del golf de Califórnia." *Estudis Universitaris Catalans* 4:81–98.

Engelhardt, Zephyrin. 1924. *Un misionero santo, o sea, Vida, virtudes y milagros del Padre Magín Catalá, natural de Montblanch, hijo de la Seráfica Provincia de Cataluña y misionero de Santa Clara en California. Traducción de 'Holy Man of Santa Clara,' por el padre Pedro Sanahuja, O.F.M.* Barcelona: Arte Católico, José Vilamala.

Engstrand, Iris H. Wilson. 1998. "Los naturalistas Moziño y Maldonado y sus viajes a Nueva España." In *Nutka 1792* 1998, 98–107.

———. 2000. "Los resultados antropológicos de la expedición: José Mariano Moziño y las noticias de Nutka." In *El águila y el nopal: La Expedición de Sessé y Mociño a Nueva España, 1787–1803—Catálogo de los fondos documentales del Real Jardín Botánico de Madrid*, ed. María Pilar de San Pío and Miguel Ángel Puig-Samper. Madrid: Real Jardín Botánico, and Barcelona: Lunwerg.

Espinosa y Tello, José, ed. 1802. See [Alcalá and Valdés] 1802.

———. 1805. *Memoria sobre las observaciones astronómicas que han servido de fundamento a las Cartas de la costa Noroeste de América, publicadas por la Dirección de Trabajos Hidrográficos, a continuación del viaje de las goletas Sutil y Mexicana al estrecho de Juan de Fuca.* Madrid: [Dirección de Hidrografía].

———. 1809. *Memorias sobre las observaciones astronómicas hechas por los navegantes españoles en distintos lugares del globo.* 2 vols. [Madrid]: Imprenta Real. Vol. 1 contains: "De las costas del continente de América, y sus islas, desde Montevideo por el cabo de Hornos, hasta los 60° de lat. N.," 1–224 (note that each section of this volume es paginado separately).

———. 1885. "Noticia de las principales expediciones hechas por nuestros pilotos del Departamento de San Blas al reconocimiento de la costa del Noroeste de América, desde el año de 1774 hasta el 1791, extractada de los diarios originales de aquellos navegantes." In Malaspina 1885, 420–33.

Esponera Cerdán, Alfonso. 1994. "Un andaluz misionero en la Baja California: el dominico Francisco Galisteo (1771–1788)." *Communio* (Seville) 27, nos. 2–3:271–336.

Estrada Arnaiz, Rafael. 1930. "El viaje de las corbetas 'Descubierta' y 'Atrevida' y los artistas de la expedición, 1789–1794. (Conferencia dada por el Capitán de Fragata Don Rafael Estrada Arnáiz el día 20 de junio de 1930 en el Museo de Arte Moderno)." *Revista General de Marina* 107 (July): 193–205, (August): 193–205, (September): 377–93, and (October): 551–67. Also published separately as: *El viaje de las corbetas "Descubierta" y "Atrevida" y los artistas de la expedición, 1789–1794*. Madrid: Ministerio de Marina, Revista General de Marina, 1930.

———. 1951. "Discurso marginal de la exposición de dibujos y grabados de la expedición Malaspina en el Museo Naval de Madrid, año 1951." *Revista General de Marina* 141 (August): 189–94.

Estrella, Eduardo, ed. 1996. *La expedición Malaspina (1789–1794). Tomo VIII. Trabajos zoológicos, geológicos, químicos y físicos en Guayaquil de Antonio Pineda y Ramos*. Madrid: Ministerio de Defensa, Museo Naval; Barcelona: Lunwerg.

Fernández Duro, Cesáreo, ed. 1894. "Vocabulario de los idiomas Runsien y Eslem formado por el Padre Fr. Francisco Garcés en sus expediciones a California en el año 1774." In *IX Congreso Internacional de Americanistas. Actas de la novena reunión: Huelva (España), 7–11 octubre 1892*, 317–21. Madrid: Tip. de los Hijos de M.G. Hernández.

———. 1901. "Tadeo Haenke, naturalista en el viaje alrededor del mundo de las corbetas *Descubierta* y *Atrevida* al mando de Don Alejandro Malaspina." *Boletín de la Real Academia de la Historia* (Madrid) 39 (November): 386–98.

———. 1903. "Monumentos erigidos en California a Vancouver y a Bodega y Cuadra." *Boletín de la Real Sociedad Geográfica* 45:330–34.

Fernández Galiano, María Josefa. 1987. *Misiones de California, 1750–1800*. PhD diss., Universidad de Sevilla.

———. 1988. "Los dominicos en la Baja California, 1773–1790." In *Actas del I Congreso Internacional: "Los dominicos y el Nuevo Mundo," Sevilla, 21–25 de abril de 1987*, 497–519. Madrid: Deimos.

———. 1989. "El régimen misional de la orden de Santo Domingo en las misiones californianas." *Communio: Commentarii Internationales de Ecclesia et Theologia. Studium Generale, O.P.* (Seville) 22, no. 2:209–22.

Fernández de Navarrete, Martín. 1802. "Introducción en que se da noticia de las expediciones executadas anteriormente por los españoles en busca del Paso del Noroeste de la América." In *Relación del viaje hecho por las goletas "Sutil" y "Mexicana" en el año de 1792 para reconocer el estrecho de Fuca*, ed. José Espinosa y Tello, i–clxviii. Madrid: Imprenta Real.

Fernández de Navarrete, Martín. 1881. "Examen del viaje de Lorenzo Ferrer Maldonado." In Novo 1881, 123–65.

———— and Eustaquio Fernández de Navarrete. 1849. "Examen histórico-crítico de los viajes y descubrimientos apócrifos del Capitán Lorenzo Ferrer Maldonado, de Juan de Fuca, y del Almirante Bartolomé de Fonte." In [*CODOIN España*] 1842–95, 15:5–214 (with documentary appendix, 15:215–363.)

Fernández González, Alicia. See Higueras, Pimentel, and Fernández 1993.

Fernández y Somera, Blas. 1959. "Diario al Norte de Baja California" (1766). In *Noticias y documentos* 1959.

Ferrer Maldonado, Lorenzo. 1849. "Lorenzo Ferrer Maldonado. De la *Gaceta* de Madrid, martes 18 de febrero de 1812, núm. 49, pág. 149, col. 2ª. Inserta dos artículos publicados en Biblioteca británica, núms. 431 (dic. 1813): 517–528, y 457–458 (enero 1815)." In *CODOIN España*] 1842–95, vol. 15 (1849), pp. 251–61.

————. 1866. "Relación del descubrimiento del Estrecho de Anián que hice yo, el capitán Lorenzo Ferrer Maldonado, el año 1588, en la cual está la orden de la navegación y la disposición del sitio y el modo de fortalecerlo, y asimismo las utilidades desta navegación, y los daños que de no hacerla, se siguen." In [*CODOINAO*] 1864–84, vol. 5 (1866), pp. 420–47. Also appears in Novo 1881, 54–83, and in Malaspina 1885, 137–44.

Fita [Colomé], Fidel, S.J. 1908. "Noticia de la California, obra anónima del P. Andrés Marcos Burriel, emprendida en 1750, impresa en 1757, y traducida después en varias lenguas de Europa: datos inéditos e ilustrativos de su composición, aprobación y edición." *Boletín de la Real Academia de la Historia* 52:396–438.

Fluviá, Francisco Xavier, ed. 1754. See Consag 1754.

Font Obrador, Bartolomé [Bartomeu]. 1966. *El Padre Boscana, historiador de California*. Palma de Mallorca: Cort.

————. 1966–67. "La obra del Padre Payeras en California." *Boletín de la Sociedad Arqueológica Luliana* (Palma de Mallorca) 33, nos. 804–7:470–78.

————. 1968. *Contribución mallorquina al conocimiento de los indígenas de California*. Barcelona: Universidad de Barcelona.

————. 1969. "El Padre Lector Junípero Serra (en la conmemoración del 200 aniversario de la Misión de San Diego de Alcalá, 16 de julio de 1769)." *Boletín de la Sociedad Arqueológica Luliana* (Palma de Mallorca) 33:121–29.

————. 1976. *El Padre Francisco Palou, O.F.M. Fundador de la Misión de San Francisco, biógrafo del Venerable Junípero Serra y el primer historiador de California. Discurso biográfico del nuevo Hijo Ilustre de Palma*. Palma de Mallorca: Ayuntamiento de Palma de Mallorca.

————, ed. 1977. See Palóu 1977.

————. 1985. "Acotaçions a l'obra civilitzadora de Fra Juníper Serra. L'horitzó d'un destí providencial." *Comunicació. Revista del Centre d'Estudis Teològics de Mallorca*, 37–38 (March–June): 25–32.

————. 1987. See Coronado 1987.

————. 1988a. *Juníper Serra: l'empremta mallorquina a la Califòrnia naixent*. Palma de Mallorca: Ajuntament de Palma de Mallorca.

———. 1988b. *Junípero Serra*. Col. Biografías de Mallorquines. Palma de Mallorca: Ayuntamiento de Palma de Mallorca.

———. 1989a. *Fra Juníper Serra: les Balears i el Nou Món*. Palma de Mallorca: Caixa de Balears, Sa Nostra.

———. 1989b. *El apóstol de California, sus albores*. Palma de Mallorca: Conselleria de Cultura, Educació i Esports, Direcció General de Cultura.

———. 1991. *Padre Viejo: Semblança de Fra Juníper Serra/A Portrait of Fray Junípero Serra*. [Palma de Mallorca]: Comissió de les Illes Balears per la Commemoració del Vè Centenari del Descobriment d'Amèrica, Miramar.

———. ca. 1992. *La Sierra Gorda de Fray Junípero*. N.p.: n.p.

———, ed. [1994]. *El P. Juan Crespí, explorador de la costa pacífica. Introducció a l'estudi dels Diaris, transcripció i bibliografia pel Dr. Bartomeu Font i Obrador*. [Palma de Mallorca]: Institut d'Estudis Baleàrics.

———. 1994. *Joan Crespí: explorador i cronista franciscà a l'Alta Califòrnia*. Palma de Mallorca: Ajuntament de Palma de Mallorca.

———. 1998. *Fray Junipero Serra. Doctor de gentiles*, Palma Imatge-70. Palma de Mallorca: Miquel Font, Govern Balear.

——— and Norman Neuerburg. 1992. *Fray Junipero Serra: Mallorca, México, Sierra Gorda, Californias*. [Palma de Mallorca]: Comissió de Cultura, Consell Insular de Mallorca.

Force, Maryanne, and Roland Force. 1989. "Captain William Trotter: The Spanish Connection." In *Culturas de la costa noroeste de América* 1989, 299–314.

Frost, Alan. 1988. "Una ciencia para fines políticos: exploraciones del Océano Pacífico por las naciones europeas, 1764–1806." In *El Pacífico español de Magallanes a Malaspina*, ed. Carlos Martínez Shaw, 89–105. Madrid: M.A.E.

Fuca, Juan de, and Miguel Lok. 1849. "Correspondencia" (1596). In [*CODOIN España*] 1842–95, vol. 15 (1849), pp. 262–63.

Fúster Ruiz, Francisco. 1997. *El final del descubrimiento de América: California, Canadá y Alaska (1765–1822). Aportación documental del Archivo General de la Marina*. Murcia: Universidad de Murcia.

Galán García, Agustín. 1988. "Conflicto entre la autoridad militar y los religiosos de la Alta California (1781–1792)." *Hispania Sacra. Revista de Historia Eclesiástica de España* 40 (July–December): 807–24.

Galera Gómez, Andrés. 1987. "La aportación científica de la Expedición Malaspina a la historia natural." *Asclepio* 39, no. 2:85–102.

———, ed. 1990. See Malaspina 1990.

Galmés Más, Lorenzo, O.P. 1988. *Fray Junípero Serra, apóstol de California*, Biblioteca de Autores Cristianos. Madrid: La Editorial Católica.

Galvin, John, ed. 1996. See Garcés 1996.

Garcés, Fr. Francisco. 1994. "Diarios" (1771, 1775, and other documents, 1768–81). In Oltra and Martínez 1994, 83–119, 120–215 and 216–71.

———. 1996. *Diario de exploraciones en Arizona y California (1775–1776)*. Ed. John Galvin, foreword by Alejandro Salafranca. 3rd ed. Col. Nuestra América 3. Málaga: Algazara.

García [Rodríguez], Casiano. 1932. "Fr. Francisco Lasuén." In *Misiones Franciscanas* (October).

Garriga, Pere C. 1986. "Ginebró Serra i Gaspar de Portolà a Califòrnia." In *Catalans a Amèrica: En el segon centenari de la mort de Gaspar de Portolà (1786) i el primer de la fundació del Centre Catalá de Buenos Aires (1886)*, 66–72. Barcelona: Fundació Jaume I.

Gascón de Gotor, Anselmo. 1950. *Aragón en América. Aventurero genial. Soldado-navegante-descubridor*. Saragossa: Estilo.

Geiger, Maynard J., O.F.M. 1987. *Vida y época de fray Junípero Serra, O.F.M., o el hombre que nunca retrocedió. (Obra completa)*. Trans. Jacinto Fernández-Largo, O.F.M., ed. Bartolomé Font Obrador. 2 vols. Palma de Mallorca: Gobierno de la Comunidad Autónoma de Baleares and Caja de Ahorros "Sa Nostra"; Curia Provincial de la O.F.M. de Valencia, Aragón y Baleares; Asociación Amigos de Fray Junípero Serra.

Gibson, James. 1994. "Nootka and Nutria: Spain and the Maritime Fur Trade of the Northwest Coast." In Palau Baquero and Orozco 1994, 137–60.

Gicklhorn, Renée. 1966. "Tadeo Haenke, como socio de la expedición Malaspina." In vol. 4 of *XXXVI Congreso Internacional de Americanistas. Barcelona-Sevilla (España), 31 agosto–9 septiembre de 1964. Actas y Memorias*, 643–45. Seville: Católica Española.

Gómez, Vito T., O.P. 1988. "Los dominicos exclaustrados de la provincia de Aragón y sus aportaciones a la evangelización de California (siglo XIX)." In *Actas del I Congreso Internacional: "Los dominicos y el Nuevo Mundo," Sevilla, 21–25 de abril de 1987*, 521–36. Madrid: Deimos.

Gómez Canedo, Lino, O.F.M. 1969. *De México a la Alta California. Una gran epopeya misional*. Mexico: Jus.

———. 1982. "Fray Junípero Serra y su noviciado misional en América (1750–1758)." *Archivo Ibero-Americano* 42, nos. 165–68:881–918.

———. 1983. *Un lustro de administración franciscana en Baja California (1768–1773)*. La Paz: Gobierno de Baja California Sur.

———. 1989. "Fray Junípero Serra, misionero." *Verdad y Vida* 47:151–68.

González Claverán, Virginia. 1987. "La expedición Malaspina y la cartografía novohispánica." *Revista de Historia Naval* 5, no. 19:91–112.

——— and María Dolores Higueras. 1989. *Malaspina en Acapulco*. Foreword by J. Wimer. Madrid: Turner.

González Montero de Espinosa, Marisa. 1990. *La antropología en la expedición de Alejandro Malaspina: las ciencias antropológicas en la España ilustrada*. PhD diss., Universidad Complutense de Madrid.

———. 1991. "Expedición Malaspina: la antropología." In *La ciencia española en Ultramar. Actas de las I Jornadas sobre España y las expediciones científicas en*

América y Filipinas, ed. Alejandro R. Díez Torre, Tomás Mallo, Daniel Pacheco Fernández, and Ángeles Alonso Flecha, 265–75. Aranjuez: Doce Calles.

González Rodríguez, Luis. 1985. "Hernán Cortés, la Mar del Sur y el descubrimiento de la Baja California." *Anuario de Estudios Americanos* 42:573–644.

Gough, Barry. [2006]. "From Nootka Sound to Trafalgar: Commodore Dionisio Alcala Galiano." In Soler Pascual [2006], 231–43.

Gracia Rivas, Manuel. 1988. "Pedro Porter y Casanate, Almirante de la Mar del Sur (1612–1662)." In vol. 1 of *Temas de Historia Militar: II Congreso de Historia Militar, Saragossa, 1988*, 615–60. Madrid: Estado Mayor del Ejército.

———. 1989. *Sueño del Nuevo Reino de Aragón: la California de Pedro Porter*. Saragossa: Mira Editores.

Grijalva, Hernando. 1870. "Relación y derrotero de una armada de dos navíos, 'Concepción' capitana, y 'San Lázaro', que salió del puerto de Santiago en el Mar del Sur, de orden de Hernán Cortés, mandada por el capitán Hernando de Grijalva y el piloto Martín de Acosta, portugués, a descubrir en el Mar del Sur. Año 1533." In [*CODOINAO*] 1864–84, vol. 14 (1870), pp. 128–42.

Grunfeld, Federico V. 1986. "Faces in the Forest: Moziño's Noticias de Nutka." In *To the Totem Shore* 1986, 158–75.

———. 1988. "El arte en la cultura del noroeste del Pacífico." In *El Ojo del Tótem* 1988, 26–47.

Guest, Francis F. 1988. "Principles for an Interpretation of the History of the California Missions (1769–1792)." *Hispania Sacra* 40 (July–December): 791–806.

Guillén y Tato, Julio Fernando. 1932. *Repertorio de los manuscritos, cartas, planos y dibujos relativos a las Californias, existentes en este Museo [Naval]*. Madrid: Museo Naval.

———. 1952. *Exposición de dibujos y grabados de los artistas que figuraron en las expediciones científicas de las corbetas "Descubierta" y "Atrevida" (1789–1794) y las goletas "Sutil" y "Mexicana" (1792)*. Las Palmas de Gran Canaria: Casa de Colón.

Guirao, Angel. 1989. "Notas para una comparación entre las expediciones a la Patagonia y a las costas del Noroeste americano." In *Culturas de la costa noroeste de América* 1989, 265–76.

Gutiérrez de la Concha, Juan. 1993. "Extracto de los sucesos acaecidos en el reconocimiento de la costa Noroeste de América." In Higueras, Pimentel, and Fernández 1993, 153–68.

Haberland, Wolfgang. 1989. "Remarks on the 'Jacobsen Collections' from the Northwest Coast." In *Culturas de la costa noroeste de América* 1989, 183–94.

Hausberger, Bernard. 2009. "El padre Eusebio Francisco Kino, S.J. (1645–1771), la misión universal y la historiografía nacional." In *El Gran Norte Mexicano. Indios, misioneros y pobladores entre el mito y la historia*, ed. Salvador Bernabeu Albert, 213–50. Madrid: C.S.I.C.

Henckel, Carlos. 1956. "Las actividades del naturalista Tadeo Haenke en la Expedición de Malaspina, 1789–1794." *Boletín de la Real Sociedad Española de Historia Natural* 54.

Hernández Aparicio, Pilar. 1975. *Los viajes a las pesquerías de perlas de California en el siglo XVII*. PhD diss., Universidad Complutense de Madrid.

———. 1976. "La Compañía de los Cardona y sus viajes a las pesquerías de perlas de la costa de California." *Anuario de Estudios Americanos* 33:405–30.

———. 1979. "Los viajes de Francisco Ortega a las pesquerías de perlas de California." In vol. 1 of *Homenaje al doctor Muro Orejón*, ed. Luis Navarro García, 85–98. Seville: Universidad de Sevilla.

———. 1980. "Los viajes de Isidro Atondo y Antillón a California, 1683–1685." *Anuario de Estudios Americanos* 37:3–43.

———, ed. 1989. See Cardona 1989.

Hernández de López, Ana María. 1991. "Un viaje científico del siglo XVIII por la costa norte de California." In *Impacto y futuro de la civilización española en el Nuevo Mundo. Actas del Encuentro Internacional Quinto Centenario/ X Asamblea General de la Asociación de Licenciados y Doctores Españoles en Estados Unidos. San Juan de Puerto Rico, 17–22 de abril de 1990*, ed. Gloria Castresana Waid, 77–86. Madrid: Sociedad Estatal V Centenario, Instituto de Cooperación Internacional, Universidad Complutense, Siruela.

Hernández Sánchez-Barba, Mario. 1953. "Españoles, rusos e ingleses en el Pacífico norte durante el siglo XVIII." *Información Jurídica* 121:549–66.

———. 1957a. "Individualismo y colectivismo en la pacificación de una periferia de tensión americana del siglo XVIII." *Revista de Estudios Políticos* (Madrid) 59, no. 91 (January–February): 169–98.

———. 1957b. *La última expansión española en América*. Madrid: Instituto de Estudios Políticos.

———. 1962. *Juan Bautista de Anza, un hombre de fronteras*. Temas de España ante el mundo 18. Madrid: Publicaciones Españolas.

———. 1982. "California, región de origen español." *Quinto Centenario* 4:245–48.

Hidalgo Sereno, Jacinto. 1961. "Un viaje de descubrimiento por la costa del Pacífico norteamericano." *Revista de Indias* 21, no. 84:271–93.

Higueras Rodríguez, M. Dolores. 1985–93. *Catálogo crítico de los documentos de la Expedición Malaspina (1789–1794) del Museo Naval*. 3 vols. Madrid: Museo Naval.

———. 1988a. "La expedición Malaspina (1789–1794). Una empresa de la Ilustración española." In *El Pacífico español de Magallanes a Malaspina*, ed. Carlos Martínez Shaw 147–63. Madrid: M.A.E..

———. 1988b. "Cuestionarios científicos y noticias geográficas en la expedición Malaspina (1789–1794)." In *Cuestionarios para la formación de las Relaciones Geográficas de Indias. Siglos XVI–XIX*, ed. Francisco de Solano, 107–29. Madrid: C.S.I.C.

―――. 1991. *Costa Noroeste de América. Album Iconográfico de la Expedición Malaspina/ Northwest Coast of America. Iconographic Album of the Malaspina Expedition.* Madrid: Museo Naval; Barcelona: Lunwerg.

―――. 1998. "Aportación de la expedición de Malaspina y Bustamante al conocimiento de la Costa Noroeste de América Septentrional, 1791–1792." In Palau Baquero, Calés, and Sánchez 1998, 27–32.

―――, ed. 1999. *La expedición Malaspina (1789–1794). Tomo IX. Diario general del viaje de la corbeta "Atrevida" por José Bustamante y Guerra.* Madrid: Ministerio de Defensa, Museo Naval; Barcelona: Lunwerg.

Higueras Rodríguez, M. Dolores, Juan Pimentel Egea, and Alicia Fernández González, eds. 1993. *La expedición Malaspina (1789–1794). Tomo V. Antropología y noticias etnográficas.* Madrid: Ministerio de Defensa, Museo Naval; Barcelona: Lunwerg. (Contains: Alejandro Malaspina, "Descripción física de las costas del NO de la América visitada por las corbetas," 91–126; Antonio Tova Arredondo, "Acaecimientos en el Puerto Mulgrave," 127–37; Antonio Tova Arredondo, "Acaecimientos en el Puerto de Nutka," 139–52; José Mariano Mociño, "Vocabulario del idioma de los habitantes de Nutka," 147–68; Juan Gutiérrez de la Concha, "Extracto de los sucesos acaecidos en el reconocimiento de la costa NO de América," 153–68.)

Higueras Rodríguez, M. Dolores and María Luisa Martín-Merás. 1986. "La cartografía española en la costa noroeste de América: el cuerpo de Pilotos de la Armada." In *To the Totem Shore* 1986, 90–119.

―――, eds. 1991. See [Alcalá and Valdés] 1802.

Hilton, Sylvia L., ed. 1981. See Abbad 1981.

―――. 1987a. *Junípero Serra.* Col. Protagonistas de América. Madrid: Historia 16, Quorum.

―――. 1987b. "Apuntes sobre rivalidades internacionales y expediciones españolas en el Pacífico, 1763–1794." *Revista de Indias* (Madrid) 47, no. 180:431–48.

―――. 1992. *La Alta California Española.* Madrid: Mapfre.

―――. 1994. "La empresa de Gálvez en Alta California: las difíciles relaciones entre sus protagonistas, 1769–70." In vol. 1 of *El reino de Granada y el nuevo mundo. Actas del V congreso internacional de historia de América, mayo de 1992,* 247–80. Granada: Diputación Provincial de Granada.

―――, ed. 1999. *Las Raíces Hispánicas del Oeste de Norteamérica: Textos Históricos.* Biblioteca Digital Clásicos Tavera, ser. 2: Temáticas para la historia de Iberoamérica CT021. CD-ROM. Madrid: Fundación Mapfre-Tavera, Digibis. This CD includes digital reproductions of: *Relación del viaje hecho por las goletas 'Sutil' y 'Mexicana' en el año de 1792 para reconocer el estrecho de Fuca, con una introducción* [by M. Fernández de Navarrete] *en que se da noticia de las expediciones executadas anteriormente por los españoles en busca del paso del noroeste de la América.* Ed. José Espinosa y Tello. Madrid: Imprenta Real, 1802; [Fr. Luis Sales]. *Noticias de la provincia de Californias en tres cartas de un sacerdote religioso, hijo del real convento de predicadores de Valencia a un amigo suyo, 1794.* Valencia: Hermanos de Orga, 1794; and [Miguel Venegas, S.J. and Andrés Marcos Burriel, S.J.]. *Noticia de la California, y de su conquista temporal y espiritual hasta el tiempo presente. Sacada de la Historia manuscrita, formada en México año de 1739, por el P. Miguel Venegas, de la Compañía de Jesús, y de otras noticias y relaciones antiguas y modernas,* 3 vols. Madrid: Viuda de Manuel Fernández, Supremo Consejo de la Inquisición, 1757.

Holm, Bill. 1989. "Cultural Exchange Across the Gulf of Alaska: Eighteenth Century Tlingil and Pacific Eskimo Art in Spain." In *Culturas de la costa noroeste de América* 1989, 105–14.

———. 1999. "La función del arte entre los indios de la costa noroeste." In Basso, Bello, and Sauquet 1999, 53–59.

Ibáñez Montoya, María Victoria. 1994. "Las reliquias botánicas y etnológicas de Tadeo Haenke en Praga." In Palau Baquero and Orozco 1994, 79–84.

Ibáñez Montoya, María Victoria, and Carmen Sanz, eds. 1992. *La expedición Malaspina (1789–1794). Tomo IV. Trabajos científicos y correspondencia de Tadeo Haenke.* Madrid: Ministerio de Defensa, Museo Naval; Barcelona: Lunwerg.

Igual Úbeda, Antonio. 1958. *Fray Junípero Serra.* Col. Vidas de grandes hombres. Barcelona: Seix Barral.

Infiesta Pérez, José Luis [Josep Lluis Alcofar Nassaes, pseud.]. 1985. Gaspar de Portolá. Gent nostra 40. Barcelona: Nou Art Thor.

———. 1986. "Don Gaspar de Portolá, primer gobernador de California." *Historia 16* 11, no. 124: 95–102.

Inglis, Robin. 1994. "The Noble Savage: Myth and Reality on the Northwest Coast at the End of the Eighteenth Century." In Palau Baquero and Orozco 1994, 50–60.

———. 1995. "Maquinna of Nootka: Portrait of an Indian Chief on the Edge of Empire." In *De la ciencia ilustrada a la ciencia romántica. Actas de las II Jornadas sobre "España y las expediciones científicas entre América y Filipinas."* Ed. Alejandro R. Díez Torre, Tomás Mallo, and Daniel Pacheco Fernández, 33–54. Aranjuez (Madrid): Ateneo de Madrid, Doce Calles.

———. 1997. "Malaspina y la costa noroeste americana; el legado de una gran expedición de exploración." In *España y el Pacífico,* ed. Antonio García-Abásolo, 239–44. Córdoba: M.A.E., Asociación Española de Estudios del Pacífico.

———. 1998. "Otras dos iniciativas: Caamaño en Alaska, y Fidalgo en Núñez Gaona." In *Nutka 1792* 1998, 108–21.

———. [2006]. "The Nuu-Chah-Nulth as Recorded in Eighteenth-Century Spanish Records." In Soler Pascual [2006], 89–106.

Jewitt, John R. 1990. *Diario y aventuras en Nootka,* Crónicas de América 60. Ed. Leoncio Carretero Collado. Madrid: Historia 16.

Jiménez Núñez, Alfredo. 1969. "Panorama etnológico de la presencia española en el Noroeste." *Revista de Indias* 29, nos. 115–18 (January–December): 279–302.

Jiménez Pelayo, Águeda. 1997. "Tomás de Suria, un dibujante de la expedición de Malaspina. Su contribución al conocimiento del occidente de Norteamerica." *Anuario de Estudios Americanos* (Seville) 54, no. 2:489–509.

Jonaitis, Aldona. 1989. "The Recreation of Haida Art at the American Museum of Natural History." In *Culturas de la costa noroeste de América* 1989, 151–62.

Jordán de Urríes y Ruiz de Arana, Juan (Marqués de Ayerbe). 1907. "Sucesos ocurridos en Nootka en 1789." In *Tres hechos memorables de la marina española en el siglo XVIII. Estudios históricos*, 183–239. Madrid: Fortanet. 2nd ed., Barcelona: Arcadia, 1957.

Kai, Zhang. 1994. "China y la expedición del Pacífico Noroeste en la época de Malaspina." In Palau Baquero and Orozco 1994, 341–44.

Kendrick, John. 1994a. "Dionisio Alcalá Galiano, un egabrense insigne." In Palau Baquero and Orozco 1994, 199–204.

———. 1994b. "The Art of Navigator in the Time of Malaspina." In Palau Baquero and Orozco 1994, 215–26.

———. 1995. "On the Persistence of Error: The Case of Cook and Mourelle on the Northwest Coast of America." *Revista Española de Estudios Canadienses* (Madrid) 2, nos. 2–3 (November): 45–60.

———. 1998. "Españoles en el Estrecho de Fuca. Última exploración Alcalá Galiano y Cayetano Valdés." In *Nutka 1792* 1998, 86–97.

Keys, James M. 1950. *Las misiones españolas de California.* Foreword by Amando Melón. Madrid: C.S.I.C., Instituto Juan Sebastián Elcano.

Kino, Eusebio Francisco. 1958. "Viajes misionales por la Pimería Alta." Ed. Mario Hernández Sánchez-Barba. In *Viajes por Norteamérica.* Bibliotheca Indiana, Viajes y viajeros 2, series ed. Manuel Ballesteros Gaibrois, 87–255. Madrid: Aguilar.

Kippis, Andrew. 1795. *Historia de la vida y viages del Capitán Jaime Cook,* trans. Cesáreo de Nava Palacio. 2 vols. Madrid: Imprenta Real.

Lafarga Lozano, Adolfo. 1949. "Expediciones españolas en busca del paso del Noroeste de la América, el estrecho de Fuca y Semblanza de un ilustre marino de noble estirpe vizcaína: Don Juan Francisco de la Bodega y Quadra." *Vida Vasca. Revista Regional Española* 26 (1949): 228–32.

Lamadrid Jiménez, Lázaro. 1963. *El alavés fray Fermín Francisco de Lasuén (1736–1803), fundador de misiones en California.* 2 vols. Vitoria: Diputación Foral de Álava, Montepío Diocesano.

Landín Carrasco, Amancio. 1968. "Los últimos descubridores (España, Rusia e Inglaterra en el N.E. del Pacífico)." In *Estudios de Derecho Internacional Marítimo (Homenaje al Profesor José Luis de Azcárraga),* [ed. Camilo Barcia Trelles and Luis García Arias], 197–202. Madrid: Sindicato Nacional de la Marina Mercante.

———. 1970. "Mourelle de la Rúa y sus viajes por el Pacífico." *Revista General de Marina* 179 (October 1970): 351–65.

———. 1971. *Mourelle de la Rúa: explorador del Pacífico*. Madrid: Ediciones de Cultura Hispánica. Reprint, 1978. Contains: "Diario de la navegación... 1775," 169–215; and "Diario de la navegación... 1779," 217–70.

———. 1988. "Mourelle de la Rúa en el Mar del Sur." In *El Pacífico español de Magallanes a Malaspina*, ed. Carlos Martínez Shaw, 133–44. Madrid: M.A.E.

———. 1989. "Nota sobre el descubrimiento de las Hawai." In *Estudios sobre Filipinas y las islas del Pacífico*, 13–16 Madrid: Asociación Española de Estudios del Pacífico.

———. 1991. "Guía de descubridores: Sebastián Vizcaíno (1602)." *Revista General de Marina* 221 (November): 577–84.

———. 1992a. "Guía de descubridores: Pérez, Heceta, Bodega." *Revista General de Marina* 222 (March): 321–30.

———. 1992b. "Guía de descubridores: Arteaga, Bodega, y Mourelle." *Revista General de Marina* 222 (April): 453–61.

Landín Carrasco, Amancio and Luis Sánchez Masía. 1992. "Capítulo XX. Los viajes de Mourelle de la Rúa." In vol. 3 of *Descubrimientos españoles en el Mar del Sur*. Foreword by Amancio Landín Carrasco, 789–844. Madrid: Naval.

Larriñaga, Juan R[uiz], O.F.M. 1915. "Cartas de América [written by Father Pablo de Mugártegui]. De los misioneros de la Nueva California." *Archivo Ibero-Americano* 2, no. 10 (July–August): 104–20.

Lefán, Luis. 1942. "Un departamento marítimo español del siglo XVIII en el Pacífico." *Revista General de Marina* 123 (July): 19–24.

Lejarza, Fidel de. 1948. "Descubrimientos y exploraciones de California por mar y tierra." *Boletín de la Real Sociedad Geográfica* 534, nos. 7–12 (July–December): 397–439.

———, ed. 1949. "Seis cartas de Fr. Junípero Serra." *Archivo Ibero-Americano* 9:413–72.

Lens Tuero, Jesús. 1998. "El influjo de la cultura grecorromana sobre la *Vida de Fray Junípero Serra* de Francisco Palou y *La Historia de la Antigua o Baja California* de Francisco Xavier Clavijero." In *VII Congreso Internacional de Historia de América: ponencias y comunicaciones, 1996, Zaragoza. Tomo II: España en América del Norte*, ed. José A. Armillas Vicente, 1093–1102. Saragossa: Diputación General de Aragón.

Lenz, Mary Jane. 1989. "Myth and Memory at Lituya Bay." In *Culturas de la costa noroeste de América* 1989, 127–38.

Léon Portilla, Miguel. 1985. *Hernán Cortés y la Mar del Sur*. Madrid: Ediciones de Cultura Hispánica.

———. 1998. "Loreto, la madre de las Californias." *Historia 16* (Madrid) 262 (February): 112–16.

Llabrés Bernal, Juan. 1934. *Breve noticia de la labor científica del capitán de navío D. Felipe Bauzá y de sus papeles sobre América (1764–1834)*. Palma de Mallorca: Guasp.

Llabrés Martorell, Pere. 1985. "Fra Juniper Serra i Ferrer: fill de Mallorca i del seu temps." *Comunicació. Revista del Centre d'Estudis Teològics de Mallorca* 37–38 (March–June): 3–17.

Longinos Martínez Garrido, José. 1994. *Diario de las expediciones a las Californias de José Longinos*. Ed. Salvador Bernabeu Albert. Madrid: Doce Calles, C.S.I.C.

López Bonet, Miquel, 1989. "Estudi de les cartes autògrafes de Fra Juníper Serra." *Estudios Franciscanos* 90, no. 396:477–513.

López y Sebastián, Lorenzo E. 2000. "Arte y expediciones en la geografía histórica del noroeste americano." *Revista Complutense de Historia de América* (Madrid) 26:377–79.

López Urrutia, Carlos. 2000. *El real ejército de California*, illus. Juan Carlos Carrasco Torrecilla and Juan Ignacio Cuesta Millán. [Madrid]: Medusa. Reprint, 2001.

Lorenzana, Francisco Antonio. 1958. *Viaje de Hernán Cortés a la Península de las Californias*. Madrid: Porrúa.

Majó Framis, Ricardo. 1956. *Vida y hechos de Fray Junípero Serra, fundador de la Nueva California*. Madrid: Espasa-Calpe.

Malaspina, Alejandro. 1849a. "Disertación sobre la legitimidad de la navegación hecha en 1588 por Ferrer Maldonado." In [*CODOIN España*] 1842–95, 15:228–50.

———. 1849b. "Viaje político-científico alrededor del mundo por las corvetas Descubierta y Atrevida." In [*CODOIN España*] 1842–95, 15:268–320.

———. 1885. *Viaje político-científico alrededor del mundo por las corvetas Descubierta y Atrevida, al mando de los capitanes de navío D. Alejandro Malaspina y D. José de Bustamante y Guerra desde 1789 a 1794. Publicado con una introducción de D. Pedro de Novo y Colson*. Madrid: Viuda e Hijos de Abienzo.

———. 1979. *Descripción de la California. Expedición Malaspina-Bustamante, Mar Pacífico, 1791*. Facsimile of "Memoria de Alejandro Malaspina y sus colaboradores," MS. 621,

Biblioteca del Museo Naval de Madrid. [Madrid]: [Museo Naval].

———. 1984. *Viaje científico y político a la América Meridional, a las costas del Mar Pacífico y a las islas Marianas y Filipinas, verificado en los años 1789–90–91–92–93 y 94 a bordo de las corbetas "Descubierta" y "Atrevida" de la Marina Real, mandadas por los capitanes de navío don Alejandro Malaspina y don José F. Bustamante. Diario de viaje de Alejandro Malaspina*. Ed. Mercedes Palau, Aránzazu Zabala, and Blanca Saiz. Madrid: El Museo Universal.

———. 1990. *En busca del paso del Pacífico*, Crónicas de América. Ed. Andrés Galera Gómez. Madrid: Historia 16.

———. 1991. "Descripción física de las costas del noroeste de la América o visitadas por nosotros, o por los navegantes anteriores." In Monge and Olmo 1991, 163–235.

———. 1993. "Descripción física de las costas del NO." In Higueras, Pimentel, and Fernández 1993, 91–126.

Mañá Alvarenga, Tibisay. 1992. "Las contribuciones de la ingeniería militar al desarrollo científico-tecnológico de las colonias ultramarinas del siglo XVIII. Miguel Costansó en Nueva España (1764–1814)." In vol. 2 of *Europa e Iberoamérica: Cinco siglos de intercambios. Actas: IX Congreso internacional de Historia de América*, ed. María Justina Sarabia Viejo, 445–60. Sanlúcar de Barrameda: Universidad de Sevilla, Junta de Andalucía.

Mandelstamm, Valentín. 1978. "California hubiera podido ser rusa." *Historia y Vida* (Barcelona) 121 (April): 114–24.

Manjarrés y Bofarull, Ramón de. 1913. "La comunicación del Atlántico con el Pacífico. Ensayo sobre la parte de España en las investigaciones y proyectos." *Boletín del Instituto de Estudios Americanistas* (Seville), 1, no. 2 (June): 1–28 and no. 3 (September): 1–28.

———. 1914. "Proyectos españoles de canal interoceánico." *Revista de Archivos, Bibliotecas y Museos* 18, nos. 1–2 (January–February): 73–94 and nos. 3–4 (March–April): 283–97.

Mariñas Otero, Luis. 1967. "El incidente de Nutka." *Revista de Indias* 27, nos. 109–10 (July–December): 335–407.

Martín-Merás, María Luisa. 1984. "Vocabularios indígenas recogidos en las expediciones de Malaspina y las goletas *Sutil* y *Mexicana*." *Revista de Historia Naval* 2, no. 6:57–74.

———. 1986. See Higueras and Martín-Merás 1986.

———. 1990a. "La búsqueda del paso del Noroeste y el relato de Lorenzo Ferrer Maldonado. I." *Ingeniería Naval* 665:496–98.

———. 1990b. "La búsqueda del paso del Noroeste y el relato de Lorenzo Ferrer Maldonado. II." *Ingeniería Naval* 666:542–45.

———. 1991. "El estrecho de Anián y el viaje de Juan de Fuca." *Ingeniería Naval* 670:173–74.

———, ed. 1991. See Alcalá and Valdés 1991.

———. 1998. "Fondos cartográficos españoles de la Costa Noroeste de América en el Museo Naval de Madrid." In Palau Baquero, Calés, and Sánchez 1998, 67–82.

Martinell, Emma, and María José Martínez. 1998. "El interés por la lengua de los pobladores de la Costa Noroeste." In Palau Baquero, Calés, and Sánchez 1998, 37–42.

Martínez, Esteban José. 1964. "Diario de la navegación que yo el alférez de navío de la Real Armada Don Esteban Josef Martínez boy a ejecutar al puerto de San Lorenzo de Nuca, mandando la fragata *Princesa* y paquebot de *San Carlos* en el presente año de 1789." In *Colección de diarios y relaciones* 1943–75, 6:19–148.

Martínez, María José. 1998. See Martinell and Martínez 1998.

Martínez Grácia, Valentín. 1994. See Oltra and Martínez 1994.

Martínez Salazar, Ángel. 1991. "Dos gobernadores de California: Joaquín de Arrillaga y Diego de Borica (I)." *Muga* (Bilbao), no. 78 (September): 64–71.

———. 1992. *Diego de Borica y Retegui (1742–1800), gobernador de California*. [Vitoria]: [Diputación Foral de Álava].

———. 1994. "Vascos en la California colonial." *Historia 16* (Madrid) 19, no. 220 (August): 46–54.

Martínez Shaw, Carlos. 1988. "Los españoles en el Pacífico." In *El Pacífico español de Magallanes a Malaspina*, ed. Carlos Martínez Shaw, 13–31. Madrid: M.A.E.

Martínez-Cañavate Ballesteros, Luis Rafael, ed. 1994. *La expedición Malaspina (1789–1794). Tomo VI. Trabajos astronómicos, geodésicos e hidrográficos*. Madrid: Ministerio de Defensa, Museo Naval; Barcelona: Lunwerg.

Martínez-Valverde, Carlos. 1946. "Los buques de la expedición misionera de la Alta California." *Revista General de Marina* 103 (February): 227–33.

Mathes, W. Michael, ed. 1965. *Californiana I: Documentos para la historia de la demarcación comercial de California, 1583–1632*. 2 vols. Madrid: José Porrúa Turanzas.

———. 1969. "Sebastián Vizcaíno y los principios de la explotación comercial de California." In *Homenaje a don José María de la Peña y Cámara*, [ed. Ernest J. Burrus, S.J.], 221–48. Madrid: José Porrúa Turanzas.

———, ed. 1970–71. *Californiana II: Documentos para la historia de la explotación comercial de California, 1611–1679*. 2 vols. Madrid: José Porrúa Turanzas.

———, ed. 1974. *Californiana III: Documentos para la historia de la transformación colonizadora de California, 1679–1686*. 2 vols. Madrid: José Porrúa Turanzas.

———, ed. 1981. "El gobernador Felipe de Neve recomienda la fundación de Los Ángeles." *Quinto Centenario* 2:159–73.

———, ed. 1987. *Californiana IV: Aportación a la historiografía de California en el siglo XVIII*. 2 vols. Col. Chimalistac 45–46. Madrid: José Porrúa Turanzas.

———. 1987. See Coronado 1987.

Meade, Teresa. 1995. "Matrimonio, clase e identidad: testimonios procedentes de la frontera de la Alta California, 1770–1850." In *De palabra y obra en el Nuevo Mundo. 4. Tramas de la identidad*, ed. J. Jorge Klor, Gary H. Gossen, Miguel León-Portilla, and Manuel Gutiérrez, 9–24. Madrid: Siglo XXI de España, Extremadura En-Clave.

Medel Valpuesta, M. Asunción. 1966 [1967]. "Los indios de la Baja California en el siglo XVIII." In vol. 2 of *XXXVI Congreso Internacional de Americanistas, España 1964. Actas y Memorias*, [ed. Alfredo Jiménez Núñez], 167–75. Seville: Católica Española.

Melón y Ruiz de Gordejuela, Amando. 1946. "Las exploraciones españolas en América del Norte alentadas por la obra misional de Fray Junípero Serra." *Estudios Geográficos* 7, no. 22 (February): 29–46.

———. 1950. "Prólogo." In James M. Keys, *Las misiones españolas de California*, 5–11. Madrid: C.S.I.C., Instituto Juan Sebastián Elcano.

Menchaca Careaga, Antonio. 1989. *De California a Alaska. Vida y descubrimientos de don Juan Francisco de la Bodega-Quadra.* Madrid: Instituto de Cooperación Iberoamericana, Ediciones de Cultura Hispánica.

———. 1998. "Juan Francisco de la Bodega y Quadra y su tiempo." In *Nutka 1792* 1998, 2–19.

Mesquida, Sebastià. 1985. "La teología de la missió i Fra Juníper Serra en el segon centenari de la seva mort (1784–1984)." *Comunicació. Revista del Centre d'Estudis Teològics de Mallorca*, 37–38 (March–June): 43–51.

Miguélez Martínez, Armando. 1999. "Antonio de los Reyes (1729–1789): un Bartolomé de las Casas alicantino en el siglo XVIII." *Alquibla: Revista de Investigación del Bajo Segura* 5:383–405. A separate ed., Alicante: Biblioteca Virtual Miguel de Cervantes, 2006, is also available online in the Biblioteca Virtual Miguel de Cervantes, at http://www.cervantesvirtual.com/servlet/SirveObras/01361697566793303202802.

Mociño, José Mariano. 1993. "Vocabulario del idioma de los habitantes de Nutka." In Higueras, Pimentel, and Fernández 1993, 147–68.

———. 1999. *Las Noticias de Nutka*. Ed. Fernando Monge and Margarita del Olmo. Aranjuez (Madrid): Doce Calles.

Moncada Maya, J. Omar. 1995. "Los ingenieros militares en California. Siglo XVIII." In *De la ciencia ilustrada a la ciencia romántica. Actas de las II Jornadas sobre "España y las expediciones científicas entre América y Filipinas."* Ed. Alejandro R. Díez Torre, Tomás Mallo, and Daniel Pacheco Fernández, 447–500. Aranjuez (Madrid): Ateneo de Madrid, Doce Calles.

Monge Martínez, Fernando. 1989. "Sobre indios e ilustrados: la antropología y la expedición Malaspina en la Costa Noroeste (1791)." In *Culturas de la costa noroeste de América* 1989, 51–60.

———. 1994. "Pueblos de una sola nación. La costa Noroeste según Alejandro Malaspina, 1791." In Palau Baquero and Orozco 1994, 61–66.

———. 1999. "Mamalni e indios en Nootka. Apuntes para un escenario." *Revista de Indias* 59, no. 216 (May–August): 499–508.

———. 2002. *En la costa de la niebla. El paisaje y el discurso etnográfico ilustrado de la expedición Malaspina en el Pacífico.* Col. Tierra nueva e cielo nuevo 44. Madrid: C.S.I.C.

Monge Martínez, Fernando and Margarita del Olmo, eds. 1991. *Expediciones a la Costa Noroeste.* Crónicas de América 67. Madrid: Historia 16. Contains: Francisco Antonio Mourelle, "Acaecimientos en el puerto de Bucareli," 49–88; Tomás de Suria, "Diario," 89–162; Alejandro Malaspina, "Descripción física de la costa noroeste," 163–235.

———, eds. 1999. See Mociño 1999.

Morales Padrón, Francisco. 1955. "Descubrimiento y toma de posesión." *Anuario de Estudios Americanos* (Seville) 12:321–80. (Also paged 1–60).

———. 1986. "Galleons, Pirates, Pearls and Fantastic Straits." In *To the Totem Shore* 1986, 8–21.

Mourelle, José María. 1856. "Biografía del Excmo. Sr. D. Francisco Antonio Mourelle, Gefe de Escuadra de la Armada." In *Crónica Naval de España*. Madrid: Viuda de Calero. 2nd ed., Madrid: E. Teodoro, 1877.

Mourelle de la Rúa, Francisco Antonio. 1971. "Diario de la navegación... 1775" and "Diario de la navegación... 1779." In Landín 1971, 169–215 and 217–69. Reprint, 1978.

———. 1991. "Acaecimientos en el puerto de Bucareli (4 de mayo–1 de julio 1779)." In Monge and Olmo 1991, 49–88.

Mourelle-Lema, Manuel, 1967. "Un navegante ilustre: el Jefe de Escuadra Francisco Antonio Mourelle." *Revista General de Marina* 172 (June): 50–754.

Moziño, José Mariano. See Mociño, José Mariano.

Muñoz Garmendía, Félix, and Carmen Sanz Álvarez, eds. 1992. *La expedición Malaspina (1789–1794). Tomo III: Diarios y trabajos botánicos de Luis Née*. Madrid: Ministerio de Defensa, Museo Naval; Barcelona: Lunwerg.

Navarro García, Luis. 1964. *Don José de Gálvez y la Comandancia General de las Provincias Internas del norte de la Nueva España*. Seville: E.E.H.-A.

———. 1989. "Política indígena de España en el noroeste." In *Culturas de la costa noroeste de América* 1989, 209–22.

———. 1994. *Francisco de Ulloa (Explorador de California y Chile Austral)*. Badajoz: Diputación Provincial de Badajoz. Contains "Account of voyage to California, 1539," 181–238.

Neve, Felipe de. 1994. *Reglamento para el gobierno de la provincia de California. 1781*. Ed. Salvador Bernabeu Albert. Madrid: Doce Calles.

Noticias y documentos acerca de las Californias, 1764–1795. 1959. Col. Chimalistac, [ed. José Porrúa Turanzas and José Porrúa Venero]. Madrid: José Porrúa Turanzas. Contains: Francisco de Ajofrín, "Descripción de Californias" (1764); Blas Fernández y Somera, "Diario al Norte de Baja California" (1766); "Extracto sobre Monterey" (1769); Gaspar de Portolá, "Diario por tierra a San Diego y Monterey," (1769); Miguel de Costansó, "Diario histórico" (1770); "Noticia breve de la expedición militar de Sonora y Sinaloa de Elizondo" (1768–71); Juan Bautista de Anza, "Descubrimiento de Sonora a Californias en el año de 1774. Ruta del primer viaje"; Juan Francisco Bodega y Cuadra, "Navegaciones 1779"; Miguel de Costansó, "Distancias Santa Fe-Sonora-Monterey" (1776); Miguel de Costansó to Marqués de Branciforte, "Informe sobre proyecto fortificar presidios Alta California" (1794); Sánchez y Fidalgo Costansó, "Informe sobre proyecto enviar auxilios a Alta California" (13 July 1795).

Novi, Carlos. [2006]. "La expedición de las goletas Sutil y Mexicana al estrecho de Juan de Fuca en 1792. Circunstancias del viaje y Diario del Comandante D. Dionisio Alcalá-Galiano." In Soler Pascual [2006], 67–78.

Novo y Colson, Pedro de, ed. 1881. *Sobre los viajes apócrifos de Juan de Fuca y de Lorenzo Ferrer Maldonado. Recopilación y estudio*. Madrid: Fortanet.

———. 1882–83. "¿Son apócrifos los viajes de Juan de Fuca y de Lorenzo Ferrer Maldonado?" In vol. 1 of *IV Congreso Internacional de Americanistas. Actas* de la Cuarta Reunión: Madrid, 25–30 septiembre 1881, 122–28. Madrid: Fortanet.

———, ed. 1885. See Malaspina 1885.

Nutka 1792. Viaje a la Costa Noroeste de la América Septentrional por Juan Francisco de la Bodega y Quadra del orden de Santiago, Capitán de Navío de la Real Armada y Comandante del Departamento de San Blas, en las fragatas de su mando "Santa Gertrudis," "Aránzazu," "Princesa," y goleta "Activa." Año de 1792. 1998. Ed. Mercedes Palau Baquero, Freeman Tovell, Pamela Sprätz, and Robin Inglis. Madrid: M.A.E.

Ojo del Tótem, El: Arte y cultura de los indios del noroeste de América [exhibition catalogue]: *Centro Cultural de la Villa, Madrid, Abril–Mayo 1988: Museu Etnòlogic, Barcelona, Junio–Julio 1988.* 1988. Ed. José Alcina Franch, Frederic V. Grunfeld, and Mercedes Palau Baquero. Madrid: Excmo. Ayuntamiento de Madrid; Barcelona: Excmo. Ayuntamiento de Barcelona, Comisión Nacional V Centenario.

Olmo, Margarita del. 1989. "De la territorialidad nativa a la soberanía europea: análisis de la 'apropiación' del concepto de soberanía territorial por parte de los indios de la Columbia Británica." In *Culturas de la costa noroeste de América* 1989, 93–104.

———, ed. 1991. See Monge and Olmo 1991.

Olson, Wallace, and Enrique J. Porrúa. 2002. "Los viajes españoles a las costas de Alaska entre 1774 y 1792 y su contribución a la etnografía del área." *Anales del Museo de América* (Madrid) 10:177–83.

Oltra Perales, Fr. Enrique, O.F.M. 1988. *Vida de fray Junípero Serra, narrada para el hombre de hoy.* Valencia: Asís.

———. 2004. *El beato fray Junípero Serra: misiones y misioneros franciscanos en la Alta California (1769–1823).* Biblioteca Franciscana-Americana 25. Valencia: Librería San Lorenzo Franciscanos.

Oltra Perales, Fr. Enrique, O.F.M. and Valentín Martínez Grácia. 1994. *Vida y diarios del Rdo. P. Fray Francisco Hermenegildo Garcés, Maestro.* Franciscanos en el Nuevo Mundo 15. Valencia: Publicaciones V Centenario del Descubrimiento y Evangelización de América.

Omaechevarría Martitegui, Ignacio, O.F.M. [Fr. Peregrino, pseud.]. 1950. "Un colaborador marquinés de Fr. Junípero Serra. Fray Pablo-José de Mugártegui." *Misiones Franciscanas* 34, no. 358 (January): 7–1.

———. 1956. "De Texas abajo. Fray Pedro Pérez de Mezquía, maestro y precursor de Fr. Junípero Serra." *Missionalia Hispanica* 133, no. 39:541–59.

———. 1958. "Fr. Pedro Pérez de Mezquía, O.F.M., Maestro y precursor de fray Junípero Serra en las Misiones." *Boletín de la Real Sociedad Bascongada de los Amigos del País* 14:308–34.

———. 1959. *Heraldos del Gran Rey en California. Fray Pablo de Mugártegui en su marco social y misionero.* Bilbao: Desclée de Brouwer.

———. 1963. *Pedro Pérez de Mezquía, O.F.M. (1688–1764). Maestro y precursor de fray Junípero Serra en las Misiones.* Vitoria: Diputación Foral de Álava.

———. 1964a. "El que llevó a Fray Junípero Serra. (Con ocasión del II Centenario de la muerte de Fr. Pedro Pérez de Mezquía [1688–1764].)" *Misiones Franciscanas* 50, nos. 423, 424, 425 and 426 (March, April, May, and June): 88–92, 124–28, 147–59, 185–88.

———. 1964b. "Los Frailes de Aránzazu en la Edad de Oro de las Misiones de California." *Misiones Franciscanas* 50, no. 429 (September): 280–81.

———. 1966. "Los adelantados de Alaska y las expediciones descubridoras del siglo XVIII." *Missionalia Hispanica* 23, no. 67 (May–August): 245–52.

Ortega Soto, Martha. 1989. "Los indios del Noroeste americano en las colonias rusas." In *Culturas de la costa noroeste de América* 1989, 237–49.

[Páez, Juan]. 1870. "Viaje por las costas de las Californias de Juan Rodríguez Cabrillo, y piloto Bartolomé Ferrelo, descubriendo Cabo Mendocino y rebasando 42°N, en 1542." In [*CODOINAO*] 1864–84, 14:165–91.

Palau Baquero, Mercedes. 1986. "The Spanish Presence on the Northwest Coast: Sea-Going Expeditions (1774–1793)." In *To the Totem Shore* 1986, 38–89.

———. 1988. "Presencia española en la Costa del Noroeste, 1774–1796." In *El Ojo del Tótem* 1988, 86–123.

Palau Baquero, Mercedes and José Alcina Franch. 1998. "Introducción a los viajes españoles a la Costa Noroeste y Nutka." In *Nutka 1792* 1998, 122–36.

Palau Baquero, Mercedes and Salvador Bernabeu Albert. 1998. "Relación de manuscritos." In *Nutka 1792* 1998, 220–23.

Palau Baquero, Mercedes, Marisa Calés, and Araceli Sánchez, eds. 1998. *Nootka. Regreso a una historia olvidada. Catálogo de la exposición celebrada en el Museu Etnològic de Barcelona y en el Museo Naval de Madrid.* Madrid: M.A.E.; and Barcelona: Lunwerg. Catalan edition, *Nootka: Retorn a una història oblidada.*

Palau Baquero, Mercedes and Antonio Orozco Acuaviva, eds. 1994. *Malaspina '92. I Jornadas Internacionales, Madrid-Cádiz-La Coruña, 17–25 de Septiembre de 1992.* Cádiz: Real Academia Hispano-Americana.

Palau Baquero, Mercedes and Pamela Sprätz. 1998. "Catálogo de dibujos y mapas del Album del 'Viaje.' Ms. 146 del Archivo del Ministerio de Asuntos Exteriores" and "Bibliografía." In *Nutka 1792* 1998, 194–205, and 224–41.

Palau Baquero, Mercedes, Aránzazu Zabala, and Blanca Saiz. 1984. *La Expedición Malaspina, 1789–1794. Viaje a América y Oceanía de las Corbetas "Descubierta" y "Atrevida"* [catalogue of an exhibition at the Centro Cultural de la Villa, Madrid, November 6–December 15, 1984]. Madrid: Ministerio de Defensa, Ministerio de Cultura, Ayuntamiento de Madrid. Items relevant to the Californias and Northwest Coast appear on pp. 90–113.

———, eds. 1984. See Malaspina 1984.

Palau de Iglesias, Mercedes. 1980. *Catálogo de los dibujos, aguadas y acuarelas de la Expedición Malaspina, 1789–1794 (donación de Carlos Sanz).* Madrid: Ministerio de Cultura.

Palma, Andrés de, O.F.M. 1949. "Cartas y noticias de Junípero Serra." *Estudios Franciscanos,* 50:249–64 and 387–413.

Palóu, Fr. Francisco, O.F.M. 1787. *Relación histórica de la vida y apostólicas tareas del V. Padre Fray Junípero Serra y de las misiones que fundó en la California Septentrional y nuevos establecimientos de Monterrey.* Mexico: Felipe de Zúñiga y Ontiveros.

———. 1857. *Noticias de la Antigua y Nueva California* (1777–1783). Mexico: n.p.

———. 1944. *Evangelista del Mar Pacífico: Fray Junípero Serra, Padre y fundador de la Alta California.* Ed. Lorenzo Riber [Llorenç Riber]. Madrid: Aguilar.

———. 1958. "Relación histórica de la vida y apostólicas tareas del V. Padre Fray Junípero Serra (viajes misionales)." Ed. Mario Hernández Sánchez-Barba. In *Viajes por Norteamérica.* Bibliotheca Indiana, Viajes y viajeros 2, series ed. Manuel Ballesteros Gaibrois, 629–782. Madrid: Aguilar.

———. 1977. *Biografía de Fray Junípero Serra, O.F.M. (1713–1784)* [*Relación histórica de la vida y apostólicas tareas del V. Padre Fray Junípero Serra*]. Ed. Bartolomé Font Obrador. Palma de Mallorca: Cort, Caja de Ahorros de las Baleares.

———. 1988. *Junípero Serra y las misiones de California.* Ed. José Luis Anta Félez. Crónicas de América 44. Madrid: Historia 16. 2nd ed., Las Rozas (Madrid): Dastin, 2002.

———. 1989. *Noticias de la Nueva California.* Facsimile edition. Ed. Fr. Salustiano Vicedo. 4 vols. Petra (Palma de Mallorca): Apóstol y Civilizador.

Pantoja y Arriaga, Juan. 1849. "Extracto de la navegación . . . 1791." In [*CODOIN España*] 1842–95, 15:111–21.

Patronato Nacional para la Conmemoración del nacimiento de Fray Junípero Serra. 1963. *CLL Anniversary of the Birth of Junipero Serra. Mallorca, 29 May–4 June 1963.* Bilingual Spanish-English text. [Palma de Mallorca?]: n.p.

Pazos, Manuel, O.F.M. 1941. "El V.P. Fr. Juan Antonio Joaquín de Barreneche, martirizado por los indios yumas del Río Colorado el 19 de julio de 1781." *Archivo Ibero-Americano* 4:455–73.

Peregrino, Fr. See Omaechevarria Martitegui, Ignacio, O.F.M.

Pereyra, Carlos. 1942. "El bautizo de California." *Estudios Geográficos* 3, no. 7 (May): 385–404.

Pérez Baltasar, Dolores. 1995. "La historiografía de California y la obra del padre Francisco Palou." *Cuadernos de Historia Moderna* (Madrid) 16:391–409.

Pérez Embid, Florentino. 1951. "La expansión geográfica de la Nueva España en el siglo XVII." *Revista de Indias* 11, no. 45 (July–September): 501–31.

Pérez Miguel, Aurora. 1973a. *Las costas del Noroeste de América en el siglo XVIII.* PhD diss., Universidad Complutense de Madrid.

———. 1973b. *Las costas del Noroeste de América en el siglo XVIII.* Extract of PhD diss., Universidad Complutense de Madrid.

———. 1988. "La presencia rusa en las costas del Noroeste: expediciones científicas e intereses comerciales." In *El Ojo del Tótem* 1988, 124–37.

———. 1989. "Relaciones diplomáticas de los europeos con los indios de la Costa Noroeste de América." In *Culturas de la costa noroeste de América* 1989, 223–36.

---. 1991. "Expediciones náuticas de europeos y americanos a la costa NO de América en el siglo XVIII." *Revista de Historia Naval* 9, no. 32:77–94.

---. 1993. *Impacto ecológico en la costa noroeste de América tras la llegada de los europeos (siglos XVII a XX)*. Foreword by Francisco de Solano. Col. Biblioteca de Historia de América 8. Madrid: C.S.I.C.

Peset, José Luis, ed. 1989. *Culturas de la costa noroeste de América*. Madrid: Turner, Comisión Nacional del V Centenario.

Picazo Muntaner, Antoni. 1999. "El viaje por el Mississipi de Fray Luis Hennepin, OFM, y la búsqueda del paso al mar del sur." *Archivo Ibero-Americano* (Madrid) 59, no. 232 (January–April): 89–110.

Píccolo, Francisco María, S.J. 1962. *Informe del estado de la nueva cristiandad de California, 1702, y otros documentos*. Ed. Ernest J. Burrus, S.J. Col. Chimalistac 14. Madrid: José Porrúa Turanzas.

Pimentel Egea, Juan Félix. 1991. "La riqueza forestal de las costas del Pacífico. Noticias e informes sobre maderas en la expedición Malaspina (1789–1794)." In *El bosque ilustrado. Estudios sobre la política forestal española en América*, ed. Manuel Lucena Giraldo, 45–61. Madrid: Instituto Nacional para la Conservación de la Naturaleza, Instituto de la Ingeniería de España.

---, ed. 1993. See Higueras, Pimentel, and Fernández 1993.

---. 1993. "Los hombres tras el cristal. Antropología y noticias etnográficas en la expedición Malaspina." In Higueras, Pimentel, and Fernández 1993, 11–19.

---, ed. 1995. *La expedición Malaspina (1789–1794). Tomo VII. Descripciones y reflexiones políticas*. Madrid: Ministerio de Defensa, Museo Naval; Barcelona: Lunwerg. (Includes "Examen político de las costas del NO de la América," 93–112).

Piña Homs, Román. 1985. "El magisteri de Juniper Serra a la Universitat de Mallorca." *Comunicació. Revista del Centre d'Estudis Teològics de Mallorca*, 37–38 (March–June): 19–23.

---. 1988. *Catalanes y mallorquines en la fundación de California*. Barcelona: Laia.

---. 1991. "Gobierno y administración de justicia en la génesis de la Nueva California: el papel del misionero en la disciplina de los indígenas y la administración de las misiones." In vol. 2 of *IX Congreso del Instituto Internacional de Historia del Derecho Indiano (1990)*, 297–304. Madrid: Universidad Complutense.

---. 1992. "Testamento de la marquesa de las Torres de Rada y la Fundación Piadosa para las misiones de California." In *Homenaje a Ismael Sánchez Bella*, ed. Joaquín Salcedo Izu, 441–53. Pamplona: Universidad de Navarra.

Pino Díaz, Fermín del. 1982. "Los estudios etnográficos y etnológicos en la expedición Malaspina." *Revista de Indias* 42, nos. 169–70 (July–December): 393–468.

Piquer, Jordi. 1984. "Junípero Serra, el mallorquín que conquistó California." *Historia y Vida* (Barcelona) 17, no. 201 (December): 26–33.

Piqueras Céspedes, Ricardo. 1992–93. "Alfinger y Portolá: dos modelos de frontera." *Boletín Americanista* (Barcelona) 42–43:107–22.

Porter Casanate, Pedro. 1868. "Carta relación de Pedro Porter Casanate, caballero de la Orden de Santiago, desde que salió de España el año 1643 para el descubrimiento del Golfo de la California, hasta 24 enero 1649, escrita a un amigo suyo." In [*CODOINAO*] 1864–84, 9:5–18.

———. 1868. "Memorial del Almirante D. Pedro Porter Casanate al Rey, recomendando una nueva expedición a la California." In [*CODOINAO*] 1864–84, 9:19–29.

Porter Casanate, Pedro and Alonso Botello y Serrano. 1849. "Declaración . . . 1636." In [*CODOIN España*] 1842–95, 15:215–27.

Portillo [y Díez de Sollano], Alvaro del. 1947. *Descubrimientos y exploraciones en las costas de California, 1532–1650*. Seville: E.E.H.-A. 2nd ed., Madrid: Rialp, 1982.

Portolá, Gaspar de. 1959. "Diario por tierra a San Diego y Monterey" (1769). In *Noticias y documentos* 1959, 49–76.

Poupeney, Catherine. 1986. "Una opinión personal de la costa noroeste: el diario de Tomás de Suria (1791)." In *To the Totem Shore* 1986, 176–89.

Price, A. Grenfell, ed. 1985. *Los viajes del capitán Cook (1768–1779)*. Foreword by Percy G. Adams. Barcelona: El Serbal.

Quadra-Salcedo Gayarre, Ana de la. 1960. "La *Atrevida* y su viaje alrededor del mundo en el siglo XVIII." *Boletín de la Real Sociedad Bascongada de Amigos del País* (San Sebastián) 16, no. 4:463–74.

Ramis Alonso, Miguel. 1959. *Fray Junípero Serra. El gran misionero mallorquín*. Panorama Balear. Palma de Mallorca: Mossèn Alcover. Reprint, 1967.

Ramos Catalina Bardaxí, María Luisa. 1956. "Expediciones científicas a California en el siglo XVIII." *Anuario de Estudios Americanos* 13:217–310.

Rey Tejerina, Arsenio. 1991. "Tomás Suria (1761–1840), un ilustrado valenciano en Alaska." In *La expedición Malaspina, 1789–1794. Bicentenario de la salida de Cádiz*, ed. Antonio Orozco Acuaviva, 301–8. Cádiz: Academia Hispanoamericana.

———, ed. 1995. *Tomás de Suria a l'expedició Malaspina: Alaska 1791*. Foreword by Miquel-Angel Fabra i Sánchez. Valencia: Generalitat Valenciana.

———. 2003. *Alaska—Nutka. Colofón del imperio hispánico*. Seville: Arboleda.

Rey-Stolle Pedrosa, Alejandro, S.J. [Adro Xavier, pseud.]. 1986. *Junípero Serra. Su incógnita, su siglo*. Barcelona: Casals.

Riber, Lorenzo [Llorenç], ed. 1944. See Palóu 1944.

Ribes, Vicente, ed. 1989. See Sales 1989.

Río, Ignacio del. 1992. "La guerra de la chichimeca y la misión de la Baja California." In *De palabra y obra en el Nuevo Mundo. 2. Encuentros interétnicos. Interpretaciones contemporáneas*, ed. Manuel Gutiérrez Estévez, Miguel León-Portilla, Gary H. Gossen, and J. Jorge Klor de Alva, 173–94. Madrid: Siglo XXI de España, Extremadura En-Clave.

Rodeja Galter, Eduardo. 1960. "Gaspar de Portolá en el descubrimiento y colonización de California." *Revista de Gerona* 6, no. 10:61–64.

Rodríguez Cabrillo, Juan. 1870. "Viaje por las costas de las Californias de Juan Rodríguez Cabrillo, y piloto Bartolomé Ferrelo, descubriendo Cabo Mendocino y rebasando 42°N, en 1542." In [*CODOINAO*] 1864–84, 14:165–91.

———. 1943. "Juan Rodríguez Cabrillo, 1542." In *Colección de diarios y relaciones* 1943–75, 1:27–42.

Rodríguez Casado, Vicente. 1950. "El Pacífico en la política internacional española hasta la emancipación de América." *Estudios Americanos* 2, no. 5:1–30.

———. 1985. "España en el Pacífico Norte (1588–1614)." *Revista General de Marina* 209 (October): 297–310.

Rosenberg, S[olomon] L[eopold] Millard. 1933. *Huellas de España en el estado de California. Discurso leído en la Academia Española.* Madrid: Tipografía de Archivos.

Rosselló Vaguer, Joan. 1985. "Crònica del centenari [of Junípero Serra's death]." *Comunicació. Revista del Centre d'Estudis Teològics de Mallorca* 37–38 (March–June): 53–60.

Rubí Darder, Sebastián. 1985. *Miguel Josep Serra i Ferrer. ¿Ideal o utopía?* Petra, Mallorca: Apóstol y Civilizador.

Ruiz de Gordejuela Urquijo, Jesús. 2007. "La independencia de México y las misiones de las Californias: españoles versus mexicanos, 1821–1833." *Boletín Americanista* 57, no. 57:219–32.

Sabater, Gaspar. 1944. *Junípero Serra (colonizador de California).* Madrid: Editora Nacional.

Saiz, Blanca. 1984. See Palau Baquero, Zabala, Saiz 1984.

———, ed. 1984. See Malaspina 1984.

———. 1992. *Bibliografía sobre Alejandro Malaspina. Y acerca de la expedición Malaspina y de los marinos y científicos que en ella participaron.* Madrid: El Museo Universal.

———. 1994. *Alejandro Malaspina. La América imposible. Biografía de A. Malaspina por Dario Manfredi.* Foreword by José de la Sota. Madrid: Compañía Literaria.

Salazar, Buenaventura, O.F.M. 1935. *Misioneros franciscanos en América; colección de artículos publicados por fr. Buenaventura Salazar en la revista 'Misiones franciscanas.'* Bilbao: E. Verdes Achirica.

Sales, Fr. Luis de, O.P. 1794. *Noticias de la Provincia de las Californias en tres cartas de un sacerdote religioso hijo del real convento de predicadores de Valencia a un amigo suyo.* Valencia: Hermanos de Orga. Digital facsimile in *Las Raíces Hispánicas del Oeste de Norteamérica: Textos Históricos.* Ed. Sylvia L. Hilton. Biblioteca Digital Clásicos Tavera, ser. 2: Temáticas para la historia de Iberoamérica CT021, CD-ROM. Madrid: Fundación Mapfre-Tavera, Digibis, 1999.

———. 1960. *Noticias de la Provincia de California, 1794.* Col. Chimalistac 6. Madrid: José Porrúa Turanzas.

———. 1989. "Noticias de la provincia de Californias." In vol. 2 of *Misioneros valencianos en Indias*, ed. Vicente Ribes, 15–320. Valencia: Generalitat Valenciana.

———. 2003. *Noticias de la Provincia de Californias*. Ed. Salvador Bernabeu Albert. Ensenada, Mexico: Fundación Barca.

Salva, Jaime. 1950. "El naturalista Tadeo Haenke." *Revista General de Marina* 139:102–3.

Salvatierra, Juan María de, S.J. 1946. *La misión de la Baja California*. Ed. Padre Constantino Bayle, S.J. Madrid: La Editorial Católica.

San Pío Aladrén, María Pilar. 1989. "El diario de 1792 de Juan Francisco de la Bodega y Quadra." In *Culturas de la costa noroeste de América* 1989, 291–98.

———. 1992. *Expediciones españolas del siglo XVIII. El paso del Noroeste*. Madrid: Mapfre.

San Pío Aladrén, María Pilar and María Dolores Higueras Rodríguez, eds. [2001]. *La armonía natural : la naturaleza en la expedición marítima de Malaspina y Bustamante (1789–1794)*. Madrid: C.S.I.C., Real Jardín Botánico; Barcelona: Lunwerg.

Sanahuja [i Vallverdú], Pedro [Pere], O.F.M. 1945. "Don Gaspar de Portolá, gobernador y explorador de la Alta California." *Ilerda* (Lérida) 3, no. 5 (July–December): 59–117. Also published separately: *Don Gaspar de Portolá, gobernador y explorador de la Alta California*. Lérida: Instituto de Estudios Ilerdenses de la Excma. Diputación Provincial de Lérida, 1945.

Sánchez Diana, José María. 1965. "Los españoles en busca del paso del Noroeste. Consecuencias internacionales." *Universidad. Revista de Cultura y Vida Universitaria* (Saragossa) 7–12:7–40.

Sánchez Montañés, Emma. 1989. "El papel del artista en la cultura de la Costa Noroeste." In *Culturas de la costa noroeste de América* 1989, 115–26.

———. 1991. "Arte indígena de la costa Noroeste (British Colombia) en el Museo de América de Madrid." *Revista Española de Estudios Canadienses* 1, no. 2 (May): 230–49.

———. 1998. "Cambio y continuidad en el arte de las culturas nativas de la Costa Noroeste de América: el caso de los Nuu-chah-nulth." In Palau Baquero, Calés, and Sánchez 1998, 43–54.

———. 1999. "Culturas nativas de la costa noroccidental de América: una introducción general." In Basso, Bello, and Sauquet 1999, 15–17.

———. 2008. "Fuentes españolas y etnografía: la costa pacífica estadounidense a finales del siglo XVIII." In *Norteamérica a finales del siglo XVIII: España y los Estados Unidos*, ed. Emma Sánchez Montañés, Sylvia L. Hilton, Almudena Hernández Ruigómez, and Isabel García-Montón, 45–68. Madrid, Barcelona, and Buenos Aires: Marcial Pons and Fundación Consejo España-Estados Unidos.

———. 2009. "Los pueblos nativos de América del Norte en revistas americanistas de Madrid. Una revisión crítica." *Revista Española de Antropología Americana* 39, no. 2: 270–80.

Sanfeliú Ortiz, Lorenzo, ed. 1944. See Tova 1944.

Sanz y Díaz, José. 1956. *Fray Junípero Serra, evangelista y fundador de la Alta California*. Temas Españoles 42. Madrid: Publicaciones Españolas. 250th anniversary reprint, 1963.

Sariego del Castillo, José Luis. 1975. *Historia de la Marina Española en la América Septentrional y Pacífico*. Seville: José L. Sariego del Castillo.

Serra, Fr. Junípero, O.F.M. 1984. *Escritos*. Ed. Salustiano Vicedo, O.F.M., and Jacinto Fernández-Largo. 5 vols. Col. Petra Nostra 7–11. Petra, Mallorca: Apóstol y Civilizador.

Serrano y Sanz, Manuel, ed. 1916. *Relaciones históricas de América, primera mitad del siglo XVI*. Madrid: Sociedad de Bibliófilos Españoles. (Includes a narrative of Francisco de Ulloa's 1539 discovery of California, 181–240).

Serrera Contreras, Ramón María. 1978. "Pedro de Fages, colonizador y cronista de la Alta California." In *Actas del Congreso de Historia de los Estados Unidos. Universidad de La Rábida, 5–9 de julio de 1976*, 243–53. Madrid: Ministerio de Educación y Ciencia.

———. 1980. "Un andaluz, pionero en la explotación argentífera de la Baja California (1753–1783)." *Gades. Revista del Colegio Universitario de Filosofía y Letras de Cádiz* 5:113–28.

———. and María Dolores Fuentes. 1988. "Panorama estadístico de los asentamientos dominicos en la Baja California, 1797–1812." In *Actas del I Congreso Internacional: "Los dominicos y el Nuevo Mundo," Seville, 21–25 de abril de 1987*, 537–55. Madrid: Deimos.

Sintes Obrador, Francisco. 1961. *Tras las huellas de fray Junípero Serra en California*. Palma de Mallorca: Casa de Menorca (Nazaret).

Soler Pascual, Emilio. 1996. "Floridablanca y la crisis de Nutka." *Revista Española de Estudios Canadienses* (Barcelona) 3, no. 1 (September): 37–52.

———. 1997. "Nutka. Una crisis en el Pacífico Norte." In *España y el Pacífico*, ed. Antonio García-Abásolo, 245–52. Córdoba: M.A.E., Asociación Española de Estudios del Pacífico.

———. 1998. "El lento declinar del Imperio español: la crisis política de Nutka." In *Nutka 1792* 1998, 60–71.

———. 1999. *La aventura de Malaspina: la gran expedición científica del siglo XVIII por las costas de América, las Filipinas y las islas del Pacífico*. Barcelona: Ediciones B.

———, ed. [2006]. *Trafalgar y Alcalá Galiano. Jornadas Internacionales, Cabra (Córdoba), 17 al 23 de octubre de 2005*. Madrid: M.A.E., A.E.C.I., Asociación Cultural Dionisio Alcalá-Galiano.

Soler Vidal, Joseph, ed. 1953. *Pere Fages, descobridor, cronista y governador de Nova California*. Mexico: Ediciones Catalanes de Mèxic.

———. 1980. "Pere Fages guissonés: primer colonitzador i descobridor de l'Alta California (USA)." *Issauna* (Guisona, Lérida) 3, no. 18 (March): 2 pp.

———. 1988. *Catalans als inicis de San Francisco de California*. Barcelona: Rafael Dalmau.

Sota Ríus, José de la. 1985. *Bodega y Quadra y la expedición de límites*. Masters thesis, Universidad Complutense de Madrid.

———. 1986. "Nootka: la crisis de 1789." In *To the Totem Shore* 1986, 190–213.

———. 1988. "Presencia inglesa, francesa y norteamericana en la Costa del Noroeste." In *El Ojo del Tótem* 1988, 138–51.

———. 1989. "Acerca de la documentación histórica de la exposición 'El Ojo del Tótem.'" In *Culturas de la costa noroeste de América* 1989, 335–42.

Soto Pérez, José Luis, O.F.M. 2008. "Cuatro cartas de Fray Francisco Palou (1787)." *Archivo Ibero-Americano. Revista franciscana de estudios históricos* 68, no. 261 (October–December): 437–46.

Sotos Serrano, Carmen. 1981. *La expedición de Alejandro Malaspina: los trabajos de sus pintores*. 3 vols. PhD diss., Universidad Complutense de Madrid.

———. 1982. *Los pintores de la expedición de Alejandro Malaspina*. 2 vols. Madrid: Real Academia de la Historia.

———. 1984a. "Relación de documentos del Archivo General de la Nación de México para el estudio de las expediciones marítimas españolas del siglo XVIII a la costa del noroeste americano." *Revista de Historia Naval* 2, no. 4:101–14.

———. 1984b. "Los artistas de la expedición Malaspina." In *La Expedición Malaspina, 1789–94. Viaje a América y Oceanía de las Corbetas "Descubierta" y "Atrevida," Catálogo de la exposición celebrada en el Centro Cultural de la Villa, Madrid, 6 noviembre–15 diciembre 1984*, lxvi–lxxvi. Madrid: Ministerio de Defensa, Ministerio de Cultura, and Ayuntamiento de Madrid.

———. 1989. "Los indios de la Costa del Noroeste en la obra de Tomás de Suria." In *Culturas de la costa noroeste de América* 1989, 173–82.

———. 1991. "La América que conoció Malaspina. Imagen artística de un viaje." In *La Expedición Malaspina, 1789–1794. Bicentenario de la salida de Cádiz*, 239–67. Cádiz: Comisión Nacional V Centenario, Real Academia Hispanoamericana de Cádiz.

Sureda Trujillo, Juana. 1986. "Influencias notables de la medicina balear en California." *Minutos Menarini* (Barcelona) 146 (June): 20–28.

Suria, Tomás de. 1991. "Diario de Tomás de Suria en su viaje a la costa noroeste con la expedición Malaspina (1789–1794)." In Monge and Olmo 1991, 89–162.

Suttles, Wayne. 1989. "They Recognize No Superior Chief: The Strait of Juan de Fuca in the 1790s." In *Culturas de la costa noroeste de América* 1989, 251–64.

———. 1994. "The Northwest Coast in World Ethnography." In Palau Baquero and Orozco 1994, 43–48.

Taraval, Segismundo. 1996. *La rebelión de los Californios, 1734*. Ed. Eligio Moisés Coronado. Foreword by Salvador Bernabeu Albert. Aranjuez: Doce Calles.

To the Totem Shore. The Spanish Presence on the Northwest Coast. 1986. Madrid: Ministerio de Transportes, Turismo y Comunicaciones, El Viso. There are two versions of this volume: one in Spanish and one in English. Pagination is the same in both. Only the English title is listed in this bibliography.

Tobar y Tamariz, José. 1960. "Informe que yo DonTobar y Tamariz, primer piloto de la Real Armada doy al Exmo. Sr. Virrey de Nueva España en obediencia de su superior orden, comunicada con fecha de 29 de agosto de 1789 [concerning the expedition commanded by Esteban José Martínez in 1789]." In Sales 1794, 57–86 and Sales 1960, 95–117.

Torréns y Nicolau, Francisco. 1913. *Bosquejo histórico del insigne franciscano V.P.F. Junípero Serra, fundador y apóstol de la California Septentrional*. [Felanix: Estab. Tip. de B. Reus].

Torres Campos, Rafael. 1892. "España en California y en el Noroeste de América. Conferencia leída el día 17 de mayo de 1892 [in the Ateneo in Madrid]." In *El Continente Americano. Conferencias con motivo del cuarto centenario del descubrimiento de América. Tomo II*, 1–60. Madrid: Sucesores de Rivadeneyra. Available online in the Internet Archive at: http://www.archive.org/details/espaaencalifornoocampgoog.

Torres Santo Domingo, Marta. 2003. "Los viajes del capitán Cook en el siglo XVIII. Una revisión bibliográfica." *Biblio 3W. Revista Bibliográfica de Geografía y Ciencias Sociales* (Universidad Barcelona) 8, no. 441 (20 April). http://www.ub.es/geocrit/b3w-441.htm.

Toschi, Larry. 1991. "St. Joseph, Father of the Birth of Christianity in Alta California." *Estudios Josefinos* (Valladolid) 45, nos. 89–90 (January–December): 705–24.

Tóth, Ágnes. 1998. "Los descendentes de Chininigchinich en la misión de San Juan Capistrano, Alta California, ss. XVIII–XIX." *Trienio. Ilustración y Liberalismo* (Madrid) 31 (May): 5–12.

Tova Arredondo, Antonio de. 1944. *62 meses a bordo—La expedición Malaspina según el diario del teniente de navío don Antonio de Tova Arredondo, Segundo Comandante de la "Atrevida," 1789–1794*. Ed. Lorenzo Sanfeliú Ortiz. Col. Biblioteca de Camarote de la Revista General de Marina 13–14. Madrid: Naval. Reprints, Madrid: Naval, 1988 and Madrid: Ministerio de Defensa, 1990.

———. 1993a. "Acaecimientos en el Puerto Mulgrave." In Higueras, Pimentel, and Fernández 1993, 127–37.

———. 1993b. "Acaecimientos en el Puerto de Nutka." In Higueras, Pimentel, and Fernández 1993, 139–52.

Tovell, Freeman. 1998a. "Rivales amigos. Quadra y Vancouver." In *Nutka 1792* 1998, 72–85.

———. 1998b. "Notas al Diario del 'Viaje.'" In *Nutka 1792* 1998, 186–93.

Ulloa, Francisco de. 1844. "Relación del armada del Marqués del Valle, capitaneada de Francisco de Ulloa que salió del puerto de Acapulco y descubrió el río de la Culata; y de la que el virey de Nueva España envió con un Alarcón para el mismo efecto." In [*CODOIN España*] 1842–95, 4:218–19.

———. 1916. "Relación del viaje que hizo el capitán Francisco de Ulloa, por orden de Hernán Cortés, por la costa de Nueva España, desde Acapulco hasta la isla de los Cedros, y las posesiones que tomó en nombre del mismo Cortés." In Serrano y Sanz 1916, 181–240.

———. 1994. "Memoria y relación. (Actas de tomas de posesión)." In Navarro García 1994, 181–238.

Valdés, Cayetano. 1991. See Espinosa y Tello 1802, and Alcalá and Valdés 1991.

Vaughan, Thomas, and E.A.P. Crownhart-Vaughan. 1986. "Russian, French, British and American Incursions into 'The Spanish Lake.'" In *To the Totem Shore* 1986, 22–37.

Velázquez de León, Joaquín. 1874. "Memoria de la observación del Paso de Venus por el disco del sol, hecha el 8 de junio de 1796 en la aldea de Santa Ana, situada en la Baja California." *Anuario del Depósito Hidrográfico* 12:549–65.

[Venegas, Miguel, S.J. and Andrés Marcos Burriel, S.J.]. 1757. *Noticia de la California, y de su conquista temporal y espiritual hasta el tiempo presente. Sacada de la Historia manuscrita, formada en México año de 1739, por el P. Miguel Venegas, de la Compañía de Jesús, y de otras noticias y relaciones antiguas y modernas*. 3 vols. Madrid: Viuda de Manuel Fernández, Supremo Consejo de la Inquisición. Digital facsimile in *Las Raíces Hispánicas del Oeste de Norteamérica: Textos Históricos*. Ed. Sylvia L. Hilton. Biblioteca Digital Clásicos Tavera, ser. 2: Temáticas para la historia de Iberoamérica CT021, CD-ROM. Madrid: Fundación Mapfre-Tavera, Digibis, 1999.

Verde Casanova, Ana María. 1980. "Notas para el estudio etnológico de las expediciones científicas españolas de América en el siglo XVIII." *Revista de Indias* 40, nos. 159–162: 81–128.

Vicedo Vicedo, Fr. Salustiano, O.F.M. 1977. *El Padre Fray Buenaventura Sitjar, O.F.M. Discurso biográfico del nuevo Hijo Ilustre de Porreres con motivo de su proclamación el día 22 de enero de 1977*. Porreres, Mallorca: Ajuntament de Porreres.

———, ed. 1984. See Serra 1984.

———, ed. 1989. See Palóu 1989.

———, 1989. "Fray Junípero, el hombre de quien mucho se ha escrito." *Verdad y Vida* 47:241–53.

———, 1991. *Convento de San Bernardino de Sena: escuela del Beato Junípero Serra*. Petra (Mallorca): Apóstol y Civilizador.

———, 1992. *Fray Francisco Palou, O.F.M. Un mallorquín, fundador de San Francisco de California*. Franciscanos en el Nuevo Mundo 10. Valencia: Publicaciones V Centenario del Descubrimiento y Evangelización de América, Editorial San Lorenzo.

———, ed. 1994. *El mallorquín fray Juan Crespí, O.F.M., misionero y explorador. Sus diarios*. Franciscanos en el Nuevo Mundo 14. Valencia: Publicaciones V Centenario del Descubrimiento y Evangelización de América, Unión Misional Franciscana.

———. n.d. "Beato Junípero Serra (1713–1784), Apóstol de Sierra Gorda y California." Directorio Franciscano, Santoral Franciscano, http://www.franciscanos.org/ santoral/junipero02.html.

Vidal Isern, José. 1949. *La estela de fray Junípero Serra*. Barcelona: Viuda de Francisco Soler.

Vila Vilar, Enriqueta. 1965. "Los rusos en América." *Anuario de Estudios Americanos* (Seville), 22:569–672. Also published separately: *Los rusos en América*. Seville: E.E.H.-A., 1966.

Vilchis, Jaime. 1992. "Ciencia novohispana en la frontera (1792), José Mariano Mociño en Nutka." In *Ciencia colonial en América*, ed. Antonio Lafuente and José Sala Catalá, 272–84. Madrid: Alianza.

Villar Raso, Manuel. 1994 [1995]. "La conquista de California en el siglo XVIII." In *La frontera, mito y realidad del Nuevo Mundo. Actas del Congreso celebrado en la Universidad de León los días 13 a 17 de septiembre de 1993*, ed. M. José Alvarez, Manuel Broncano, and José Luis Chamosa, 335–44. León: Universidad de León.

Viniegra, Juan Manuel de. 1984. "Apuntamiento instructivo" (1771). In Cano, Escandell, and Mampel 1984, 263–87.

Vizcaíno, Sebastián. 1944. "Relación o diario muy circunstanciado del viaje que hizo el General Sebastián Vizcaíno" (1602–3). In *Colección de diarios y relaciones* 1943–75, 4:39–68.

Voltes Bou, Pedro. 1989. "Conexiones entre España y la Rusia de Catalina II." In vol. 3 of *Actas del Congreso Internacional sobre Carlos III y la Ilustración. III: Educación y pensamiento*, 391–96. Madrid: Ministerio de Cultura.

Weber, Francis J. 1979. *Junípero Serra, pionero religioso de California*. Foreword by Bartolomé Font Obrador, trans. Harold J. Greenberg. Palma de Mallorca: Miramar.

Wright, Robin K. 1989. "Western Washington Indian Art: A Collection History." In *Culturas de la costa noroeste de América* 1989, 163–72.

Xavier, Adro. See Rey-Stolle Pedrosa, Alejandro, S.J.

Ybarra y Bergé, Javier de. 1945. *De California a Alaska: Historia de un descubrimiento*. Madrid: Instituto de Estudios Políticos.

———. 1946. *La cuestión de Nutka*. Bilbao: Imprenta Provincial de Vizcaya.

———. 1964. "Juan Francisco de la Bodega y Quadra." In *Los vascos y la Hispanidad*, 113–19. Bilbao: Instituto Vascongado de Cultura Hispánica.

Zabala, Aránzazu. 1984. See Palau Baquero, Zabala, and Saiz 1984.

———, ed. 1984. See Malaspina 1984.

Zdenek, Joseph W. 1974. "La relación entre California y el Estrecho de Anián, según el cronista fray Antonio de la Ascensión." *Revista de Occidente* (Madrid) 132:375–86.

Selected Bibliography

Abad Pérez, Antolín. *Los Franciscanos en América*. Madrid: MAPFRE, 1992.

Almaraz, Felix D. "San Antonio's Old Franciscan Missions: Material Decline and Secular Avarice in the Transition from Hispanic to Mexican Control." *The Americas* 44, no. 1 (July 1987).

———. *The San Antonio Missions and Their System of Land Tenure*. Austin: University of Texas Press, 1989.

Asisara, Lorenzo. "Personal Narrative of a Former Neophyte Born at Santa Cruz Mission in 1819." In *History of Santa Cruz County, California*, ed. Edward Harrison. San Francisco: Pacific Press Publishing Co., 1892.

Aviña Levy, Edmundo, ed. *Códice Mendieta: Documentos Franciscanos siglos XVI y XVII*. Guadalajara: Edmundo Aviña, 1971.

Barbastro, Francisco Antonio. *Sonora hacia fines del siglo XVIII*. Introductory study by Lino Gómez Canedo. Guadalajara: Librería Font, 1971.

Baudot, Georges. *La pugna franciscana por México*. Mexico: CONACULTA, 1990.

Beebe, Rose Marie, and Robert M. Senkewicz, eds. *Testimonios: Early California through the Eyes of Women, 1815–1848*. Berkeley, Calif.: Heyday Books, 2006.

Bianchi, Hermenegildo. *La Regla de los Frailes Menores*. Tolosa, Spain: Editorial Guipuzcoana, 1924.

Bolton, Herbert E. "The Iturbide Revolution in the Californias." *Hispanic American Historical Review* 2 (1919): 188–242.

Borges, Pedro, ed. *Historia de la Iglesia en Hispanoamérica y Fillipinas*. 2 vols. Madrid: Biblioteca de Autores Cristianos, 1992.

Brading, David A. *The Origins of Mexican Nationalism*. Cambridge: Centre of Latin American Studies, 1985.

———. *The First America: The Spanish Monarchy, Creole Patriots, and the Liberal State, 1492–1867*. Cambridge: Cambridge University Press, 1991.

Bringas, Diego Miguel. *Friar Bringas Reports to the King: Methods of Indoctrination on the Frontier of New Spain, 1796–1797*, ed. Daniel S. Matson and Bernard L. Fontana. Tucson: University of Arizona Press, 1977.

Caplan, Karen. *Indigenous Citizens: Local Liberalism in Early National Oaxaca and Yucatán*. Stanford, Calif.: Stanford University Press, 2009.

Castañeda Delgado, Paulino. "Los franciscanos y el Regio Vicariato." In *Actas del II Congreso Internacional sobre los Franciscanos en el Nuevo Mundo*. Madrid: DEIMOS, 1988.

Castells, Manuel. *The Power of Identity*. The Information Age: Economy, Society, and Culture 2. Massachusetts and Oxford: Blackwell Publishers, 1997.

Castro-Klarén, Sara, and John Charles Chasteen, eds. *Beyond Imagined Communities: Reading and Writing the Nation in Nineteenth-Century Latin America*. Baltimore: Johns Hopkins University Press, 2003.

Caulfield, Sueann, Sarah C. Chambers, and Lara Putnam, eds. *Honor, Status, and Law in Modern Latin America*. Durham, N.C.: Duke University Press, 2005.

César, Julio. "From the Reminiscences of Julio César." In *Lands of Promise and Despair: Chronicles of Early California, 1535–1846*, ed. Rose Marie Beebe and Robert Senkewicz. Berkeley, Calif.: Heyday Press, 2001.

Chambers, Sarah. *From Subjects to Citizens: Honor, Gender, and Politics in Arequipa, Peru, 1780–1854*. University Park: University of Pennsylvania Press, 1999.

Cook, Sherburne F., and Woodrow Borah. *Essays in Population History: Mexico and California*. Berkeley: University of California Press, 1979.

Da Silva, Owen. *Mission Music of California*. Los Angeles: Warren F. Lewis Publisher, 1941.

Deeds, Susan M. *Defiance and Deference in Mexico's Colonial North: Indians under Spanish Rule in Nueva Vizcaya*. Austin: University of Texas Press, 2003.

de la Torre Curiel, José Refugio. *Vicarios en entredicho: Crisis y desestructuración de la provincia franciscana de Santiago de Xalisco*. Zamora, Mexico: El Colegio de Michoacán, 2001.

———. "Conquering the Frontier: Contests for Religion, Survival, and Profits in Northwestern Mexico, 1768–1855." PhD diss., University of California, Berkeley, 2005.

Elliott, John. *Empires of the Atlantic World: Britain and Spain in America, 1492–1830*. New Haven, Conn., and London: Yale University Press, 2006.

Escandón, Patricia. "Los problemas de la administración franciscana en las misiones sonorenses, 1768–1800." In *Actas del IV Congreso Internacional sobre los Franciscanos en el Nuevo Mundo*. Madrid: DEIMOS, 1993.

Eshleman, Jason A., Ripan S. Malhi, John R. Johnson, Frederika A. Kaestle, Joseph Lorenz, and David Glenn Smith. "Mitochondrial DNA and Prehistoric Settlements: Native Migrations on the Western Edge of North America." *Human Biology* 76 (2004): 55–75.

Esparza Sánchez, Cuauhtémoc. *Compendio histórico del Colegio de Propaganda Fide de Nuestra Señora de Guadalupe Zacatecas*. Zacatecas, Mexico: Universidad Autónoma de Zacatecas, 1974.

Espinosa, Isidro Félix de. *Crónica de los Colegios de Propaganda Fide de la Nueva España*. Madrid: Academy of American Franciscan History, 1964.

Esteva-Fabregat, Claudio. *Mestizaje in Ibero-America*. Translated by John Wheat. Tucson: University of Arizona Press, 1995.

Florescano, Enrique, and Isabel Gil Sánchez. "La época de las reformas borbónicas y el crecimiento económico, 1750–1808." In *Historia General de México*, vol. 1, ed. Daniel Cosío Villegas. Mexico: El Colegio de México, 1976.

Frank, Ross. *From Settler to Citizen: New Mexican Economic Development and the Creation of Vecino Society, 1750–1820*. Berkeley and London: University of California Press, 2000.

Geiger, Maynard J. *Franciscan Missionaries in Hispanic California, 1769–1848: A Biographical Dictionary*. San Marino, Calif.: Huntington Library, 1969.

Geiger, Maynard, and Clement W. Meighan. *As the Padres Saw Them: California Indian Life and Customs as Reported by the Franciscan Missionaries, 1813–1815*. Santa Barbara, Calif.: Santa Barbara Mission Archive-Library, 1976.

Gerhard, Peter. *The North Frontier of New Spain*. Rev. ed. Norman: University of Oklahoma Press, 1993.

Gómez-Quiñones, Juan. *Roots of Chicano Politics, 1600–1940*. Albuquerque: University of New Mexico Press, 1994.

González, Michael J. *This Small City Will Be a Mexican Paradise: Exploring the Origins of Mexican Culture in Los Angeles, 1821–1846*. Albuquerque: University of New Mexico Press, 2005.

Green, Lance D., James N. Derr, and Alec Knight. "mtDNA Affinities of the Peoples of North-Central Mexico." *American Journal of Human Genetics* 66 (2000): 989–98.

Guardino, Peter. *Peasants, Politics, and the Formation of Mexico's National State: Guerrero, 1800–1857*. Stanford, Calif.: Stanford University Press, 1996.

———. *The Time of Liberty: Popular Political Culture in Oaxaca, 1750–1850*. Durham, N.C.: Duke University Press, 2005.

Gutiérrez, Ramón A. "Ethnic and Class Boundaries in America's Hispanic Past." In *Social and Gender Boundaries in the United States*, ed. by Sucheng Chan. Lewiston, N.Y.: Edwin Mellon Press, 1989, 37–53.

Haas, Lisbeth. *Conquests and Historical Identities in California, 1769–1936*. Berkeley: University of California Press, 1995.

———. "Pablo Tac: Memory, Identity, History." In *James Luna: Emendatio*. Venice, Italy: Biennale and Smithsonian National Museum of the American Indian, 2006. An exhibition catalogue.

Hackel, Steven W. *Children of Coyote, Missionaries of Saint Francis: Indian-Spanish Relations in Colonial California, 1769–1850*. Chapel Hill: University of North Carolina Press, 2005.

Hale, Charles A. *Mexican Liberalism in the Age of Mora, 1821–1853*. New Haven, Conn.: Yale University Press, 1968.

Haley, Brian D., and Larry R. Wilcoxon. "How Spaniards Became Chumash and Other Tales of Ethnogenesis." *American Anthropologist* 107 (2005): 432–45.

Hansen, Woodrow J. *The Search for Authority in California*. Oakland, Calif.: Biobooks, 1960.

Hera, Alberto de la. *Iglesia y Corona en la América Española*. Madrid: MAPFRE, 1992.

Hinton, Leanne. *Flutes of Fire: Essays on California Indian Languages*. Berkeley, Calif.: Heyday Books, 1994.

Hunefeldt, Christine. *Liberalism in the Bedroom: Quarreling Spouses in Nineteenth-Century Lima*. University Park: University of Pennsylvania Press, 2000.

Hutchinson, C. Alan. *Frontier Settlement in Mexican California: The Híjar-Padres Colony and Its Origins 1769–1835*. New Haven, Conn.: Yale University Press, 1969.

Hyde, Villiana Calac, and Eric Elliott. *Yumáyk yumáyk = long ago*. Berkeley: University of California Press, 1994.

Iriarte, Lázaro. *Historia Franciscana*. Valencia: Editorial Asís, 1979.

Jenkins, Richard. *Social Identity*. London and New York: Routledge, 1996.

Jerónimo Romero, Saul. *De las misiones a los ranchos y las haciendas: La privatización de la tenencia de la tierra en Sonora, 1740–1860*. Hermosillo, Mexico: Gobierno del Estado de Sonora, 1995.

Johnson, John R., and Joseph G. Lorenz. "Genetics, Linguistics, and Prehistoric Migrations: An Analysis of California Indian Mitochondrial DNA Lineages." *Journal of California and Great Basin Anthropology* 26 (2006): 33–64.

Johnson, John R., and William M. Williams. "Toypurina's Descendants: Three Generations of an Alta California Family." *Boletín: The Journal of the California Mission Studies Association* 24 (2007): 30–55.

Katzew, Ilona. *Casta Painting: Images of Race in Eighteenth-Century Mexico*. New Haven, Conn.: Yale University Press, 2004.

Keeling, Richard. "Music and Culture Areas of Native California." *Journal of California and Great Basin Anthropology* 14, no. 2 (1992): 146–58.

Kemp, Brian M. "Mesoamerica and Southwest Prehistory and the Entrance of Humans into the Americas: Mitochondrial DNA Evidence." PhD diss., University of California, Davis, 2006.

Kemp, Brian M., Ripan S. Malhi, John McDonough, Deborah A. Bolnick, Jason A. Eshleman, Olga Rickards, Cristina Martinez-Labarga, John R. Johnson, Joseph G. Lorenz, E. James Dixon, Terence E. Fifield, Timothy H. Heaton, Rosita Worl, and David Glenn Smith. "Genetic Analysis of Early Holocene Skeletal Remains from Alaska and its Implications for the Settlement of the Americas." *American Journal of Physical Anthropology* 132 (2007): 605–21.

Lorenz, Joseph G., and David Glenn Smith. "Distribution of Sequence Variation in the mtDNA Control Region of Native North Americans." *Human Biology* 69 (1997): 749–76.

Lynch, John. *The Spanish American Revolutions 1808–1826*. 2nd ed. New York: W. W. Norton, 1986.

Malhi, Ripan S., Holly M. Mortensen, Jason A. Eshleman, Brian M. Kemp, Joseph G. Lorenz, Frederika A. Kaestle, John R. Johnson, Clara Gorodezky, and David Glenn Smith. "Native American mtDNA Prehistory in the American Southwest." *American Journal of Physical Anthropology* 120 (2003): 108–24.

Martin, Cheryl English. *Governance and Society in Colonial Mexico: Chihuahua in the Eighteenth Century.* Stanford, Calif.: Stanford University Press, 1996.

Mason, William Marvin. *The Census of 1790: A Demographic History of Colonial California.* Ballena Press Anthropological Papers 45. Menlo Park, Calif.: Ballena Press, 1998.

Merriwether, D. Andrew. "Mitochondrial DNA." In *Environment, Origins, and Population.* Vol. 3, *Handbook of North American Indians,* ed. Douglas H. Ubelaker. Washington, D.C.: Smithsonian Institution Press, 2006.

Milliken, Randall. *A Time of Little Choice: The Disintegration of Tribal Culture in the San Francisco Bay Area, 1769–1810.* Menlo Park, Calif.: Ballena Press, 1995.

Miranda, Gloria E. "Racial and Cultural Dimensions of *Gente de Razón* Status in Mexican California." *Southern California Quarterly* 70 (1988): 265–78.

Monroy, Douglas. *Thrown among Strangers: The Making of Mexican Culture in Frontier California.* Berkeley: University of California Press, 1990.

Mutnick, Dorothy G. *Some Alta California Pioneers and Descendants.* 5 vols. Pleasant Hill, Calif.: Contra Costa County Historical Society, 1989.

Navarro García, Luis. *Don José de Gálvez y la Comandancia General de las Provincias Internas del Norte de Nueva España.* Seville: Escuela de Estudios Hispano-Americanos, 1964.

Newell, Quincy D. *Constructing Lives at Mission San Francisco: Native Californians and Hispanic Colonists, 1776–1821.* Albuquerque: University of New Mexico Press, 2009.

Northrop, Marie E. *Spanish-Mexican Families of Early California.* 3 vols. Burbank, Calif.: Southern California Genealogical Society, 1984–2004.

Ortega Soto, Martha, *Alta California: una frontera olvidada del noroeste de México, 1769–1846.* México, D.F.: Universidad Autónoma Metropolitana, Unidad Iztapalapa [División de Ciencias Sociales y Humanidades], 2001.

Radding, Cynthia. *Wandering Peoples: Colonialism, Ethnic Spaces, and Ecological Frontiers in Northwestern Mexico, 1700–1850.* Durham, N.C.: Duke University Press, 1997.

———. "Cultural Boundaries between Adaptation and Defiance: The Mission Communities of Northwestern New Spain." In *Spiritual Encounters: Interactions between Christianity and Native Religions in Colonial America,* ed. Nicholas Griffiths. Lincoln: University of Nebraska Press, 1999.

Ray, Mary Dominic, and Joseph H. Engbeck Jr. *Gloria Dei: The Story of California Mission Music.* [Sacramento]: State of California, Department of Parks and Recreation, 1974.

Reff, Daniel T. *Disease, Depopulation, and Culture Change in Northwestern New Spain, 1518–1764.* Salt Lake City: University of Utah Press, 1991.

Renfrew, Colin, ed. *America Past, America Present: Genes and Languages in the Americas and Beyond.* Cambridge: McDonald Institute for Archaeological Research, 2000.

Reséndez, Andrés. *Changing National Identities at the Frontier: Texas and New Mexico, 1800–1850.* Cambridge: Cambridge University Press, 2005.

Reséndez, Andrés, and Brian M. Kemp. "Genetics and the History of Latin America." *Hispanic American Historical Review* 85 (2005): 283–98.

Rodríguez, Jaime. *The Independence of Spanish America*. New York: Cambridge University Press, 1998.

Russell, Craig H. "Juan Bautista Sancho: Tracing the Origins of California's First Composer and the Early Mission Style." In *J. B. Sancho, Pioneer Composer of California*, ed. Antoni Piza. Palma, Spain: Universitat de les Illes Balears, 2007.

———. *From Serra to Sancho: Music and Pageantry in the California Missions*. New York: Oxford University Press, 2009.

Sáiz, Félix. "La expansión misionera en las fronteras del imperio español." In *Franciscanos en América*, ed. Francisco Morales. Mexico: Conferencia Franciscana de Santa María de Guadalupe, 1993.

Sánchez, Rosaura. *Telling Identities: The Californio "Testimonios."* Minneapolis and London: University of Minnesota Press, 1995.

Sandos, James A. *Converting California: Indians and Franciscans in the Missions*. New Haven, Conn.: Yale University Press, 2004.

Sauer, Carl. *The Distribution of Aboriginal Tribes and Languages in Northwestern Mexico*. Ibero-Americana 5. Berkeley: University of California Press, 1934.

———. *The Aboriginal Population of Northwestern Mexico*. Ibero-Americana 10. Berkeley: University of California Press, 1935.

Senkewicz, Robert M., and Rose Marie Beebe. "Uncertainty on the Mission Frontier: Missionary Recruitment and Institutional Stability in Alta California in the 1790s." In *Francis in the Americas: Essays on the Franciscan Family in North and South America*, ed. John F. Schwaller. Berkeley, Calif.: Academy of American Franciscan History, 2005.

Summers, William. "Spanish Music in California, 1769–1840: A Reassessment." In *International Musicological Society Report of the Twelfth Congress, Berkeley 1977*, ed. Daniel Heartz and Bonnie Wade. Basel: American Musicological Society, 1981.

Tajfel, Henri, ed. *Social Identity and Intergroup Relations*. Cambridge: Cambridge University Press, 1982.

Turner, John C. *Rediscovering the Social Group: A Self-Categorization Theory*. Oxford: Basil Blackwell Ltd., 1987.

Twinam, Ann. *Public Lives, Private Secrets: Gender, Honor, Sexuality, and Illegitimacy in Colonial Spanish America*. Stanford, Calif.: Stanford University Press, 1999.

Voss, Barbara L. *The Archaeology of Ethnogenesis: Race and Sexuality in Colonial San Francisco*. Berkeley: University of California Press, 2008.

Weber, David J. *The Mexican Frontier, 1821–1846: The American Southwest under Mexico*. Albuquerque: University of New Mexico Press, 1982.

———. *The Spanish Frontier in North America*. New Haven, Conn.: Yale University Press, 1992.

———. *Bárbaros: Spaniards and Their Savages in the Age of Enlightenment*. New Haven and London: Yale University Press, 2005.

CONTRIBUTORS

Steven W. Hackel, Associate Professor of History at the University of California, Riverside, is general editor of the Huntington's Early California Population Project and author of *Children of Coyote, Missionaries of Saint Francis: Indian-Spanish Relations in Colonial California, 1769–1850* (University of North Carolina Press, 2005). He is currently writing a biography of Father Junípero Serra for Hill & Wang's American Portraits Series.

Rose Marie Beebe is a professor of Spanish literature at Santa Clara University. With Robert M. Senkewicz, she is translator, editor, and annotator of *Testimonios: Early California through the Eyes of Women, 1815–1848* (Heyday Books, 2006); translator, editor, and annotator of *Lands of Promise and Despair: Chronicles of Early California, 1535–1846* (Heyday Books, 2001); and translator, editor, and annotator of *The History of Alta California by Antonio María Osio* (1996), which received the Norman Neuerburg Award from the Historical Society of Southern California. With Senkewicz, she is the co-editor of two series for the Arthur H. Clark Company: *Early California Commentaries* and *Before Gold: California under Spain and Mexico*.

José Refugio de la Torre Curiel is an associate professor of history at the University of Guadalajara. He is the author of *Vicarios en entredicho* (El Colegio de Michoacán, 2001) and has published articles on Franciscan missions and the development of frontier societies in New Spain's Northwest in *Colonial Latin American Historical Review* and *Historia Mexicana*, among others.

Lisbeth Haas is a professor of history at the University of California, Santa Cruz. *Conquests and Historical Identities in California, 1769–1936* was published by University of California Press in 1995. University of California Press will also publish her two forthcoming books on early California: "Horses, Saints, and Citizens: Indigenous Histories of Colonial Missions and Mexican California," and an edition of a translated manuscript, "Pablo Tac, Luiseño Indian Scholar: Writing from Rome, c. 1841."

Sylvia L. Hilton is professor of History of the Americas at the Complutense University in Madrid. She has published extensively on Spanish Borderlands in colonial North America. Recent books are, with Cornelis A. van Minnen, *Teaching and Studying U.S. History in Europe: Past, Present, and Future* (VU University Press, Amsterdam, 2007), and with Gene A. Smith, *Nexus of Empire: Negotiating Loyalty and Identity in the Revolutionary Borderlands, 1760s–1820s* (University Press of Florida, 2010).

Albert L. Hurtado has taught Native American and Western history at the University of Maryland, Indiana University-Purdue University, Arizona State University, and the University of Glasgow. He now holds the Travis Chair in Modern American History at the University of Oklahoma. His publications on California history include *Indian Survival on the California Frontier* (Yale University Press, 1988), *Intimate Frontiers: Sex, Gender, and Culture in Old California* (University of New Mexico Press, 1999), and *John Sutter: A Life on the North American Frontier* (University of Oklahoma Press, 2006). His *Herbert Bolton and the Challenge of American History* will be published by the University of California Press in 2011.

John R. Johnson is Curator of Anthropology at the Santa Barbara Museum of Natural History and Adjunct Professor of Anthropology at the University of California, Santa Barbara. He has published a number of ethnohistorical, archaeological, and genetic studies of California Indians, particularly emphasizing the use of mission records as an important source of primary data about the region's original inhabitants.

Joseph Lorenz is an assistant professor in the Department of Anthropology and Museum Studies at Central Washington University in Ellensburg. His research focuses on the distribution of genetic variation within and among human populations and other primate species and what these data tell us about our recent evolutionary history.

Louise Pubols is Chief Curator of History at the Oakland Museum of California. Her book, *The Father of All: The de la Guerra Family, Power, and Patriarchy in Mexican California* (Huntington Library and University of California Press, 2009), explores how patriarchy informed the economic and political systems of the Mexican era. This volume received the William P. Clements Prize for Best Non-Fiction Book on Southwestern America published in 2009.

James A. Sandos is the Farquhar Professor of the Southwest in the History Department at the University of Redlands. His history of the California missions, *Converting California: Indians and Franciscans in the Missions*, was published by Yale University Press in 2004 and issued in paperback in 2008. His current research focuses on choirs and choristers in building Indian community in California's missions.

Robert M. Senkewicz is a professor of history at Santa Clara University and the author of *Vigilantes in Gold Rush San Francisco* (Stanford University Press, 1985). With Rose Marie Beebe, he is translator, editor, and annotator of *Testimonios: Early California through the Eyes of Women, 1815–1848* (Heyday Books, 2006); translator, editor, and annotator of *Lands of Promise and Despair: Chronicles of Early California, 1535–1846* (Heyday Books, 2001); and translator, editor, and annotator of *The History of Alta California by Antonio María Osio* (1996), which received the Norman Neuerburg Award from the Historical Society of Southern California. With Beebe, he is the co-editor of two series for the Arthur H. Clark Company: *Early California Commentaries* and *Before Gold: California under Spain and Mexico*.

David J. Weber founded the William P. Clements Center for Southwest Studies at Southern Methodist University in 1996 and directed it up until his death in August 2010. Among his significant contributions to the study of the U.S. Southwest, the Spanish and Mexican Borderlands, Mexico, and colonial Latin America are a number of prize-winning books, including *Bárbaros: Spaniards and Their Savages in the Age of Enlightenment* (2005), *The Spanish Frontier in North America* (1992), and *The Mexican Frontier, 1821–1846: The American Southwest under Mexico* (1982). Weber was a fellow of the American Academy of Arts and Sciences, and both the Spanish and Mexican governments honored him with the highest awards they bestow on foreigners.

INDEX

Page numbers in bold refer to illustrated material.

A

Abbad y Lasierra, Iñigo, 242, 247, 273n21
Abella, Ramón, 117
Abenodia (San Juan Bautista), 122
Aconchi (Sonora), 57, 58, 60
Adams, Ephraim D., 205, 208, 209
Africa, genetic origins in, 158, 165–66, 168–69
Africans, 132, 136, 222
Agreda, María de Jesús de, 29, 30
agriculture, 69n20, 252, 255
  adoption of, by Indians, 163, 172, 182
  Indian practices of, 81
  and manual labor, 216
  prayers and, 19–20
  reform of, 135
Ahern, Maureen, 225
Ajofrín, Francisco, 240, 275n46, 276n52
Akimel O'odham. *See* Pima
alabado (song of praise), 112
Álamos (Sonora), 173, 180
Alaska, 162–63, 236–37, 245, 249, 254
Albarracín, Agustín, 259
Alberni, Pedro de, 256, 260
Alcalá Galiano, Dionisio, 246, 267, 273n22, 276n56, 278n76
alcaldes (Indian officials), 26, 61, 116, 117, 121, 124
Alfonso VIII (king of Spain), 28
Alonso, Ana María, 221
Alonso de la Fuente, José Andrés, 255

Altamira y Crevea, Rafael, 244
Alvarado, Juan Bautista de, 140–41, 145, 147–48, 152n43, 153n57
Amador, José María, 137–38, 149n8
Amamix, Agapito, 87–88, 107n20
Anderson, Benedict, 132, 278n74
Anderson, Gary Clayton, 222
Anglo Americans. *See also* United States
  activities in the North Pacific, 247
  economic views of, 197
  and fantasy heritage, 201, 221, 226
  as hard working, 202, 204–5, 217, 228
  historical identity of, 198
  history of, 215
  individualism of, 202
  Mexicanization of, 224
Anglo-Americanization, of Mexicans, 224
Aniceto Abendaño (San Jose), 114–19, 123, 127n18, 127n21
anthropology, 157
  and definition of culture, 216
  and ethnohistory, 252–53
  and group identity, 228
  molecular, 158, 161, 163, 179
  and the "other," 221
  and syncretism, 26
  and use of term "identity," 219–20
anti-Catholic sentiment, of Spaniards, 238
anti-Church sentiment, of Mexicans and Spaniards, 88
anti-Semitism, of Mallorcans, 25, 27
anti-Spanish sentiment
  and Black Legend, 243
  of Creoles, 142
  in Mexican government, 148
  of Mexican soldiers, 144
  of revolutionaries, 135, 136
  in Santa Barbara, 145

335

Index

Anza, Juan Bautista de, 256, 260
Apache, 163
    autonomy of, 221
    changing identity of, 222
    in Chihuahua, 221
    and dance, 100
    descriptions of, 225
    and intermarriage, 218
    in Luiseño dictionary, 80, 103
    as the "other," 221
    wars with, 221, 222
Apess, William, 104
Apostolic College of Guadalupe. *See* College of Guadalupe (Zacatecas)
Apostolic College of San Fernando. *See* College of San Fernando (Mexico City)
Apostolic College of Santa Cruz. *See* College of Santa Cruz (Querétaro)
Aranegui y Coll, Manuel de, 257, 263, 278n81
Arco, Ricardo del, 262, 265
Argüello family, history of, 257, 263
Argüello, Luis Antonio, 138
Ariza Torres, Cristóbal, 259
Arizona, 165, 176, 178
Arizpe (Sonora), 52, 69n21
Armillas Vicente, José Antonio, 262, 265
Arrieta Elizalde, Idoia, 263, 265
Arrillaga, José Joaquín de, 256, 260, 263
Arroyo de la Cuesta, Felipe, 113, 114, 128n25
Arteaga y Bazán, Ignacio de, 246, 276n56
Ascensión, Antonio de la, 238, 240, 276n52
asistencias, 79, 86, 105n2. *See also* missions
assimilation, 219
    of Indians, 26, 34
Athabaskan languages, 163
Atondo y Antillón, Isidro, 246, 276n56
Augustinian historians, 259
Augustinian missionaries, 34
Ausaima (village), 121
autobiography. *See* oral histories, in Bancroft Library
ayuntamientos (Mexican town councils), 141, 146–47
Aztecan, 163–64, 174–76, 178, 182

B

Bacadehuachi (Sonora), 52, 69n21, 73n56
Bacoachi (Sonora), 59
Baja California, 256
    Dominicans in, 39, 48, 239–40, 255
    expulsion of Jesuits from, 37–38, 47, 65
    languages of, 164, 182

missions, 18, 37–39, **39**, 238–41, 255, 265
    pearl fisheries of, 246, 255
    population of, 169
    Serra in, 37–40
    settlers from, 133
    settlers to, 37–38
Balantín (San Juan Bautista), 121–23
Balearic Islands, 21, 264–65, 279n97
Baltazar (San Carlos), 26
Bancroft, Hubert Howe, 41n1, 208
    on California's "Golden Age," 201–2
    on Californios' lifestyle, 202, 217
    and fantasy heritage of Californios, 201, 204
    on gold miners, 202
    on missionaries, 201
Bannon, John Francis, 206, 217, 221
baptism. *See also* sacramental registers
    and godparents, 80, 114–15
    of Indian adults, 4, 116–17, 121, 124
    of Indian children, 1, 4, 18–20, 115–18, 121–22, 124
    and land rights, 79
    of Luiseños, 82–86
    by Serra, 18–20
    of Spanish children, 2, 4, 8, 144
barbarism. *See* civilization vs. savagism
Barbastro, Antonio, 51–60
    accusations against, 56–58
    conflict with Villaseca, 58–59
    on Indian labor, 52
    on mission administration, 51–52
    on reform of missions, 55–56
Barcelona, 88, 252
Bardavío Gracia, José María, 251, 262, 265
Barker, Eugene C., 206–8
Barker, Matilda, 207–8
Barr, Juliana, 224
Barras y de Aragón, Francisco de las, 250, 261
Barreiro-Meiro, Roberto, 259, 264, 265
Barreneche, Juan Antonio Joaquín de, 239
barter system, and missionaries, 51–52
Barth, Fredrik, 220
Bartroli i Nogué, Tomás, 251, 265
Batista González, Juan, 260
Bauzá, Felipe, 249, 260, 265, 280n98
Bayle, Constantino, S.J., 239, 244, 259
Becerra, Diego de, 244
Beebe, Rose Marie, 9, 49, 64, 70n29, 74n74
Bering land bridge, 162

Berkhofer, Robert F., Jr., 225
Bernabeu, Salvador, 240–41, 251–52, 255–57, 267, 270
Bernardino de Jesús (San Carlos), 18–19
Bernardino de Sena (San Jose), 116–19
Beya Alonso, Ernesto, 264
Biblioteca dell'Archiginnasio (Bologna), 85, 90–91, 93, 96–97, 101
Black Legend, 243
Blessed Sacrament, 112
blood purity, 88, 221
blood quantum, 228
blue robes, 52–53, 62
Bodega y Cuadra, Juan Francisco de la, 246, 263, 276n56, 278n83
Bolton, Frederick, 206, 214n36
Bolton, Herbert Eugene
  California's Story, 205, 208–9
  career of, 10–11, 198, 206, 210, 214n36
  on fantasy heritage, 198, 204, 210
  and myths of California, 202–3
  and Native Sons of the Golden West, 203–4
  papers of, 213n21, 214n36
  photos of, **199**, **207**
  The Spanish Borderlands, 204–5, 211n5, 216–17
  on Spanish character, 215–17, 221, 228
  students of, 198, 204–5, 210, 213n32
  textbooks written by, 205–10
  on vigilantes, 209
Boneu Companys, Fernando, 256, 264, 265
Borah, Woodrow, 218
Borderlands, Spanish
  Bolton on, 198, 204–5, 211n5, 216–17
  as cultural meeting place, 210
  ethnic boundaries in, 7–8, 220
  genetic research on, 169
  historians of, 198, 204, 213n23, 215–29
  and nationalism, 261
Borges Moran, Pedro, O.F.M., 259
Borica, Diego de, 256, 260, 263
Borrego Plá, María del Carmen, 265
Boscana, Gerónimo, 87, 107n26, 240, 264, 276n52, 279n96
  on dance, 99–100, 109n53
Bouchard, Hipólito, 136
Bourbon Reforms, 23–24, 36, 65, 132–33
Bravo, José Marcelino, 19
Bringas, Diego Miguel, 55–60, 72n39
Bringas, Señor (merchant), 141
Brooks, James F., 222–23

Brown, Alan K., 27
Bruno (San Jose), 116, 118–19
Buache de Neuville, Jean-Nicolas, 247
burials
  Franciscan notions of, 94
  Franciscan records of, 126n1
  of Indians, 111
Burriel, Andrés Marcos, 238–39, 258
Burrus, Ernest, S.J., 259
Bustamante y Guerra, José de, 246

C
Caamaño Moraleja, Jacinto, 246, 264
Caballero, Francisco, 52, 69n21
Cabeza de Vaca, Lucas, 34
Caborca (Sonora), 59, 69n20, 74n73
Cabot, Pedro, 111, 124–25
Cahita language, 173, 174–75, 180, 182–83
"Californeses," 89. *See also* Luiseño
California (territory of Mexican Republic). *See* Mexican California
California (territory of New Spain), economy of, 65, 82
California (U.S. state), 3, 123, 148
  education in, 205–10
  gold rush, 197–98, 200, 202–4, 208–9
Los Californianos, 164
Californios, 5, 10, 149n3. *See also gente de razón*; settlers
  and allegiance to Mexican Republic, 137–39
  and alliances with Indians, 103
  appearance of, 132, 134, 138, 149n8
  Bancroft on, 201–2
  Bolton on, 204, 217, 228
  broadsides of, 133, 145
  and civilian rule, 139, 141, 146, 147
  and climate, 204, 216–17
  Creole identity of, 142–43
  descendants of, 165, 203
  distribution of land to, 87
  economic relationships of, 8, 254
  education of, 140, 146
  ethnic boundaries of, 132
  hospitality of, 145, 217
  isolation of, 144, 217
  and kinship networks, 8, 9
  memoirs of, 125, 140
  and mission sacramental registers, 3
  notions of honor, 58, 113, 132, 145, 221
  political conservatism of, 137–39, 148

Californios (continued)
  political views of, 139, 141, 146, 147
  population of, 133, 160
  pronunciamientos (declarations) by, 148
  racial mixing of, 157
  reminiscences of, 125, 140
  republicanism of, 139–41, 144, 146
  reputed lifestyle of, 201–2, 204–5, 217, 228
  and royalism, 138, 143
  second generation, 10, 132–33, 139–41, 144–48
  self-rule of, 147
El Camino Real, 82, 83, 203
Campa Cos, Miguel de la, O.F.M., 241, 274n31, 276n52
Canada, 162–63, 245, 255
Cañizares, José, 251
Canny, Nicholas, 7
Cano Sánchez, Angela, 264, 265
cantores, 114, 123, 124. *See also* music; musicians (*músicos*)
Cardona, Nicolás, 246, 251
Cardona, Tomás, 246
Carlos (San Diego), 1
Carlos III (king of Spain), 25
Carlos IV (king of Spain), 135
Carlota (San Jose), 117
Carmel mission. *See* Mission San Carlos Borromeo (Carmel)
Carner-Ribalta, Joseph, 264, 265
Carretero Collado, Leoncio, 252, 255
Carrillo, Baltasar, 54
Carrillo, Joaquín, 131, 142
Carrillo, Julio, 148
Carrillo, Raymundo, 131, 142
Carrillo y Lugo, Anastasio, 131
Carrillo y Lugo, José Antonio, 136
Carrillo y Lugo, María Antonio, 131, 136
Casas, Bartolomé de las. *See* Las Casas, Bartolomé de
Casilda (San Jose), 116
Casilda de la Cruz, María (Santa Barbara), 8
casta system, 232n30. *See also castiza*; *coyote*; *español*; *indio* (casta term); *mestizo*; *mulato*; *negro*
  and 1790 census, 168, 182
  abolished in 1824, 88
  and Apache, 80, 103
  and legal rights, 103
  simplification of, in Alta California, 133–34, 157, 159, 183, 221

Castellanos, Bonifacio, O.F.M., 259
castiza, 181. *See also casta* system
Castro, José, 140, 145–47, 153n57
Catalá, Magín, 239, 263, 276n52
Catalonia, 251, 263–64, 267, 269, 279n84
Catalonian Volunteers, 19
Catholicism
  and Church privileges, 132, 137
  and daily life, 5
  doctrine of, 29, 84
  and European music, 111–12
  and festival of the Virgin of Guadalupe, 146
  and history writing, 238–41, 258–59, 269
  Holy Days, 120, 124
  and Mass, 80, 112–13, 120, 123, 137–38
  opposition to, in Spain 238
  sacraments of, 1–5, 51, 94, 124
  and saints, 21, 103, 272n19
  and syncretism, 84
  and theology, 29
cattle trade, 50
Cayapa Indians, 178
Cayetano (San Jose), 117
Ceballos, Juan Bautista, 60–64
Cebreiro Blanco, Luis, 259
Cecilia (San Juan Bautista), 121
census. *See* population (Alta California)
Cerezo Martínez, Ricardo, 259
Chamorro, María del Carmen, 19
Chañichñis, 84, 103. *See also* Chinigchinich
Chappe d'Auteroche, Jean-Baptiste, 251
Charles III (king of Spain), 23
Charles IV (king of Spain), 245
Cherokee, 104
Chevalier, François, 218
Chicanos, 227
Chico, Mariano, 147
Chihuahua, 35, 164–66, 169–81, 221
Chinigchinich, 99, 102. *See also* Chañichñis
choirs. *See* music; musicians (*músicos*)
Choris, Louis, 27
Chrisanta (San Jose), 115, 127n21
Chrisanto (San Jose), 115, 127n21
Christianity. *See* Catholicism; missions
Chumash, 172, 183
  and dance, 100
  and disease, 82
  in Santa Barbara Channel region, 163, 170, 179
Church. *See* Catholicism; missions

citizenship
    and Indians, 10, 89
    in Mexican Republic, 136, 141
    political ideas about, 81
    in Spain, 148
Ciudad Juárez, 164
civilian rule, by Californios, 139, 141, 146, 147
civilization vs. savagism, 201–2, 209, 216, 220–21. *See also* Hispanicization
clades. *See* mitochondrial DNA (mtDNA)
Claret, Pompeyo, 256
class identity
    and honor, 221
    in Mexican Republic, 132
    in Mission San Gabriel, 159–60
    and Spanish frontiersmen, 217
    in United States, 226
climate, and Californio cultural traits, 204, 216–17
clothing
    of Indian musicians, 113
    of Indians, 40, 101, 102
Coahuila, 69n23, 169
Cochimí, 163, 176, 182
Cocopa, 167, 185
Cocóspera (Sonora), 61, 71n33
Collazo, Ángel, 59
College of Guadalupe (Zacatecas)
    founding of, 32
    Zacatecans, 36
College of San Fernando (Mexico City), **31**
    and Escandón, 34–35
    Fernandinos, 34–37, 39
    founding of, 32
    missionaries sent to California, 49
    and *padres descontentos*, 70n29
    Serra at, 30
    and Sierra Gorda, 34, 35, 37
College of Santa Cruz (Querétaro)
    Barbastro at, 70n30
    and conflicts among missionaries, 62–63
    Discretory of, 55–57, 59–60, 63, 72n37, 72n45, 72n46
    Fontbona punished by, 74n69
    founding of, 30, 67n12
    and group identity, 49–50
    Queretans, 48–54, 60, 62–63, 65n1
    and Sonoran missions, 37, 47, 71n32
    and staffing for College of San Fernando, 34–35
Collegium Urbanum de Propaganda Fide (Rome), 88

colonialism
    and allegiance of Indians, 66n5
    and effect on language, 22, 92, 94
    and hierarchy, 81, 134–35
    and indigenous power, 81, 114
    and oppression, 32, 37, 40, 74n74, 135
    and religious conversion, 237
    and subjectivity, 7
colonization (Mexican), and Híjar-Padrés colony, 147
colonization (Spanish)
    and Borderlands, 222
    in California, 79, 133, 157
    historiography of, 256
    in Sierra Gorda, 32, 34–36
colonizers. *See* settlers
Colorado River, 54–56, 59, 132, 251
Columbus, Christopher, 17, 243, 245
comisionados (commissioners), 38
commerce. *See* trade
Communion. *See* Mass
conquistadors, 37, 216
Consag, Fernando, 238, 258
conservatism, political
    of Governor Victoria, 146
    of Iturbide, 136–37
    of older Californios, 137–39, 148
    of soldiers and settlers, 217
Constant, Benjamin, 140
constitutions
    Mexican (1824), 138–39
    Mexican (1835–36), 147
    Spanish (1812), 61, 64
conversion, religious, 66n4, 103, 222. *See also* missionaries, Franciscan
    authenticity of, 25–26
    as fundamental task of missionaries, 25, 47
    of Indians, 84, 107n20, 197, 237
    and music, 111
conversos, 25
convicts, 143, 144
Cook, James, 247, 249, 273n22
Cora (Indians), 164, 173
Coronado, Eligio Moisés, 240
corporal punishment, 81
Corredor García, Antonio, 259
Cortés, Hernán, 201, 210, 246, 256, 260
Cosalá (Sinaloa), 177
Costansó, Miguel, 252, 256, 260, 263
Cot, Antonio José, 143–44

coyote, 168, 175–77. *See also casta* system
Creo, Matías, 61, 63
Creoles, 7, 54, 132, 133, 135–36, 142–44
   on Mexican independence, 137
Crespí, Juan, 27, 241, 264, 276n52
Croix, Teodoro de, 47, 69n23
Crosby, Harry, 38
cross-cultural unions. *See* intermarriage
Cucurpe (Sonora), 59, 67n8
Cueva, Pedro de la, 117
Cugat Bonet, Josep María, 264, 265
Culiacán (Sinaloa), 174–75, 177
curatos (parishes), 34–35, 74n66, 87, 144

D

dance (Californio), 113, 138, 145–46
dance (Indian), 99–102, **101**
   coming-of-age, 95
   and fertility, 111
   and group identity, 100
   Luiseño, 92, 95
   Ohlone, 27
   and the spiritual world, 84, 94, 99–100, 102–3
Dativo (San Juan Bautista), 121–23
de la Cueva, Pedro, 117
de la Guerra y Carrillo, Angustias, 139, 143, 146, 148
de la Guerra y Carrillo, Francisco, 148
de la Guerra y Carrillo, José Antonio, 131, 133, 142, 147
de la Guerra y Carrillo, Rita de Jesus, 136
de la Guerra y Noriega, José Antonio Julián, 144, 149n8
   captured during civil war, 135–36
   as deputy to congress, 142–43, 145
   loyalty to Spain, 135, 138, 148
   at Santa Barbara presidio, 131, 147
   and social hierarchy, 133
de la Ord, Angustias. *See* de la Guerra y Carrillo, Angustias
de la Peña, Tomás, 4
de la Teja, Jesús F., 221, 231n27
de la Torre Curiel, José Refugio, 9
de Nava, Pedro, 53–55, 65
death
   and burials, 94, 111, 116, 126
   from diseases brought by Spanish settlers, 81–82, 84
   Franciscan notions of, 94
   and Indian rituals, 94
   and last rites, 144

mission records of, 114, 122, 124, 126
   and short expectancy of life, 120, 122
Deeds, Susan, 223
deities (Indian), 84, 102–3
del Arco, Ricardo. *See* Arco, Ricardo del
depopulation
   of California Indians, 3, 5
   at Mission San Carlos, 128n24
   of Sinaloa and Sonora, 170, 174
depositarios (depositaries), and missionaries, 55
Diegueño, 100. *See also* Kumeyaay
Díez, Antonio, 59, 71n32
diputacíon (territorial legislature), 145–47
discourse analysis, 225, 241
disease
   among missionaries, 83
   among sedentary Indian groups, 223
   brought by Spanish settlers, 81–83
   Indian healing practices for, 81, 93
   Indians' limited immunity to, 166
   in Luiseño territory, 83
   measles, 122
   in Sierra Gorda, 34
   in Sinaloa and Sonora, 170
dishonor. *See* honor/shame
divinities. *See* deities (Indian)
DNA analysis. *See* mitochondrial DNA (mtDNA)
doctrina, 62, 112
Dolores mission. *See* Mission San Francisco de Asís (Dolores)
Dominicans, 48, 259, 264–65, 276n52
   and Baja California missions, 39, 239–40, 255
   histories of, 242
drought, 19–20, 38
Duhaut-Cilly, Auguste, 27
Durán, Narciso, 117, 133, 140, 147
   and liturgical music, 113–14, 117, 124
Durango (Mexico), 47, 137, 169, 176

E

Early California Population Project (ECPP)
   categories of, 7–8
   development of, 5–6, 13n11
   and genealogical research, 191n27
   musicians listed in, 111, 114, 124, 126
ecclesiastical records. *See* sacramental registers
Echeandía, José María de, 87, 89, 139–40, 142–44

economy
    Anglo Americans and, 197
    barter, 51–52
    and Indians, 82, 227
    of Luiseños, 83, 86–87
    of Mexican California, 139–40
    of Mission San Luis Rey, 83, 86–87
    of New Mexico, 227
    and the "other," 222
    and second-generation Californios, 139–40
    and settlers, 47, 64, 254
    and social mobility, 221
    of Sonora, 47–48
    of Spanish California, 65, 82
    and women, 20–21, 98
Ecuador, 178
Eliza, Francisco de, 246, 276n56
Elizondo, Domingo de, 225, 256
Elliott, Eric, 94, 108n43
emigration. *See* migration
Engelhardt, Zephyrin, O.F.M., 17, 203, 259, 263
epidemics, 34, 83, 170. *See also* disease
Epifanio (San Juan Bautista), 121–23
Escandell Tur, Neus, 264, 265
Escandón, José de, 32, 34–37
Escolástica (San Jose), 117
español, 8, 133–34, 168, 175–78, 181, 218.
    See also casta system; Spaniards, European-born
Espinosa y Tello, José, 242, 259, 260, 273n22
Esponera Cerdán, Alfonso, 259
Esquibel, José Antonio, 223
Estrada Arnaiz, Rafael, 244, 249, 260
Estudillo, José María, 121
Estudio General Lulliano, 22
ethnogenesis, 222, 232n30
ethnohistory, 158, 222, 242, 252–55, 269
ethnolinguistics, 161–63, 170, 180
ethnology, 249–53, 255, 261, 270
Eulalia (San Juan Bautista), 121
evangelization. *See* missionaries, Franciscan
exploration (Spanish), 237–38, 242–45, 248, 251, 261, 263
explorers (Spanish), 252–53, 256, 263, 264
    Bolton on, 216–17
    as heroes, 208, 217

F
Fages, Pedro, 19, 20, 256, 260, 264
Familia Ancestral Research Association, 165

fantasy heritage of California. *See also* romanticization
    fostering of, 200, 201, 226
    promulgated in textbooks, 206
    reinforced by Bolton, 11, 198, 210
Fausto (San Jose), 118–20
Feijóo, Benito Jerónimo, 23–24
female lineages. *See* mitochondrial DNA (mtDNA)
Fénelon, François, 140
Fermín (San Jose), 115
Fermina (San Jose), 116
Fernández de Navarrete, Martín, 242, 247, 259
Fernández de San Vicente, Agustín, 87, 137–38
Fernández Duro, Cesáreo, 238, 247, 249, 259–60, 273n27
Fernández y Somera, Blas, 256
Fernandino Indians, 100
Fernandino missionaries, 34–37, 39. *See also* College of San Fernando (Mexico City)
Fernando Librado (Kitsepawit), 100
Fernando VII (king of Spain), 135–38, 243
Ferrer Maldonado, Lorenzo, 243, 247, 273n22, 276n56
Fidalgo, Salvador, 246, 276n56
Fita Colomé, Fidel, S.J., 239, 259
Florescano, Enrique, 218
Fluviá, Francisco Xavier, 238, 259
Font Obrador, Bartolomé (Bartomeu), 264–65
Fontbona, Francisco, 61, 63, 74n69
Forbes, Jack D., 218
Fortuny, Buenaventura, 124
forty-niners. *See* gold rush (California)
Francis of Assisi, Saint, 21, 22
Francis Solano, Saint, 29
Franciscans. *See* missionaries, Franciscan
Francisco (San Diego), 1
Francisco Antonio (San Diego), 1
Francisco Antonio (San Juan Bautista), 122
Franco, Francisco, 239, 244–45, 247, 249
    death of, 240, 250, 261–62
Frank, Ross, 221, 231n28
Freemasonry, 139, 140, 145
Frémont, John Charles, 148, 210
frontier
    Anglo-American, 215, 216
    definitions of, 216, 220
    and fluid identities, 131
    historiography of, 235–37, 239, 268

frontier (continued)
  and intermarriage, 166
  Mexican, 10
  and the military, 133–34
  and shaping of character, 216–18
  Sonora as, 47, 50, 53–54, 56–57
  Spanish, 135–36, 157, 164, 183, 217–18, 235
Fuca, Juan de, 243, 246
Fuentes, María Dolores, 255
fueros (privileges), in Mallorca, 20, 23
fugitive Indians, 26, 81
Fuster, Vicente, 83

G

Gabrielino, 100
Gachupines, 53, 141, 144, 153n48
Galán García, Agustín, 256
Galmés Más, Lorenzo, O.P., 259, 264, 265
Gálvez, José de, 38, 47, 50, 69n23, 225, 256
Garau, Francisco, 25
Garcés, Francisco, 68n15, 251, 262, 276n52
  biographies of, 238, 240–41
  ethnological work by, 249, 275n44
  on temporalities, 50
García Rodríguez, Casiano, 259
Garriga, Pere C., 265
Gascón de Gotor, Anselmo, 262, 265
Gates, Henry Louis, Jr., 158
Gaudiosa (San Jose), 117–20, 125
Gavino/Gabino (San Juan Bautista), 121–23
Geiger, Maynard J., O.F.M., 17, 30, 46n56, 259
  photos by, 31, 39
gender, and historiography, 257
genetic origins, 157–58. *See also*
  mitochondrial DNA (mtDNA)
  phylogenetic relationships, 158, 161, 175, 176–77
genízaros, 221, 228
gente de razón
  as racial category, 7–8, 134, 157, 197
  in Mission San Gabriel, 159–60
  social identity of, 183
gente sin razón, 134, 197
gentiles
  and baptism, 19, 115, 117
  vs. neophytes, 226
  Serra on, 40, 46n56
Gil, Diego, 62
Gila River, 47, 54–56, 59, 67n8
godfathers (*padrinos*), 19, 80, 113–16, 120–21, 124
godmothers (*madrinas*), 19, 116, 122

gold rush (California), 197–98, 200, 202–4, 208–9
Gómez Canedo, Lino, O.F.M., 34, 239–40, 259
Gómez, Vito T., O.P., 259, 265
Gómez-Farías, Valentín, 146–47
González, Miguel, 131, 132, 142, 145
González Montero de Espinosa, Marisa, 261
Gracia Rivas, Manuel, 259, 262, 265
gray-robes, 53, 65
Green, Lance D., 180
"Grito de Dolores," 135
Guadalajara, 38, 47, 147
Guadalupe, Virgin of. *See* Virgin of Guadalupe
Guaicura, 182
Guanajuato, 38, 169, 176
Guasabe (village), 173–74
Guasave (Indians), 174, 182
Guechi, 82
Guerra, Angustias de la. *See* de la Guerra y Carrillo, Angustias
Guerra, Francisco de la. *See* de la Guerra y Carrillo, Francisco
Guerra, José Antonio de la. *See* de la Guerra y Carrillo, José Antonio
Guerra, José de la. *See* de la Guerra y Noriega, José Antonio Julián
Guerra, Rita de la. *See* de la Guerra y Carrillo, Rita de Jesus
Guest, Francis F., O.F.M., 17, 259
Guida (San Jose), 117
Guillén y Tato, Julio Fernando, 244, 259
Gutiérrez de la Concha, Juan, 246, 276n56
Gutiérrez, María de los Santos, 174–75
Gutiérrez, Narciso, 59, 62, 71n32
Gutiérrez, Nicolás, 147
Gutiérrez, Ramón A., 220–21
Guzmán, Nuño de, 170

H

Haas, Lisbeth, 10, 66n5, 113–14, 220
Hackel, Steven W., 81, 106n12, 126, 128n24, 220
Haenke, Tadeo, 249–50, 252, 260
hagiography, 258, 265
haplogroups/haplotypes. *See* mitochondrial DNA (mtDNA)
Hartnell, William, 140
Hausberger, Bernard, 241
Hawaii, 104, 169, 191n28
Heceta, Bruno de, 246, 274n31, 276n56

Henckel, Carlos, 261
Hennepin, Luis, 251
Hernández Aparicio, Pilar, 251, 255
Hernández, María Rufina, 164
Hidalgo y Costilla, Miguel, 135–36
hide-and-tallow trade, 143–44
Higueras Rodríguez, María Dolores, 260
Híjar, José María, 147
hijos del país (sons of the country). *See* Californios
Hilton, Sylvia L., 11, 66n6
Hispanic culture
    Bolton on, 198
    and California settlers, 237
    secular, 257
Hispanicization
    Bolton on, 216
    and cultural identity, 237
    on the frontier, 268
    of Indians in Sonora, 74n66
    Juan Bautista Muñoz on, 238
    by missionaries, 17, 197, 252
    by Tlaxcaltecans, 170
Hispanos
    and fantasy heritage, 226
    and identity, 222
    in New Mexico, 227

historiography, 11
    discourse analysis, 225, 241
    of international relations, 247–49
    of maritime expeditions, 242–47
    of missions, 237–42
    and nationalism, 10, 235, 243, 261–66, 268
    science and, 249–55
    and tourism, 268
Holy Days (Catholic), 120, 124
honor/shame
    and autonomy, 221
    and masculinity, 145
    and missionaries, 58
    and music, 113
    and national identity, 132
Hopi, 227
Horcasitas (Sonora), 176, 180
Hoyzela (San Jose), 116–19
Huichol, 164, 167, 178
Huite, 182
Huntington Library, 5, 11
Hurtado, Albert H., 10–11, 217
Hutchinson, C. Alan, 218

I

Ibáñez, Florencio, 60, 73n53
Ibáñez Montoya, María Victoria, 261
identity
    Anglo-American, 226
    Chicano, 227
    Creole, 7
    definitions of, 216, 219, 221
    Franciscan, 48–50
    Mexican, 132
    as social construction, 157, 221
identity (Californio)
    and appearance, 132, 134
    and class, 159–60
    construction of, 157
    and genetic origins, 160
    and race, 10, 132–34
identity (Indian), 128n21, 228
    and dance, 100
    and genetic origins, 162
    in historical literature, 222
    and individuals, 219–20
    and music, 10
    and shift to Spanish identity, 1–2
identity (Spanish), 133, 136
    and class, 217
    in frontier regions, 237
    and language, 224–25
images
    and Mexican national identity, 136, 139
    petroglyphs, 95
Immaculate Conception, 29
immigration. *See* migration
Indian languages. *See* languages (Indian)
Indian officials (*alcaldes*), 26, 116–17, 121, 124. *See also* cantores; pages (*pajes*); sacristans
Indians. *See also* Indian officials (*alcaldes*); *individual groups*; music; musicians (*músicos*); neophytes
    and agriculture, 81
    and allegiance, 95
    and alliances with Spanish, 63, 84, 103
    and authority, 26, 81, 84, 94–95, 104
    and autonomy, 81–82, 89, 98, 104, 221
    baptisms of, 1–2, 82, 84, 116–17, 121, 124
    Bolton on, 216
    burials of, 111
    characterized as deceptive, 92
    clothing of, 40, 57, 101, 102
    conflicts with missionaries, 64

Indians (continued)
  conversion to Catholicism of, 84, 107n20, 134, 197
  corporal punishment of, 81
  and dance, 27, 92, 95, 111
  depopulation of, 122, 128n24, 170
  descriptions of, 83, 225, 226
  descriptions of mission life, 113
  detribalization of, 221, 228
  and economy, 82, 227
  education of, 98
  emancipation of, from missions, 89
  Europeanization of, 103
  and evangelism, 26, 40, 225
  fugitive, 26, 81
  as *gente sin razón*, 134, 197
  and group identity, 10, 128n21, 162, 228
  Hispanicization of, 17, 74n66, 170, 197, 237, 252
  impact of Spanish presence on, 82
  intermarriage of, 160, 162, 166, 180, 224
  as interpreters, 104, 116, 120, 121, 124
  and isolation from Spaniards, 223
  as laborers, 20–21, 53, 79, 98
  land ownership by, 47, 53, 61, 79, 87
  legal rights of, 80
  and liberalism, 140
  life expectancy of, 120, 122, 128n24
  loss of political autonomy by, 10, 82
  as Mexican citizens, 10, 89, 136
  mortality, 120, 122, 128n24
  oppression of, 36, 140, 225, 226
  persistence of traditions among, 219
  and political equality, 87, 89
  population of, 133, 197
  precontact ethnic boundaries of, 227–28
  rights of, 63, 87, 103, 140
  romanticization of, 225
  self-rule of, 79
  shamans, 94, 95
  and soldiers, 17, 36, 134, 225
  and syncretism, 26, 84
  tattooing of, 100
  tribute and slavery, 36, 79, 135
  uprisings by, 1, 24, 109n53
  warfare among, 81, 222
indio (*casta* term), 8, 80, 157, 168, 181. *See also casta* system
  at bottom of social hierarchy, 133–34
individualism
  of Anglo Americans, 202
  of soldiers and settlers, 217

indoctrination. *See* missionaries, Franciscan
Infiesta Pérez, José Luis, 264, 265
Inquisition, Spanish
  comisarios of, 25
  in Mallorca, 21, 24–26
  in New Spain, 35
intermarriage
  among Indian groups, 180
  of Indian women and European men, 166, 224
  in Pre-Columbian Americas, 160, 162
international relations, history of, 245, 247–49
interpreters (Indian), 104, 116, 121, 124
Ipai. *See* Diegueño; Kumeyaay
Iturbide, Agustín de, 87, 136–37
Iturralde, Francisco, 54, 59–60, 73n53, 73n56

J

Jachucoy (San Jose), 115–19
Jackson, Helen Hunt
  Father Junípero and the Mission Indians of California, 41n1
  Ramona, 202–3, 212n14
Jackson, Robert H., 33
Jaime I (king of Aragón, Mallorca, and Valencia), 23, 27
Jalisco
  Cora and Huichol of, 164, 173, 178
  missionary district of, 37, 54, 62, 74n66
Jalpan (Sierra Gorda), 32–35, **33**
Jayme, Luis, 1
Jesuits, 25, 48, 52, 54, 88, 259
  ex-missions of, 37, 71n32, 173
  expulsion from New Spain, 37–38, 47, 65, 75n77
  historical studies of, 238–41
  religious program of, 26, 40
Jiménez, Fortún, 244
Jiménez Núñez, Alfredo, 253
Jiménez Samaniego, José. *See* Ximénez Samaniego, José
John, Elizabeth A. H., 218–19
Johnson, Hiram, 208
Johnson, John R., 3, 10–11, 126
Jonace, 34, 35
Jones, Oakah L., Jr., 217–18
Jordan, David Starr, 208
Jordán de Urriés y Ruiz de Arana, Juan, 247, 260
José Elías (San Jose), 117
Juan Capistrano (San Juan Bautista), 121–23

Juan Carlos I (king of Spain), 248, 250
Juan José (San Jose), 117
Juaneño, 95, 98, 99, 100
Julio (San Juan Bautista), 121
Junípero (companion of St. Francis), 21
Jupagtac (village), 121

K
Kamen, Henry, 25
Kastor, Peter J., 228
Keen, Benjamin, 225
Kemp, Brian, 163, 173–76, 178, 180
Kendrick, John, 267
Kessell, John, 218
Keys, James M., 239
king. *See* monarchy (Spanish)
Kino, Eusebio Francisco, 239, 241, 276n52
Kippis, Andrew, 247, 273n22
Kitsepawit (Fernando Librado), 100
Kumeyaay, 1, 24. *See also* Diegueño

L
La Purísima Concepción mission, 87
labor
 Anglo-American, 217
 Californios' dislike for, 216–17
 by Indian women, at missions, 21, 98
 by Indians, for settlers, 53, 197, 201, 217
 at missions in New Spain, 52, 79
 at Pimería Alta missions, 48, 50, 61
 on ranchos, 201, 216–17
 in Sierra Gorda, 35–36
 soldiers' dislike for, 134
Lafarga Lozano, Adolfo, 263, 265
Lamadrid Jiménez, Lázaro, 259
land ownership
 and Alta California missions' near-monopoly, 133
 by Californios, 200–201
 in Chihuahua, 221
 Hopi and Zuni, 227
 Luiseño, 79–81, 87, 103
 and Mexican identity, 132
 and mission secularization, 79, 87, 140, 147
 in Pimería Alta, 47, 53
 in San Diego, 159
 in Sierra Gorda, 34–35
Landín Carrasco, Amancio, 259, 264–65
languages (Indian)
 Apache, 163

Athabaskan, 163
 in Baja California, 164, 182
 Cahita, 173, 174–75, 180, 182–83
 ceremonial, 93
 Christian words translated into, 26, 84
 Chumash, 170
 and colonialism, 92
 and genetic origins, 160–61
 Luiseño, 79, 84, 89, 99, 108n43
 Tahue, 174–75, 182
 Tewa, 223
 Uto-Aztecan, 163–64, 174–76, 178, 182
 Yuman-Cochimí, 163, 176, 182
 Zuni, 170
Larriñaga, Juan Ruiz de, O.F.M., 259, 263, 265
Las Casas, Bartolomé de, 36
Lasuén, Fermín Francisco de, 82–83, 86, 239–41, 263, 276n52
latifundia, 201
Lejarza, Fidel de, 259
Leonardo (San Carlos), 19
liberalism
 Alta California as experiment for, 132, 138–40, 147
 and Californios, 139–40, 146–47
 and Governor Echeandía, 87, 89
 and language, 89
 and Mexican Constitution of 1824, 138
 and political ideas, 139–40
 and women, 152n44
Lightfoot, Kent G., 228
Lima, 143, 144, 263
limpieza de sangre, 88, 221
Linck, Wenceslaus, 256
Liquithe (San Juan Bautista), 121–23, 128n25
literacy, of Californios, 136, 151n20, 152n44
Llabrés Bernal, Juan, 249, 265
Llinás, Antonio, 30
Llomoi (San Juan Bautista), 121
Llorens, Juan Bautista, 54, 62, 73n56
Llull, Ramón, 22–24, 29
Longinos Martínez Garrido, José, 246, 252, 260, 276n56
López Bonet, Miguel, 259, 265
López, María Rosa, 180
López Urrutia, Carlos, 256
Lora, Juan Ramos de, 36
Lorenz, Joseph G., 10–11
Lorenza (San Jose), 116
Loreto (Baja California), 164, 177
Loreto presidio, 38
Los Angeles, 2, 3, 133, 141, 159

Lovato, Andrew Leo, 227
loyalty
   of European-born Spaniards, 143
   of religious and military leaders, 137
   of soldiers and settlers, 10
   of territorial assembly, 138
Lucas (San Jose), 115–19
Luis Antonio (San Juan Bautista), 121–23
Luis Gonzaga (San Jose), 116, 121
Luiseño, 66n5, 80
   authority of, 81, 84, 94–95, 98, 103–4
   autonomy of, 81–82, 98
   and ball games, 95, 98
   baptism of, 84, 107n20
   and dance, 92, 99
   deities, 84, 99, 102, 103
   and disease, 81–82, 83
   grammar and dictionary of, 79, 89, 99
   history of, 79
   ideas about the sacred, 84, 93–94, 103
   identity of, 103
   intermediaries, 95
   lands owned by, 79, 87
   language, 79, 84, 89, 99, 108n43
   oral traditions of, 89, 99
   paternalism, 98
   petroglyphs, 95
   and political defeat, 81, 84, 94–95
   and political equality, 87, 89
   religion of, 92–93, 102
   translation of, 84, 90–91, 94
   uauquiii (ball game), 95
Lummis, Charles F., 203

M

Machado, Juana, 137, 138
madrinas. *See* godmothers (*madrinas*)
maestro de la música. *See* musicians (*músicos*)
Maitorena, José Joaquín, 131, 145
Malaspina expedition, 244–46, 249–51, 253, 265, 276n56
Mallorca, 19, 22–30, 35, 124, 264–65. *See also* Palma de Mallorca; Petra (Mallorca)
   anti-Semitism in, 25, 27
Mampel González, Elena, 264, 265
Mañá, Tibisay, 265
Mancisidor, Juan Ignacio, 143–44
Manjarrés y Bofarull, Ramón de, 244, 260–61
Maquipa (village), 173
Marcos José (San Jose), 116

María de Buen-año (San Carlos), 19
María de los Santos (San Juan Bautista), 122
María Ester, 144
María Jacinta (Santa Barbara), 8
María Plácida (San Jose), 117
maritime expeditions, Spanish, 242–47
marriage, 83, 86, 144, 257
   Franciscan investigations of, 8
   Franciscan records of, 2–3, 114–15, 118–19, 121, 123
   intermarriage, 160, 162, 166, 180, 224
   witnesses to, 114–24
Marta (San Juan Bautista), 121–22
Martínez, Esteban José, 246, 276n56
Martínez Grácia, Valentín, 259
Martínez, Luis Antonio, 143–44, 147
Martínez Salazar, Ángel, 263, 265
Martínez-Cañavate Ballesteros, Luis Rafael, 261
Martínez-Valverde, Carlos, 259
Martín-Merás, María Luisa, 260, 270
Mary. *See* Virgin Mary
Masonic lodges, 139, 140, 145
Mass, 62, 80, 112–13, 120, 123, 137–38
Mathes, W. Michael, 255
Mayo, 174, 175, 183
Mayo River, 174
Mayo Valley, 173
mayordomos (foremen), 32
McWilliams, Carey, 212n6, 226
Meade, Teresa, 257
Melón y Ruiz de Gordejuela, Amando, 261
Menchaca Careaga, Antonio, 259, 263, 265
merchants, 65, 140–41, 143–44
Merrill, William L., 219, 221, 232n30
mestizaje, 157, 161, 166
mestizo, 168, 173, 175–76, 180, 254. *See also casta* system
   and "ethnic migration," 218
   and intermarriage, 181
   and masking of racial origins, 8, 11
   at middle of social hierarchy, 133
   and simplification of *casta* system, 8
   and vanished Indian groups, 223
Mexican Americans, 158, 164, 167–69, 176
   and Chicano identity, 227
   as Spanish Americans, 226
Mexican California
   economy of, 139–40
   governors of, 73, 75, 117, 133, 136–43, 146–48
   legislature of, 87, 138, 145–47

Mexican Republic. *See also* New Spain
  authority of, 141, 147
  Californios' allegiance to, 131, 137–39
  centralism, 139, 147
  ceremonies to acknowledge
    independence, 87, 137–38
  and citizenship, 136, 141
  as constitutional monarchy, 137
  control of Alta California, 132, 136
  efforts to build national identity, 136–38
  and elections, 141, 147
  and equality
  and European-born Spaniards, 143
  federalism, 139, 147
  Franciscan allegiance to, 87, 137
  ideology of republicanism, 139–41, 144, 146
  Independence Day celebrations, 87, 144–46
  independence movement of, 135
  law on expulsion of Spaniards, 142–43
  law on Indian land rights, 79
  liberalism, 139
  and missions, 86–87, 197
  and national unity, 132
  and trade, 86
  war of independence, 134–36, 142, 153n67
Mexicana, 242
Mexican-American War. *See* U.S.-Mexico War
Mexicanization
  of Anglo Americans, 224
  and Independence Day celebrations, 146
Mexico City, 18, 29–32, **31**, 81, 131. *See also* College of San Fernando (Mexico City)
  and liberalism, 143–44, 146
  missionaries in, 34–35, 37–38, 88
  during war of independence, 135–37
Mezzofanti, Carlos Giuseppe, 89, 91–93, 104
Michoacán, 169
migration. *See also* colonization (Spanish)
  from Europe to America, 6–7, 166, 168, 209, 237
  from Mexico to California, 147, 157, 160, 164–65
  pre-Colombian, 160, 162, 179, 183
  slow pace of, 237
Miguel Francisco (San Jose), 118–19, 124
Miguélez Martínez, Armando, 267
military (Mexican). *See also* soldiers (Mexican)
  appearance of, 136

authority of, 141
conflicts within, 145
governing privileges of, 132, 137, 141
and liberalism, 139
and loyalty, 132
and oaths of allegiance, 137–38
and race, 142
resentment against, 141–42, 145
and social hierarchy, 142
military (Spanish). *See also* soldiers (Spanish)
  appearance of, 134, 149n8
  conflicts with Indians, 34, 225
  conflicts with missionaries, 56, 59
  deprivation of, 136
  descriptions of Indians by, 224–25
  desertion within, 134
  governing privileges of, 69n23, 141
  historiography of, 255–56, 260, 263–64
  and Indian labor, 36
  Jesuit control over, 37
  loyalty of, 136
  and missionaries, 20, 24, 39, 56, 197
  and mission-presidio system, 32
  and race, 133
  and social hierarchy, 133
Milliken, Randall T., 3, 82, 126
Ministerio de Guerra y Hacienda, 32
Miqueas (San Jose), 116, 118–19
Mission Dolores. *See* Mission San Francisco de Asís (Dolores)
Mission La Purísima Concepción, 87
Mission Nuestra Señora de la Luz de Tancoyol (Sierra Gorda), 34
Mission Nuestro Padre San Francisco del Valle de Tilaco (Sierra Gorda), 34
Mission San Antonio, 1, 29, 87, 111–12, 124–25
Mission San Buenaventura, 87
Mission San Carlos Borromeo (Carmel), 18–19, 26, 82, 83, 136
  establishment of, 1
  sacramental registers of, 3
Mission San Diego, 1, 5, 82
Mission San Fernando Rey de España de Velicatá (Baja California), **39**
Mission San Francisco de Asís (Dolores), 27
Mission San Francisco del Ati (Pimería Alta), 50, 68n13
Mission San Gabriel, 26, 82, 159–60, 164
  establishment of, 1
  sacramental registers, 3

348 Index

Mission San Jose, 27, 80, 87
   music at, 10, 112–21
Mission San José de Vizarrón (Sierra Gorda), 34, 35
Mission San Juan Bautista, 87
   music at, 10, 112, 121–22
Mission San Juan Capistrano, 82, 84, 87, 99
Mission San Luis Obispo, 1, 26, 143
Mission San Luis Rey, 84–87, 105n1. *See also* Peyri, Antonio
   asistencia of, 79, 86
   boundaries of, 86
   Indians at, 79, 82, 234n51
   Peyri at, 27, 86–87, 99
Mission San Miguel de Concá (Sierra Gorda), 34
Mission San Xavier del Bac (Pimería Alta), 50, 61, 68n15, 71n33
Mission Santa Barbara, 8, 134, 147, 159
Mission Santa Clara, 4, 87
Mission Santa Cruz, 87, 127n14
Mission Santa Inés, 87
Mission Santa María de la Purísima Concepción del Agua de Landa (Sierra Gorda), 34
Mission Santiago de Jalpan (Sierra Gorda), 32–35
Mission Soledad, 87
missionaries, Franciscan. *See also* Augustinian missionaries; Dominicans; *individual missionaries*; Jesuits; Paulines; *specific apostolic colleges*
   as agents of civilization, 17
   and allegiance to Mexican Republic, 87, 143
   and authority, 12n5, 55, 56, 58, 64
   biographies of, 6, 9, 239–42
   Bolton on, 216
   books banned by, 140
   conflicts with Indians, 64
   conflicts with soldiers, 12n5, 24
   and corporal punishment, 81
   on de Nava's reforms, 54
   and *depositarios*, 55
   descriptions of Indians by, 57–58, 225
   desertion of, 62
   disagreements among, 18, 49, 54, 56, 60, 221
   and disease, 34, 83
   as evaluated by historians, 201
   Fernandinos, 34–37, 39
   financial hardships of, 53, 56, 58
   financial support for, 32, 53, 58, 68n13, 69n21
   goals of, 9, 25, 32, 47, 52, 60
   and group identity, 48–50
   handling of money by, 51
   as heroes, 37, 208, 217
   idealization of Alta California by, 18, 40
   on Indian music, 111–12
   Interrogatorio of 1813, 158–60
   and loyalty to Spain, 136, 137–38, 143
   management of labor and production by, 48
   naming practices, 1–2, 19, 116–17, 127n21
   notions of burial, 94
   oaths of allegiance to Mexican Republic by, 87, 137–38, 143
   omnímoda jurisdicción (universal jurisdiction), 56
   as protectors of Indians, 37, 47
   Queretans, 48–54, 60, 62–63, 65n1
   religious program of, 26, 51, 84, 112, 124
   and religious syncretism, 26, 84
   return to Spain by, 87
   role in providing sacraments, 144
   rules and precepts of, 48–49, 54, 58, 64
   and sacramental registers, 1–5
   from settlers' perspective, 47
   shaping of Indians' environment by, 17
   and temporalities, 38, 48, 50–56, 59, 64
   tensions with Indians, 1, 48
   threatened with expulsion, 142, 143
   at top of social hierarchy, 133
   training for, 87
   treatment of Indians by, 140
   as villains, 17
   vow of obedience, 21, 49
   vow of poverty, 21, 49–50, 56
   welcomed by Indians, 82–83
   Zacatecans, 36
Missionary College of Guadalupe. *See* College of Guadalupe (Zacatecas)
missions. *See also* secularization of missions; *specific missions*
   and agriculture, 20
   asistencias, 79, 86, 105n2
   converted to parishes, 34–35
   and disease, 82, 83, 222–23
   Dominican, 39
   economy of, 20, 47–48, 55, 65, 68n15, 83, 86–87
   establishment of, 34–35, 37, 54, 82–84, 112, 114, 197

father presidents of, 18, 32, 63, 112
Fernandino, 34–37, 39
historiography of, 237–42
and identity transformation, 222
Jesuit, 37–38, 47
life span of Indians at, 120, 122, 128n24
and medical assistance, 83
monopoly of land by, 79, 133, 140
poverty of, 38
property of, 50–56
romanticization of, 203
as sanctuaries, 222
and temporalities, 38, 48, 50–56, 59, 64
and textile production, 102
weaknesses of, 64
mitochondrial DNA (mtDNA), 10–11, 158, 161, 165–77, 182. *See also* genetic origins
  clades, 161
  DNA analysis of, 160–62
  female lineages, 161, 164–69, 174, 179–82
  haplogroups/haplotypes, 161
Miwok, 163
Mixtec, 175–76
Mociño, José Mariano, 252, 253, 260
monarchy (Spanish), 236
  Alfonso VIII, 28
  authority of, 68n13, 135, 197
  Carlos III, 25
  Carlos IV, 135
  Charles III, 23
  Charles IV, 245
  collapse of, 135
  emphasis on conversion, 47, 237
  Fernando VII, 135–38, 243
  Juan Carlos I, 248,250
  loyalty to, 132, 138, 142, 217
  Philip V, 23
  rights of, 68n13, 79
  submission to, 134
Monterey (California), 20, 127n14, 136, 144
  California nativism in, 145, 147–48
  and disease, 81
  Mexican political ceremonies in, 87, 137–38, 203
  Mexican town council of, 141
  Spanish expedition to, 28
Monterey presidio, 19, 143, 151n20
Montes, Miguel, 61
Montesquieu, Baron de, 140
Montgomery, Charles H., 226–27
Moorhead, Max L., 219, 229n1

Moraga, Gabriel, 256, 260
Mourelle de la Rúa, Francisco Antonio, 243, 246, 264, 276n56
Moyano, Francisco, 54, 61–63
Moziño, José Mariano, 252, 253, 260
Mugártegui, Pablo de, 239, 263, 276n52
mulato, 8, 133, 159, 168, 218. *See also* casta system
Muñoz Garmendía, Félix, 261
Muñoz, Juan Bautista, 238
Muñóz, Pedro, 136
Murguía, José Antonio, 4
music, 10, 111–25, 137. *See also* Russell, Craig; Summers, William John
  alabado (song of praise), 112
  and colonialism, 99
  European forms of, 111, 113, 124
  Indian, 111–12
  and instruments, 112–14, 116–17, 124, 125
  and Serra, 28, 112–13, 120
  and women, 111–12, 118–20, 125
musicians (*músicos*), 10, 114–25
  cantores, 114, 123, 124
  clothing of, 113
  female, 117–20, 125
  and instruments, 114, 124
  maestro de la música, 114, 115, 123, 124
  at Mission San Antonio de Padua, 124–25
  at Mission San Jose, 114–21
  at Mission San Juan Bautista, 121–23
  in sacramental records, 114

N
Na-Dene, 163
Nahua, 110n65, 175–76
Namiquipa (village), 221
Napoleon, 135, 243
Narciso (San Jose), 114–19, 124
nation building
  and Californios, 141, 148
  and Mexican liberalism, 139, 146–47
national identity, 6, 9
  among Spanish-Mexicans, 131, 148
  of Californios, 142, 146
  Reséndez on, 223
  rituals of, 132, 136–39
nationalism (Mexican), 223
  among Californios, 80, 139
  and anti-Spanish sentiment, 142, 144
nationalism (Spanish), 241
  and historiography, 11, 235, 243, 261–66, 268

Native Americans. *See* Indians
Native Hawaiians, 104, 169, 191n28
Native Sons of the Golden West, 203–4
nativism (California), 146–48
nativism (Mexican), 136
naturalists (Spanish), 249–50, 252–53, 260–61
Nava, Pedro de. *See* de Nava, Pedro
Navajo, 163, 222
Naval Museum (Madrid), 250, 260
Navarro García, Luis, 256
negro, 133. *See also casta* system
neophytes. *See also* Indians
  identification of, 3, 197, 226
  and mission regime, 254
  as peons, 197
  in Sonora, 61
Neve, Felipe de, 25–26, 256, 260
New Mexico, 54, 69n23, 146, 163, 223, 227
  historiography of, 215, 220
  and national identity, 223–24
  population of, 165, 169–79
  and Spanish-American identity, 226
New Spain, 18, 24, 36–37. *See also* Mexican Republic
  apostolic colleges in, 30, 32
  colonial legacy of, 32, 36–37, 135–36
  and isolation of Alta California, 132, 135
  mission-presidio system in, 32
  northwestern expansion of, 170, 216, 247
  royalism in, 135
  wars of independence, 134–36, 142
Nicolás (San Gabriel), 26
Nieto-Phillips, John M., 226–27
Nio, 175, 182
Nominanda (San Jose), 116
Nootka, 247–49, 252, 254, 256, 260
Northrop, Marie E., 3
Northwest Passage, 242
Novo y Colson, Pedro de, 259
Nuestra Señora de Guadalupe. *See* College of Guadalupe (Zacatecas)
Nueva Galicia, 47
Nueva Planta, 23
Nueva Vizcaya, 69n23, 160, 223
Nuevo Santander, 36

O

Ocio, Manuel de, 38, 262
O'Conor, Hugo, 225
Ocoroni, 175, 182
officers (Mexican), 142. *See also* military (Mexican); soldiers (Mexican)
officers (Spanish). *See also* military (Spanish); soldiers (Spanish)
  descriptions of Indians by, 224–25
  European-born, 133
  naval officers, 259–61, 263, 265, 269
  quarrels with Serra, 24
Ohlone, 27
Ojinaga, Chihuahua, 164
Olbés, Ramón, 134
Oltra Perales, Enrique, O.F.M., 259
Omaechevarría Martitegui, Ignacio, O.F.M., 259, 263, 265
Ópata, 52, 69n21, 74n66, 167, 176, 180
Oppenheimer, Stephen, 157–58
Oquitoa (Sonora), 61
oral histories, in Bancroft Library, 113, 125, 140
Ord, Angustias. *See* de la Guerra y Carrillo, Angustias
Orozco Acuaviva, Antonio, 260
Ortega, Francisco, 246
Ortés de Velasco, José, 35
Osante, Patricia, 36
Osio, Antonio María, 138, 148

P

Pablo Tac. *See* Tac, Pablo
Pacheco, Romualdo, 144
Pacific coast, historiography of, 235, 242–43, 247, 255, 260
Padrés, José María, 139–40, 142, 146–47
padrinos. See godfathers (*padrinos*)
Pagden, Anthony, 7
pages (*pajes*), 115–17, 121, 123–24
Pala (*asistencia*), 80, 82, 86
Palau Baquero, Mercedes, 260
Palma, Andrés de, O.F.M., 259, 264, 265
Palma de Mallorca, 20–25, 28–30, 40, 265. *See also* Petra (Mallorca)
Palóu, Francisco, 18, 27, 241, 259, 265
  biographies of, 239, 264, 276n52
  biography of Serra by, 21, 24, 29, 34, 238
  Noticias de California, 38
  in Sierra Gorda, 32–36
Pames, 34, 40
Papago, 62
Papaguería (region), 57, 60
Parra, Juana Paula, 174
Pascual, Antoní Ramón, 23–24
pasquinades (satirical broadsides), 145

Index   351

Paulines, 259
Payeras, Mariano, 87, 137, 240, 264, 276n52
Pazos, Manuel, O.F.M., 259
Pearce, Roy Harvey, 225
Pedro Alcántara (San Jose), 115, 117–19, 121
Pedro Antonio (San Jose), 117, 127n21
Pedro Bautista (San Juan Bautista), 122
Peña, Tomás de la, 4
peninsulares. *See* Spaniards, European-born
Pennybacker, Mrs. Percy V., 207–8
Pequot, 104
Peregrino (San Jose), 116–19
Pérez de Mezquía, Pedro, 240, 263, 276n52
Pérez Miguel, Aurora, 252
Pericú, 182
Perpetua (San Jose), 117
Peru, 143, 144, 263
Petaluma (Indians), 27
Petra (Mallorca), 19–21, 264. *See also* Mallorca; Palma de Mallorca
Petra (San Jose), 116
Petra Antonia (San Jose), 117, 127n21
petroglyphs, 95
Peyri, Antonio, 27
  on Indian dance, 99, 109n53
  on Indian secrecy, 92–93
  return to Spain of, 86–88
Philip V (king of Spain), 23
phylogenetic relationships. *See* genetic origins
Picazo Muntaner, Antoni, 251
Píccolo, Francisco María, S.J., 239, 258
Pico de Avila, María Inocenta, 138
Pico, José Miguel (Santa Barbara), 8–9
Pico, Pío, 141
Picurís (village), 223
Pima, 67n8, 74n66, 176–77, 180
Pimentel Egea, Juan, 252
Pimería Alta, 67n8, 68n16, 74n69
  Barbastro removed from, 59
  de Nava's reforms in, 54
  missions in, 56–57, 61
  Queretans in, 48, 52, 55, 59–63, 71n33
Piña Homs, Román, 240, 265
Pious Fund, 239
Piqueras Céspedes, Ricardo, 264, 265
Pizarro González, Francisco, 201
Plácida (San Jose), 117
Plan de Iguala, 87, 136, 142. *See also* Mexican Republic
Pliego, Rodrigo del, 145–46
pobladores, 10, 159

political ceremonies, 136–38, 247
population (Alta California). *See also* depopulation; Early California Population Project (ECPP)
  in 1790, 8, 133, 158, 160, 165, 174, 180–82
  in 1821, 133
  decline in Indian population, 5, 128n24, 170, 174
  female, 168, 172–74, 177, 180
  growth in Indian population, 163
  and Interrogatorio of 1813, 158
Porter y Casanate, Pedro, 246, 262, 276n56
Portilla, Pablo de la, 141
Portolá, Gaspar de, 260, 264, 279n87
  administration of, 38, 256
  expeditions of, 28, 39, 158, 256
Posadas, Vicente de, 35
Powell, Philip Wayne, 218
presidios, 32, 36, 133–34
  impact of, 81–82
  Indian labor at, 79
  Loreto, 38
  Monterey, 19, 143, 151n20
  and political ceremonies, 138
  San Diego, 24, 86, 138, 159
  San Francisco, 106n7, 143, 151n20
  Santa Barbara, 2, 3, 121, 131, 142, 159, 174
priests. *See* missionaries, Franciscan
procuradores (purchasing agents), 55
property. *See* land ownership
proselytism. *See* missionaries, Franciscan
Pubols, Louise, 10, 80
Pucules (San Jose), 115, 117–19, 121, 127n21
Pudenciana (San Juan Bautista), 122
Pueblo Indians, 221–23, 231n28
Pumusi (village), 84
purchasing agents (*procuradores*), 55

Q

Quadra-Salcedo Gayarre, Ana de la, 263, 265, 278n83
Quechán, 100, 132
Quechinga (village), 84, 86
Quechla, 80, 95, 103, 104
Quechnajuis, 80
Queretans, 48–54, 60, 62–63, 65n1. *See also* College of Santa Cruz (Querétaro)
Querétaro, 32, 34, 36, 67n12
Quilchocho (San Jose), 117
Quimper, Manuel, 246, 276n56

R

Rabasa, José, 225
race
   and honor/shame, 221
   and identity, 8, 132
   language of, 133, 142
   mixing of, 133–34, 142, 157, 160, 222, 226
   purity of, 8, 134, 204, 221
   and social hierarchy, 132, 134
   Spanish categories of, 7–8, 133, 157, 218, 220
Ramírez, Potenciana, 175
Ramis Alonso, Miguel, 265
rancheros, 140, 200, 208
ranchos, 50, 63, 64, 138, 159, 200–201
rebellions. *See* uprisings
recuerdos. *See* oral histories, in Bancroft Library
Redondo, María Antonia, 175
Reff, Daniel T., 225, 233n42
religion (Indian), 26–28, 227. *See also* conversion, religious
   and astrology, 100
   and dance, 27, 100, 102
   and music, 111
   and secrecy, 92–93
   syncretism, 26, 84
   and teleology, 103
religious orders. *See also* Dominicans; Jesuits; missionaries, Franciscan
   Augustinians, 34
   Paulines, 259
reminiscences. *See* oral histories, in Bancroft Library
Republic of Mexico. *See* Mexican Republic
republicanism (Mexican), 139–41, 144, 146
Reséndez, Andrés, 146, 223, 229
revolution. *See* war of independence, in Mexico
Rey Tejerina, Arsenio, 267
Reyes, Antonio de los, 54, 58, 71n31, 71n32, 241, 276n52, 278n76
Rey-Stolle Pedrosa, Alejandro, S.J., 259
Riber, Lorenzo (Llorenç), 264, 265
Ribes, Vicente, 265
Rickards, Olga, 178
Ritchie, Robert C., 5, 11
Rivera, María Ignacia, 174
Rivera, Pedro de, 32
Rivera y Moncada, Fernando, 24, 38, 42n21, 256, 260
Robinson, Alfred, 144
Robles, Vito Alessio, 218
Rodeja Galter, Eduardo, 264, 265
Rodrigo (San Juan Bautista), 121–23
Rodríguez, Pascual, 60, 72n39
Roman Catholic Church. *See* Catholicism
romanticization. *See also* fantasy heritage of California
   of California's missions, 203
   of California's past, 200, 210
   of Indians, 225
Romero, Catalina, 255
Romero, Diego, 218
Romero, María Francisca, 180
Rosario (Sinaloa), 176
Rousseau, Jean-Jacques, 140
Royal Academy of History (Spain), 238
royalism, of Californios, 131–32, 135–38
Rubí Darder, Sebastián, 259, 265
Rubio, Petra, 172–73
Ruiz de Gordejuela Urquijo, Jesús, 256
Ruíz, Francisco María, 138
Ruiz, Pedro, 61
Russell, Craig, 125, 126n3

S

Sabater, Gaspar, 265
Sabina (San Jose), 116
sacramental registers, 157, 160. *See also* Early California Population Project (ECPP); godfathers (*padrinos*); godmothers (*madrinas*); witnesses (*testigos*)

   baptisms recorded in, 4, 41n4, 118–19, 122, 126, 173
   burials recorded in, 116–18, 121, 126
   importance of, 1–5
   Indian musicians listed in, 111, 114, 124
   marriages recorded in, 119, 123, 126
   numbering system of, 2–3, 12n6
   and Serra, 18–19
Sacramento Valley, 256
sacraments (Catholic), 1–5, 112, 124, 134, 144. *See also* sacramental registers
sacristans, 123–24
   at Mission San Jose, 80, 115, 121
   at Mission Santa Cruz, 127n14
sailors
   Basque, 278n83
   English, 144
   Spanish, 244, 263–65
saints (Catholic), 21, 103, 272n19
Saiz, Blanca, 260

Index   353

Salafranca, Alejandro, 251
Salazar, Buenaventura, O.F.M., 239, 263, 265
Sales, Luis de, O.P., 238, 239, 241, 259, 265
Salgado, Lugarda, 178
Salvatierra, Juan María de, S.J., 239, 258
Samaniego, José Ximénez. *See* Ximénez Samaniego, José
San Antonio (Texas), 221, 222
San Antonio de Pala (*asistencia*), 79, 86
San Antonio mission. *See* Mission San Antonio
San Bernardino (church in Mallorca), 19
San Blas, 20, 136
San Buenaventura mission, 87
San Carlos de Sonora, Custodia of, 54–55, 71n31, 71n32
San Carlos Borromeo mission. *See* Mission San Carlos Borromeo (Carmel)
San Diego, 82, 89, 102, 138. *See also* Mission San Diego
   Californios in, 140
   described by Serra, 39–40
   expedition to establish, 246
San Diego presidio, 24, 86, 138, 159
San Fernando College. *See* College of San Fernando (Mexico City)
San Fernando Rey de España de Velicatá (Baja California), 39
San Francisco (city), 202, 209
San Francisco del Valle de Tilaco (Sierra Gorda), 34
San Francisco presidio, 106n7, 143, 151n20
San Francisco region, 27
San Gabriel mission. *See* Mission San Gabriel
San Ignacio (Baja California), 61
San Jose (town), 141
San Jose mission. *See* Mission San Jose
San Juan (pueblo), 223
San Juan Bautista mission. *See* Mission San Juan Bautista
San Juan Capistrano mission. *See* Mission San Juan Capistrano
San Luis Obispo mission. *See* Mission San Luis Obispo
San Luis Rey mission. *See* Mission San Luis Rey
San Luis Rey River, 84
San Mateo (village), 86
San Miguel de Concá (Sierra Gorda), 34
San Pedro (church in Mallorca), 19

Sanahuja i Vallverdú, Pedro, O.F.M., 259, 263, 264, 265
Sánchez Masía, Luis, 259
Sánchez Montañés, Emma, 255
Sancho, Juan, 111, 124–25, 128n31
Sandos, James A., 10, 80, 272n18
Sanfeliú Ortiz, Lorenz, 259
Sant Francesc (church in Palma de Mallorca), 22, 24
Santa Anna, Antonio López de, 147
Santa Barbara, 134, 143–45, 147. *See also* Mission Santa Barbara
Santa Barbara Channel region, 3
   Chumash in, 163, 170, 179
Santa Barbara Mission Archive-Library, 17, 191n25
Santa Barbara presidio, 2, 121
   baptismal register at, 3, 174
   prank staged at, 131, 142
   soldiers at, 159
Santa Clara mission, 87
Santa Cruz de Mayo (pueblo), 141, 173–74
Santa Cruz mission. *See* Mission Santa Cruz
Santa Fe (New Mexico), 227
Santa Inés mission, 87
Santa Margarita (region), 86
Santa María, Vicente de, 27
Santa Ynez mission. *See* Mission Santa Inés
Santiago de Jalpan (Sierra Gorda), 32–35, **33**
Santiesteban, Juan, 54
Sargentaruc (village), 19
Sarría, Vicente Francisco de, 87, 241, 263
Saucillo (Chihuahua), 35
savagism. *See* civilization vs. savagism
science, historiography of, 249–55
Scottish Rite masons, 139. *See also* Freemasonry
Scotus, John Duns, 28–29
Sebastian José (Santa Clara), 4
secularization of missions
   in central Mexico, 36–37
   and liberalism, 139–41, 146–48
   mission life after, 114–15, 117, 120–21
Secundo (San Jose), 116
self-rule
   of Californios, 147
   of Indian communities, 79
Señán, José Francisco de Paula, 134
Senkewicz, Robert M., 9, 49, 64, 70n29
Sequoyah, 104
Seri, 163–64, 182, 225

Serra, Junípero, 9, 17–40
  academic career of, 29–30
  admission to Franciscan order, 21
  antipathy toward military, 9, 24
  in Baja California, 37–40
  Bancroft on, 201
  baptisms performed by, 4, 4, 18–19, 41n4
  biographies of, 21, 238, 239, 241, 264
  childhood in Petra, Mallorca, 19–20, 74n74, 264
  chosen name of, 21–22
  as *comisario* of the Inquisition, 25–26, 35
  and Crespí's diaries, 27
  criticisms of, 18
  disagreements with Neve, 25–26
  distrust of Indian traditions, 27
  education of, 20–21
  on Escandón, 35
  and Fages, 20
  as father president, 18, 32, 112
  on Father Santa María, 27
  as hero, 208
  on the Immaculate Conception, 29
  in Jalpan, 32
  on liturgical art, 28
  in Mexico City, 30, 32
  as missionary, 29–30
  and music, 28, 112–13, 120
  proposed canonization of, 9, 17, 241, 272n19
  religious fervor, 29–30, 37
  in San Diego, 40
  sermons of, 24
  in Sierra Gorda, 32–36
Serrera Contreras, Ramón María, 255, 257, 265
settlers. *See also* Californios; *gente de razón*
  in New Mexico, 221
  in New Spain, 17, 47
  on Pacific coast, 237
  in Sierra Gorda, 35–38
shame. *See* honor/shame
ships, 265
  María Ester, 144
  Mexicana, 242
  Sutil, 242
Sierra Gorda, 18, 21, 30–37, 40
  Spanish colonization of, 32, 34–36
Sierra Madre mountains, 47
Silvestre (San Jose), 115–20
Simó, Lorenzo, 54, 59, 73n56

Simón (San Juan Bautista), 122
Sinaloa, 11, 133, 158, 160, 164, 166–84
Sinaloa River, 173, 175, 176, 180
Sintes Obrador, Francisco, 264–65
sistema de castas. *See casta* system
Sitjar, Buenaventura, 241, 264
slaves
  African, in Mexico, 132
  Escandón as trader of, 34
  and Grito de Dolores, 135
  Indian, in Querétaro, 36–37
  Spaniards labeled as masters of, 142
social hierarchy, in Alta California, 132, 133, 157
social mobility
  for Hispanics in New Mexico, 221
  for Indian musicians, 112
  for Mexican soldiers, 142
  for soldiers of New Spain, 133
Solá, Pablo Vicente de, 133, 137, 138, 263
soldiers (Mexican), 132. *See also* military (Mexican)
  and disobedience, 142
  firsthand accounts by, 94
  loyalty of, 137
  racial mixing of, 242
  at Santa Barbara presidio, 131
  uprisings of, 143
  views on independence, 137
soldiers (Spanish). *See also* military (Spanish)
  ancestry of, 10
  appearance of, 134
  assistance to missions, 32
  authority over missions, 39
  dislike for manual labor, 134
  as heroes, 200
  and Indian women, 26, 168
  and Indians, 36, 134, 225
  individualism of, 217
  and oppression of Indians, 17
  in Pimería Alta, 56, 65
  racial mixing of, 80, 133–34, 158–60
  tensions with missionaries, 12n5, 24, 27, 37
Soledad mission, 87
Soler, José, 51, 68n15
Soler Vidal, Joseph, 264, 265
Solís, Joaquín, 143, 153n56
Sonora, 37, 132
  and Apache, 80

missions in, 47–48
population, 158, 167–84
and Seri, 163
settlers from, 11, 160, 164–65
and Tarahumara, 164
Sotelo, Micaela, 175
Soto Pérez, José Luis, O.F.M., 259
Spain. *See also* monarchy (Spanish)
   authority of, 256
   centralization in, 23–24
   and citizenship, 148
   emphasis on conversion of Indians, 47
   exploration by, 237–38, 242–45, 248, 251, 261, 263
   histories published in, 235–36
   identification with, 133
   invasion of, by Napoleon, 135
   involvement in New World, 198, 237
   law on structure of religious orders, 49
   loyalty to, 131, 136, 143
   and nationalism, 235
   Second Republic (1931–36), 238, 244
   Spanish Civil War (1936–39), 238, 244, 249, 264
Spaniards, European-born, 54, 132, 133
   rights of, 142
   sentiment against, 135, 136, 142–45, 148
Spanish Americans
   on invasion of Spain, 135
   in New Mexico, 226–27
Spanish Borderlands. *See* Borderlands, Spanish
Spanish California. *See* California (territory of New Spain), economy of; New Spain
Spanish Californians. *See* Californios; *gente de razón*
Spanish Revival movement, 17
Spanish settlers. *See* Californios; settlers
Spicer, Edward H., 219, 230n17
Ssaches (San Jose), 114–19, 124
stereotypes of California, reinforced by Bolton, 198, 210, 212n6
suffrage
   of Mexican Americans, 227
   in Mexican Republic, 141, 147
Summers, William John, 112, 120
Suria, Tomás de, 253, 260, 267
Sutil, 242
Sykes, Bryan, 157
syncretism, 26, 84

T
Tac, Pablo, 9–10, 66n5
   on dance, 99–100, **101**, 102
   on disease, 83–84
   education of, 87–89
   ethnographic sketches by, 89, 95, 98–99, **105**
   on Indian-Spanish alliances, 103
   letter to Mezzofanti by, 91–92, **93**
   Luiseño dictionary by, 79, 89–91, **90–91**, 94, **96–97**, 102
   Luiseño grammar by, 79, 89–91, 94, 98–99
   Luiseño history by, 79–81, 84, **85**, 92, 98
   on political equality, 81
   in Rome, 88–89, 104
   on sacred words, 84, 94, 103
   travels of, 88
Tacayame, 84
Tahue language, 174–75, 182
Tampico, Tamaulipas, 143
Tancama Valley (Sierra Gorda), 35
Tancoyol mission. *See* Mission Nuestra Señora de la Luz de Tancoyol (Sierra Gorda)
Tarahumara, 164, 167, 174, 176, 180, 232n30
Taraval, Segismundo, 240, 276n52
Teggart, Frederick, 205
Teja, Jesús Frank de la. *See* de la Teja, Jesús F.
Telesforo/Thelesforo (San Juan Bautista), 121–23, 128n25, 128n26
Temecula (village), 80, 86
Temple, Thomas Workman, 3
temporalities (*temporalidades*), 38, 48, 50–56, 59, 64, 70n26, 74n66
Tepic, Nayarit, 37, 145
testigos. See witnesses (*testigos*)
testimonios. See oral histories, in Bancroft Library
Tewa language, 223
Texas, 69n23, 70n26, 146, 221
   and national identity, 223–24
   population of, 165, 169, 174, 178–81
textbooks on California history, 205–10
Third Order of Penitence, 58
Tipai. *See* Diegueño/Digueño; Kumeyaay
Tjarks, Alicia Vidaurreta, 218
Tlaxcaltecans, 80, 170
Tobar y Tamariz, José, 246, 276n56
Topome (village), 86

Torre Curiel, José Refugio de la, 9
Torréns y Nicolau, Francisco, 238–39, 259, 265
Torres Campos, Rafael, 243
tourism, and historiography, 200, 203, 212n17, 227, 248, 268
Tova Arredondo, Antonio de, 246, 276n56
town councils, 141, 146–47
trade
  among Indians, 83
  hide-and-tallow, 143–44
  between Indians and Spanish settlers, 81
  and Mexican liberalism, 139
  between missions and foreign merchants, 86
  sea otter, 255
  by Yuman and Apache Indians, 100–101
traders. *See* merchants
trueque (barter), 51–52
Tubutama (town), 61
Tumacácori (town), 61
Tupatu, Luis, 223
Turner, Frederick Jackson, 198, 215–16, 220

U
Ulloa, Francisco de, 244, 246, 276n56, 318
United States
  conquest of Mexico by, 148, 201–2, 208, 226
  economy of, 7, 223
universal jurisdiction (*omnímoda jurisdicción*), 56
uprisings
  of Indians, 1, 24, 109n53
  in Santa Barbara, 147
  of soldiers, 143
Ures (Sonora), 61
U.S.-Mexico War, 7, 197, 208, 223
Uto-Aztecan languages, 163–64, 174–76, 178, 182

V
Valdés, Cayetano, 246, 273n22, 276n56
Valencia (Spain), 253, 262, 265, 267
Valencia, María Dolores, 180
Valentín (San Juan Bautista), 121–23
Vallejo, Guadalupe, 125
Vallejo, Mariano Guadalupe, 125, 140, 147, 153n57
Vargas, Diego de, 223
Vatican, 29, 88–89, 93

vecinos
  in New Mexico, 70n27
  in Sonora, 65, 74n73
Velasco, José Ortés de. *See* Ortés de Velasco, José
Velázquez de León, Joaquín, 251
Venegas, Miguel, 238–39, 258
Ventureño Chumash, 170
Veracruz, 32
Vicedo, Salustiano, O.F.M., 259, 264
Victoria, Manuel, 146
Vidal Isern, José, 264, 265
vigilance committees, as depicted by Bolton, 208, 209
Vila, Pablo, 220
Villa de Herrera (settlement), 35
Villa Sinaloa, 175–77, 180
Villaseca, Francisco, 57–59, 72n45
Virgin Mary, 19–20
Virgin of Guadalupe, 135, 146
Virmond, Enrique, 140
visitador, 55–57, 59–60
Vizcaíno, Juan González, 241, 246, 267
Vizcaíno, Sebastián, 238, 244, 246, 276n56
Voltaire, 140
von Langsdorff, Georg Heinrich, 27
voting. *See* suffrage

W
Wallace, Douglas, 162
war of independence, in Mexico, 134–36, 142, 153n56
War of the Spanish Succession, 23
Weber, David J., 11, 66n4, 66n6, 79
Weber, Francis J., 259
Wells, Spencer, 158
Wheeler, Benjamin Ide, 208
Williams, Mary Floyd, 209, 214n50
Wilson, Chris, 226
witnesses (*testigos*), 114–24
women (colonial California)
  in 1790 census, 168, 172–74, 177, 180
  and female lineages, 161, 164–69, 174, 179–82
  and literacy, 152n44
  and virtue, 201
women (Indian)
  economic role of, 20–21, 98
  as godmothers, 116
  hospitality of, 224
  and music, 111–12, 118–20, 125
  and soldiers, 26, 168

Wood, Stephanie, 103, 109n65
work. *See* labor

X

Xalisco. *See* Jalisco
Xavier, Adro, 259
Ximénez Samaniego, José, 30

Y

Yaqui Indians, 167, 172–73, 174, 183
Yaqui River, 173
Yaqui Valley, 47
Ybarra y Bergé, Javier de, 263, 265, 278n82
Yldefonso (San Jose), 117
Yocitaye. *See* Gaudiosa (San Jose)
Yokuts, 163
York Rite masons, 139
Yuma, 59, 100, 132
Yuman-Cochimí languages, 163, 176, 182
Yumete (San Jose), 117

Z

Zabala, Aránzazu, 260
Zacatecans, 36. *See also* College of Guadalupe (Zacatecas)
Zapotec Indians, 175
Zavala, Silvio, 218
Zuni, 163, 170, 227